D1022396

Jenny Lind, the Swedish Nightingale

Books by Gladys Denny Shultz

JENNY LIND, THE SWEDISH NIGHTINGALE

LETTERS TO JANE

IT'S TIME YOU KNEW

HOW MANY MORE VICTIMS?

By Gladys Denny Shultz and Daisy Gordon Lawrence

LADY FROM SAVANNAH: THE LIFE OF JULIETTE LOW

Courtesy of The New York Historical Society, New York City

Courtesy of The New York Historical Society, New York City

JENNY LIND, FROM THE PORTRAIT BY MAGNUS

JENNY LIND

The
Swedish Nightingale

BY

GLADYS DENNY SHULTZ

J. B. Lippincott Company
Philadelphia & New York

COPYRIGHT © 1962 BY GLADYS DENNY SHULTZ
PRINTED IN THE UNITED STATES OF AMERICA
LIBRARY OF CONGRESS CATALOG CARD NUMBER 62-10537
THIRD PRINTING

Library
University of Texas
at San Antonio

"Jenny Lind was a wonder and a joy. She passed *through* life, that is what she made one feel. She was on her way somewhere else. It was a movement across a scene—her life. On she passed; often in perplexity and surprise at what she found here; never quite at home, never comfortable, and settled, and at rest. On she went travelling; and as she passed, she left all eyes following after her, and all hearts wondering over her, as after a sudden vision."

From a letter of Henry Scott Holland,
Canon of St. Paul's, to his ward, Evelyn Holland

CONTENTS

Contents

Jenny Lind, the Swedish Nightingale

Foreword

A LITTLE MORE THAN A
hundred years ago, first Europe and then the United States were gripped
by what was variously called the Jenny Lind Mania, the Jenny Lind Fever,
or more concisely, Lindomania. Never before or since has an artist so
appealed to the imagination of the public at large, or exerted such an
impact on the society of her time, as did Jenny Lind. And her influence
did not end with her death in 1887.

A young American, Leonidas Westervelt, acquired the infection in
1903, through his studies in the drama courses of Professor Brander
Matthews at Columbia University. From then until his death in 1952,
what time he could spare from business was spent in following Jenny
Lind's footsteps over the world and assembling material about her. He
came to feel that Jenny was his companion and guide on these excursions.
"Together we have poked into odd nooks and corners of New York,
Boston, Havana, London, Stockholm and Copenhagen, searching among
dusty packets of old letters and bundles of manuscripts for holographs,
pictures, music sheets and programs; through numismatic material for
the many medals and tokens struck in Jenny's honor; through antique
shops for souvenirs of all kinds."

There were the Royal Worcester candle snuffers, for instance, with
a woman's body and a nightingale's head, which were among the countless Jenny Lind souvenirs turned out by manufacturers during the height
of the singer's popularity. The Royal Worcester ones were made in pairs,

[11]

each pair differing in design from every other. Who but Jenny herself, Mr. Westervelt maintained, could have led him to the antique shop in Blue Point, Long Island, where he found one of a Royal Worcester pair; and then to the stall in the Caledonia Market in London, where its mate was displayed?

Every spot where Jenny had lingered gave up some bit of treasure trove for Mr. Westervelt's collection, either from the antique shops of the region or from private homes, whose owners were touched by Mr. Westervelt's enthusiasm for the singer. Many ancestral diaries and letters containing references to Jenny came into his possession in this way. Jenny Lind's daughter, Mrs. Raymond Maude, gave him choice items from her own collection of mementos of her famous mother.

In time, the Jenny Lind collection filled the Westervelt home, and contained such intriguing items as the original contract drawn up between P. T. Barnum and the diva, letters exchanged between Barnum and Jenny, daguerreotypes, pictures and statues galore. Among the four hundred volumes dealing with Jenny and her contemporaries was Jenny's Bible, with her name written in her own hand, faintly but distinctly, on the title page of the New Testament. Because Jenny Lind was woven inextricably with American history of the pre-Civil War era, Mr. Westervelt in 1945 presented his collection to the New York Historical Society. The items mentioned, along with many others, may be seen in the Jenny Lind section of the Society's museum at 170 Central Park West in New York City.

The letters and diaries contain information not previously published. And the innumerable American newspapers and magazines collected by Mr. Westervelt for the years 1850 to 1852 (the time of her American visit), furnish a vivid picture of the United States of the decade before the Civil War, when farm produce was sold at stalls set up beneath the dome of the Capitol in Washington, D.C., and work had stopped on the monument to George Washington because Congress had refused to appropriate the $100,000 needed to complete it.

In addition to this hitherto untapped vein of material about her American stay, facts concerning Jenny's origin and childhood, kept secret until all the principals in her life story had died, have been revealed in recent years. First in biographies of her by Swedish writers, and in the latest biography of her in English, Joan Bulman's excellent *Jenny Lind*, published in 1956 by James Barrie of London. There is no doubt in the minds of Swedish scholars that Jenny was born out of wedlock, and had to endure rejection and hostility from her mother throughout her early years. Hers was a background which could explain one of the too frequent tragedies of lives of great promise, ruined, or brought to untimely death, by emotional instability. How it came about that, from a homely, unwanted and unloved illegitimate child, Jenny Lind became the most idolized woman of her time, and the first woman ever to be memorialized in Westminster Abbey, is known to few Americans. Yet the resolution of her personal story, the throwing off of the feelings of inferiority and fear which had haunted her throughout her unbelievably successful stage career, took place in the United States.

This book does not pretend to be a scholarly discussion of Jenny Lind as singer and actress, or to give a full account of her unparalleled triumphs in England and on the continent. These matters have been covered in many books. Its purpose is to tell the inner, human story of the nameless little girl from a poor section of Stockholm, who became the most adored performer in the world's history; of what she did for America, and of what America did for her.

No one can write of Jenny Lind without drawing heavily upon the official biography of her by Holland and Rockstro, though it does not contain the more unpleasant facts about her parents and her childhood, out of respect for the wishes of Jenny's husband, Otto Goldschmidt, who worked closely with the authors. These facts, however, together with the evidence of her parents' nagging greediness when Jenny began to make money, are described in two Swedish biographies entitled *Jenny Lind*, one written by Moses Pergament and published by Norstedts, the other by K. Rootzen and T. Meyer, published by Lindfors. There is much about Jenny's American visit in the several editions of P. T. Barnum's autobiography, but some of his statements about their relationship must be taken with a grain of salt, and weighed against the testimony of other persons on the scene. Biographies of Jenny by her daughter, Mrs. Raymond Maude, E. Wagenknecht, Laura Benét and many others, round out the picture.

The New York and Boston Public Libraries contain much material about Jenny Lind in addition to their files of daily papers of 1850 to 1852; issues of *Punch* and the *London Illustrated News* of the late 1840's are full of her. Interesting personal bits and sidelights are taken from the store of unpublished material collected by Leonidas Westervelt.

All the events described in this book are as they happened, though the author has drawn on her imagination in some places for the exact way in which they happened. For example, it is not known who told Jenny that her parents had finally legalized their union, when their daughter was fourteen and a half, but somebody had to. The date of their marriage is known, and it is also known that Jenny at this time was living at the Royal Theater School in Stockholm, and that her mother was about to go into court to force the Theater School to surrender the girl to her parents. It would seem logical that the person for this delicate and not very pleasant task would have been the titular head of the Royal Theater School, who would be representing the school in the court proceedings, and who had taken a fatherly interest in Jenny from the time she entered the school at the age of ten. In a similar way, all the imagined conversations are based on known happenings, and on ideas and attitudes known to have been expressed by the persons involved.

In only one instance has a liberty been taken with the public record. The often told story about Hans Christian Andersen's courtship of Jenny is that, wearied by his constant proposals of marriage, the singer one day simply handed him a mirror as her reason for refusing him yet again. Andersen was far from being a handsome man and such an action would have been unforgivably cruel, completely foreign to Jenny Lind as one comes to know her. There is no doubt that this incident inspired Andersen's story, "The Ugly Duckling," which symbolized Jenny in his mind. Stories can become altered in the telling, and the author has recorded this incident in the way that it seems to her it must have taken place.

Grateful acknowledgments are due officials of historical societies in a number of states and cities, who confirmed facts and dates in connection with the American tour; to Dr. Brandberg, Director of the Swedish Institute for Cultural Relations in London, for his patient replies to many questions; to O. K. Armstrong, who, inspired by Leonidas Westervelt's interest in Jenny Lind, visited every city on her American tour and is responsible for many of the gleanings from local newspapers in the South and Middle West; and above all to Mrs. Leonidas Westervelt, who generously allowed free access to her husband's personal notes and writings about Jenny Lind, as well as to the many papers in his collection.

CHAPTER ONE

Merely Jenny

THANKS be to heaven, the child was asleep! Crumpled uncomfortably in the corner of the opposite seat, her face smudged from crying, her head with its tow-colored braids bobbing with every jolt and jerk of the carriage, nevertheless she slept. Now Anna Marie Fellborg could lean her head back and close her eyes, too. She must force herself to relax, she knew, or she would get one of her headaches.

Anna Marie, at thirty-one, was a handsome woman still in spite of the lines that were beginning to be etched down from the mouth corners, the worry wrinkles grooved between the eyes. Her clothes, neat and of good material though somber and much worn, made her look like an extremely respectable schoolmistress, which was what Anna Marie was.

She was accustomed to strict self-discipline, but try as she would, Anna Marie could not banish from her mind the disastrous events of the day. If only she hadn't gone to Ed-Sollentuna, had made some excuse! But she had felt it her duty to go when word came that Fru Ferndal was so ill. Besides, it would have appeared odd to the Ferndals if she had not.

Fru Ferndal did look very ill. Perhaps that was the reason why she had brought up the old question, about which the few other persons acquainted with the child's origin had learned long ago it was useless to argue. It was a matter of principle with Anna Marie. Fru Ferndal should know by this time that on a matter of principle Anna Marie was not to be swayed.

[17]

Jenny Lind, the Swedish Nightingale

I shouldn't have lost my temper, I suppose, Anna Marie thought regretfully. She hadn't meant it when she had said angrily that if this was the way the Ferndals viewed matters, it would be best for her to take Jenny away. The Ferndals had always professed to be so fond of Jenny. How could Anna Marie have anticipated that Carl Ferndal would so promptly take her at her word? She felt her face grow hot again, as it had when Carl said gravely, "We will be sorry to lose her, Anna Marie, but perhaps that will be best. The doctor has told me Karen will not recover. It is not right that so small a girl should stay on in a house where there is no mother."

And he had stood firm. Finally Anna Marie had rushed off, walking blindly over hills and thrusting through thickets, to keep from saying things she would really be sorry for, and to give the Ferndals time to reconsider. But when she returned to the farmhouse, it was to find Jenny's little wardrobe packed, a hired carriage ordered. Anna Marie's mouth twisted bitterly. If he had loved Jenny as he had claimed, Carl Ferndal would never have been able to withstand the child's tears and pleadings when the carriage arrived and it was time to go back to Stockholm.

Now Anna Marie had to think what she was to do with a four-year-old. She had her hands full with her private school, and no help beyond what Amelia could give her. The tired, strained face softened at the thought of Amelia. This daughter was the one recompense the Lord had allowed her, while making her lot so difficult in every other way. But Amelia was only thirteen, and had never been very strong.

Anna Marie had not been able to arrive at any solution for her problem when the carriage drew up in front of the tall, narrow house at No. 40 Mäster Samuelsgrand Street in Stockholm. The driver got down from his seat, opened the carriage door and, seeing that the little one was asleep, spoke softly. "I'll carry her in if you like, Madam. I've two of my own."

"If you would," Anna Marie replied gratefully. "It's three flights up and I am very tired. Right straight ahead, and my place is at the top of the stairs, if you will be so kind."

"Three flights—good thing she don't weigh hardly more than a feather!" When they reached the top of the stairs, Jenny opened her

[18]

eyes, and the driver set her down carefully. The child looked about her dazedly, saw a dark hall and a strange man bending over her. The wailing began again. Anna Marie, toiling up the stairs after them with Jenny's little portmanteau, felt the first stab of the dreaded headache.

A door opened, and a slender young girl came hurrying into the hall. "You're back, Mama!" She kissed her mother affectionately, took the bag from her hand. "Did you have a nice day? It's the funniest thing. I thought I heard someone crying out here." Jenny, who had stopped crying at Amelia's sudden appearance, began again. "Why, it *is* someone. Who is she, Mama?"

It was beyond Anna Marie's strength to explain about Jenny. She fumbled in her purse for a tip for the driver—Carl Ferndal had at least had the decency to pay for the carriage he had ordered—and said wearily to Amelia, as the man went clumping back down the stairs, "The little girl from Ed-Sollentuna. Fru Ferndal is too sick to care for her any longer, so she will stay with us until some other place can be found for her. Take her in the kitchen and give her something to eat, will you, darling? I must go lie down."

Amelia looked at her with concern. "One of your headaches, Mama?"

"Yes, a bad one. You will just have to manage as best you can."

Amelia gently propelled the weeping child first through a large, bare-looking room equipped with school desks, and then into an equally bare, inhospitable little kitchen, as different as could be from the big, warm kitchen at Ed-Sollentuna, with its gay curtains and rugs and pots of plants in every window. When Amelia had finished getting cheese and bread and milk from the cupboard, and placed them on the table, she found that the child had backed into a corner and refused to leave it.

"I want to go home, I want to go home!" she wailed over and over. Amelia was on the point of giving up when a merry-faced young man with dark, curly hair stuck his head around the kitchen door. "Where is your mother, Amelia? Is she back yet from Ed-Sollentuna?"

"Yes, Uncle Niklas, but she has one of her headaches. She is in her bedroom lying down. Uncle Niklas, she brought the Ferndals' little girl back with her from Ed-Sollentuna. I'm trying to give her some supper, but she won't eat a thing."

"A little girl from Ed-Sollentuna?" Niklas Lind came into the kitchen, knelt down before the little rebel in the corner, took her hands in his. "What is your name, little girl from Ed-Sollentuna?" When Jenny only went on crying, he said softly, "I can tell you what your name is, I bet you. Your name is Jenny. Didn't I guess right?"

Jenny nodded shyly, and Niklas swept her up in his arms, danced with her around the room. "I knew it, I knew it! Such a sweet little Jenny, such a dear little Jenny! Do you know something, Jenny? I love you, and we are going to be great friends. I'll tell you what we're going to do." Niklas seated himself at the table, with the child on his knee. "You shall be the baby bird and I shall be the papa bird. Now ordinary everyday little baby birds eat wriggly worms, but this baby bird is a very special one, who eats bread and cheese. So Papa Niklas brings a bit of cheese and puts it in the baby's mouth—so! And a bit of bread, and puts it in the baby's mouth—so!" And Jenny obediently swallowed the cheese and bread Niklas popped into her mouth. After it was gone, she nestled against him. Niklas's merry face was sober now, he pressed the little girl to him gently.

"This little Jenny-Bird is getting sleepy, I can tell. Where did your mother want her to sleep?" he asked Amelia.

"She didn't say. Her head was so bad she just went off to her room. Do you think it would be all right if I take Jenny in with me? It's vaca-time, you know, and Louise Johansson isn't here."

"I think that would be excellent. See, Jenny, Amelia will be with you all night. If you should wake up, you won't be lonely."

Niklas removed Jenny's dress and shoes, drew the covers over her and kissed her good night. Then he went into Anna Marie's room, and the two girls heard him say, "You didn't tell me you were bringing her back with you."

Anna Marie's voice came, high and fretful, "I didn't intend to. They made me. Oh, Niklas, what ever will I do?"

Anna Marie Fellborg did have a difficult life; made no easier by the fact that, in the opinion of those who knew her best, she had created her worst difficulties herself.

She had been married at eighteen to a handsome, dashing army officer, Captain Erik Johan Rådberg, and was not yet twenty when she divorced

him, on grounds of infidelity, in the High Ecclesiastical Court. She had
then undertaken to support herself and her eight-month-old baby,
Amelia.

Resuming her maiden name, Anna Marie opened a school for girls on
the third floor of the house at No. 40 Mäster Samuelsgrand (later renamed Mäster Samuelsgata). There she and little Amelia also had their
living quarters. It was a respectable address, though far from select, the
street in that section being lined mainly with small shops, with flats
above them.

The rent was low, but even so Anna Marie barely managed to make
ends meet. Daughter of a respected Stockholm harbor master, she had
received a somewhat better education than was the usual lot of middle-
class Swedish girls in the early 1800's. Nevertheless it had stopped when
she was seventeen. Her principal asset was the Fellborg name, and her
own excellent reputation. The terms of Anna Marie's divorce had stipulated that she might marry again whenever she chose, whereas Captain
Rådberg might not remarry during her lifetime. This unusual provision
was proof of Anna Marie's entire innocence in the break-up of her
marriage.

At the same time Anna Marie had declared over and over that she
would not avail herself of the privilege of remarrying granted her by
the Ecclesiastical Court. A deeply religious young woman, Anna Marie
contended that she was still Captain Rådberg's wife in the sight of God,
for so long as he lived.

But Anna Marie was a lonely woman and a passionate one, though
this last she would have denied indignantly. She had seen no harm in
the friendship that developed after a few years between herself and young
Niklas Lind. He was five years younger than she was, he had no way of
supporting a wife and there was little indication that he ever would have.
He had quickly lost the little lace-manufacturing business his father had
left to him; he never kept very long the bookkeeping jobs he took from
time to time. More than once he had had to go to jail because of debt.

But Niklas was as gay and light-hearted as Anna Marie was sober and
hard-working. He had an agreeable baritone voice, which made him a
favorite in the taverns he frequented—a voice which Anna Marie also

liked to listen to. Moreover, she felt that she was a good influence in the young man's life.

Anna Marie began to look forward to his evening visits. She could forget her troubles when Niklas sang to her accompaniment on the guitar. Niklas's company afforded practically the only pleasure Anna Marie had in the bleak way of life she had elected for herself, and she needed it. For Anna Marie was becoming embittered by her struggle against poverty, with its concomitant burdens of overwork and deprivation. As the years went by, her voice grew sharper, her angry outbursts more frequent. Niklas's admiration and respectful devotion were salve for the affronts fate had put upon her.

When, therefore, Anna Marie had to face the fact that she was pregnant by young Niklas, her chief reaction was outrage. It was not in her nature to blame herself, and she could not find it in her heart to blame Niklas too much. Her resentment concentrated on this new, unthinkable burden.

Niklas begged Anna Marie to marry him. But she had already made one bad marriage; she did not intend to make another which would be even more unsuitable from every practical standpoint. She told Niklas, however, and the few close relatives who had to know her secret, that she could not marry him because she still felt bound to Captain Rådberg.

Luckily, the baby would not be born until mid-fall. Anna Marie finished the school year as usual, then delayed reopening her school after the summer vacation had ended, pleading illness. No one in the outside world knew that a little girl was born to Anna Marie Fellborg on October 6, 1820. The baby was christened the next day, privately. As soon as possible after that, the infant was sent to Ed-Sollentuna to the Carl Ferndals. Anna Marie's school opened again after the Yuletide season as though nothing had happened.

Anna Marie could convince herself very easily that little Jenny would be better off with the Ferndals, who were distant cousins, than in the dingy flat at No. 40 Mäster Samuelsgrand. Ed-Sollentuna was an unspoiled country hamlet, about fifteen miles north of Stockholm. The Ferndals were well-to-do, and it was a religious home. Carl was the parish clerk, he played the organ and led the singing in the little country church. From the time Jenny could walk, she had the freedom of Fru

Ferndal's garden. As she grew a little older, she tagged her "brothers," as she had been taught to regard the two Ferndal boys, through the fields and woods that surrounded the little town. She was the darling of the Ferndal household; the family and servants united in spoiling her.

Anna Marie continued to do her duty conscientiously by the child, visiting her from time to time. But since Jenny looked upon the Ferndals as her parents, it seemed advisable for her to know the seldom smiling woman who appeared at infrequent intervals as Aunt Anna Marie.

It was not until Fru Ferndal had been forced to stay abed for a long time, suffering ever increasing pain, requiring more and more attention from the servants and her worried husband, that the Ferndals began to feel they ought to ask Anna Marie to take her child. Fru Ferndal had broached the matter at Anna Marie's last visit, rashly suggesting that if Anna Marie were to marry Jenny's father quietly, the embarrassing aspects would be done away with. Anna Marie's temper had flared out at the sick woman, and Carl Ferndal had decided sorrowfully that only by caring for the child herself could Anna Marie be brought to a realization of her duty.

To be wrenched from the Ferndals, the big comfortable house and the entrancing surroundings, was in itself a traumatic experience for a child of four. And Jenny's new environment was not of a kind to reconcile her to the change. After she had recovered from her initial fright and shyness, Jenny showed that she had a strong will of her own. She would race through the flat, she would sing at the top of her voice, she would chatter endlessly. Anna Marie screamed at her furiously to stop running, to be quiet.

At first Jenny screamed back, stamped her foot, flew into rages which were an admirable imitation of Anna Marie's own. But her tempests would end in heartbroken sobs. She could not understand why the woman who seemed to be in charge of her destiny disapproved of everything she did and was.

A redeeming factor was that thirteen-year-old Amelia was fond of children and made much of the little girl. So did the one boarding pupil, Louise Johansson, also thirteen. The two girls appointed themselves mothers to the child. The happiest times for Jenny, though, were the evenings when the young man who called himself Papa Niklas would appear. She soon learned to recognize the quick steps, taking the stairs two at a time, and would run to the door to meet him. Too, Aunt Anna Marie was usually in a better temper when Papa Niklas was there. Sometimes her mouth would draw into a straight line when he fussed over Jenny, calling her his little baby bird and similar silly names, but she never said anything. When she was in a particularly good mood, she would get her guitar and strum an accompaniment of chords while Papa Niklas sang the sentimental ballads of Bellman and other popular Swedish composers. Jenny, sitting on his knee in the circle of his arm, felt warm and safe and happy at these times.

A four-year-old child takes relationships as she finds them, and it never occurred to Jenny that there was anything incongruous about the relationships at No. 40 Mäster Samuelsgrand. Anna Marie remained "Aunt," as she had been at Ed-Sollentuna. The gay, affectionate young man who came in now and then of an evening was Papa Niklas, because that was what he called himself with Jenny. Amelia, who called Aunt Anna Marie "Mama" and Papa Niklas "Uncle Niklas," was Jenny's big sister. That was Amelia's idea. She had asked Anna Marie if she might not play that Jenny was her sister, and Anna Marie, a rather peculiar expression on her face, had given permission. As for Jenny herself, explanations and a last name had proved unnecessary. To those about her she was merely Jenny.

It seemed perfectly natural to Jenny, therefore, that when Anna Marie's mother, Fru Tengmark, came back from a visit to relatives, she should be Grandma to both Amelia and Jenny. Fru Tengmark, who had remarried after her husband's death and had again been widowed, was waiting until there should be a vacancy in the Stockholm Widows' Home, spending her time with various relatives meanwhile.

Grandma seemed very fond of Jenny, and Jenny soon became very fond of Grandma. It was an added bond that both suffered from Anna Marie's attacks of ill temper, and neither was able to cope with her. Grandma's refuge was her strong, simple Lutheran faith, and she shared it with Jenny. When the child would come running into the old lady's room, her face puckered in an effort to keep the tears back, Grandma would open her Bible and seek out a comforting text or story. In after

[24]

years, Jenny attributed her own strong religious bent to Grandma Teng-mark's early teaching.

Jenny owed something else to Grandma Tengmark, too, and it was something that had required considerable courage on the part of the gentle, timorous lady. In the dull routine of life at No. 40 Mäster Samuelsgrand, there was one colorful interlude. Every day a military band would march down the street, playing, on its way to the Palace. There was a certain fanfare which the band played often as it passed the house.

One day Grandma heard someone playing this fanfare on the piano. She supposed it was Amelia, who had been taking piano lessons from her mother for some time. The fanfare was a long one and rather diffi-cult, Grandma thought it very nice that Amelia could play so well by ear, and called to Amelia to say so. Receiving no answer, she went to the door and looked into the room. No one was there. She was about to turn away, perplexed, when she heard a little sound, and saw Jenny crowding still farther underneath the piano. It was she who had played the fanfare. She had hidden because she was sure she would be scolded for it. That night Fru Tengmark nerved herself to tell Anna Marie of the incident, and also of Jenny's pitiful assumption that she would be punished.

Anna Marie bristled. "She was right in thinking that she should be punished for banging on my piano. It is the only nice thing I have. Since she hid, she knew she was doing wrong. She shall certainly be punished!"

"But she wasn't banging, Anna Marie. She was playing, and playing very well! It was really remarkable." Then seeing that Anna Marie re-mained angry, Fru Tengmark exclaimed in spite of herself, "Anna Marie, why do you hate the child so?"

"How can you say such a thing!" Anna Marie's face began to quiver, the harsh lines broke up. To Fru Tengmark's astonishment, her stern strong daughter was crying.

"I don't hate the child, Mother. It is myself that I hate!" Anna Marie struck her chest with her fist. "It is something here! Oh, I have tried. I don't want to do the things I do, I don't want to be cross with Jenny. But when I see her something rises up in me and I can't help myself.

Oh Mother, what ails me? Where have I gone wrong? Why do these things happen to me?"

Fru Tengmark wished desperately that she were a cleverer woman. Never before had Anna Marie spoken in this way. If only she could know the right thing to say, it might be a turning point in her daughter's dreary, mistaken life. But the words did not come, and while she hesitated, Anna Marie raised her head with the old gesture of proud defiance and dabbed angrily at the tears.

"After all, though, it isn't easy. If you had to raise two children all alone, with no help from anyone, and support them too, you might find yourself tired and cross at times!"

Sighing to herself, Fru Tengmark returned to the incident of the afternoon. "I wish you could have heard Jenny play the fanfare," she said. "When I praised her and asked her how she could do it, she said such a strange thing for a little child. She said, 'I felt the music in my fingers.' Anna Marie, she has inherited your talent for music! Mark my words, some day she is going to make you very proud of her. As proud as your father and I were when you played the piano so much better than anyone else at the recitals."

And how proud indeed they had been of this daughter, Fru Tengmark's thoughts continued sadly. Had they been too proud, given her her own way too much? Yet how could they have helped it when she was so good-looking, so brilliant, so talented? Always a leader, always first in her studies, always the star of the pupil concerts the piano teacher sponsored.

It had been bad luck that at seventeen, a most impressionable age, Anna Marie caught the eye of the much older Captain Erik Johan Rådberg. It had done no good to point out that the captain was a divorced man whose five children had been awarded to their mother, that he had a reputation for being irresponsible. Anna Marie must have her own way in this, as in all other things. Yet eighteen months after the wedding, Anna Marie herself brought suit for divorce. The high-spirited, confident girl had become a stony-faced woman. Her husband had been unfaithful to her. And though he pleaded that his lapse had been unintentional and would not be repeated, she refused to see or speak to him again. She would not even accept the financial aid—one-half of the captain's salary, in fact—which had been granted her by the court.

Merely Jenny

All this was nothing, however, compared with Fru Tengmark's bewilderment when told that Anna Marie was to bear a child by young Niklas Lind, and was determined, moreover, to bear it out of wedlock, insisting that she was Niklas's wife in the sight of God. But hardest of all to understand had been Anna Marie's attitude toward the baby after it was born. Dutifully she had allowed the infant to suckle from her overflowing breasts, but without tenderness. Fru Tengmark, who was there for the accouchement, ached for the little thing. And how explain the fact that Anna Marie christened the baby Johanna Marie, combining the Johan of her discarded husband's name with her own middle name? It was Fru Tengmark, secretly scandalized, who had started calling the baby Jenny. Anna Marie still professed to love Niklas Lind as a true wife, yet turned toward his child the same stony face she had turned toward Erik Johan Rådberg when he fell from grace! It was all too much for Grandma Tengmark.

However, in attributing Jenny's musical feat to talent inherited from Anna Marie, Fru Tengmark had struck the right chord. Jenny was permitted to take music lessons from Amelia. And after the allotted practice time for the scales and chords and arpeggios prescribed by Amelia, she was allowed to play the music that ran through her head. Whatever music penetrated Jenny's ears remained with her—strains floating upward from passers-by on the street; Papa Niklas's songs; tunes sung by the pupils, in the classroom or out of it. And Jenny's fingers seemed to know where to go on the keyboard to reproduce it.

Before long, the music she made on the piano became Jenny's only escape. Grandma Tengmark left them in August of 1824, a vacancy having occurred at the Stockholm Widows' Home. Now that there was no one to look after her during school hours when Amelia and Louise Johansson were busy at their lessons, the four-year-old must sit in the schoolroom too. The pupils were much older than she was, and there was little to interest her in what went on. She would drift into dreaming that she was back in Ed-Sollentuna. Sometimes in the big, sunny, kitchen, full of delicious smells, sometimes in the meadow with her "brothers," the Ferndal boys. They would stop their play to listen when the sound of the church organ came to them. Papa Ferndal was practicing the hymns for the next service. Jenny would hurry to the church. Papa Ferndal would lift her up onto his knee, she would feel the rhythm through her whole body as his feet pumped the pedals. He would put his big fingers over her little ones and guide them over the keys, so that she could imagine she was making the sonorous music herself.

One day Jenny disappeared. Amelia and Louise Johansson, going in search of her, found her far up the street. She told them she was going home, to her papa and mama in the country. Amelia knelt down in the dust and put her arms comfortingly around the little girl. "You can't go back to Ed-Sollentuna, pet; your mother is dead." Jenny did not know what "dead" meant, but the word had a sound of finality. She did not try to run away again, and the pictures of Ed-Sollentuna grew fainter and fainter, until Jenny could not distinguish between her own imaginings and the things she had experienced there. But all the rest of her life Jenny Lind was to yearn for the country—for open fields and woods and birds and flowers.

The years between 1824 and 1828 were increasingly dreary for Jenny. Things were going badly with the school. As pupils dropped out, Anna Marie became more and more sharp-tempered. And the more sharp-tempered she became, the faster pupils dropped out.

Everyone felt Anna Marie's displeasure, with the possible exception of Amelia, but Jenny usually felt it most. She learned to recognize the signs—the red that would flame in Aunt Anna Marie's cheeks, the hard, steely look in her eyes—and would make herself as inconspicuous as possible.

One bright spot was that she was allowed to visit Grandma Tengmark fairly often at the Widows' Home. Away from the depressing atmosphere of No. 40 Mäster Samuelsgrand, she would skip and sing. She said years afterward that she probably sang for Grandma Tengmark, too. But no one seems to have seen anything remarkable in her voice during this period. It was her piano playing that drew whatever favorable attention she received in her own home. She was frequently asked to play for visitors, who were usually parents of Anna Marie's pupils. Anna Marie was all smiles on these occasions, taking the compliments Jenny received as a tribute to the quality of her teaching.

Thus Jenny learned that by working hard at the musical tasks assigned her, she could command respect in the forbidding adult world.

Merely Jenny

She was approved and applauded, even though she was little and homely and had nothing but her facility at the piano to recommend her.

Jenny was eight when Louise Johansson left, unable to stand Anna Marie's moods and tempers any longer. This was a fatal blow, since Louise's board money had been a mainstay. Anna Marie had to close her school and look about for employment. She was offered a position as governess in Linköping, a town at a considerable distance from Stockholm. She could take the now seventeen-year-old Amelia with her, to help with her charges, but she could not take Jenny.

Nothing at all is said about Niklas Lind during this period. He could hardly have accompanied Anna Marie to Linköping, but evidently there was no thought that he might assume the responsibility for Jenny. He had a very respectable aunt, Fru Strömberg, who had taken him into her home, after he was orphaned, and with whom Jenny herself found refuge some years later. It is unlikely that Fru Strömberg knew as yet of Jenny's existence. Relations with the family at Ed-Sollentuna had been broken off. Anna Marie's moods grew darker, her temper flared more frequently, as she was held in Stockholm by her inability to find a home for Jenny.

It was at this point, the lowest so far in Jenny's life, that Providence decided to take a hand in her affairs. At least, Grandma Tengmark so regarded it, and with some reason. For one day the new steward of the Stockholm Widows' Home knocked at the door of Fru Tengmark's room. When she opened it he told her, beaming, that he had a surprise for her. Then out from behind the man, where she had been hiding, Jenny ran, threw her arms around her grandmother and announced that she had come to live at the home! In the lodge at the entrance, that was to say, with the steward and his wife.

The steward was full of the strange coincidence, which had all come about, so he said, through an advertisement in the newspaper.

"An advertisement in the newspaper?" murmured Fru Tengmark.

"Why yes. You see, my wife and I never had any children, though we always wanted them. We've talked, off and on, about taking one in. Then we came to this new job, with the lodge to live in and an extra bedroom, so we put a notice in the paper, asking for a little girl to keep us company. Your daughter, Fru Fellborg, answered it. And here we are!"

Jenny Lind, the Swedish Nightingale

Grandma Tengmark was convinced that her God had personally engineered the whole thing.

Jenny always remembered the next year of her life as the time when she could jump and run and sing and chatter as much as she liked. She was the pet not only of her grandmother and the kindly steward and his wife, but of all the old ladies in the home. Now she sang all the time. The old ladies delighted in teaching her their own favorite songs and the folk songs of the sections of Sweden where they had grown up.

Jenny was even permitted to have a pet, a cat. When the steward and his wife were busy and the old ladies were resting, she would sing to the cat. The place she liked best of all in the lodge was the window looking out on the busy street which led to the Church of St. Jakob's. She would sit there on the broad window sill, holding the cat, and sing and sing. Her voice even then had a clear, bell-like quality and an oddly moving sweetness. Passers-by, we are told, would hear the clear, piercingly sweet young voice, and pause to listen and wonder.

Among the frequent passers-by, as it happened, was the maid of a Mademoiselle Lundberg, one of the dancers at the Royal Opera House. Members of the Royal Theater were expected to help recruit fresh new talent for the Royal Theater School, where gifted children were trained for the stage. This was to insure a steady stream of home-grown performers for the Royal Theater, which was supported by the state, and was dear to the King and Queen. The maid reported to Mademoiselle Lundberg that never in her life had she heard such a beautiful voice as that of the little girl who sat in the window of the lodge at the gate of the Stockholm Widows' Home. Mademoiselle simply must hear this child sing.

When Mademoiselle Lundberg told the story in later years, as she did very often, she said that she had been skeptical at first. But she yielded finally to the maid's persuasion. Anna Marie was in Stockholm at this time and Mademoiselle Lundberg hunted her up, urging her, "You must have the child sing for the Directors of the Royal Theater School. I believe they will take her into the Royal Theater School and educate her for the stage."

(In that day, "the stage" covered opera, as well as strictly theatrical performances. Jenny always spoke of her opera sphere as "the stage," and of her performances there as "acting.")

Anna Marie received the idea coldly. The stage was not considered respectable; the private lives of actresses and opera singers were rumored to be very scandalous, and frequently were. But Mademoiselle Lundberg was insistent, and Anna Marie finally consented to an appointment with Herr Croelius, the singing master at the Royal Theater School.

Herr Croelius was a heavy-set man with a sharp nose, shrewd, kindly eyes and thick, tousled hair. But Jenny was no beauty herself. She was small for her age, and has described herself as ugly, shy and awkward, "with little, piggy eyes and a big, broad nose."

The homely, undersized child sang an aria from a now forgotten opera by Winter. Where she had learned it, no one could imagine. But somewhere she had heard it and her retentive ear had picked it up. When she finished, Herr Croelius's eyes were filled with tears.

Herr Croelius went off to get Count Pucke, who was above Croelius in the Theater School hierarchy. When Count Pucke learned that the child Herr Croelius wanted him to listen to was only nine, he refused to waste his time. "We are not running a nursery here, after all." Herr Croelius persisted, finally exclaiming, "If you do not come, I will teach her myself for nothing. Some day you will hear her sing, and she will astonish you." Count Pucke yielded, to please the singing master. When he heard the child sing, his eyes, too, filled with tears. This is the first recorded instance of what was to be an outstanding characteristic of Jenny Lind's voice—its power to play on the heartstrings of the listener.

Count Pucke at once offered to take Jenny into the Royal Theater School. Not only would she receive instruction in the skills needed by an actress, but the school would also pay for her maintenance and general education. It was expected that after Jenny's preparation for the stage was finished she would pay back the money that had been advanced. But this would be her responsibility. Anna Marie would be relieved henceforth of any financial burden in connection with Jenny.

Nevertheless, Anna Marie refused. To subject the child to the godless atmosphere of the stage and the temptations that would surround her as she grew older was unthinkable, she declared.

Count Pucke and Herr Croelius came back with more and more

enticing offers. It was the custom of the school to board its pupils out, paying for their maintenance and also for their education in subjects not in the school curriculum. They would board Jenny with Anna Marie, they said, paying her for the child's keep, and also pay her to teach Jenny the outside subjects. When this offer failed, they volunteered to place three other pupils with Anna Marie, under the same arrangement. By now, Anna Marie's impatience and temper had cost her her job as governess, and she was thinking of reopening her school. Four boarding pupils would have solved her financial problems. Yet she still refused.

Anna Marie had been at the Widows' Home a great deal while the negotiations were going on, and her mother had agreed fully with her viewpoint. All the old ladies, in fact, had to be given full accounts of the conversations with the gentlemen of the Theater School, and nodded their heads approvingly over Anna Marie's continued staunch refusals.

The steward and his wife had received the impression, without being told any actual falsehoods, we may be sure, that Jenny was the orphaned daughter of another child of Fru Tengmark. Since Grandma Tengmark did not want to reveal Jenny's illegitimacy, the idea had become prevalent in the home. The old ladies believed that Anna Marie had nobly assumed the responsibility for her niece's care. Now she was nobly resisting the efforts of the powers of darkness to get hold of the child.

There was a great clucking of tongues and shaking of heads when Anna Marie reported the latest offer. It said much for Fru Fellborg's principles, the old ladies declared, that she was not moved by it in the least. But as Grandma Tengmark thought it over, she began to wonder.

One day Anna Marie found Fru Tengmark and Jenny alone in the grandmother's room, and Grandma Tengmark told Anna Marie what she had been thinking.

"Do you remember I said to you once, years ago, that some day Jenny would make you very proud of her? I thought it then because of the way she had played the fanfare on the piano, when she was such a tiny mite. But now those people at the theater—Mademoiselle Lundberg, Herr Croelius, Count Pucke himself—seem to think Jenny has a voice that some day will make all Sweden proud of her.

"Isn't it possible that this offer is God's way of bringing it about? Didn't God bring her here to the lodge when you had to go off to

Linköping? Perhaps He did it so that Mademoiselle Lundberg's maid would hear Jenny sing, and persuade Mademoiselle to have Herr Croelius hear her sing. Perhaps it is by His will that these gentlemen still keep on, after you have said no so many times.

"I haven't a great deal longer to live, Anna Marie, and my prayer to our dear Lord has been that He would look after you and Jenny. These gentlemen have offered to leave Jenny at home with you. Now they are offering such terms that you won't have to wear yourself down with hard work and worry.

"Jenny is a good girl, she will be a good woman. Just think how many prettier faces Count Pucke and Herr Croelius could find if *that* was what they wanted. They ask only to cultivate the talents God has given Jenny. Can this be wrong? And how can harm come to her when she is living in your home, under your moral and spiritual care?"

Perhaps Anna Marie had secretly wanted some encouragement in a course that would be so advantageous to her, for she did not argue the points her mother had made. She raised another one.

"I don't think you realize, Mother, that if Jenny enters the Theater School, a contract will have to be made, papers will have to be signed. Consent will have to be obtained from both parents. Did you know that?"

"But surely Niklas will agree?"

"Of course he will, if I do. But don't you see, Mother, *everything would have to come out?*"

Fru Tengmark did see now what had lain behind Anna Marie's steadfast refusals. She would have to reveal the truth about Jenny's parentage. Anna Marie's twisted "principles" were closing the door to what Fru Tengmark had come to look upon as the salvation of both Jenny and Anna Marie herself.

She exclaimed, in a voice shaking with emotion, "Anna Marie, this child is God's lamb. I feel it, I know it! His hand has been laid upon her. You must not, you shall not, sacrifice her any longer to your selfish blindness and foolish ideas!"

Anna Marie was not accustomed to criticism from her meek little mother. "So I'm blind, I'm selfish, and my ideas are foolish!" she retorted angrily. Jenny, looking up at the sharp tones, saw the angry color surge into Anna Marie's cheeks, the steely look come into her eyes. "Very

[33]

well, if that is the way you want it." Anna Marie turned to Jenny and said in a hard, angry voice, "Your grandmother has decided you are to enter the Theater School. It seems I have nothing to say about it. I am only your mother, after all."

Jenny stared in wild disbelief, not realizing she was clutching her cat so hard that it was struggling and crying to be released.

"You are my aunt! My mother is dead! Amelia told me so!"

"It was your foster mother who died," Anna Marie went on in the same hard voice. "I am your real mother, and Papa Niklas is your father. Your name is Jenny Lind, and that is what you will be called at the school."

Anna Marie's manner, more than the revelations themselves, made the news unbearable to Jenny. She dropped the cat and ran to her grandmother sobbing, "It isn't so, Grandma, I know it isn't so!"

Fru Tengmark lifted the child onto her lap. "It is true, dearest, that Fru Ferndal was your foster mother. Aunt Anna Marie is your real mother. Some day you will understand. And just think, your mother is going to let you go to the Theater School! You will learn all sorts of nice things there, and some day you will be famous. Jenny, my love, my darling, I have talked to God so much about you, and I believe this is the answer to my prayers."

Jenny cried for a long time, not quite knowing why she cried. But the next time Anna Marie went to the Opera House, Fru Tengmark and Jenny went with her. Jenny stayed with Fru Tengmark while Anna Marie, at her own request, had a private conference with Count Pucke and Herr Croelius in another room.

Presently they returned, Anna Marie sweeping into the room with her head held high and the red spots burning brightly in her cheeks. She did not appear angry, however, and the two gentlemen displayed a markedly deferential attitude toward her. Throughout the discussion of details that followed, it was Madam this, and Madam that, as though Anna Marie had been a great lady.

After the visitors had been bowed out, Count Pucke dropped into the nearest chair. "What a woman! I thought I had seen everything in the way of stage mothers, but Fru Fellborg is something new. She makes it seem a positive virtue to have borne a child out of wedlock!"

Herr Croelius chuckled. "Never mind. It was well worth some bowing and scraping to get a chance to make something of that child." Then he grew serious. "But what about the other pupils we have promised to place with Madam? We didn't know the full story then."

"My dear Croelius, we can be sure that Fru Fellborg would never countenance in anyone else the kind of behavior she justifies so convincingly in her own case. If anything, she will be likely to look after the moral character of our girls rather more carefully than they will appreciate."

In fact, Anna Marie felt it her duty to warn Jenny against the bad women she would undoubtedly encounter at the theater, and against yielding to the temptations surrounding the stage, as soon as the door of the Opera House had closed behind them. Grandma Tengmark said nothing, but pressed Jenny's hand reassuringly. After the old lady and the little girl were back at the Widows' Home, Grandma Tengmark opened her Bible and read aloud the passage about the pure of heart.

"God has given you your voice, precious," she said earnestly. "He has opened the way now for you to cultivate it. Use it always as God would want you to use it, and He will protect you from harm."

For a while, Jenny wondered about the "bad women" Anna Marie had warned her against. But the only women she ever encountered at the school were the teachers, and the actresses and dancers of the Royal Theater. The latter were so pretty, wore such lovely clothes and were so kind to the pupils, that Jenny knew they couldn't be bad. Before long, she forgot both the bad women and the mysterious "temptations" Anna Marie had spoken of.

Because Grandma Tengmark was kind and loving, her gentle admonition sank deep into the child's mind, and remained there.

CHAPTER TWO

The Training of a Star

JENNY became an *"aktris-elev"* of the Swedish Royal Theater School in September of 1830, a month before her tenth birthday on October 6. She was to receive lessons in singing, elocution, dancing, French and "such other branches as belong to the education of a cultivated woman, and are requisite for the theatrical profession," according to the contract Anna Marie had signed. Anna Marie was to be paid for seeing to her daughter's food, shelter, warmth, furniture, clothing, bedding and laundry and "supplying a mother's tender care"; and also for teaching Jenny and the three other boarders from the Theater School piano, religion, history, geography, writing, arithmetic and drawing.

Jenny herself was to receive two *Riksdaler Banco* a month (about eighty cents) for pocket money, but the contract specified that out of this she was to pay for the needles, thread and materials needed to mend her clothes.

The Royal directors were to be the judges as to the time when Jenny would be considered competent to become an actress in the Royal Theater, draw a salary from the Civil List and start paying back the money her education had cost; and they were also to determine the salary she would receive. At this time a new contract was to be drawn up, by which Jenny was to pledge herself to remain for ten years in the service of the Royal Theater. On the other hand, should *Aktris-elev* Lind prove to be of no use to the Royal Theater, or fail in the obedience she owed the Royal

Directors, she could be discharged with three months notice and the contract would lapse.

If Anna Marie felt any qualms at agreeing to what would amount to virtual bondage for Jenny throughout the first ten years of her professional life, she gave no indication of it. She rented a flat at No. 4 Quarteret Hammeren in the Parish of St. Jakob's (the Jakobsbersgata), near the handsome Opera building, which also housed the Theater School. She tried to dress Jenny in a manner befitting their new economic status, but in vain. Jenny declared later that she had never cared for frills and furbelows, and would pull the feathers from her hat and the ribbons from her dress as soon as she got out of sight of home.

The contract had been read to Jenny before it was signed, and Count Pucke had explained to her solemnly that she would have to work very hard in order to continue to receive the benefits of the school. But to Jenny, who had had little experience with the usual childish games, it was as though, in studying dancing and acting and music, she were being exhorted to "work" at the most delightful play one could imagine.

She was by far the youngest child who had ever been taken into the school, the average age for entrants being fourteen, and the heads of the school and the teachers took a special interest in this unusually young and unusually gifted student. Herr Forsberg, a war office official who handled the financial affairs of the school and had the title of Honorary Superintendent, looked on Jenny as a daughter, and she was often in his home. Herr Croelius naturally considered Jenny his special protégé, giving her much extra time and care, while Mademoiselle Bayard, the school matron, petted and mothered her. Jenny skipped and sang all the way to school and back again because she was so happy.

It cannot be disputed that Jenny Lind owed much of her later success to the fact that from the age of ten onward, she was trained in all the skills essential to a dramatic artist. In the dancing classes, she learned to carry herself well and to walk with a unique grace and distinction which counteracted the angular thinness that was to characterize her for a number of years. It was as a child actress that she first appeared in public. When she had become a great opera singer, the critics customarily devoted as much space to analyzing her interpretations of her roles and praising her acting as to her singing.

Jenny also, however, displayed a natural bent for all the skills the theater brings into play. She was a beautiful dancer, though after she became a prima donna she did not dance much socially for fear of becoming overfatigued. She could have excelled equally at the piano, except that she feared the long hours of necessary practicing would, like dancing, tire her too much and affect her voice. But she was completely at home with the piano, loved to improvise, and when she sang her Swedish folk songs, either at private parties or in concerts, accompanied herself in a way that added much to their charm. She was a "quick study." The blue-gray eyes may have been as small and "piggy" as Jenny always claimed, but they were bright with intelligence. Anything to do with music, in particular, seemed to come to her as effortlessly as her lungs took in the air she breathed.

It proved an actual advantage that Jenny was small for her age. The combined Swedish Royal Theater and Opera presented every kind of production from grand opera and concerts to comedy burlesques. The December following Jenny's entrance into the school in September, she was given a fat role as the seven-year-old Angela in the Royal Theater's production of a melodrama, *The Polish Mine*. In March 18, 1831, a few months later, she received her first newspaper notice, for her acting of the part of Johanna in a play called *Testamentet, a Drama*. *Heimdall*, a periodical devoted to literature and art, apologized for not having called attention before this to the young *aktris-elev*. "She shows in her acting a quick perception, a fire and feeling, far beyond her years," denoting, in the opinion of *Heimdall's* critic, "an uncommon disposition for the theater."

In 1833, she appeared in twenty-two performances at the Royal Theater, including one opus called *Thirty Years of a Gambler's Life*, which proved so popular that it was repeated many times in 1834. In 1833 also, before Jenny was thirteen, she entered so wholeheartedly into the "coquetry, boldness and heartlessness" of the role assigned her in a French farce, *La Fausse Agnes*, that the newspaper *Daily Allehanda* felt she had rendered her part with "an almost incomprehensible, a really unnatural cleverness." The *Daily Allehanda's* critic complained of the immoral character of this play and called upon the young girl's instructors and guardians to pay more attention to their responsibilities for guarding "her happy natural gifts, high-spirited as they are." The directors evidently took heed, for they did not again give Jenny a role of this nature.

So far, the special attention Jenny had attracted from the critics had been because of her acting and dancing, though she had had a few singing parts by the time she was fourteen. But her voice was not neglected. Herr Croelius was privileged to instruct his protégée only for a year, for when Jenny was eleven he retired and was followed by Herr Izak Berg as singing master. (Croelius wrote Jenny, not long before his death, "Your fame, your success, are the comfort of my old age and a balm for my sufferings.") Herr Berg took a more intense interest in Jenny than Herr Croelius had done, if that were possible. The new singing master was a popular figure in Stockholm society. He had Jenny singing duets with him at parties almost from the first moment that she came under his guidance. In November, 1832, just a month after she turned twelve, she sang a duet with Berg at a concert in the Royal Theater.

Heimdall lavished praise for Jenny's mastery of difficult musical passages, her quick receptiveness, ending with a prophecy that was also a warning. "If this young genius does not ripen too prematurely, there is every reason for expecting to find in her an operatic artist of high rank."

It was well for Jenny that she had these successes to buoy her, for conditions at home were becoming more and more difficult. Anna Marie at first had been impressed by her daughter's new importance and that she had eased life for all of them; the fact that Jenny now bore openly the name of a man her mother had never married seems not to have injured Anna Marie's reputation in the least, so formidable was her air of respectability. But self-pity had become chronic with Anna Marie. Before long she began to complain because of the work connected with boarding the four Theater School pupils and teaching them, though it was less than the work of building up and maintaining her own school would have been.

It was no trick at all for Anna Marie to persuade herself that Jenny was responsible. For was it not in order to give Jenny her great chance that Anna Marie had taken on this heavy burden? Presently her ill-humor extended to the other boarders as well, and the time came when they would stand it no longer. The three who had been awarded Anna Marie as an extra inducement to let Jenny enter the Theater School—one of them was Fanny Westerdahl, who later became a famous singer—presented themselves to Mademoiselle Bayard, the school matron, and said they had left Anna Marie's for good.

Mademoiselle Bayard found rooms for them on the top floor of the Opera House and acted as their chaperon. Jenny often visited the girls in their new quarters and saw how happy they were under Mademoiselle Bayard's kindly guardianship. There Jenny made her first friendship with a girl her own age, Mina Fundin; for by this time Jenny was approaching the age at which pupils usually were taken into the school. The friendship with Mina lasted as long as Jenny lived.

Anna Marie had taken it for granted that Jenny, being her own child, would have to stay with her, and for a while Jenny did. But she was no longer the cowed, apprehensive little creature of No. 40 Mäster Samuels-grand Street. She had learned to call Anna Marie "Mama," but respected her less as a mother than she had as an aunt. For as Jenny came to understand that she was as much Anna Marie's own child as Amelia was, a hard core of resentment grew within her. Once again she began to flare up angrily in response to Anna Marie's nagging. And at the end of October, 1834, having turned fourteen on the sixth, Jenny too presented herself to Mademoiselle Bayard and asked to be allowed to live at the Opera House. By this time the directors knew Anna Marie's character very well indeed. They gave their approval to the arrangement.

Anna Marie was furious. Until she had accepted the offer from the directors of the school, Jenny had merely represented an incumbrance to her. But now her daughter's presence in the home was a source of income. Also, Jenny's talent was attracting attention in the world, and her defection was a blow to Anna Marie's pride. Wrathfully, Anna Marie went to the theater and demanded that Jenny be sent back home, basing her claims on the contract the directors had signed with her. She had carried out her part of the bargain, Anna Marie insisted. But the directors could have shown, had they wished to do so, that Anna Marie had not supplied a "mother's tender care"—one wonders if that clause might have been put in the contract to cover such a contingency as this. In any event, they let Jenny stay at the Opera House.

It has always been assumed that the year-and-a-half Jenny lived at the Opera House was an especially happy time for her, and no doubt it was in many respects. To have Mademoiselle Bayard's kindly supervision in place of her mother's tantrums and petty tyrannies, to have the assurance of the love and interest of the heads of the school, to have a full part in the fun and pleasures enjoyed by the other girls, perhaps above all to have at last a friend of her own age, meant much to Jenny. The summer of 1835, she went with several girls from the school, including Mina Fundin, to a little inland lake for a holiday. The first of Jenny's letters to be preserved were written from there—perhaps the first she wrote, for her life up to this time had hardly called for letter writing—and they display the happy exuberance of a middle-teen-ager who feels secure in her world.

But there were matters for wondering and apprehension and heartache, too, during this period. The May following Jenny's flight to Mademoiselle Bayard, Herr Forsberg called Jenny to his office, for there were important developments she had to know about. First, Anna Marie had renewed her efforts to get Jenny back. Second, Jenny's father and mother had finally married on May 5, 1835.

Niklas Lind drops from sight with the break-up of Anna Marie's school at No. 40 Mäster Samuelsgrand and her departure to Linköping. There is no mention of him at all during the intervening years, but evidently the alliance had continued and now Anna Marie had not only dragged poor, feckless Niklas into her fight with the Theater School, but at long last had married him. There was a face-saving aspect for Anna Marie in the fact that Captain Erik Johann Rådberg had died. However, Anna Marie was taking her case against the Theater School into court, and that she was not as blind to material considerations as she liked to pretend was to become obvious before very long. It must have occurred to her that she would stand in better light before the court if she were married legally to the father of the child she wished to reclaim, as well as in the eyes of God.

Herr Forsberg could not tell what Jenny was thinking as she received this news. The face that sparkled with animation when she played a lively role on the stage was dull and lifeless now. The eyes were downcast. She said nothing at all.

Herr Forsberg went on to explain that it was very unpleasant to have family affairs aired in a courtroom. Jenny might have to testify. The directors were prepared to fight the case if that was what Jenny wanted. But first they must find out if Jenny preferred to return home.

"I would rather stay here if you will let me."

The very next month, Herr Forsberg had even more distressing news for Jenny. Amelia, who had recently been married, had incurred what her doctor called "nerve fever," and had died. Jenny had loved Amelia. This was a serious blow, and she knew, moreover, what a loss it would be to Anna Marie. Perhaps if her mother had stretched out loving arms to Jenny at this time, their whole future might have been different. But no word came from the Linds, Anna Marie continued her efforts to get Jenny back by way of the courts, and Jenny stayed on at the Opera House.

The directors had, of course, long since written Anna Marie down as a pious hypocrite. But how did Jenny regard all this? Her preceptors at the school had shielded her from ugliness as far as was humanly possible. Nevertheless, Jenny was at an age when the most sheltered young girl wonders about the origins of life, picks up knowledge of the relations between men and women, and applies it to the men and women she knows. How account for the fact that her parents had waited to marry until their daughter was fourteen and a half?

That Jenny came through this period with no outward evidence of harm was due no doubt partly to the support she received from everyone at the Theater School, partly to the fact that already she was a disciplined professional, with firmly established work habits. She could forget her troubles in the gay companionship at the school and in study. Yet there are signs that her career languished a little. During 1836, she was seen on the stage only eighteen times. She made her first appearance in an opera, one composed by Adolf Linblad, the leading Swedish composer of the time, but the opera was never repeated after the first few performances. Years later Lindblad sent Jenny a copy of the score, with a notation that the opera was so bad "even your genius could not save it."

The fact remains that Jenny's performance did not create any stir whatsoever.

The court judging the Linds' suit against the Theater School handed down its verdict on June 23rd of that year. It was a complete victory for Jenny's parents. Jenny must return home. The Theater School was required to pay the lawyer fees and all other expenses incidental to the case, and also to pay Anna Marie for her daughter's board, lodging and teaching during the time Jenny had lived at the Opera House.

Once more Jenny was called to Herr Forsberg's office. She was now fifteen and a half and had shot up in the last year or two, so that she was no longer so small for her age, though still thin and coltish. Looking at her, Herr Forsberg was amazed, as he frequently was, that so much talent could be contained in this pale, plain creature. Grandma Tengmark had been right in saying the Royal directors could have found many prettier girls than Jenny, who having long ago accepted her lack of beauty, did nothing to make herself more attractive.

"Well, Jenny," Herr Forsberg sighed, "we have lost the suit your parents brought against us. The court says you must return to your parents' home by July 1—that is just a week away. I am afraid there is nothing more the directors can do, and we are all very sorry it has turned out this way." He got up from his chair, paced back and forth.

"What troubles me most, Jenny, since you must return home, is that we may have made a mistake in fighting the case. I hope, my dear, that it won't make your situation at home more unpleasant. It is very hard to know what is best to do in such a situation. For your own sake, Jenny, I would like to suggest that you conceal any resentment you may feel. You are compelled to live at home now until you marry, and I would like to see you make the best of it."

"I am afraid I have made the directors a great deal of trouble," Jenny said. "I should have thought of that."

Herr Forsberg smiled. "We consider you a very valuable property, Jenny. We didn't want anything to stand in the way of your success, and we were afraid that unhappiness in your home might interfere with your progress. But more than that, we all love you. We felt you deserved happiness, and we wanted you to have it."

The plain face underwent one of those marvelous transformations for which one day it would be famous. The gray eyes lighted; Jenny momentarily was beautiful.

"I will try, Herr Forsberg. I will try very hard."

Just prior to the date when Jenny must return to No. 4 Quarteret Hammeren, she received a visit from Niklas Lind. "We want you to know, Jenny," he said, "that it wasn't just for the money that we brought our suit. You are our daughter. We love you and we want you with us. Your mother wants me to tell you that things are going to be different now.

"You can't imagine how hard it was on your mother, losing Amelia that way. She needs you, Jenny-bird. She doesn't mean half what she says, you know. She wants to do right, but something seems to get hold of her and make her do and say things she doesn't feel in her heart. Many's the night she has cried herself to sleep because she drove you away with her crossness. She won't be cross now. Don't you worry, Jenny-bird."

Her father's pleas to start again with a clean slate touched Jenny. "I was pretty cross myself sometimes, Papa," she acknowledged. "I guess it was the same way with me. Something would rise up in me and I would say things I didn't really mean."

So Jenny's homecoming did not prove to be the ordeal that Herr Forsberg had feared. Jenny tried hard and Anna Marie did too. Later that summer Anna Marie took Jenny to the country for a holiday. She wove flower crowns for her daughter and wrote Niklas of the good times they were having "among the haystacks." Jenny added a postscript. "Welcome home, sweet Papa, and do take care of your health. This is the wish of your faithful daughter, Jenny."

By January of 1837, the directors decided Jenny had amply fulfilled her early promise and placed her on a fixed salary as an actress of the Royal Theater. She would not be seventeen until October 6 of that year, yet already she had appeared on the Royal Theater stage one hundred and eleven times, not counting the concerts in which she had taken part. Her salary, set by the directors in accordance with the contract Anna Marie had signed when Jenny entered the school, was 700 *Riksdaler Banco* a year, about the equivalent of sixty English pounds of that day.

In addition, however, she was to receive what was called "play money"—a small bonus each time she appeared on the Royal Theater stage.

To earn her sixty pounds in 1837, Jenny appeared in the theater ninety-two times. The pieces she played in ranged from burlesque comedy to deep tragedy, and her roles from song-and-dance parts to the Second Genius in Mozart's *Magic Flute*. They included Zoë, the title role in a comedy by Scribe; Dafne in Victor Hugo's *Angelo Malipieri*; Fräulein Neubrunn in *The Death of Wallenstein*; and a boy's part in an operetta, *The Fisherman*.

A budding dramatic singer could hardly have asked for a wider range of experience. But Jenny was barely sixteen when she entered upon this strenuous routine. In later life, Jenny used to urge that during her sixteenth and seventeenth years a girl's voice should have a rest. In this she echoed the great singing master Manuel Garcia, to whom it fell eventually to try to undo the damage done to Jenny's voice by her own failure to observe this precept. For Jenny herself, at sixteen, welcomed all the opportunities that came her way.

Toward the end of 1837, she was presented with a very special opportunity. Meyerbeer's was the leading name among contemporary opera composers. His works were the rage in Paris and Berlin, but as yet none had been heard in Stockholm. Would they appeal to a Swedish audience? The directors of the Royal Theater were uncertain. They decided upon a test before presenting a Meyerbeer opera in toto.

A scene from *Robert de Normandie* would be given in a concert. It included a short passage from the part of Alice, and Jenny was chosen to sing it. Brief though it was, the passage was particularly melodious, and it ended in a pathetic cadence which brought out, as her previous singing roles had not done, the peculiarly moving quality of Jenny's voice. Her official biographers, Holland and Rockstro, wrote many years later, "The tradition still lives of the instantaneous effect she produced on all who heard her. It was a short flight, she merely tried her wings."

But it opened the way to flights that carried her far and high.

The scene from *Robert de Normandie* was repeated four times that December. Meyerbeer's music was acclaimed, but the critics' most enthusiastic enconiums were for Jenny's singing in the bit she had played. The newspapers were demanding to hear her in a full opera, and Jenny was assigned the role of Agatha in Weber's *Der Freischütz*, opening March 7. While studying it—a very heavy, exacting score for a girl barely seventeen —she also played throughout January and February in a melodrama called *The American Monkey*. This was followed by three performances of a tragedy, *The Sons of King Edward*. Any time she could snatch from rehearsals and appearances in these dramas, she worked on the role of Agatha with Madam Eriksson, a former opera singer, who coached the pupils in their dramatic roles.

Madam Eriksson was a favorite of Jenny's, and one day, to please her, Jenny resolved to give everything she had to the part. It was the first time she had ever released all her powers, both of singing and acting. When she had finished, Madam Eriksson said not a word. Jenny was thinking she must have done very badly indeed, until she saw that tears were running down the woman's face. When Madam Eriksson could speak she said, "My child, I have nothing more to teach you. From now on do as your nature tells you."

Der Freischütz was an important opera and a favorite with Stockholm's theater-goers. Agatha was Jenny's first leading role in opera. The day of her debut, March 7, 1837, was spent in agonizing apprehension that she would fail miserably. She was thoroughly accustomed to appearing in public, but this time was different. This time the whole production would stand or fall on her performance.

When she came on stage she was pale and shaking. But with her first notes, confidence surged through her. Giving herself to the part as she had done for her teacher, she thrilled the audience as she had thrilled Madam Eriksson. It was one of those memorable evenings in the theater when a great new talent is recognized. The audience saw that Sweden had a new singing star of magnitude, and Jenny's youth made her all the more appealing.

A tremendous ovation followed her first number, and at the end of the performance, the audience rose and cheered her for many minutes, the members of the orchestra laying down their instruments and joining in the applause. The members of the cast remained on stage after the curtain fell, talking excitedly among themselves. All, that is, except the new star herself. Important persons in the audience began streaming backstage to felicitate Jenny, but she could not be found. Herr Forsberg hurried toward the dressing rooms, calling Jenny's name, until he saw Madam Eriksson coming toward him, gesturing for silence.

"She is in her dressing room," Madam Eriksson whispered. "I looked in just now, but she was on her knees. I think she must be praying."

"Praying! All Stockholm is waiting to congratulate her!"

"I suppose the child is thanking God for her success," Madam Eriksson murmured, tears filling her eyes. "Herr Forsberg, we have never before had a pupil so talented, and so *good!* A prima donna who prays to God *after* a success—what will become of her?"

Jenny's was more than a personal success that night. March 7, 1838, stood thereafter as a notable date in the Swedish theater's history. The Royal directors recognized its importance by presenting Jenny with two silver candlesticks inscribed, "In Remembrance of March 7th." Jenny herself regarded the seventh of March as a second birthday. "I got up, that morning, one creature. I went to bed another creature. I had found my power!" Always thereafter, she would ask her friends to remember her on that day with their prayers.

Jenny sang Agatha nine times during 1838, interspersed between sixty-four appearances in other roles. The directors showed their appreciation by raising her salary, in January, 1839, to 900 *Riksdaler Banco* (about 75 English pounds). On May 10, the Royal Theater presented *Robert de Normandie* in full, with Jenny in the role of Alice. She played it twenty-three times before the year was out, and twenty-three times the next year. August Bournonville, a distinguished Danish composer and ballet master, declared that though Jenny was only eighteen when he first heard her, her performance of Alice could stand comparison with the best he had seen and heard in Paris.

In June, 1839, Jenny gave a concert at Uppsala, where the venerable University of Sweden was located, in connection with the great Whitsuntide festivities which were held there annually. The students went wild with enthusiasm. When she started back to her lodging after the concert, they unhitched the horses from her carriage and pulled it through the streets themselves by long ropes decorated with their corps colors, singing their students' song the whole way. This was the first time Jenny was accorded this accolade, but by no means the last.

The Swedes loved Jenny the more because her head was not turned by her new prominence; she assumed none of the airs of a prima donna. The first female stage performer ever to be accepted in Sweden's highest social circles, she took this, too, entirely as a matter of course. When Jenny attained her full growth, she was around five feet four, the average height for women, but for some years her body retained the thinness and angularity of its upward shoot, though her arms and shoulders were round and lovely. She continued to wear her hair parted in the middle, with bunches of tight little curls at either side of her forehead, a style that made her appear particularly girlish and unsophisticated. She used no cosmetics and her clothes offstage were so simple, they may very well have been run up by Jenny herself and the little maid, Annette, whom Anna Marie had insisted she acquire when she became a star.

Her features were strong and somewhat coarse, her mouth wide, though very mobile and expressive. Her face seemed plain at first sight, but what made her the focus of attention wherever she went was the transformations that would come over it when she sang, or when she became interested or moved. "It was a delightful face to watch," wrote her official biographers. "Her countenance expressed everything with a graphic intensity that made one laugh from pure joy. It could brim over with fun, it had an irresistible archness when she was amused. It was capable of an almost awful solemnity and it could, when she was suspicious and on her guard, become absolutely stony."

Jenny herself was unaware of these transformations. When she looked in a mirror, she saw only the eyes that were too small, and the mouth and nose that were too big.

She would appear at the most elegant soirees, a plain, pale girl in a simple dress, her only ornament a flower stuck in her ringlets or a nosegay tied to her wrist. A murmur would run through the room, "It's Jenny Lind, it's Jenny Lind!" and the whole company would press toward her. As her host presented her to the other guests, she would bow with restraint and say little, as a rule. When she did speak, it was with an honesty that could be disconcerting. A tale that went all over Stockholm concerned a fatuous admirer who asked her what "divine thoughts" had filled her mind the night before when, as Alice, she embraced the cross.

"I believe I was thinking about making over my old bonnet," Jenny replied.

The Training of a Star

Jenny's triumph in *Der Freischütz* had come at a most auspicious time. The older, long-established stars of the Swedish Royal Opera were fading, the Swedish public was ready to welcome new, young performers, with young, fresh voices, and soon Jenny was joined in the top rank of singers by a tenor, Julius Günther, of Swedish origin, though brought up in Germany.

Günther, the son of an organist and singing teacher, had gone into the German army, expecting to make it his career, and had put in three years as a warrant officer before it was discovered that he had developed a fine tenor voice. The summer following Jenny's initial triumph on March 7, he was passing through Stockholm on a concert tour and had an audition at the Opera House. The Royal directors offered to take him on as an actor-pupil, such as Jenny had been, but his father would not hear of this. Günther was twenty-one, too old to become a pupil. He must have a regular appointment to the Royal Theater or nothing. The directors gave in and Günther made his debut on November 8, 1838, in the ambitious role of Fra Diavolo. His training had been scanty, but he was an immediate success with the audience. He attracted the attention of Emily Högqvist, a reigning, though aging, star of the opera whose salons, the liveliest and most brilliant in Stockholm, were not attended by any woman who valued her reputation. Thanks to Madam Högqvist's favoritism, Günther quickly became the Opera company's leading dramatic tenor, nearly always playing opposite Jenny when she had the leading soprano role.

These two youngsters—Jenny, the bright particular star, was only eighteen now, following her birthday on October 6—were joined in early 1839 by Giovanni Belletti, an Italian baritone. His case, however, was very different from that of the other two. Endowed with a superb voice, he had had as well five years of instruction in the famous music school at Bologna, Italy. He had been urged to go on the stage, but had lacked the confidence to do so until an eminent Swedish sculptor, Herr Byström, heard him sing in Italy and felt that the young man, so cultured and so thoroughly schooled in the Italian style of singing, would contribute something then lacking in the Swedish Royal Opera. Herr Byström offered to pay Belletti's way to Stockholm, keep him in his home as a guest until the singer had made his debut, and if the debut proved unsuccessful, pay his way back to Italy. Belletti did not see how he could lose by accepting such a proposition, and Herr Byström was sure the singer would be received enthusiastically in Stockholm. In this, the sculptor proved to be badly mistaken. Nine days after the successful debut of the almost untutored Günther, Belletti appeared with Jenny in a concert and was all but hooted off the stage. To make the more unmistakable its disapproval of Belletti's bel canto singing, the audience shouted the house down with cheers after each of Jenny's numbers.

It was Jenny who persuaded Belletti not to return at once to Italy. She had enough musical instinct to appreciate his voice and technique—bel canto, in fact, was the most highly rated style of singing in the outside world—and was very indignant at the discourteous treatment the Italian had received. At Jenny's insistence, the two appeared again in concert the following January. This time Belletti had a more friendly reception, which led to his successful operatic debut as Figaro in *The Barber of Seville*. Jenny, Günther and Belletti became a triumvirate, singing the leading soprano, tenor and baritone roles respectively in opera upon opera.

Belletti was fully as attractive in his dark, Latin way as the blue-eyed, blond Günther was in his Nordic fashion, but he was shy and reticent, possessing none of the aggressiveness and self-confidence which marked the younger Günther. Though barely twenty-five himself, Belletti felt immeasurably older than his two colleagues, since both were innocent of real knowledge of their art. Günther had little more to go on than an unusually good natural voice. Jenny's voice, with its wild-bird sweetness and strangely moving quality, had been badly trained, as events were to prove. Belletti was deeply grateful to Jenny, but felt unable to do more than watch over her from the background. Jenny, though very fond of Belletti, thought of him only as a confidant and always dependable friend.

It is possible, indeed, that Jenny had already lost her heart to Günther before Belletti appeared on the scene. The young tenor had a flair and dash which had quickly made him the idol of Stockholm's society ladies, as well as the accepted lover of the notorious Emily Högqvist. Mature for her age in many ways, Jenny was exceedingly naïve in others, and it is doubtful that she realized the nature of his relationship with Emily Högqvist or knew of the passing affairs he had with other women. He became, in her thoughts and imaginings, the unstained hero he played in the operas they performed together.

The Training of a Star

It was probably fortunate for Jenny that she was far too much the *jeune fille* offstage to appeal romantically at this time to a young man who could have his pick among Stockholm's susceptible females. And Jenny, of course, was too modest to make any overtures. Belletti and Jenny's other warm friends at the theater realized what was happening because of the way the young prima donna's eyes would follow the tenor during rehearsals, the added tenderness of her voice when she sang love duets with Günther. Herr Forsberg and Madam Eriksson talked the situation over, but decided that it was time Jenny should fall in love; and that no harm could come to her so long as Günther was hardly aware that she existed, except as a fellow player.

CHAPTER THREE

Second Flight from Home

HERR FORSBERG had been delighted that Jenny's return to the Linds' home in the summer of 1836 had apparently worked out so well. But Jenny was developing very rapidly, her perceptions were quickening and deepening. Though she retained her childhood fondness for Papa Niklas for a long time, she could not help but see him more and more clearly. Niklas's waist had thickened, his hair had thinned. He had the red-veined nose and eyes of the habitual hard drinker, he dressed carelessly and sloppily, he no longer made any pretense of working. Anna Marie's attitude toward him was half indulgent, half scornful. His attitude toward her was fawning and anxious. With Jenny, he was embarrassingly doting, and boasted of her successes endlessly. But he would never stand up to Anna Marie in Jenny's behalf. When there was trouble at home, Niklas sneaked out and made the rounds of his favorite taverns, staying away until he thought it was safe to return, or until somebody brought him back, reeling and singing.

Jenny was also becoming uncomfortably aware of the difference between her mother's standards of conduct for herself, and the harsh, suspicious judgments she made of other people. But what was most disconcerting was to discover the ways in which she herself resembled Anna Marie. Jenny undoubtedly had inherited her strength from her mother, since Niklas had none to impart, and she had not entirely escaped Anna Marie's faults—the quick temper, the moods, the tendency to imagine slights where none were intended.

Second Flight from Home

Anna Marie was perhaps the last person in the world whom Jenny wished to resemble. She fought her own tendency to temper and irritation by trying to achieve the Christian virtues of kindness, humility and tolerance which had been presented to her so persuasively by Grandma Tengmark from the time she was a tiny child. She strove for purity in thought and action, even refusing to play a role on the stage that she considered in any way degrading. She started the charities for which she was later to become famous as soon as she had finished paying the Royal directors for her education, and had a tiny surplus left over from her own needs and those of her parents. She remembered Grandma Tengmark's injunction to use her God-given voice in the way God would want her to, and sang outside the theater, for nothing, for anyone to whom her singing would give special pleasure—thereby coming into fresh conflict with her mother.

Anna Marie's first reaction was to deplore the fact that "this good, this incomparable Jenny" received no material compensation when she gave a private concert to someone who had been unable to hear her at the Opera House. Presently her mild deprecation changed to resentment that Jenny was not making better use of her opportunities to swell the family income. And before long, Anna Marie was demanding prima donna status for herself.

Her vanity and pettiness in this respect would be unbelievable if Anna Marie had not seen fit to record it, describing to a friend, in a letter that has been preserved, the fuss she created when she decided to attend one of Jenny's performances with no advance notice, and found that no ticket had been set aside for her. The curtain had already gone up when Anna Marie arrived at the theater, and every seat had been sold.

Anna Marie wrote indignantly that "M—— with his insinuating smile asked me to wait on the chance of there being room after the second act had begun. But I answered, 'As no place is accorded to me, I shall go without altogether,' and so I left."

Everyone would have been much happier if Anna Marie had indeed left the Opera House at this point, but she left the "insinuating M——" only to hunt up another member of the staff, designated as "Z," who was no better. "He is always overbearing and rude. This is the gratitude we get for our leniency with these people!"

Jenny Lind, the Swedish Nightingale

Though the performance had started and Jenny was to go on stage before long, Anna Marie sent for her. Jenny, white-faced with anxiety, not knowing what had happened, hurried to the foyer in her first-act costume, to receive an indignant account of the slights Anna Marie felt she had received. Jenny then hunted up Z herself and asked him to get Anna Marie a seat. His reply, according to Anna Marie, was a mutter to the effect that "there couldn't be room for everybody's mother," so that Jenny had to speak to him quite sharply, whereupon Z dispatched a page to Anna Marie with a ticket for a seat in the front row. Only there was no Anna Marie to be found! "To Jenny's surprise, Mother was gone," Anna Marie concluded her spiteful chronicle, "and best so."

About this time, Jenny renewed an old friendship. Louise Johansson had been the star boarder when Anna Marie had her school at No. 40 Mäster Samuelsgrand, and had helped make life there bearable for Jenny when she had been brought from Ed-Sollentuna at the age of four. Since then Louise's parents had died, and the young woman, now in her late twenties, was supporting herself by working as a saleswoman. It was a drab, lonely existence, and when Jenny learned of Louise's circumstances, she suggested that her old friend come to live at the Linds. It was a happier situation for Louise, and furnished Jenny with companionship at home.

For a while, Anna Marie withheld her usual complaints before the outsider, but presently, in her rising greed for money, demanded that Louise pay more for her board and room. Louise felt this was unreasonable; besides, she could not afford to pay what was demanded. Jenny had been trying with all her might to treat her mother's eccentricities, too, with Christian charity, but when Anna Marie chose the unfortunate Louise as a butt for her ill temper, it was too much and Jenny said so. Anna Marie flew into one of her tantrums, declaiming that Louise was welcome to leave at any time if she were not satisfied, and Jenny could go with her, as far as Anna Marie was concerned.

Anna Marie didn't mean this. But Jenny saw a chance to escape from a situation that was rapidly becoming past bearing. The court had decreed that Jenny must live in her parents' home. But what if she were ordered out of the home by the very person who had insisted on her presence there—her mother? Jenny and Louise together concocted a plot which would confront Anna Marie with a fait accompli. For Jenny knew very well what storms there would be if Anna Marie found out in advance that Jenny proposed to take her at her word.

First of all the two conspirators applied to Niklas's aunt Fru Ström-berg, whom Jenny now called "Grandmother," and who lived with a relative, Mademoiselle Apollonia Lindskog, a well-to-do spinster. Jenny and Louise told these ladies what they planned to do, and asked if they might find refuge there. The older women said the girls would be most welcome.

The next step was to get their belongings out of the Lind flat. Jenny packed her clothes in a big laundry basket, saying they needed altering. The basket went off under the supervision of Annette, Jenny's maid, but it ended up at Mademoiselle Lindskog's instead of at the dressmaker's. Then Jenny gave her parents box seats for that evening's performance of *Robert de Normandie*, in which Jenny was playing Alice. While Jenny sang, and Anna Marie and Niklas received congratulatory bows and smiles from members of the audience, Louise packed her clothes and took them over to Mademoiselle Lindskog's. But she returned to the Linds' flat to sleep, for this was part of the plot.

Next morning, at breakfast, Louise dropped her carefully prepared bombshell. Fru Lind had requested that Louise leave, she said, and she was leaving. This would be her last meal with the Linds. Anna Marie fell into the trap that had been so skillfully laid for her. The red spots flared in her cheeks as she told Louise, "Don't think *I* shall be sorry! I'll be only too glad to see you go." Then turning angrily on Jenny, she spoke the words the girls had been waiting for. "I only wish I could be rid of you, too!"

Jenny laid down her spoon, pushed back her chair. "Very well, Mama, if that is what you want." Before Anna Marie realized what she had done, both girls were out of the flat, Louise going off to her job, and Jenny to Mademoiselle Lindskog's.

Anna Marie's fury can be imagined when she found the two bedrooms stripped of the girls' personal possessions. It did not take long to trace them to Mademoiselle Lindskog's, and she dragged Niklas there with her to demand that his relatives give Jenny up. It was late 1839, and

Jenny was now nineteen. Her protectors pointed this out, and also that Jenny was famous all over Sweden. She could hardly be yanked through the streets by the ear, like a recalcitrant child. The Linds had to go home without their daughter.

Nevertheless, it had been a most unpleasant scene, and Jenny feared that Fru Strömberg and Mademoiselle Lindskog would not be able to hold out indefinitely against Anna Marie's iron determination and the violence and false accusations of which she was capable. A few days later Jenny dropped in at the Lindblads after a rehearsal. Adolf Fredrik Lindblad, the composer, at this time was around forty and at the height of his creative powers, a fine-looking, charming man, with his full share of artistic temperament. His wife, Sophie, was as gentle and sweet as Lindblad was moody and impetuous. They had a handsome apartment in the Bonde Palace, not far from the Opera House, and had long been numbered among Jenny's admirers and dear friends.

When Jenny explained her situation, and that she felt she should not involve the Royal directors in her troubles with her mother another time, the Lindblads at once invited her to come and live with them. Adolf Lindblad would be more than a match for Anna Marie, and would welcome an encounter with her. So Jenny moved to the Lindblads forthwith. But Anna Marie did not pursue her there. She had enough sense to realize that while she might hector Niklas's elderly relatives with impunity, she could not take her case to the outside world a second time without appearing ridiculous.

March 7, 1838, had been the date of Jenny's birth as a star performer. Her removal to the Lindblads marked her true entrance into the world of art. Lindblad was a musical scholar of the first rank, having studied in both Paris and Germany following his course at Uppsala. In Germany, he had been a fellow student of Felix Mendelssohn-Bartholdy, and it was at the Lindblads' that Jenny first heard the music of the man whose *Songs Without Words* had enraptured all of Europe. The Lindblads' home, in contrast to the high social circles Jenny had been frequenting, was a gathering place for scholars and artists—for anyone who was doing serious work in the arts or in fields allied with the arts. Here was heard the finest music and the best talk in Sweden. Above all, here was warm, loving acceptance and appreciation of Jenny, which she had never had in her parents' home.

And Jenny could repay the Lindblads by helping Adolf with his songs. Those for which he was most famous were in a minor key, tinged with melancholy, and Jenny's voice, with its unconscious note of pathos, was the perfect instrument for them. Jenny became both his pupil in a deeper understanding of music, and his inspiration for making further music of his own. They would spend hours at the piano, Lindblad improvising, Jenny quickly catching the melodic line, the two working it over and over until each note and phrase brought out the full beauty of Jenny's voice. Then she popularized the songs by singing them in drawing rooms and as encores at her concerts.

Jenny had not realized how much strain and tension she had been undergoing while subject to Anna Marie's whims and tempers, until she was freed of them. She bloomed. Little by little she was losing the feelings of inferiority, the depressions under which she became dull and lumpish. The blue-gray eyes now were almost always alight, the face smiling. She was on the way to becoming pretty, offstage as well as on.

Jenny had gone to live with the Lindblads in late 1839, and the year 1840 was one for her of triumph heaped upon triumph. It began on January 1, when the Royal directors, of their own volition, raised her yearly salary to 1,100 *Riksdaler*—around 95 English pounds, and an advance of 20 pounds over her 1839 salary.

On January 13, 1840, Jenny was appointed Court singer by His Majesty, Karl Johann. This was the highest official recognition possible in Sweden, and it carried a stipend with it, though a small one. Anna Marie, writing to Niklas, spoke of the honor, and how proud it should make them to be Jenny's parents. But she must also have done some gnashing of teeth at having shut herself off from participation in the exciting developments that were coming faster and faster.

Later in the year, Jenny was made a member of the Swedish Royal Academy of Music, the highest honor in the power of her fellow musicians to bestow. Now she was appearing only in opera. To the roles she had been singing—Alice, Agatha, Euryanthe, Pamina, Julia in *La Vestale*, and Marie in the operatic drama of that name—she added two very important new ones: Donna Anna in *Don Giovanni* and Lucia in *Lucia di Lammermoor*. This last opera she introduced to Stockholm and her Lucia created a tremendous furore. It became one of her most famous roles, and she was asked to play it twenty-eight times that year.

That Whitsuntide she went to Uppsala again, again she charmed and enchanted. The Uppsala *Correspondenten* began one of those panegyrics that Jenny was to inspire until they became monotonous, with this statement: "In addition to Nature's beautiful singing birds, there came, flying thither on Whitsun Eve, a nobler nightingale, the famous Jenny Lind." From that time on, Jenny was known as "The Swedish Nightingale," first to her fellow artists and admirers in Stockholm, then throughout Sweden and the other Scandinavian countries, and finally to the whole world.

But there was one member of the audience at Uppsala who saw Jenny's situation with the same clarity as Belletti. Erik Gustaf Geijer, professor of history at the University, was a man of many parts. In addition to being an authority on history, Herr Geijer was a composer of delightful songs and a prominent figure in Swedish literary circles. Jenny had met him on her first visit to Uppsala the previous Whitsuntide, and a friendship had sprung up at once between the young singer and the subtle, accomplished scholar. Geijer was a good friend of the Lindblads and a frequent visitor in their home. Early in January, 1840, when Jenny had not been with the Lindblads very long, Geijer wrote to a friend boasting of the fine, close friendship he had established with Jenny, adding, "She is a simple, attractive being. Lindblad and Madam Lindblad both stand to her in almost a fatherly and motherly relation, which becomes both parties very well. All the same, I am afraid she is a kind of 'comet' which may interfere with their domestic peace."

Geijer detected a weariness and huskiness in Jenny's voice and an unevenness in her greatly applauded *Lucia*. Jenny herself had begun to be aware of a roughening in her voice, and had spoken to Herr Berg about it. But Herr Berg, whose misguidance of Jenny's voice had been due entirely to ignorance of the way so choice an instrument should be handled, had nothing to offer.

Failing to get any help from her singing master, Jenny took her problem to Belletti, whose technique she had always considered the best of any of the singers at the theater. At last Belletti had his chance, and he made the most of it. He was too kind to criticize Herr Berg and the others at the Royal Theater who had permitted Jenny to all but sing her fabulous voice away. (Jenny herself, in fact, never blamed these people, even when she knew the worst. The Bergs always remained among her closest friends.) But he did seize the opportunity to turn Jenny's thoughts toward further training, telling her how he himself would love to study, if he could, with Manuel Garcia in Paris.

"He is the greatest voice teacher in the world," Belletti assured Jenny. Manuel Garcia's father, also named Manuel and a Spaniard, had been both a composer of operas and an opera singer, Belletti told her. His operas had been successful in their day, but the elder Garcia, trained in the Italian style, had achieved greater fame as a singer. He developed a teaching method for which he soon became even more famous than for his operas or his singing, and had trained some of the most celebrated singers of the first third of the century.

Among his pupils were his three children, who became opera stars. One of his daughters, Malibran, was the most celebrated singer in Europe during the short span of life allotted to her, and today is considered one of the great singers of all time. The other daughter, Madame Viardot, was a leading singer, though she never attained the brilliance of her sister. The son, Manuel, had a creditable career in opera, then, like his father, retired from the stage and devoted himself to teaching.

Jenny's imagination was fired by Belletti's stories about Malibran's fabled voice, and the method that had produced so many fine singers. Belletti himself was thinking of the fact that the two Garcias, father and son, had a good deal of the scientist about them. The younger Garcia had studied the structure of the throat and vocal organs more intensively than had any anatomist up to that time. (He invented the laryngeal mirror, and opened a new era in medical treatment of afflictions of the throat as well as in voice production.) The havoc wrought in Jenny's voice was greater than Belletti wanted her to know. But if anyone could restore it, Manuel Garcia could.

Jenny needed no persuasion to wish to study with the brother of the incomparable Malibran. But it would mean going to Paris, and Jenny up to that time had never been out of Sweden. It would take a great deal of money, to pay for lessons with Garcia and to live in Paris. Meanwhile she would be earning nothing. These were the obstacles Jenny saw to carrying out her wish. It did not enter her mind that Garcia might not accept her as a pupil.

Studying with Garcia would probably have remained only a dream for Jenny, if another complication had not arisen in her life. Adolf Fredrik Lindblad, her great friend and protector and teacher, the man she admired as a musician and loved as a father, developed an unfatherly passion for her. This would have been a trying situation for any girl not yet out of her teens, but it was especially damaging for Jenny that her first openly avowed suitor should have been a married man, and one whom she esteemed so highly. She felt she must have been guilty of some wrong, and the incident threw her back into the soul-searching and inhibitions she had been on the way to abandoning.

She felt guiltier still when Sophie Lindblad, generous and self-sacrificing to a fault, proposed to step aside and let Lindblad marry the younger woman. Jenny loved both the Lindblads, and was always to love them. Many years later she wrote that they had such deeply noble natures "so unusually pure, each in their way, that one has to be fonder of them than of anyone else. At any rate that is how it has been with me. They were my first home, the two of them my first warm love. But they nearly drained me of all strength and energy through the topsy-turvy way they treated life and its responsibilities. I do not think I could ever have been induced to leave Sweden, had it not been for the terrible Tragedy they were both proposing to enact, with me as Prima Donna!"

Geijer had perhaps foreseen the development of this odd triangle, in which each of the three persons involved loved both the others deeply and high-mindedly. In any event, his poet's sensibility made him quickly aware of it and of Jenny's feeling of helplessness in the situation.

So Geijer wrote a little poem, for Jenny's eyes alone, a copy of which, in her own handwriting, was found among her most cherished keepsakes after she died. On the margin was written, also in Jenny's hand, "On these words I was launched into the open sea." Or, as Jenny expressed it to friends, "With a poem, Geijer kicked me out into the great world."

The poem which played such a part in Jenny's life was entitled by Geijer "Courage and Renunciation," and consisted of two short stanzas:

"Oh if, from yon eternal fire, —
Which slays the souls that it sets free,
Consuming them as they aspire, —
One burning spark have fallen on thee,

"Fear not! Though upward still it hastes,
That living fire, that tongue of flame,
And turns thy days to bitter waste,
From Heaven, ah, from Heaven it came!"

Jenny recognized at once what Geijer was trying to say to her. Heretofore, hard as she had worked, nevertheless every step of her way had been mapped out for her. She had had only to take advantage of the opportunities fate had dropped continually into her lap since she was nine. The only times Jenny had initiated any action were in her two flights from home, and on both those occasions she had fled to persons with whom she knew she would be safe and cared for. Was she not still playing the part of the timid child who always looks about for a protector, a rescuer, when a situation grows unpleasant? Geijer was telling her that she could no longer hold back, shirk decisions and action and consequences. She must go on to meet her destiny, whatever the cost.

Not long after Geijer had sent her the poem, Jenny asked Belletti to come to her dressing room following a rehearsal, and then sent Annette on an errand.

"Belletti, I have made up my mind. I am going to Paris. I am going to study with Garcia."

Belletti seized both her hands in his, kissed one and then the other. "Jenny dear, how happy you make me. It will open up a new world for you, believe me."

Before Jenny could go to Paris, two things had to be done. She had to raise the money to pay for her lessons and for a year's stay in Paris, and she had to be freed of her obligation to the Royal directors, which Anna Marie had assumed in Jenny's behalf when she signed the contract with the Theater School. By that contract, Jenny was bound to sing for the Royal Theater until 1846, and for whatever salary the Royal directors saw fit to set.

First in order, however, was the money. Immediately after Whitsuntide, the summer of 1840, she set out on a round of concerts in the

Swedish hinterlands, Niklas Lind accompanying her. It rained constantly and travel was grueling. Jenny wrote Louise Johansson from Malmö that the roads were so bad the wheels of the carriage often sank into mud up to the hub, and Jenny and Niklas would have to sit patiently until they were pulled out.

"It was very horrid sitting about in the atrocious weather. But then as soon as I arrive in a town, and see the exceeding kindness and friend-liness the people have for me, I feel it is wicked to grumble. You cannot think to what an extent they all vie with each other in serving me. It is quite astonishing."

In this letter Jenny asked Louise to take to Brühn, a sick painter, the monthly allowance Jenny had been giving him and which she had been too busy to take him before she left Stockholm. She told Louise that she was not certain whether the number was Kirkogata 13 or 25, in Clara Vestra. "But after you have crossed the Clara churchyard, and when you arrive at the gate on the Vestragatan, turn to the left, then it is the first door on the right-hand side, on the ground floor. Ask for Brühn, the painter, a poor sick man ill in bed these last fourteen years. Give him warm greetings from me, and his wife too, and forgive your friend who puts you to this trouble."

The amount of the "allowance" was only 8 *Riksdaler Banco*, for the months of July and August, but the smallness of the amount may be taken as a measure of the slenderness of Jenny's own resources.

By the end of August, Jenny was back in Stockholm again, singing Lucia and facing a full fall and winter schedule at the theater without having had any rest at all. Nevertheless, the audiences cheered her to the skies and called her back time and time again. When January 1, 1841, came around, it was evident that the Royal directors had been giving much thought to the case of their little Jenny. It had become known that she was looking forward to study abroad, and they were worried lest their prize might be snatched from them once managers in other countries were allowed to hear her.

In submitting a new contract for her consideration, they mentioned they were making her the highest offer their regulations empowered them to, in their wish "to most particularly to attach to the Swedish stage a talent so eminent as the Court-Singer Frökken Jenny Lind." They were advancing her salary to 150 pounds a year—a notable jump from the previous 95 pounds a year—with extra "play money" for the parts in which she appeared and the privilege of one benefit for herself each year. The theater would provide her costumes, which hitherto Jenny had had to furnish. There was an added lure in that the directors offered to let her off for the months of July and August to study abroad, if she wanted to; and intimated that this period for further study might even be made a bit longer.

Some biographers of Jenny Lind have believed the Royal directors had it in their power to make Jenny a much better offer than this, and have criticized them because they did not. On the other hand, the directors had reason to feel that they were being generous with a girl who had been trained and educated at the expense of the state and whose annual salary had been 60 pounds just three years ago. They were taken aback to receive in reply a polite, but firm, letter of rejection.

Belletti had helped Jenny compose it. Alone, she would not have had the courage—for the letter plunged at once into the inadequacy of the training Jenny had received at the Royal Theater, as though anticipating the claim the directors might make on her services because of this training.

"I have the honor to state as follows: The musical and dramatic capabilities which, from my earliest years, I have felt myself to possess have, thanks to the cultivation received at home, though hitherto insufficient, still been able to attract some attention to my dawning talent. But it is not with half-developed natural gifts, however happy, that an artist can keep his ground; and greatly as I prize the appreciation I have been fortunate enough to win, I feel I ought to consider it not so much homage to the artist I was and am, as an encouragement to what I might become."

The letter made it clear that she was determined to have her year of study. The Royal directors released Jenny from her obligation to them with no further parley.

They had done very well financially, in fact, out of their venture in underwriting the support, training and education of a nine-year-old child. Jenny had become the greatest drawing card the Royal Theater had ever had, and Holland and Rockstro figured that her some sixty-nine appearances in the fiscal year 1840-1841 had cost the directors only a little over $5 a performance!

A voice student could hardly have had better references or sponsors than those with which Jenny Lind went to Paris. She arrived under the protecting wing of the Swedish Minister himself, and the Consulate remained a refuge and a contact with home. Even more important, she carried with her a letter of introduction from Queen Desideria of Sweden to Madame la Duchesse de Dalmatie, in Paris.

These two great ladies were old and close friends, for the husbands of both had been Marshals of France under Napoleon Bonaparte. Queen Desideria had been Désirée Clery, of Marseille, before she married Bernadotte, who had afterwards been adopted by the Swedish King as a son and had succeeded to the throne after the King's death. The Duc de Dalmatie had been the famous Soult before his elevation to the peerage. His wife's salon was one of the most distinguished in Paris.

The Duchess of Dalmatia knew that Garcia accepted only students with exceptional voices and talent, and was aware, as Jenny was not, that Paris and Stockholm might have very different ideas as to what constituted an exceptional voice and talent. Thinking to have Garcia hear Queen Desideria's protégée under the most favorable circumstances possible, the Duchess arranged an afternoon reception at which Jenny was to sing, and invited Garcia.

When the moment came, the pale, unfashionably dressed young woman from Stockholm made her way to the piano with her peculiar, gliding walk, sat down and proceeded to sing the songs of Lindblad and Geijer, accompanying herself. But what a contrast from the reception accorded her and her songs in the drawing rooms of Stockholm! Jenny had harmed her voice dreadfully by overusing it in fulfilling her contract with the Royal Theater and raising the money to come to France. She was tired from her journey, and more than ordinarily nervous and unsure of herself in facing these strangers who did not understand the Swedish words of her songs, and would only have smiled pityingly if told that they were listening to the Swedish Nightingale. Her voice was shaky, it had none of the electrifying effect upon her listeners it had always had before. The guests had resumed their conversations before Jenny had finished singing, and there was only a polite spattering of applause when she rose from the piano, bowed, and tried to find a place in the large drawing room to hide herself. Garcia, asked by one of the guests what he thought of the Swedish girl, replied that she possessed none of the qualities necessary for singing before a truly discriminating audience.

And so the Duchess of Dalmatia's kindly meant gesture very nearly proved fatal to Jenny's hopes, for Garcia's mind was already made up when she came to his studio in the Square d'Orleans, near the Rue Saint Lazare. Nevertheless he received her graciously, asked her to sing some scales and then the *Perche non ho* from *Lucia di Lammermoor*. This should have been an easy test for Jenny, for she knew the part thoroughly, having sung it many times in Stockholm. But halfway through she broke down completely, stumbled to a chair and sitting there, head bowed in misery and shame, awaited Garcia's verdict.

One of Garcia's pet abominations was the ruining of promising young voices by overuse during the adolescent years. His impatience was directed at those who had done this thing to Jenny, rather than at Jenny herself. But he saw no use, either, in mincing words.

"My dear young lady," he said, "you had better go back to Stockholm. It would be useless for me to take you as a pupil. However fine a voice you may have had at one time, you have none left now. Absolutely none."

CHAPTER FOUR

Year of Humility

WHEN Jenny later described this incident to Felix Mendelssohn-Bartholdy, she told him that never in her life had she suffered such anguish. She had known that her voice was roughening, that she had had to force it. But the possibility that it might be ruined, gone forever, had not once occurred to her.

In that catastrophic moment many agonizing images flashed through Jenny's mind. There was the disappointment to her countrymen, who had been so proud of this Northern Nightingale of theirs that her downfall would be in the nature of a national calamity. Queen Desideria would have to learn that her protégée was not even considered worthy to receive instruction. Jenny thought of her friends and teachers. Herr Berg would be completely crushed, kind Madam Eriksson and Herr Forsberg devastated. What would become of her parents, whose support she had been for years now; what of her little group of pensioners? She thought of the crowd of admirers who had gathered at the dock in Stockholm to wave farewell to her. How could she return defeated, a failure?

The tears poured down her cheeks. "What am I to do?" Jenny implored Garcia. "How can I go back to Sweden and tell them I have no more voice left?"

Garcia had been sincere in refusing Jenny as a pupil, thinking it would only waste her money. But he could not resist her evident distress. He told her finally, "There is one thing you may try, if you wish to. Your voice is seriously fatigued. Give it a complete rest. Do not sing a note, speak only when you have to, and then in as few words as you can manage. If you will do this for six weeks, you may come back at the end of that time and I will hear you sing again. But I beg of you, Mademoiselle, do not develop any hopes."

Jenny's initial reaction to the blow had been one of sheer panic. But after she had recovered somewhat and her mind had begun to function again, she quietly but firmly rejected, in her own thinking, Garcia's dictum that her voice would never return. She knew how deathly tired and depleted she was. She felt that her voice would recover along with her bodily strength and vitality. Besides, she knew, with a conviction rooted in her earliest memories, that Grandma Tengmark's God would not have led her thus far, only to slam in her face the door to the promised achievement. Jenny had used her voice unwisely, it was true, but never with evil intent. God would not permit that the career started so brilliantly when she was seventeen should be ended before she was twenty-one.

Jenny went back to the highly respectable boarding-house in which Count Löwenhjelm, the Swedish Minister, had arranged for her to stay, and made arrangements to exist for six weeks without talking aloud. But she determined the six weeks should not be wasted. She was so sure her career was not over that she studied Italian, a language she would need in operatic singing, and brushed up on her French grammar. There are still in existence large sheets of foolscap filled, in Jenny's handwriting, with declensions and conjugations of Italian nouns and verbs, and with columns of French irregular verbs in all their moods and tenses.

At the end of the six weeks of silence, Garcia found her voice so much smoother and stronger that he thought it might be possible to restore it. At any rate, he consented to take her as a pupil. But she would have to learn completely new methods of breathing and voice production. If she were willing to start again from the bottom, he would give her two lessons a week, of one hour each.

Jenny agreed gladly and found a cheaper boardinghouse, that of a Mademoiselle de Puget—she could no longer afford the one Count Löwenhjelm had placed her in, now that she would be paying Manuel Garcia for two lessons a week. Herr Berg was in Paris at this time, and she delayed starting with Garcia until he had left, out of consideration for her old singing master's feelings. But she wrote a friend in Stockholm on September 10, 1841, that she had already had five lessons with Garcia.

"I have to begin again, from the beginning. To sing scales, up and down, slowly and with great care; then to practice the shake—awfully slowly; and try to get rid of the hoarseness, if possible. Moreover, he is very particular about the breathing. I trust I have made a happy choice. Anyhow he is the best master, and expensive enough—twenty francs an hour! But what does that signify, if only he can teach me to sing?"

As though it were not enough that she must start her voice training over from the very beginning—after nearly eleven years of it—Jenny found that in her new environment she herself was nobody at all. Garcia still had no great enthusiasm about her voice, and did not have any for some years to come. He had consented to take her as a pupil mainly because he saw it meant so much to her. Henrietta Nissen, another very promising Swedish girl, had been studying with Garcia for two years, and he considered her much the more talented of the two.

What impressed Garcia most at this time about Jenny were her intelligence and her capacity for hard work. Once more, the lesson Jenny had learned so well as a small child came to her aid. Garcia said that Jenny never made the same mistake twice—he believed she would have cut her throat before she would have done that. He is reported to have said that if only Jenny had possessed Henrietta Nissen's talent, or Henrietta Jenny's brains, the composite artist would have made the greatest singer the world had ever seen.

However, since there was no way to amalgamate the outstanding qualities of the two girls, it was upon Nissen that Garcia pinned his great hopes, and Jenny was ignored outside of her lesson periods with him. As for Paris society, which Queen Desideria had thought to open to Jenny with her warm letter of introduction to the Duchess of Dalmatia, Jenny never showed her face again in a Paris salon.

Jenny and Henrietta Nissen became great friends, in spite of their teacher's obvious preference for Henrietta, and often sang together for their own pleasure. They were frequent guests at the home of Count Löwenhjelm. Aside from this, Jenny's only diversion was to attend operas, plays and concerts, slipping alone into one of the cheapest seats in the most remote gallery.

She confessed later that it was "the divine song" alone which gave her the heart to continue the struggle throughout this year of humiliation and discouragement. She heard Beethoven symphonies for the first time in her life in concerts at the Paris Conservatoire, and was at a loss to express her rapture. Among the many Swedish friends to whom she wrote innumerable letters that winter—in letters, Jenny seemed able to lay aside the inhibitions that often made her seem cold and unresponsive in company—was Jakob Axel Josephson, who was to become a well-known composer. Only two years older than Jenny, he had achieved no success as yet, but Jenny had great respect for his musicianship. The letter to Josephson in which she described the sensations Beethoven's music aroused in her consisted mainly of disconnected phrases and exclamation points. "No! I have no words! What strength, what delicacy, what softness! . . . Today I heard the Seventh Symphony. Oh! the waves of sound!"

The Paris stage and opera, however, for the most part were a disappointment to Jenny. Both were under the supervision of the government, and the fate of actors and singers was dependent upon the favor of higher-ups. All but the most prominent performers were forced to hire claques—groups paid to applaud their employer vigorously. Without the backing of a prominent politician or other protector, and money to assemble a claque, it was practically impossible for a newcomer to become established.

The system, which continued for many years, was not conducive to the development of art in the highest sense, and was most distasteful to Jenny. Though she went often to the Théâtre Italien, at that time the mecca of Europe's aspiring singers, where the great Italians appeared, she found more to criticize than to praise. She wrote the Lindblads that Persiani, one of the reigning favorites of the day, sang with perfect taste, but with not a trace of feeling. Jenny added that Persiani was a clumsy actress and did not have a very "happy" voice. "I cannot understand how she can sing so divinely with that voice." Jenny admired the equally famous Grisi more for her acting than for her singing. The great tenor Lablache was the only singer then appearing in Paris whom she considered an authentic genius. "God in heaven, what a voice! And the most perfect acting you could ever see!" Though she thought her friend Belletti quite as fine an artist as Lablache, and that he would create a sensation if he were to come to Paris. She wrote Jakob Josephson, "No one, no one of them all, sings better than he, Belletti."

Jenny never met any of the stars in person in Paris, though before many years she was to sing opposite Lablache and to outdraw the famous Grisi. Paris was the one city in Europe where Jenny stayed for more than a day or two that she did not meet the leading persons in the world of affairs, music and art and make friends among them. She was far too low in the musical scale at the moment to impose herself upon the great, and it is doubtful that they would have found her in the least interesting if she had.

However, of the various deprivations of her self-imposed exile, Jenny found that she missed her acting most of all. She wrote the Lindblads that this had been her joy, her pride, her glory. "Oh! To pour out my feelings in a beautiful part. This is, and ever will be, my continual aim. And until I stand there [on the stage] again, I shall not know myself as I really am." She went often to the theater and studied the performers, writing Josephson that among the actresses, too, she had found a great dearth of genius. "Mademoiselle Rachel is the only one. After her, there is only Grisi. That is how things stand in the theatrical world in the famous Paris. You would have to search long and hard to find an honest talent."

Rachel was the only one, in fact, whom Jenny acknowledged to be a better actress than she was herself. She wrote the Lindblads that the difference between them was that Rachel could be splendid when angry, but was unsuited for tenderness. "I am desperately ugly, and nasty, too, when in anger; but I think I do better in tender parts. Of course, I do not compare myself with Rachel. She is immeasurably greater than I."

Rachel, however, had used her voice training merely to make her speaking voice more flexible, and appeared in drama only. Jenny, thinking of herself primarily as an actress at this time, evidently did not dream that her own name would live on because of her singing.

Up to this year of 1841-1842, there had been, in fact, an amazing parallel between the careers of these two very young women, both of whom were to be fixed among the supreme stars of all time. Rachel was a year younger than Jenny, being twenty to Jenny's twenty-one, but her outstanding talent had been discovered when she was nine, as Jenny's had been, and she and her sister had been taken as free pupils of the Paris Conservatoire at an early age. Rachel, like Jenny, had had her first great triumph at the age of seventeen, and thereafter had been acclaimed in Paris as Jenny had been in Stockholm. Now, however, the parallel broke down. This season Rachel had created a great sensation in London in the plays of Corneille and Racine, whereas for Jenny there was no acting, and no singing except the practicing of breathing and scales and arpeggios—from the beginning—under Garcia's critical direction.

On November 26th, Garcia sponsored an important evening party in Henrietta Nissen's honor. She sang several solos and also sang with a chorus. It was a brilliant affair and probably had much to do with the offer Henrietta soon received from the Théâtre Italien. Jenny was one of the audience of several hundred and clapped for her friend sincerely, insisting in the account of the occasion she wrote to a Swedish friend that she would not change places with Henrietta, being content with her own life, "though my prospects for the future are so dark and poor."

Just the same it was a time of great soul-searching for Jenny. And her loneliness, heartache and depression gave her a more sympathetic view of her parents than she had had for years. Now that the silver spoon had been snatched from her so abruptly, Jenny began to appreciate the good fortune that had been hers, so far as her career was concerned, up to this time. To have so sudden and crushing a reversal, after so unusual and uninterrupted a triumph, might well have been a *coup de grace*, especially falling on one so young. In the light of the smoothness of her path in the theater heretofore, perhaps the strengthening and toughening she had acquired from the conflicts with her mother were a saving factor.

In any event, Jenny could see what it had meant for Anna Marie to have to face the world with a baby to care for and support, at the same age as Jenny when she was facing her first reversal. Numerous men and women had devoted themselves to developing the talents with which Jenny had been born. She had worked hard, it was true. But the determination to go to Paris for further training was the first step she herself had had to take of her own volition and carry out unaided. She wrote Sophie Lindblad that she loved her mother now as she had never loved her before, that the thought of Anna Marie gave her the courage to work, and try to win back the ground she had lost.

If there had been any danger that the worship Jenny had received at so early an age would turn her head, the lonely year in Paris dispelled it. She could not help being plunged into deep depression when Henrietta Nissen received her offer from the Italian Opera, early in 1842, of a three-year engagement. For the first year, Henrietta would receive 4,000 *Riksdaler Banco*. (About 325 pounds sterling, or more than twice the amount the Royal Theater had tendered Jenny in 1841 as the most generous offer within its power.) Jenny thought it likely that when the three years of her engagement with the Italian Opera were finished, Henrietta would be able to command anywhere from 480 to 560 pounds a year.

The glittering offer to Henrietta intensified Jenny's consciousness of her own obscurity. March 7, the anniversary of her first great triumph as Agatha, had a funereal quality for Jenny that spring. Had it been just four years, or was it five, since the marvelous evening when she had first learned and used her power? Jenny couldn't even remember. It had actually been four years, and her reign as the Swedish Nightingale had lasted for a little more than three years after that. She knew there were others who would be thinking of her on this day, and that one of them would surely be her old friend Herr Forsberg, the Honorary Superintendent of the Royal Theater School in Stockholm. He would remember that night in 1838 as clearly as she did, and would be wondering how it was with Jenny now. So she wrote him cheerfully, "My singing is getting on quite satisfactorily. I rejoice heartily in my voice. It is clear and sonorous, with more firmness and much greater flexibility. A great, great deal still remains to be done, but the worst is over. Garcia is satisfied with me.

"Sometimes I act by myself, and it seems to me that I am gaining more feeling, more verve, more truth in my rendering. At least, I feel I know, better than I used to, what life really is."

In the ten years following, when over and over again she had to be prodded or coaxed or inveigled into taking advantage of the dazzling opportunities that came to her, some people thought Jenny overdid her protestations of unworthiness. They even detected pride in the humility with which she would insist that this or that impresario could get performers far better than she was for the money he was offering her. These people did not know how thoroughly humility had been ground into Jenny during the year when she learned what life really is, how haunted she was by fears of failure whenever she was called upon to sing under new and strange circumstances. Her humiliating experience at the Duchess of Dalmatia's soiree, the doubts Garcia had expressed about her abilities, would not soon, or easily, be forgotten.

In May, Garcia once more threw her into deep despondency by maintaining that she would never again be able to enact an operatic role. He was still influenced, it would seem, by Jenny's failure and collapse on the two occasions when he had first heard her sing. Jenny thought she had improved a great deal, and was altogether bewildered. And there was a further complication. Jenny's place in the Royal Theater in Stockholm had been taken by Elma Ström, another pupil of Izak Berg's. Perhaps there would not be a place waiting for Jenny in Stockholm when she was ready to return there!

One day in her room, all by herself, Jenny went through the entire part of Norma and decided she had done it nearly as well as in Stockholm, when she had been supported by an orchestra and cast. She had started her study with Garcia in August of 1841 and had taken two lessons a week until the end of June, 1842. She had thought to spend two years in study, but she realized now that she could learn nothing more from Garcia. Her voice had not only recovered from the effects of overuse and bodily fatigue, but in less than one year Jenny had learned all that Garcia had taught Henrietta Nissen in three years. Her voice was better than ever before. According to H. S. Holland, who heard Jenny sing at this time, "It had acquired a rich depth of tone, a sympathetic sweetness, a birdlike charm in the silvery clearness of its upper register, which at once impressed the listener with the feeling that he had never before heard anything in the least degree resembling it."

This supremely cultivated and controlled voice had lost some quality of unearthly freshness, of the natural and untamed, which had marked Jenny's voice before. But it was an instrument now completely subservient to her bidding.

The time had come for her to decide what her next step would be. She was dismayed to learn that her friends in Sweden were expecting her to make a successful public appearance in Paris, for the very idea of such a thing repelled her. She wrote to her friend Marie Ruchman, "There is nothing to which the people here will not submit, for the sake of gain. Applause is not always given to talent, but often to vice, or to any obscure person who can afford to pay for it. Ugh! It is too dreadful to see the claqueurs sitting at the theater, night after night, deciding the fate of those who are compelled to appear. A terrible manifestation of original sin!" Rachel, young as she was, already had acquired a reputation for gallantry. Jenny wanted no part of a success that depended on "admirers."

She longed to return to Stockholm and wrote Herr Forsberg, "If they want to hear me again, in my Sweden, with what joy will I not hasten hither!" But she did not want to return to the Royal Theater if someone else had replaced her in the affections of the public.

"I do not wish to stand in the way of anyone. Rather than that, I would settle down here to give singing lessons; for Garcia's method is the best of our time, and everyone here is striving to follow it. But in any case, I shall come home, in order that people may hear what progress I have made—if I really have made any. Will they accept me, and give me a suitable engagement? If so, I shall remain. If not, I shall go abroad again."

The future, which a short year ago had seemed so assured and promising, was now a vast question mark. She wrote Papa Niklas, half jokingly, half seriously, that she might have to sit on the Common in Stockholm with a little money box in front of her, to gather in small contributions. Her final decision was to approach the whole matter in a spirit of adventure. She wrote Sophie Lindblad in April, 1842, "I am really anxious to see how a life, begun like mine, will end. . . . This journey and experience have altogether changed me. The foundation of the building was tolerably sound and needed no pulling down. But the superstructure! It has crumbled away, through not having been better put together."

Year of Humility

When Adolf Lindblad came to Paris in late May, he was aghast to learn how little attention and help Jenny had had throughout the year and plunged himself immediately into her affairs. Garcia told Lindblad that he had found Jenny to possess much spirit and feeling, but that he considered her voice was still a little tired. Nevertheless, when Lindblad heard that Meyerbeer, the outstanding opera composer of the day, had come to Paris, he took Meyerbeer to see Jenny at Mademoiselle de Puget's. She sang for the composer airs from his own *Robert de Normandie* and *Norma*, and several of Lindblad's songs.

Meyerbeer professed to be entranced by her voice and interested in having her appear in his operas in Paris or Berlin. But he wanted to hear how her voice would sound in a large opera house. He arranged with the director of the Grand Opera in Paris, M. Pillet, for Jenny to sing on the stage of the Opera, to a piano accompaniment. Only a handful of people were there, including Lindblad. M. Pillet had planned to be present, but was called away before Jenny began to sing. This audition, with Jenny alone on the unlighted stage and singing to an empty auditorium, gave rise later to a variety of conflicting stories. Some people blamed M. Pillet because he had not secured Jenny for the Paris stage. He defended himself by saying that, first of all, he had not been able to hear Jenny sing, and second, Meyerbeer had not given a very enthusiastic report of her performance.

At breakfast the next morning with Meyerbeer, Berlioz, and several other French musicians, Lindblad doubted Meyerbeer's sincerity because of the very enthusiasm with which the composer spoke of Jenny's talents, for Lindblad felt Jenny had not sung nearly so well as she was capable of doing.

"Jenny is not sorry to return home," Lindblad wrote to Sophie, "for the greatest stage reputations are won here only through sacrifice of honor and moral reputation. While the world is resounding with the praise of these ladies, every salon is closed to them, and this even in easy going Paris. Such homage as Jenny met with in Sweden, no foreigner ever received. This she feels; and it is for this vivifying atmosphere that she is longing."

CHAPTER FIVE

Out into the Great World

On APRIL 17, 1847, Jenny's good friends, Felix Mendelssohn-Bartholdy and Mrs. George Grote, were pacing anxiously up and down on the west side of Belgrave Square in London, with an eye always on the doorway of the Grote house. They had been waiting in Mrs. Grote's drawing room for Jenny to arrive from the Continent. But she had not arrived, and they had begun to fear very much that she would not. Finally, to relieve their tension, they had taken to walking up and down out of doors.

Jenny had been giving her friends in London a very bad time that spring. She had contracted to make her London debut in Her Majesty's Theatre in early April, arriving in the English capital as soon as possible after the close in March of her engagement with the Vienna Opera. But instead she had stayed on in Vienna. His Majesty, King Ferdinand of Austria, had appointed her Imperial Chamber Singer, she was making appearances at the Austrian Court; she refused even to discuss going to London with an emissary sent out from Her Majesty's Theatre.

Almost too much had happened to Jenny in the five years that had elapsed since her year of study in Paris. She had been dragged into the great world in earnest, protesting every step of the way. It appeared that she had decided she had gone far enough and had determined, with unshakable obstinacy, not to go one step farther.

To begin with, she had not been compelled, after all, as it is hardly necessary to say, to sit on the Common in Stockholm and beg for alms. She had been received back rapturously by the Royal Theater and by the public of Stockholm, alike. For her opening appearance, she had deliberately chosen to sing Norma, the last role she had sung before she left Stockholm, to let her admirers know to what extent her voice had changed and whether or not they liked the change. It had proved almost as much of an occasion as her initial triumph in *Der Freischütz*. The audience had cheered and clapped and even stamped in its wild enthusiasm. Before Paris, her voice, fresh, sweet and thrilling as it had been, had lacked the flexibility and strength to do full justice to the great operatic roles. The critics found it now a soprano voice of impressive sonority and compass, equal to any demand put upon it. One enthusiast declared that her technique was "great enough to be regarded as unique in the history of a musical world." The young woman who had substituted for her during Jenny's year in Paris remained in the company, but the best roles went to Jenny, again with Günther and Belletti in the tenor and baritone parts.

She had returned to the Lindblads, Adolf apparently having come to his senses, and her life might have gone on just as it had before, except for the improvement in her voice and technique, if the old trouble with Adolf had not begun again. Once more he stormed about, or sulked gloomily, like a lovesick adolescent. People began to talk, and Fredrika Bremer, Sweden's leading writer and a member of the Lindblad circle, became seriously concerned for Jenny's reputation. Jenny wrote to a friend to whom Fredrika Bremer had confided her worries, "Love, hate, envy, applause, flattery, intrigues, slander—they all crush me down until I do not know how I shall survive!"

She survived by finding a flat of her own, not far from the Bonde Palace, persuading Mademoiselle Apollonia Lindskog, "Tant Lona," one of the ladies who had received Jenny and Louise Johansson when they left the Linds, to live with her as her chaperon. The move also necessitated acquiring a male guardian, for Swedish law required this for every young, unmarried Swedish woman who did not live under the roof of her father or other natural protector. Her choice of Judge Henric Munthe of the Court of Second Instance proved a singularly happy one. He was a musician as well as a jurist and shrewd businessman, who could understand every side of Jenny's complex needs. Now Jenny had only to turn over her earnings to Judge Munthe. He attended to her investments and disbursements, including the allowances she made to her parents and to her growing list of pensioners, and also gave her invaluable advice about her personal affairs. He became to her, in fact, the father Niklas Lind had never been, and that Adolf Lindblad had ceased to be.

By January of 1843, when these changes had been brought about, Jenny was at last as independent as it was possible for a respectable unmarried Swedish woman to be. She had made it a condition of her re-employment by the Royal Theater that she should not be obliged to appear in more than fifty productions during a season, and was to be paid extra for any productions above that number she chose to appear in; that she should not have to appear in the theater more than twice in any one week; and that she should be granted a leave of absence each year, lasting from the fifteenth of June to the first of October. She had learned well the lesson of not exceeding her strength. But now that she knew how to handle her voice, it grew with use.

That winter she had added to her reportoire the parts of Valentine in Meyerbeer's *Les Huguenots*, the Countess in Mozart's *Marriage of Figaro*, and Amina in *La Sonnambula*. Amina, in particular, had been a tremendous success and bade fair to be one of the most popular of Jenny's roles to date.

It was her first appearance outside her native land the following autumn, however, which set her, though she did not know it at the time, on the path that was to carry her to the heights. She had given concerts in Sweden with Günther after June 15, then gone into Finland, which did not count as an outside country, having been part of Sweden until it had been gobbled up by Russia some thirty-four years previously. In Helsinki she had used Swedish folk songs for the first time as encores, and learned the great appeal they had for an audience. The university students had serenaded her, and the great Finnish poet, Runeberg, had talked to her so long and earnestly about the great things he saw in store for her that she had wept from the certainty of her inability ever to realize them.

After that she had crossed over to Copenhagen, to rest before reporting for the opera season in Stockholm. Once more, Grandma Tengmark would have detected the hand of Providence, for the results of this simple act were to be far-reaching.

Jenny, disliking hotels and inns, had accepted an invitation to stay with the Bournonvilles, anticipating nothing but a brief escape from work and travel and people. It had dismayed her that the numerous Bournonville children were turned out of their nursery to make room for her, but she made it up to them by singing with them every morning after breakfast. On her birthday, the children had appeared at the door of her room, each with a bouquet for her. Jenny had scooped the flowers into her arms and declared that she wished she had a home of her own, so that she might keep them always.

Jenny had found the Bournonville home so enjoyable and the children so delightful that the few days she had planned to spend in Copenhagen had stretched into weeks. She could not remember when she had been so happy and peaceful—until August Bournonville conceived his brilliant idea.

Robert de Normandie was playing at the Royal Theater in Copenhagen, and it occurred to August that this was a heaven-sent opportunity for Denmark to see and hear Jenny in the role of Alice. He mentioned his idea to the head of the Danish Royal Theater, who expressed enthusiastic approval. But when Bournonville broached the matter to Jenny, she was terrified.

Jenny had sung in concerts outside of Stockholm, but opera was something else. She remembered how she had broken down in the aria from Lucia when she had tried to sing for Garcia. When Bournonville suggested that she attend the theater in Copenhagen, so she could see how much the atmosphere was like that in Stockholm, he only made matters worse. The performance of the Danish actress, Louise Heiberg, impressed Jenny more forcibly even than had the acting of Rachel. August Bournonville wrote later that Jenny wept and wrung her hands and implored him to "spare her the pain of exhibiting her own insignificant person and talent on a stage which had at its disposal the genius and beauty of Fru Heiberg." The Bournonville children, who witnessed this demonstration, were amazed that a grownup could behave so childishly.

It was this childish behavior, however, which brought Hans Christian

Andersen into Jenny's life, for it reminded Bournonville that his good friend, the poet and storyteller, was better with children than anyone else in all Denmark. He appealed to Andersen to help him dispel Jenny's foolish fears.

Andersen had met Jenny two years before. When she was in Malmö on the concert tour she had undertaken in order to raise the money to study in Paris, Andersen had called to pay his respects. This had been after the trip when the carriage had frequently sunk hub-deep into the mud, and Jenny was drained, exhausted. The lanky, angular Andersen had an innocent love for striking clothes, which only emphasized his homeliness. To Jenny he had appeared a figure of fun, and she had not been in the mood for fun just then. Andersen for his part had considered Jenny cold and commonplace.

When Bournonville begged him now to intercede with the Swedish prima donna, Andersen replied that the Danes had managed to exist to date without hearing Jenny Lind sing, and that it was his opinion they would be just as well off if they never did hear her sing. The ballet master finally ended the argument by seizing Andersen's hat and walking stick, putting the first on the writer's head and the second in his hand, and practically dragging him to the Bournonville home.

There Andersen had a pleasant surprise. Instead of the dour young woman he had called on in Malmö, so unresponsive that he had decided she was hopelessly spoiled by the attention she had received, a warmly smiling Jenny, hand outstretched, hurried across the room to greet him. Fredrika Bremer was a good friend of Andersen's, as she was of Jenny's, and since the unfortunate encounter in Malmö, Jenny had heard a great deal about the tall Dane and had read some of his stories. She explained to him, as frankly and confidingly as to an old friend, why she was so terrified of appearing as Alice. She had grown up in the Royal Theater in Stockholm, she told him; the people there had known her from childhood. She could count on their kindness. But the audience in Copenhagen might not be so tolerant of her shortcomings. They might hiss! That was Jenny's recurrent nightmare when she was tired or depressed—of standing alone on a stage, facing the vigorous disapproval of a theater full of people.

Andersen saw that she had a real fear of failing to please an audience in a city of strangers. He replied with equal frankness and sincerity, "I have never heard you sing, Fröken Lind, and I therefore cannot judge the quality of your singing. I have never seen you act, so I have no idea how good an actress you may be. But I do know Copenhagen audiences. If you can sing at all, and can act moderately well, I can't imagine that you will have anything to worry about."

Jenny still hung back and protested, however, until finally August Bournonville, disgusted and hurt, suggested they forget the whole thing. By accident, Bournonville had hit upon exactly the right tactics to use with Jenny in one of her moods of mulish unreasonableness. As soon as he intimated that the idea had been a mistake in the first place, Jenny volunteered timidly that it would do no harm for her to rehearse, just once, with the Copenhagen company. Bournonville had the good sense to reply carelessly, "I suppose it can be arranged," his manner indicating that he did not expect much good to come of it.

Jenny thereupon became determined to rehearse with the company, and went off by herself when Bournonville did not offer to accompany her. On her return to the Bournonville home after the rehearsal, the family had never seen her in such a good humor. She threw her arms around August's neck and danced him about the room, begging him to forgive her. Everyone present—the director, the cast, the orchestra—had joined in an ovation to Jenny at the end of the first act. She sang the part of Alice at the Danish Royal Theater on September 10, 1843, and repeated it on the thirteenth by request. Long after the performance was over, the streets were filled with people shouting Jenny's name over and over.

Bournonville wrote that "Jenny Lind found in Denmark, a second fatherland." She gained admirers and dear friends among the eminent Danish artists, poets and writers; and an army officer, reputed to be a Norwegian, was at the Bournonville house morning, noon and night. He was never known to have had a conversation with Jenny, however, because every time she opened her mouth, he would burst into tears.

Hans Christian Andersen, also, generally managed to be where Jenny was and there now ensued, for the Bournonville youngsters, an experience surely unique in the annals of childhood. Every morning, after breakfast, they were allowed to cluster around the piano and sing hymns and folk songs with Jenny Lind. Sometime during the day Hans Christian Andersen, the storyteller loved above all others, was sure to show up. After paying his respects to their parents and Jenny Lind, if she were there, he would gather the youngsters about him and tell them his latest inventions. Ten-year-old Charlotte Bournonville soon caught on. For, while he held the children enraptured, his eyes would be on Jenny. Or if Jenny did not happen to be there, he would be watching the door for her appearance.

He found in Jenny the inspiration for some of his most poignant works. One of her acts of kindness had moved even the sophisticated August Bournonville to sentimental rapture. A friend of the Bournonvilles had been seriously ill and unable to hear Jenny sing. Jenny went to the man's home and gave a concert just for the sick man and his wife. Bournonville swore that this had materially speeded his friend's recovery and from that time on, the couple for whom she had sung called her "the Angel."

It was hardly coincidence that Hans Christian Andersen soon had a new story for the Bournonville children which he called "The Angel." And a few days later there was another story, "The Emperor's Nightingale." It told how a nightingale by its beautiful song had driven death away from the Emperor. The monarch had wanted to hang a diamond pendent around the nightingale's neck as a reward. But the nightingale, seeing the tears of happiness in the Emperor's eyes at being rescued from death, said she already had had her reward.

In fact, the Bournonville children were able to follow Andersen's wooing of Jenny through the new stories which they were privileged to hear before these appeared in book form, to become the favorites of the whole world. His story, "The Snow Queen," grew out of an episode when Andersen felt that Jenny had been particularly cold. For Jenny, alas, did not take his fervent declarations of love and frequent proposals of marriage as seriously as she might have done if her old feeling for Günther had not been reawakened.

Jenny had scarcely thought of the handsome tenor while she was fighting for her life and career in Paris; indeed, Belletti was the one she had been happiest to see on her return to Stockholm. On her concert tour with Günther through Sweden that summer, he had been merely a pleasant companion until the two had run into their friend Jakob Axel Josephson, the young composer, in Linköping. Josephson was trying to amass funds to study in Germany, just as Jenny a year or two before had been trying to get money together for her study in Paris, and they gave a benefit for him. Jenny sang one of Josephson's songs, "Believe Not in Joy!" with such an effect on the audience that Josephson was quite carried away. He reported to Jenny how Günther's thoughts about her had changed. (Emily Högqvist had gone to Italy for two years of study. Günther never resumed his relationship with her.) Günther had confessed that he could not remember ever being so thrilled by any embrace as by the one his role required him to exchange with Jenny in the last scene of *La Sonnambula* when Amina wakes, realizes her vindication and expresses her joy. "All of these things our divine Jenny does in a way that might drive colder people than I am off their head," he had written to Josephson.

Julius Günther at this time was twenty-six and better-looking than ever; the homely Dane was thirty-eight. Although she was always very fond of Andersen, Jenny could not think of him as a husband, now that she knew Günther was at least beginning to take a romantic interest in her.

Undiscouraged, Andersen would repeat his proposal of marriage nearly every time he and Jenny talked together. On one occasion, after he had importuned and entreated until Jenny was at her wit's end, she picked up a mirror and looked long at herself, then handed the mirror to Andersen. "No, dear brother," she begged him, "not me, with my potato nose!" Andersen was very thoughtful for the rest of that visit. The next time he came he had still another story for the children, "The Ugly Duckling."

The writer put on paper "The Angel," "The Emperor's Nightingale," and "The Ugly Duckling," and sent them to Jenny not long after she had left Copenhagen to rejoin Günther and Josephson in Sweden for a few more concerts. Jenny pretended not to recognize the application to herself, though she did very clearly, and merely thanked him for the "pretty tales," of which she said she had decided, upon reflection, that "The Ugly Duckling" was the prettiest of all.

Andersen remained her worshiper throughout the rest of his life, writing of her very movingly in his memoirs. "Through Jenny Lind, I first became sensible of the holiness there is in Art. . . . One feels, when she appears on the stage, that the holy draught is poured from a pure vessel."

Andersen always counted it one of his supreme achievements that he was able to be the instrument through whom Jenny was brought to the attention of the great world. Homely and awkward as he was, Andersen's talent and sincerity made him an honored guest in all the Courts of Europe. He went everywhere and knew everybody who counted, including Giacomo Meyerbeer.

The most popular operatic composer of the day, who with his *Robert le Diable* and *les Huguenots* had brought the grand manner to the opera of romance, Meyerbeer had been commissioned to compose an opera in honor of Berlin's outstanding musical event of the century—the dedication of the largest and finest opera house in Europe, rebuilt by King Frederick William IV of Prussia on the same site and on lines almost identical with the one built one hundred years before by Fredrick the Great, which had recently burned down. For the theme of his opera, Meyerbeer had chosen an incident from the Silesian campaign in which Fredrick the Great had first shown his military genius. The libretto had been written by Ludwig Rellstab, one of the leading musicologists and critics of the day.

Hans Christian Andersen, visiting Meyerbeer in Berlin the summer following Jenny's stay in Copenhagen, heard all about the new opera, which was to be called *Camp in Silesia* (*Das Feldlager in Schlesien*). Meyerbeer was not satisfied with any of the leading sopranos of the day for the part of Vielka. Andersen promptly suggested Jenny Lind for it.

"Yes, her voice is perfect," Meyerbeer said. "I heard her sing in Paris. But a good voice is not enough. The role calls for a fine actress as well."

Then Andersen told his friend how Jenny had captivated the Danes by her acting in Meyerbeer's own *Robert de Normandie*. On his recommendation, backed up by that of Paul Taglione, the dancer, who knew what enthusiasm Jenny had created in both Stockholm and Copenhagen, Meyerbeer invited Jenny, a singer then unknown outside Scandanavia, to play the leading part in his new opera, which was to be the outstanding feature of the dedication of the new opera house on December 7, 1844.

The offer could not have arrived at a more propitious time. King Karl Johann, the former Marshal Bernadotte, had died, and the Swedish Royal Theater had closed during the period of national mourning. The two-year contract Jenny had signed with the Royal Theater before she left Paris had expired. Moreover, Jenny's personal affairs were in a kind of doldrums.

She and Günther had been together so much the winter before, after her return from Copenhagen, that everyone believed them to be engaged. Günther had thrown himself ardently into the task of helping their friend Josephson complete the sum of money he needed to study abroad. Jenny had helped. She had been impressed by the tenor's new seriousness and unselfishness, as well as by Günther's deeply admiring comments about herself which Josephson reported to her from time to time. A concert Jenny and Günther gave, together with Mina Fundin, at Uppsala, brought in enough money to ensure a year of study for Josephson in Germany, but Günther had never said a word to Jenny herself about love. The conqueror of the experienced Emily Högqvist was abashed before Jenny's purity, and Jenny, deciding that she had misinterpreted Günther's attentions and the confidences he had made to Josephson, became more withdrawn. After the concert at Uppsala, Günther wrote Josephson that the only change he could note in the state of his romantic affairs was that "a realization of my inmost desires appears to me if anything more remote than ever."

Another close relationship was taking on a bitter flavor—that with Jenny's parents. Once more Anna Marie's private daemon seemed bent on ruining the affection Jenny, while in Paris, had developed for her mother and father. Although the provision she made for the elder Linds was generous, Anna Marie took the ground that the money Jenny spent on her charities was in some way stolen from them. Niklas Lind would act as Anna Marie's emissary to Jenny when Judge Munthe refused to give them more than the agreed-upon stipend.

"It makes your mother feel badly that you do so much more for outsiders than you do for us," Niklas would report meekly. The benefit for Josephson was particularly galling to Anna Marie. Jenny, bent upon avoiding the angry bickering that had gone on earlier between herself and her mother, was finding it increasingly hard to bite back an angry, "What did you and my mother ever do for me?"

Jenny Lind, the Swedish Nightingale

Jenny thought it would be a good idea to get away from Stockholm for a while. And she had always smarted a bit at the idea that she must have a successful appearance in Paris in order to prove her worth. Meyerbeer's engaging her for his new opera certainly answered that.

These various reasons apparently were impelling enough to counteract the terror at appearing before an audience outside her own country which had assailed her in Copenhagen. The correspondence between Meyerbeer and Jenny was not preserved, but the indications are that she accepted his invitation with little if any urging.

Everyone, including Jenny herself, took it that she would return to the Swedish Royal Opera after she had introduced *Camp in Silesia* to the Prussian public. At a farewell audience with Desideria, the Queen Dowager gave Jenny, in addition to portrait medals of herself and her husband, the late King, a little watch. The watch, Desideria said, was to remind Jenny "not to forget when it is time for your return to us."

Everyone, that is, but Giovanni Belletti. He knew that Jenny now was truly as great an artist as most people had claimed before she went off to study with Manuel Garcia. Once she had been heard in the great world, Belletti was sure she would not be allowed to return to the limited, though loving, confines of her native country.

This brought the realization that it was on Jenny's account he had stayed on in Stockholm, and that there would be nothing to keep him there any longer. His contract with the Royal Theater was also up for renewal, and he did not renew it. When Jenny left Stockholm, Belletti left too, never to return. Günther wrote Josephson mournfully that he would have joined the exodus himself except that his contract with the Royal Theater was still in force. So he remained, the only one left of the old triumvirate.

Jenny had undertaken the task not only of introducing a new role to the world's most exacting audience, but of learning a new language as well, in a few month's time. Meyerbeer, as expert in public relations as in music, wanted to conceal his new prima donna from the Berlin public until she had both the language and the new role well in hand. Berlin, then the musical capital of Europe, had heard all the great voices and artists of the day: Malibran and Catalani, Pasta and Schröder-Devrient, and Germany's own Sontag. Jenny would be compared with these great ones as well as with the reigning stars, such as Persiani, whose singing she had admired in Paris, and Grisi whom she had admired as an actress.

The composer therefore had Jenny go to Dresden because the German spoken there was particularly pure, and the city had a fine opera, where Jenny might hear and study the German singers. Tant Lona accompanied Jenny as her chaperon, and whom should they see as they drove to their lodgings from the railroad station but Jakob Axel Josephson! He had come over from Leipzig, where he was studying in the Conservatory recently founded by Felix Mendelssohn-Bartholdy, to attend the opera. He served as the ladies' escort when they went to hear Beethoven's *Fidelio*, and a new opera, *Rienzi*, by Richard Wagner, which Meyerbeer had been instrumental in having produced. The Swedish Consul was allowed to give a party for Jenny, where she sang her Swedish songs, including "The Herdsman," composed by her old singing master, Izak Berg, as well as several arias. The Swedish guests were delighted to find their Nightingale as good as she had been reported to be; the Germans declared they could not wait to hear her in full opera. Aside from these appearances, Meyerbeer permitted no outsiders to get a glimpse of her.

Jenny had been in Dresden only a little more than a month, however, when the plans for quiet work and study were disrupted. Karl Johann's son was to be crowned King Oskar I of Sweden. A royal command came for the Court singer Jenny Lind to add her voice to the festivities. Jenny felt she owed everything to Sweden and the Royal Theater, and Meyerbeer granted her a leave of absence to carry out her obligation.

This incident very nearly put an end to Jenny's foray into the great world before it had properly started. For Stockholm received her back so ecstatically and applauded her singing so vigorously, that a great clamor arose in the press and among theater goers to keep Jenny from returning to Germany. The Royal Theater made her an offer unprecedented in its history, a contract for eight years at a salary of 5,000 *Riksdaler* a year (about 420 English pounds) and the same salary each year as a pension for as long as she lived, when she had finished her eight-year contract! Jenny was greatly moved, and almost irresistibly tempted. Out of respect for Lindblad and Geijer and other good friends who tried to make her see that her talents were too great to be limited to Sweden alone, she did not sign the contract immediately, but she fully intended to.

In the end it was Günther who changed her mind. Still too timid to tell Jenny of his love for her, he was at this time unselfishly, almost quixotically, devoted to her interests. Calling on her one day, he found her on the point of signing the contract offered by the Royal Theater. Much as he would have liked her to stay in Stockholm, Günther protested that she owed it to herself and the world not to close the door to wider opportunities. Jenny's face set in the stubborn lines that he knew all too well and seeing that further argument was useless, he rushed out into the street distractedly. Encountering a friend who prided himself on his knowledge of musical matters, Günther poured out the story to him—how tragic it would be if Jenny were to refuse to carry out her commitment to Meyerbeer, were to bury herself in Stockholm for the remainder of her active musical life. To Günther's surprise, the man disagreed with him. Jenny was good enough for the Scandanavian countries, which after all were pretty provincial, he remarked. But doubtless Jenny herself was aware that her abilities were not equal to the challenge presented her by Berlin audiences.

Günther, returning to Jenny, told her exactly what his friend had said. At that moment Jenny looked like her mother, anger bringing bright color to her cheeks and fire to her eyes. Without a word, she picked up the contract and tore it into little pieces. On the ninth of October she sang another farewell to her homeland, once again choosing the role of Norma for her last appearance, and set off once more for Germany.

With Jenny's return to Germany, affairs began to gather the momentum which was soon to sweep her onward at breakneck speed. This time she went straight to Berlin, for scarcely more than six weeks remained until December 7, the opening night for *Camp in Silesia*. All the traveling about having proved too much for Tant Lona, Jenny had brought her old friend Louise Johansson as her chaperon and companion. Meyerbeer engaged Frau Birch-Pfeiffer, a former actress who had also written many plays, to teach Jenny German and to coach her in her role.

As the date for the opening grew closer, Jenny was seized with the fear of failure which had caused her to make a spectacle of herself in Copenhagen. Her nervousness and apprehensions so disturbed Meyerbeer that he thought it advisable to gain some support for her. He presented her to the royal family, who were so kind that Jenny felt the King and Meyerbeer were the only friends she had in Berlin, as she wrote Josephson. But she quickly acquired other friends.

The Princess of Prussia (afterwards the Empress Augusta, grandmother of Wilhelm II) gave a reception at which Jenny was invited to sing. Among the guests were the famous prima donna Henrietta Sontag, now Countess Rossi and temporarily retired from the stage, and the Countess of Westmorland, the wife of the English Ambassador. The Westmorlands were friends of Meyerbeer, who had raved to them about Jenny, calling her a "veritable diamond of genius," insisting that she would be the greatest singer-artist the nineteenth century would produce. Lady Westmorland was filled with curiosity to hear this genius, and so naturally was Sontag. The two ladies were together when Meyerbeer's "diamond" was pointed out to them—"a thin, pale, plain-featured girl, looking awkward and nervous, like a very shy country schoolgirl," as Lady Westmorland later wrote.

When Meyerbeer came up to pay his compliments to Lady Westmorland, she exclaimed, "You cannot be serious! You can't really mean to give this frightened child the lead in your new opera!"

Meyerbeer replied simply, "Wait, my lady."

Lady Westmorland wrote afterwards that when Jenny began to sing, it was the most extraordinary experience she, Lady Westmorland, had ever had. "The wonderful notes came ringing out. But over and above that was the wonderful *transfiguration*—no other word could apply—which came over her entire face and figure. Her face simply and literally shone like that of an angel." Sontag was reported to have said that Jenny was the greatest living singer.

Meyerbeer also introduced Jenny to the home of Professor Wichmann, a sculptor, who with his wife occupied much the same place in artistic circles in Berlin that the Lindblads did in Stockholm. Lady Westmorland and Madam Wichmann became very much attached to Jenny, and took it upon themselves to induce the young star to pay more attention to her appearance. They had little luck in the matter of cosmetics, for if Jenny ever used rouge, she did it so sparingly that it could not be detected. (In Havana, seven years later, the novelist Fredrika Bremer pointedly presented Jenny with a box of rouge. It was found among the singer's personal effects, unopened, after her death.) However, Jenny did yield to their suggestions about clothes. Her dresses thereafter were more modish and becoming, though she clung to simple styles and a minimum of decoration.

Just two weeks before the opening of *Camp in Silesia*, came a second unexpected interference with Jenny's plans—and Meyerbeer's. Jenny learned that a Fräulein Tuczec, her understudy for Vielka, who had been playing the role at rehearsals during Jenny's absence in Stockholm, was claiming to various prominent persons that she was entitled to perform the part on the opening night. Meyerbeer had been stoutly resisting Fräulein Tuczec's pretentions, but had to give way when Jenny promptly sided with the German singer. Jenny wrote to the Stockholm papers, which had noted the controversy, that she considered Fräulein Tuczec had right on her side, "since she had had the part for some time, and is, moreover, a great favorite with the public here, while I am unknown and a foreigner besides."

Jenny, in fact, felt that a great burden had been lifted from her. Now she could go back to Stockholm and sign the contract with the Swedish Royal Theater.

It was not to work out that way, however. Through her gracious attitude toward Fräulein Tuczec, Jenny not only had endeared herself to the Berlin public, she had made them anxious to hear her sing. By popular demand, a debut was arranged for Jenny at the Opera House on December 15. She chose to sing Norma and gave her own interpretation, as she had worked it out in Stockholm, in spite of the fact that it was very different from the interpretation of the famous prima donnas whose names had been associated with the role.

Bellini had written the part originally for Madame Pasta, and she had portrayed the Druid priestess as a fiery Amazon. Grisi had played it next, and had even exceeded Pasta in the violence and vengefulness exhibited by the wronged priestess. The other great prima donnas who had played the role, including Malibran, had followed the tradition set by Pasta and Grisi.

Jenny saw Norma as a woman, governed by womanly emotions, and in Berlin as in Stockholm, her Norma shrank back from the thought of murdering her children, in sharp contrast to the tigerish gestures toward them of Grisi and the others. In her first appearance before objective and highly sophisticated critics, she was challenging one of the dearest traditions of opera.

As it turned out, Jenny's Berlin debut might have been one of Hans Christian Andersen's pleasanter phantasies. Meyerbeer's opera, on which so much pains and money had been lavished, closed after five nights, although it contained some of the most appealing music that Meyerbeer had yet written. There was no doubt in anyone's mind as to who was to blame for the failure. Meyerbeer was first furious, then coldly bitter, that his beautiful opera should have been sacrificed to Fräulein Tuczec's vanity.

Jenny's Norma, on the other hand, had an unprecedented triumph. The audience was so enraptured by her rendering of the "Casta diva" that, for the first time in Berlin's opera history, the production was stopped by thunderous applause, and Jenny had to repeat the passage before the audience would let the opera proceed. Jenny had transposed the aria from the key of G in which it had been written, to the key of F, which she considered better suited to it. Ever since that night, "Casta diva" has been sung in the key of F.

Herr Rellstab, in his capacity of music critic, wrote that while he hoped the audience's behavior would not set a precedent, nevertheless it had been pardonable on this occasion because "until now no singer has ever sung "Casta diva as we think it ought to be sung." He approved as highly her interpretation of the role of Norma. "Pasta presents a Norma *before* whom we tremble, our present artist a Norma *with* whom we tremble. The art of the one is broader, more astonishing; that of the other more sweet and enthralling."

There followed in rapid succession two more appearances in *Norma* by popular demand, and a command performance at Court at which she was given a jeweled bracelet by the King and Queen. Next came the offer of a six months' engagement with the Prussian Royal Opera at a salary of 6,000 thalers (around 900 pounds) and a benefit. Jenny at once offered Jakob Axel Josephson the money for a year of study in Italy following his year at the Leipzig Conservatory of Music. He accepted it and, returning to Sweden afterwards, steeped in the classical tradition of music, was appointed Musical Director of Uppsala University in 1849. Josephson introduced to Sweden the great oratorios of the great masters, especially those of Handel, Haydin and Mendelssohn, which had not been heard there before.

As her first performance under her new contract with the Prussian Royal Opera, Jenny sang Vielka in *Camp in Silesia*. Meyerbeer had written the part for her voice and would not rest until she was given a chance to sing it. She had an even greater trumph as Vielka than as Norma. Particular enthusiasm was aroused by the aria with flute obligato in the third act. Jenny's tones took on so flutelike a quality that her voice could hardly be distinguished from the instruments. Meyerbeer later transferred this passage to his *L'Etoile du Nord*, and it has become one of the most famous in opera.

When it was announced that Jenny would appear a second time in *Camp in Silesia*, there was such a demand for tickets that the manager raised the price of admission. The opera was repeated over and over. There was never a night that the theater could not have been filled two or three times, and four clerks were kept busy answering letters and filling requests for tickets. Meyerbeer's opera had been saved by the young singer from Sweden.

The next notable event, three months later, was a grand performance of *Euryanthe* in honor of its composer Carl Maria von Weber, in whose opera *Der Freischütz* Jenny had scored her first outstanding success. He had died in London in 1826 and had been buried there. But now his family, aided by such friends as the English composer Jules Benedict, who was to enter Jenny's own story later on, and the then relatively unknown Richard Wagner, had brought his body back to Dresden. The special performance of *Euryanthe* was both to raise funds to erect an appropriate monument to him, and also to pay tribute to a man who had been greatly loved by his countrymen. Jenny was chosen above all the German stars to sing the leading role.

Once more, she flew in the face of tradition by emphasizing the supernatural element which she felt had been Weber's leading motif, and she had to sing in German a role she had sung previously in Swedish.

The critics applauded her interpretation as much as they did her singing. When it came time for her benefit performance of *Norma*, with which she closed the season, tickets were sold out long in advance and the stage was carpeted with flowers and wreaths when she took her bows at the end. Josephson wrote in his diary, "Jenny is oscillating between heaven and earth, not knowing, yet, on what terms she is with either."

She started back to Stockholm then, stopping for concerts on the way. At Hanover and Hamburg she was nearly smothered with flowers, and the grand Duchess of Mechklenberg-Schwerin took a valuable bracelet from her own arm and gave it to Jenny. Her steamboat was not to reach the Swedish capital until midnight, yet the port and the adjacent streets were packed with people. When a rocket signaled the approach of her ship, the assembled crowd began shouting their welcome, and an orchestra serenaded her from a boat which escorted hers into port. Jenny had come a long way from the nameless little girl of No. 40 Mäster Samuelsgrand.

Now events began to crowd thick and fast. She was given another valuable bracelet by Queen Dowager Desideria at a private supper, and at the request of King Oskar, played Marie in *La Figlia del Reggimento* at a special performance for his soldiers. The house was filled solidly with uniforms, and Jenny, loving things military ever since she had picked out the fanfare on the piano at the age of four, had devised a particularly fetching costume, a feminine version of military uniforms at the beginning of the nineteenth century. She romped exuberantly through the role of Marie, declared she had never before had so much fun, and the audience of soldiers roared with laughter, clapping so hard Jenny feared they would injure their hands. Marie quickly became one of Jenny's most popular roles and she was most often represented, in pictures and statues, in her "regimental" costume. (When the Metropolitan Opera in New York City reintroduced *Daughter of the Regiment* in December of 1940, Lily Pons's costume was a replica of the one worn by Jenny Lind.)

But her visit home was cut short by an invitation from King Fredrick William IV of Prussia to take part in the elaborate entertainments he was arranging for Queen Victoria of England, who with her consort was paying her first visit to the Continent since her accession to the throne. Nearly all the royalty of Europe were invited. And as the statue to Beethoven at Bonn was to be unveiled at the time of Victoria's visit, a host of Europe's eminent musicians, including Moscheles, Berlioz, Liszt, as well as Meyerbeer, were coming too. The opening concert, for the most distinguished guests of the King, was held in the courtyard of the Château of Brühl, not far from Bonn. In this medieval setting, lighted by torches, the program began with "God Save the Queen," sung by a chorus of seven hundred voices. Then Jenny stepped forward, wearing a long white gown, a red rose in her hair her only ornament, and sang so beautifully that those who had doubted the reports about her were converted to ardent admirers.

The Queen and the singer were very nearly the same age—Victoria had had her twenty-sixth birthday on May 24 of this year of 1845, Jenny would be twenty-five that October—and Victoria was impressed quite as much by Jenny's modesty and fine character as by her singing. The two developed such a friendship that King Fredrick William invited Jenny to go on with the Royal party to his old castle of Stolzenfels, on the Rhine near Coblenz. Then Queen Victoria and Prince Albert stopped at Frankfurt to hear Jenny in four of her most dramatic roles, *Norma*, *Lucia di Lammermoor*, Amina in *La Sonnambula*, and Agatha in *Der Freischütz*.

In Copenhagen, where Jenny went next, she was met at the pier by a great group of Danes, including Hans Christian Andersen, who had written a poem, "Welcome," especially for the occasion. Andersen said in his memoirs that when told of a plan to provide a home for children who had been deserted or were neglected by their parents, Jenny had promptly begged to be allowed to give a benefit concert for the project on her single free evening. Andersen wrote that this was the only occasion when he had heard her express self-satisfaction about her voice and the power it gave her. When told how much money the concert had raised for the children, Jenny's eyes filled with tears, he said, and she exclaimed, "Is it not beautiful that I sing so well?"

Yet Jenny was talking of retiring into private life. During her engagement in Frankfurt she had met and quickly established a close friendship with Mrs. George Grote, a Swedish woman married to an Englishman, and had confided to her her plan to leave the stage as soon as she amassed enough money to live on the rest of her life. She would like to sing for charity, she said, and for her friends and for her own pleasure, but that was all.

Also in Frankfurt she had met, at the home of Baron Rothschild, Prince and Princess Metternich of Austria, and they had heard her sing. They said she must come to Vienna, and soon after this Jenny had received a letter from Herr Pokorny, manager of the Vienna Opera, offering her an engagement with half the box-office receipts as her recompense. Jenny had asked Frau Birch-Pfeiffer to decline the offer in her behalf. "They have such excellent singers in Vienna—what could I do there?"

Jenny begged Frau Birch-Pfeiffer's forgiveness for being so difficult and stubborn, but pleaded as an excuse her "terrible nervousness which destroys all for me. I see far less well than I should, if it were not for this enemy."

When Queen Victoria had said good-bye, she had added that she hoped and expected to see Jenny soon, in England. But Jenny had shaken her head and said that would be impossible.

She had excellent reasons, or so she thought, both for confining her singing to Scandinavia and Germany, and for ending her career as quickly as she could. More honor had come to Jenny by this time than she had ever dreamed of. She had shown Garcia that she could both sing and act. She had proved to her Swedish friends that one could get along quite well without making a successful appearance in Paris. If she were to aspire to more, might she not again invite that failure which, in Jenny's mind, forever lay in wait beyond some innocent-appearing corner or other?

Throughout the period of public triumph upon triumph, moreover, there had been disillusionments in her private life which had gone far to negate the outward successes in her eyes. Josephson had written of her in his diary, "I can only pray that in her restless life peace may one day obtain the victory."

When she had returned to Stockholm that summer, Jenny had sung again with Günther in the Coronation ceremonies, but he had seemed remote, almost as though he were avoiding her. The fact was that when she had appeared with the aura about her of her great successes abroad, he had felt more unworthy of her than ever. But all Jenny knew was that she had not heard from him since she had left Stockholm.

Günther was no longer in Stockholm himself. He had finally broken away from the Swedish Royal Theater and was studying voice in earnest in Paris, with Manuel Garcia. He had written Josephson that "his heart and soul would be filled by Jenny Lind until eternity," and commissioned Josephson to tell Jenny he had said she was the greatest singer alive, now that he had had an opportunity to hear singers who were said to be better than she was in some respects. Günther was trying to make himself worthy of Jenny as an artist, but Jenny took his silence to mean that he had lost whatever interest in her he might once have had. She wrote Josephson that she would never marry. "The man who is the cause of all this is now wandering at large . . . may he be happy. He has himself chosen his lot."

There was another wrench at her heart, which only Judge Munthe knew about. When she had arrived in Frankfurt, after singing before most of the crowned heads in Europe in the entertainments for Queen Victoria, she had found waiting for her a letter from Niklas Lind, who practically never wrote to her, demanding the money to buy a house for himself and Anna Marie. And at Ed-Sollentuna, of all places.

It had been a secret aim of Jenny's ever since her return from Paris to surprise Anna Marie and Niklas with the gift of a home, as soon as she could afford it. She had even decided that the home would be at Ed-Sollentuna, where Jenny herself had been so happy as a small child. Here Jenny would be able to visit her parents, roam the fields and woods once more, hear the birds and make her own music on the organ of the little church. It destroyed all her pleasure, however, to have her parents claim this as a right.

Jenny wrote to Judge Munthe, asking him to talk to Anna Marie about the purchase. Not to Niklas—Jenny knew he was hopeless when it came to business or handling money. She told the Judge to give Anna Marie whatever she asked for, "for it is for them I work," and as much more as they would need to get settled in the house. But she wanted her guardian to investigate a bit to make sure the money would be spent wisely. The result was another of Anna Marie's temper explosions. She resented having to apply to Judge Munthe, and talked to him so insult-ingly that he refused to give her any money at all and wrote Jenny that he would never see or talk to her mother again.

Jenny implored Judge Munthe not to be angry with *her* because of her mother's behavior and went on to say rather bitterly that while ordinarily she did not hear from her parents for weeks at a time, in the last week she had received two letters, the second from Anna Marie herself, beg-ging Jenny to send the money for the house by Louise Johansson, or even just loose in the mail. Only thus, Anna Marie had written, could they be assured that Jenny "would never allow her cruel guardian to come be-tween her and her parents, and that Jenny, with her unusually beautiful character, would keep her promise to provide her parents with a home." Jenny commented that her character became unusually beautiful only when her parents wanted something from her that they were not en-titled to.

It developed that Niklas and Anna Marie had borrowed the money for a down payment on the house without having told Jenny of their inten-tion, and now they looked to her to extricate them from their predica-ment. All of this without a word of inquiry about Jenny's own affairs and whether she was able to spare the money.

"To be a plaything for their frightful, merciless selfishness does not amuse me," Jenny wrote to Judge Munthe, telling him not to give them any money at this time, but to wait a while and make sure it would be spent to good purpose. Anna Marie retaliated by refusing to accept the allowance Jenny made them. Jenny worried as to what Niklas might say when he was in his cups, assuring Judge Munthe that her father would not knowingly misrepresent the situation or do her any harm, but that he was lacking in discretion. In the end, Jenny had Judge Munthe buy the house at Ed-Sollentuna, but the hamlet was spoiled as a place where she herself might find peace and rest.

However, the cause of the nervousness and fright she had confessed to Frau Birch-Pfeiffer with regard to Herr Pokorny's offer was Mr. Alfred Bunn, manager of the Drury Lane Theater in London. Word had reached him of Jenny's great success in her debut at the Prussian Royal Opera and he had gone at once to Berlin to see if she was as good as the rumors said. He heard her sing Vielka, and knew that his fortune would be made if he could get her to London. He spoke of this to Lord Westmorland, and the British Ambassador agreed that his countrymen must have a chance to hear Jenny. When Mr. Bunn was unable to get a ticket for the second performance of *Camp in Silesia*, the Westmorlands invited him to sit in their box.

Thus, without the slightest intention of doing so, Lord Westmorland laid the trap into which Jenny was to fall. Between acts, Meyerbeer escorted Jenny to the Westmorland box. The English impresario pulled out a contract, prepared in advance, which bound her to sing at the Drury Lane Theater under what appeared to be magnificent terms, and Lord Westmorland and Meyerbeer both encouraged Jenny to sign it on the spot. The fact that she had signed in the presence of the British Ambassador and in his theater box (which made the box British territory for the time being) gave the contract legality in British courts.

In the beginning Jenny had been pleased with the contract—Mr. Bunn offered her nearly $5,000 for a month and a half!—but soon began to have misgivings, and when she expressed these to Mr. Bunn, he had made it plain that a contract was a contract and he expected her to stand by her word. Jenny had broken down in a performance at the opera and had been physically ill for a time. Thereafter she was pursued by letters from Mr. Bunn either demanding to know when he could expect her in London to fulfill her engagement, or threatening her with serious consequences if she did not.

Mr. and Mrs. George Grote had promised to see Mr. Bunn on their return to England to try to persuade him to release her. They imagined that Jenny would have to pay Mr. Bunn something and to this Jenny agreed readily, saying she would consent to anything the Grotes thought desirable in the way of "smart money," as an indemnity of this kind used to be called.

That was when Jenny had expressed a wish to retire from the stage as soon as she had amassed sufficient capital. It was not Mr. Bunn's behavior about the contract alone that influenced her, she said. There were also the inescapable incidentals of an operatic career—the crowds of curious people who constantly intruded on her; the exhaustion of acting and singing long, difficult roles; the exposure to drafts, after having been under great exertion on an overheated stage; the labor of rehearsal. She told Mrs. Grote, "My wants are few, my tastes simple, I could be content on a very small income."

Mrs. Grote got Mr. Bunn to agree that he would cancel the contract if Jenny would give him £500 forfeit money. The letter reached Jenny in Copenhagen, where she had just insured the success of the home for neglected children by her benefit concert. But she did not have £500 of her own, or anything like it. As her salary had risen, her charities had risen in proportion. The purchase of the home for her parents, on top of the year of study in Italy she had financed for Josephson, had wiped out her small capital.

Meanwhile word had got about in London that the now lengendary Swedish songstress would appear there that fall, along with a rumor that Jenny was dealing with Bunn's rival impresario at Her Majesty's Theatre, Mr. Benjamin Lumley, in order to get better terms. Actually, Jenny had had no contact with Mr. Lumley as yet, but the rumor of her negotiations with Her Majesty's Theatre had led Mr. Bunn to dicker about a release, for he could do nothing to Jenny unless she came to England and he thought he might as well salvage what he could.

When he did not get his £500, Mr. Bunn threatened to put Jenny in jail if she came to England to sing for anyone else. Jenny's natural tendency to nervousness and lack of self-confidence was greatly increased. She declared—and meant it—that she would rather die than go to England under Mr. Bunn's management.

Jenny Lind's career would probably have ended with a few more engagements in Scandanavia and Germany if it had not been for the friendship that developed during her second winter in Berlin, with Felix Mendelssohn-Bartholdy.

CHAPTER SIX

Felix Mendelssohn-Bartholdy

MENDELSSOHN was one of the distinguished persons Jenny had met at the Wichmanns' in Berlin before her debut and she had been overwhelmed when the great man went out of his way to be friendly and polite. But when he mentioned her own "great talent," she said sharply, "How can you speak like that when you have never heard me sing or seen me on the stage?"

"Well!" Mendelssohn replied, somewhat overwhelmed in his turn. "For this reason. All who have heard you have only one opinion. And that is so rare a thing that it is quite sufficient to prove what you are."

In the fall of 1845, Jenny renewed her contract with the Royal Opera House in Berlin and passed another supreme test when she sang Agatha in *Der Freischütz*. That had been the first of the romantic operas and, written by Weber, a German, it had been produced first in Berlin and had been sung by all the great German singers. Agatha had become a measuring stick of a prima donna's excellence, as far as Berlin was concerned.

When Jenny sang it, the cultured Berlin audience once again broke into the middle of a scene with tumultuous applause. The critic Rellstab wrote that her singing and interpretation of the role had given the opera "a new impulse and a new birth."

There was a person for whom Jenny's success as Agatha, in particular, would crown a life not remarkable in other ways—Madam Eriksson, who had been Jenny's teacher at the Royal Theater School in Stockholm, and had coached her for her first appearance in the role of Agatha. Madam Eriksson was now sixty-eight years old, and though she had sung in opera at one time, most of her life had been spent in teaching and coaching others. In order that her teacher might share the full glory of this triumph, Jenny wrote her a detailed description and even did some gloating, to an extent rare with her. As she told Madam Eriksson, "I have not forgotten that it was you who first guided my sensitive young mind toward higher aims, or that it was you who saw beneath the surface and fancied that you had discovered something, overlooked by others, behind those small, gray insignificant eyes of mine.

"How changed is everything now! What a position I have attained! What great things has the Almighty vouchsafed to me! . . . In seven months only I have succeeded in making my reputation here. And after seven years at home, not a creature knew anything at all about me. At this present moment all the first engagements of the world are open to me. After seven months! Is it not strange?"

It was hardly correct to say that after seven years in opera in Stockholm not a creature knew anything about Jenny. That was to make Madam Eriksson feel that she might have had a great success herself if she had not stayed in Sweden.

It was soon after *Der Freischütz* that Jenny received an invitation from Mendelssohn to sing at his Gewandhaus concerts, considered to be the finest in Europe. Mendelssohn had now had ample basis for a judgment of Jenny's talent. She accepted, was granted a leave of absence from the Berlin Opera and went to Leipzig on December 3, 1845. As soon as it was announced that Jenny Lind would sing, there was such a rush for tickets that the house could have been sold out several times over, even though the price was raised. At previous Gewandhaus concerts, students at the Leipzig Conservatory had been granted free admission. But in the face of the demand for tickets to hear Jenny, the free list was suspended, to the great indignation of the students.

They held a meeting and selected one of their number, a sixteen-year-old lad named Otto Goldschmidt, to protest to the directors. Son of a well-to-do Hamburg merchant and one of Mendelssohn's own pupils in piano and composition, young Goldschmidt bearded the lions courageously, though unsuccessfully, then managed, by paying out all of his generous allowance, to get a seat in the front row at the concert, along with H. S. Holland. (Later Holland became one of Jenny's official biographers.)

The audience was Jenny's after the first notes of her opening number "Casta diva," and excitement arose almost to frenzy when Jenny finished with a group of her Swedish songs. Jakob Josephson, now in Italy, wrote in his diary, "Mendelssohn and Jenny Lind appearing together in Leipzig! What would I not have given to be there at that time!"

For Jenny's second Gewandhaus concert, which at her suggestion was to be a benefit for the widows of orchestra members, the price was raised again, but a black market flourished in the tickets just the same, and anyone who wanted to part with a ticket could get at least five times what he had paid for it.

The program included a piano solo, played by Mendelssohn, and for her concluding numbers Jenny was accompanied by Mendelssohn at the piano. She sang his "Spring Song," a Swedish dance song and, Izak Berg's "Herdsman's Song" (Fjerran i Skog) and the audience went mad. Jenny was staying at the home of Richard Wagner's sister, Frau Friedrich Brockhaus. Mendelssohn and his wife, Cecile, had been invited to the Brockhaus home for supper that night, the only guests by Jenny's express request. Suddenly the courtyard filled with students from the Conservatory, including young Goldschmidt, and members of the orchestra with their instruments. They formed a circle and serenaded Jenny by torchlight. There came a pause in the music, and a group of the Gewandhaus directors entered the room, headed by Ferdinand David, the violinist father of the great Joachim and orchestra leader under Mendelssohn. They presented Jenny with a silver tray, gift of the grateful musicians. Jenny, who had been listening to the music from behind the window curtain, was too overcome to say a word. So Mendelssohn took her hand, led her into the courtyard and made a graceful little speech for her.

"Gentlemen!" he said. "You think that the Kappellmeister Mendelssohn is speaking to you, but in that you are mistaken. Fräulein Jenny Lind speaks to you and thanks you for the beautiful surprise you have arranged for her. But now I change myself back into the Leipzig Kappellmeister and call upon you to wish long life to Fräulein Jenny

Lind. Long life to her! And again, long life to her! And for the third time, long life!"

"Long life to Jenny Lind!" shouted the students and orchestra members and, as they departed, sang the beautiful "Waldlied."

From this moment, Mendelssohn accepted Jenny as a member of the "invisible Church" of which he often spoke to his close friends—the little company of people devoted to the finest in music and art—writing to his friend, Franz Hauser, "She pulls at the same rope with all of us who are really in earnest about that; thinks about it; strives for it. And if all goes well for her in the world, it is as pleasant to me as if all went well with me." With no intermediate period, a devoted friendship came into being between the composer and the singer, the supreme friendship of Jenny's life.

Here was a man fitted above all others to round out the ways in which Jenny's artistic education had been deficient. Grandson of the great philosopher Moses Mendelssohn, Felix had grown up in a home of wealth and culture, where every opportunity had been given him to cultivate his abilities. Felix Mendelssohn had begun playing the piano in public at the age of nine, and in 1820 when he was eleven—the year in which Jenny was born—he had composed some sixty vocal and instrumental pieces. For his general education, he had had as tutor the father of Paul Heyse, the novelist. While still a lad, Mendelssohn had sat at the feet of the poet Goethe, and established friendships with Weber, Spohr, Moscheles, Bellini, Meyerbeer and Cherubini as well as with many lesser musical lights.

He was only seventeen and a half when he became famous for his overture to A *Midsummer Night's Dream*, and began his project for rescuing the works of Johann Sebastian Bach, completely forgotten by the world at large, from the obscurity into which they had fallen. He formed a choir to study the works of the old master, and at the age of twenty conducted, with a chorus of nearly four hundred voices, the first performance of *The Passion According to Saint Matthew* since Bach's death, one hundred years after its first performance by Bach.

He was a great conductor and pianist—some called him the greatest pianist of his time—as well as a great composer, and at the same time an urbane man of the world, brilliant in conversation and extremely attractive in appearance. Uncompromising in his own standards, but generous and tolerant of the failings of others, he was entirely lacking in the kind of temperamental explosions which had made Jenny's relations with Adolf Lindblad difficult. He loved his pretty, gentle wife, Cecile, and the children she bore him; he avoided deftly the ladies who were inevitably attracted by his fame and personal charm. It has been written of Mendelssohn, "It is not too much to say that his heart and life were as pure as those of a little child."

Jenny wrote Judge Munthe about her new friend, "He is a *man*! This is in addition to possessing the most supreme talent, which is as it should be."

Here was a friendship to which Jenny could give herself without reservation, while Mendelssohn delighted in the opportunity to work closely with a singer of such superlative voice and instinctive artistry. Whenever he went to Berlin, and whenever Jenny visited Leipzig, Mendelssohn, like Adolf Lindblad before him, would sit at the piano for hours, exploring the potentialities of that glorious voice. He considered Jenny's high F sharp her loveliest tone. Engaged now in composing his *Elijah*, he filled the soprano solos with high F sharps, for Jenny to sing. When they were apart, he found time, busy as he was—he would die two years hence from overwork—to write long, charming letters of advice and encouragement to Jenny. She submitted to his guidance in all things. And it was thanks to Felix Mendelssohn-Bartholdy alone that she took her next hesitating steps out into the great world.

Another invitation came to Jenny from Herr Pokorny to sing in Vienna. Because Mendelssohn urged her to accept it, she did. This started a chain of incidents and friendships which not only widened Jenny's horizon, but in the end was to be instrumental in establishing Robert Schumann's lovely songs in public favor. For, on the way to Vienna, Jenny and Louise Johansson stopped over in Leipzig for a few days, and Mendelssohn seized the occasion to give another Gewandhaus concert. The only performers were to be Jenny and Mendelssohn himself, except for a violin solo by Ferdinand David. There would not even be an orchestra; Mendelssohn was undertaking to play all the accompaniments, besides at least one piano solo.

But Clara Schumann, Robert Schumann's wife and one of the finest pianists of her day, came over from Dresden to hear the concert. When the point on the program was reached where Mendelssohn was scheduled to play several of his own *Songs without Words*, he came down from the platform, went to where Clara Schumann was sitting and led her to the piano. She played the *Songs without Words* (numbers I and IV in the Sixth Book) and a scherzo of her own composition, with brilliant effect. For his own solo, Mendelssohn played Beethoven's Sonata in C Sharp Minor with a perfection of technique and subtlety of interpretation unique with Mendelssohn. And Jenny, with his miraculously understanding support at the piano, sang her selections from operas, and a concluding group of her Swedish songs, better than she had ever sung before. No one had the faintest idea that this would be Mendelssohn's last appearance but one in a Gewendhaus concert, but the audience knew it had been privileged to attend a legendary musical feast.

An aftermath was that while Jenny was carrying out an engagement in Vienna the next year, she was able to turn what would have been a drastic failure for Robert and Clara Schumann, into triumph. Paying a courtesy call on the couple in recognition of the part Clara Schumann had taken in the Gewandhaus concert the year before, Jenny found them greatly discouraged about a series of concerts they were giving. Each one had been more poorly attended than the one before, even though Rubenstein had appeared in the second one. Jenny begged to be allowed, as a favor, to sing in their fourth and last concert and immediately the demand for tickets soared, the hall was packed. Jenny added a number of Schumann's songs to her concert repertoire thereafter, insuring their popularity. Clara Schumann wrote of Jenny, "She is for me the warmest, noblest being I have yet found among artists."

But to get Jenny to Vienna the first time had taken a great deal of contriving, even after the tremendous success of the Gewandhaus concerts. She had come to feel entirely at home in Germany, but Austria was a strange country; they might not like her there. She was so plagued by nervousness and fears at the thought of singing in a city where she knew no one, that Mendelssohn wrote his friend Franz Hauser, who was teaching singing in Vienna, demanding, with no apologies, that Herr Hauser should make himself friendly and useful to Jenny.

It was well that he had done so. For when Jenny entered the large, handsome auditorium of the Vienna Opera House for her rehearsal—she was to sing Norma—she was sure her voice would not fill the vast room and refused even to try. No, she would return at once to Berlin. Herr Pokorny knew Mendelssohn had written to Franz Hauser, and he sent for the singing teacher, who fortunately was at home and came at once. Using Mendelssohn's name freely, Herr Hauser persuaded Jenny that it was her duty at least to do her best to carry out her obligation to Herr Pokorny and the Vienna Opera. Finally Jenny went to the middle of the stage and released her entire voice. It proved adequate for any auditorium and her debut in Vienna was a replica of her first night's triumph in Berlin. It led to her engagement in Vienna the next winter, which she undertook with no qualms whatsoever.

Mendelssohn introduced Jenny to the great oratorios—heretofore her singing had been confined to opera and lieder. And her first appearance in the new medium was at the Rhine Music Festival of 1846, which Mendelssohn conducted. There had been a near disaster because of the wild enthusiasm of the Vienna audience on Jenny's farewell appearance there, in the spring of 1846. The Opera that night was *La Sonnambula* and the house was filled with the Austrian elite—all the leading persons in the arts, nobility and society, as well as members of the Imperial family. Jenny was recalled again and again after the finale, and among the flowers showered onto the stage was a wreath dropped at Jenny's feet by the hand of the Empress Mother herself—a radical departure from Court etiquette and an honor that had never been bestowed upon any artist before.

As Jenny was driving to her lodgings, a band of young men unhitched the horses, preparing to pull her carriage themselves, and though a detachment of cavalry coming up just then stopped this maneuver, an excited crowd accompanied the carriage all the way to the house where Jenny was staying, pushing in so closely that Jenny, always made terribly nervous by a crowd, wrote Judge Munthe she was grateful to have escaped with her life. A manservant furnished Jenny by the opera house either fell or was accidentally knocked from his footman's seat, and his injuries at first were thought to be serious. Jenny, dazed herself by the experience, refused to leave Vienna until the man was out of danger.

It had been arranged that she would meet Mendelssohn at Frankfurt on May 26 and travel with him to Aachen, where the festival was being held that year, for the grand rehearsal on the 27th. Because of the delay, they were able to have only one rehearsal before the first concert. Nevertheless, the Rhine Festival of 1846 was considered the greatest ever held. Under Mendelssohn's direction, Jenny created as stupendous an effect with Haydn's "On Mighty Pens," "With Verdure Clad" and with solos from "The Marvelous Word," as she had with her most successful operatic roles. At the Artists' Concert, the main event of the festival, she so enchanted the audience with Mendelssohn's own "On Wings of Song" and "Spring Song," with their composer wielding the baton, that those who heard her referred thereafter to the 1846 Rhine Festival as "The Jenny Lind Festival."

Herr Giejer, to whom Jenny always gave the credit for first nudging her out of the security of her homeland, arrived unannounced from Uppsala with his wife, to find that the world into which he had kicked her "now turns round according to Jenny's wishes and commands," so Fru Geijer wrote to their son-in-law. Jenny decreed that Mendelssohn should play for the Geijers alone, and he did, having a piano sent to their sitting room in the hotel for the purpose. They had a delightful evening, with Mendelssohn accompanying Jenny while she sang her favorite Swedish folk songs and some of Geijer's own songs. Geijer begged Mendelssohn to visit them in Sweden, saying he should have some reindeer meat, and Mendelssohn said he would come if Geijer would guarantee that he could also have some of Jenny's rice-milk.

It had appeared to Jenny that this was a fitting time to begin her preparations to retire from the public eye. She wrote Frau Wichmann that she was determined to leave the stage the next summer or the autumn following that at the very latest. On her birthday the following October, she wrote Madam Birch-Pfeiffer, "I am twenty-six years old today and that is no joke!"

She recollected that she had not changed the will she had made just before she went to Paris to study, which left everything to her parents. She wrote Judge Munthe that to let it remain that way would be a terrible injustice. For Anna Marie and Niklas had continued to hound her for money in nearly every letter they wrote her, never thanking her when she sent extra sums, only complaining because they were not enough.

Jenny planned to make a new will, with provision for Louise Johansson and her maid, Annette. "My parents shall have no more of my property than just enough to take care of their needs." One of her reasons for wanting to retire was to stop their excessive demands, for she would be unable to give them extra money after that. Meanwhile, she always weakened.

The rumors that Jenny was planning to retire increased public interest in her and everyone wanted to hear her while it was still possible. After the Rhine Festival she filled engagements at Hanover and Frankfurt and was so tired that she planned earnestly to make her engagement in Vienna the following winter her last one. When, in the fall of 1846, pressure was renewed to get her to England, she wrote her friends in London that it was no use securing offers for her. No amount of money could ever persuade her to go to England.

This was in spite of the fact that the pressure now did not come from the feared and hated Mr. Bunn, who had not shaken his glory locks at her for some time. Mr. and Mrs. Grote could not endure that Jenny's unfortunate experience with Mr. Bunn should keep her from ever singing in England. After Jenny's failure to produce the £500 indemnity asked by Mr. Bunn, Mrs. Grote had approached Mr. Benjamin Lumley, the manager of Her Majesty's Theatre, who had subsequently made some tentative overtures toward Jenny, but to no effect.

By the fall of 1846, however, Mr. Lumley's position was such that he was prepared to go to any lengths to get a contract with Jenny. Up to this time, Her Majesty's Theatre had held a position similar to that of the Italian Opera in Paris. In fact, when the season was over in Paris, the Italian stars to whom Jenny had listened from her inexpensive seat—Persiani, Lablache, Grisi, Mario, Tamburini and others—would come on to London to Her Majesty's Theatre. These singers had had everything their own way and as a result of their unreasonable caprices, the management often lost money. When Mr. Lumley took over as manager in 1842, he had tried to bring some order into the situation, but was met with increasing hostility on the part of the stars. In 1845, all but Lablache had deserted Her Majesty's Theatre and gone to Covent Garden in a body under the name of the Royal Italian Opera Company. Lablache was the only big name remaining to Her Majesty's, and he urged Lumley to get Jenny Lind at any cost to save his theater.

Lablache had not heard Jenny sing, but he had heard a great deal about her and knew what a tremendous drawing card she was. He was also impressed by the reports of her character. He wrote Mr. Lumley, "I have been the friend of Malibran and of Pasta and I should like to be able to add that I am the friend of Lind."

Mindful of Jenny's firm rejections of his previous overtures, Lumley started his new campaign in a circuitous way. It was common knowledge that Jenny Lind was a great friend of Mendelssohn's and that he had more influence over her than anyone else. While Mendelssohn was in England in August, 1846, for the Birmingham Festival and the first production of his *Elijah*, Mr. Lumley sought his help. Mendelssohn, knowing for his part how determined Jenny was not to go to England, suggested a circuitous maneuver of his own. Mr. Chorley, one of the foremost music critics of the day and a friend of both Lumley and Mendelssohn, was already on the Continent. Mendelssohn wrote Jenny about him and asked her, as a personal favor to him, to sing some of Mendelssohn's songs for Chorley—a request he knew she would not refuse. The night Mr. Chorley heard Jenny sing, in Frankfurt, he wrote back to London that he had found Jenny, as a singer, twenty times better than he had expected. "I am really delighted to find that I am not past the old thrill, the old beating of the heart." But he had to write Mendelssohn, "She says she *will not* come to London."

Then Lumley went to Frankfurt to see her, but Jenny told him she was determined to leave the stage in six months or a year at most, and sent him on to Italy to look for a singer there. She wrote Madam Birch-Pfeiffer, "If you should hear that I have lost my mind completely, it will mean that I am on my way to London."

There was only one hope left—that Mendelssohn should bring pressure upon her directly, and this he consented to do. When next Mr. Lumley called on Jenny, he was armed with a very long letter to her from Mendelssohn, which urged her, in the strongest terms possible, to deal with the English impresario. Mendelssohn knew that Jenny would be received so warmly in London that she would remember it with pleasure throughout all the rest of her life. "When the English once entertain a personal liking for anyone, I believe that no people are more friendly, more cordial, or more constant. I believe they will entertain this feeling for you, not only about your singing, but about your personality and your whole being, and upon this last they set even more store than upon the singing itself." He spoke of the marvelous reception his *Elijah* had had in Birmingham. "It was the best performance I have ever heard of any of my compositions."

It was an additional point that Mr. Lumley was greatly interested in an opera Mendelssohn was hoping to write for Jenny, and for which Madam Birch-Pfeiffer already had submitted a number of suggestions for a libretto. Mendelssohn assured Jenny that he believed the opera could not be produced under better auspices. As a final inducement, Mendelssohn promised that if she would go to England, he would accept an invitation to return there and so would be able to give her his personal support.

Mr. Lumley wrote Mendelssohn that it had been a most pleasing picture to see Jenny's face while she was reading this letter. "No sun could have infused more joy in a beautiful landscape, than your letter did in her." Mendelssohn thought she ought to go to England, so Jenny told Mr. Lumley she would. Lumley wrote Mendelssohn that the English, as a nation, would owe him a debt of gratitude, "for I look upon the engagement of Lind as a new era in the progress of Art in England. . . . Independently of her great genius, she has that purity and chastity of manner which none but a really good person can possess, and which, in England, will gain her partisans on all sides."

Mendelssohn had refused to enter into a discussion of terms with Lumley—Jenny had no one to represent her in business, comparable to the agent every artist has today. He apologized to Jenny for being remiss but said he had such an abhorrence of financial dealings that he had not the courage to do it, even for her. He could only say that she ought to make such terms as no one else could at this moment, "since you are the *only* one upon whom alone the whole theater depends." Jenny, following Mendelssohn's example, also refused to talk about money, and left it to Mr. Lumley to set the terms of her engagement.

They seemed generous to Jenny, though Mendelssohn thought afterwards that she should have had more. The high points were that for the season which would begin April 4, 1847, and extend to August 20, Jenny was to receive a salary of £4,800, a sum close to $25,000 in that day. She was to receive a further sum, in advance, of £800 if she wished to spend a month in Italy before her debut, in order to study the language, or to rest. Emoluments included a furnished house in London, a carriage and a pair of horses for the season. Mr. Lumley engaged himself to take over all responsibility for buying off or otherwise satisfying the claims of Alfred Bunn. Until this was done, her contract with Lumley was to be kept absolutely quiet.

Even after the contract was signed, Mr. Lumley realized that all was not likely to be clear sailing, for Jenny had already expressed some of the fears that had assailed her previously at the thought of singing in a new country. He wrote Mendelssohn that he counted on the composer to keep her assured of the "absolute certainty of her great success."

Jenny, however, seemed quite serene, writing Frau Wichmann that Mendelssohn alone could have induced her to sign the contract, but that as things had shaped themselves she could see clearly "it is our Lord who brought it about, and against one's destiny one can do nothing."

But this was October, and her engagement in England did not begin until April.

Mendelssohn unintentionally reactivated her uneasiness first by finding fault with various points in the contract after he had examined it carefully. Next, it was impossible to keep secret the fact that Jenny had signed with Mr. Lumley, and when Alfred Bunn heard of it, he renewed his threats, writing Jenny that he would have her put in jail if she sang under Lumley's management. In spite of Lumley's promise to settle matters with Bunn, Jenny offered her persecutor £2,000 of her own money. When he refused, she was unable to sleep nights. She saw herself being arrested as soon as she disembarked in England; yet now she had signed a contract with Lumley, which bound her to do that very thing!

Why had she allowed herself to be persuaded to leave the Continent, where fresh honors and happy experiences were being heaped upon her constantly? Between her engagements with the opera in Berlin and Vienna, Jenny had sung in nearly every kingdom and principality in Germany, making warm friends among the rulers and notables wherever she went. She had a casket full of jeweled bracelets, gifts of royalty, which Jenny never wore, except to entertain the young people in homes where she visited. When Jenny sang in Munich, where Mendelssohn's friend Hauser had accepted the position of Director of the Conservatory, the orchestra greeted Jenny with shouts and fanfares every time she appeared at a rehearsal. Hauser wrote Mendelssohn, "I tell you it was a jubilee such as I find it impossible to describe."

In Heidelberg she was serenaded by the students after her concert. Finding her gone the next morning when they came to serenade her again, they surged into the hotel room that was pointed out to them as the one she had slept in, pulled the sheets from the bed, tore them into strips and made "Jenny Lind" rosettes, which they proudly wore. (The room was in fact that of a visiting Englishman, who decided the high-spirited Heidelberg boys must have been engaged in some kind of political demonstration. What mystified him was why they had torn up *his* bed sheets to make their emblems!) At Nuremburg a medal was struck in her honor. And so it went in Germany.

December 31, 1846, found her in Vienna again, where she was to open her engagement with *Daughter of the Regiment*, under its German title, *Marie, die Tochter des Regiment*. The Viennese welcomed her back warmly and she made such a hit in *Die Tochter* that there was scarcely a cultivated home in Vienna which did not have a picture of Jenny in her costume as Marie. Meyerbeer took advantage of Jenny's presence in Vienna to present his *Camp in Silesia* there for the first time. The famous passage to the accompaniment of two flutes stopped the show. A committee appeared to present her with a medal in the name of Die Gesellschaft der Musikfreunde of Vienna. In Austria, as in Germany, she knew she was loved, and she felt safe.

When she expressed her mounting anxiety at leaving all this for England, Mendelssohn failed in his task of reassuring her, for he himself was a prey to depression that winter. He had been unable to secure an acceptable libretto for the opera he wanted to write for Jenny, a form of music he had not yet attempted, though he had always wanted to. He told her he had a foreboding that if he did not manage to compose a fairly good opera now, for Jenny, he would never accomplish it.

He felt with special keenness his inadequacy at protecting Jenny in her business dealings and very much deplored the fact that she had offered to buy Bunn off. "I confess that, after all you have told me, I would rather that you had not promised Lumley to go to England." And though he tried to cheer her up and urged her not to be upset "by the horror outcry on this side and that," Jenny's panic deepened as the winter months wore on. Louise Johansson, not too bright though good and loyal, was inclined to nerves herself and suffered as much or more than Jenny. On one occasion, Louise wrote in her diary that she was afraid Jenny was losing her mind, she had been carrying on to such an extent.

Louise attributed Jenny's moods to the fact that she wanted to get married and there was no man in sight. (Jenny could have married Hans Christian Andersen at any time, but neither Jenny nor anyone in her circle appears ever to have viewed him seriously as a matrimonial possibility.) Louise was sure that Jenny would never find another man like Günther, and added dolefully, "Poor Jenny, who wants to change freedom for bondage, and in addition an unfaithful man who will squander her money!" Louise's conclusion was that no man could ever make Jenny happy.

It was not a man, or lack of a man, however, that was responsible for Jenny's erratic behavior. It was simply the prospect of going to London. Mendelssohn and Jenny's friend Herr Arnemann, the Swedish Consul at Frankfurt, held several anxious consultations about the matter, without arriving at any solution. When the time came to leave for England, Jenny refused to budge.

Mr. Lumley had received no direct word from her, and fewer and fewer people were attending Her Majesty's Theatre. It was as much to the advantage of the Italian stars at Covent Garden that Jenny should not show up to fulfill her contract with Mr. Lumley, as it was to that of Mr. Bunn at Drury Lane, so all manner of rumors were set in motion. Several London newspapers were declaring that Mr. Lumley never had had a contract with Jenny Lind, and that the impresario's report of having commissioned Mendelssohn to write an opera for her was another fiction.

The situation got so bad that Mrs. Grote's brother, Doctor Edward Lewin, whom Jenny had known in Stockholm, went to Vienna to bring Jenny back with him. She would talk of nothing except Mr. Bunn's threats, though Doctor Lewin had come armed with an opinion from several leading English lawyers that there was nothing Bunn could do to her.

By Easter time, it was apparent that Her Majesty's Theatre could hold out very little longer. During the last production before the Easter recess, Mr. Lumley slipped out of his theater between acts, and, still in full evening dress, started for Vienna and Jenny. He was not seen in London again until April 16, though the theater reopened on the tenth. When he reappeared, it was to announce joyfully that Jenny was on her way to London under the care of an escort he had provided. She would arrive the next day and go directly to the Grotes' home, where she was to stay until the residence Mr. Lumley was providing for her was ready.

Mendelssohn meanwhile had come to England to conduct performances of his *Elijah* in Exeter Hall, London, and in Birmingham. Going back and forth between the two cities he had rather lost track of Jenny's affairs. So when he dropped in at the Grotes' on the seventeenth to pay his respects to Jenny's friend, he was astonished and delighted to learn that Jenny was expected any minute and had stayed on to greet her.

At last, two heavily laden carriages pulled up in front of the Grotes' door and a frightened, bewildered Jenny emerged. She and Louise Johansson were both exhausted, and Jenny was thrown into such a panic at learning arrangements had been made for her to attend the performance at Her Majesty's Theatre that night, that Mendelssohn left hurriedly, after exchanging only a few words with his protégée.

CHAPTER SEVEN

"Their Sufferings Have Become Historic"

A

T FIRST few people noticed the simply dressed young woman who sat toward the back of the George Grotes' box at Her Majesty's Theatre. Nevertheless a rumor that Jenny Lind was present began to spread through the house. There was a stir of excitement when Mr. Lumley visited the box and bowed low over the hand of the mysterious lady. And when Signor Lablache followed suit between acts, a murmur ran through the entire audience. From then on all eyes were directed toward the Grotes' box, instead of toward the stage.

But Jenny refused to discuss any arrangements for her London debut, or even to meet the conductor of Her Majesty's Theatre, Mr. Balfe. At a party the Grotes gave for Jenny, with Mendelssohn, Lablache and Mr. Lumley among the guests, Mendelssohn played the piano for a little while and then asked Jenny to sing his "On Wings of Song," with which she had created so tremendous a sensation in Leipzig. Jenny began to sing, but broke down and was unable to continue, just as she had done when she sang for Manuel Garcia. Lablache bridged the awkward moment with some amusing Italian songs, and Mendelssohn played again for the company. Then Jenny tried again, this time singing some of her Swedish songs, and enchanted the group.

But talk with Mr. Lumley about her appearance at the theater she would not. Her Majesty's limped along, with Mr. Lumley giving away tickets by the hundred in order to have any audience at all. Mendelssohn, weary unto death and doubtful of the wisdom of having urged the London engagement upon Jenny in the first place, had no heart to bring further pressure to bear on her. He called on her every day, but talked mainly about the opera he was writing, and which Mr. Lumley had promised to produce as soon as it was finished. It had been no myth that Mr. Lumley was committed to this project. At his suggestion the French dramatist Scribe had actually done a libretto of Shakespeare's *The Tempest*, which Mendelssohn had turned down because he felt it took too many liberties with the work of the greatest poet-dramatist of all. But another librettist had been found; he and Mendelssohn had agreed upon the Lorelei for a theme, and Mendelssohn was writing music for it. He believed it was going to be his best work.

Nor did Mr. Lumley plead or argue when Jenny told Mrs. Grote she would never be able to face a London audience and asked her to arrange a withdrawal from Jenny's contract with Her Majesty's. He only suggested that they wait a bit to see if Jenny might change her mind.

A day or so afterwards Jenny, out for a drive with Mrs. Grote, asked casually how Her Majesty's Theatre was doing. "Very badly," Mrs. Grote replied bluntly. "No one will buy tickets, the way things are now. Everyone is waiting for the announcement of your debut. Meantime, the theater is losing money every night."

Nothing more was said until they had returned to the Grote home. Jenny then told her friend she could inform Mr. Lumley that she, Jenny, would appear for rehearsal the following Monday. Her debut was set firmly for May 4.

Very little time remained. Jenny chose Meyerbeer's *Robert de Normandie* for her first London appearance. The role of Alice had always been one of her favorites, and she had sung it many times. Also, her first entrance was onto a crowded stage and she had no important passages to sing until the chorus had departed. That would give her a chance to recover a bit from her initial nervousness. She still visualized a London audience as a whole theater full of Mr. Bunns lying in wait to destroy her.

But the Italian version—*Roberto il Diabolo*—was to be presented, and besides rehearsing, Jenny had to learn the Italian words for her role and also pick up as much English as she could. She was not easy to live with during this period, and Louise Johansson wrote in her diary that Jenny had given her some very sharp words. "Words that go right through you." Now Louise herself began having headaches, and was so ill and depressed by May 4 that all she could think of on that amazing night was the frightful pain she herself was suffering.

Louise was perhaps the only person in London who remained entirely unmoved by the debut itself. As had happened so many times before, Jenny's fears proved to be completely unjustified. The very delays and rumors and counter-rumors had only heightened the public's interest in her. By the night of her debut, it had reached fever pitch. The *Encyclopaedia Britannica*, a publication not given to hyperbole, said in its 1910-1911 edition that the furore she created "exceeded everything of the kind . . . in London or anywhere else; the sufferings and struggles of her well-dressed admirers, who had to stand for hours to get into the pit, have become historic."

The elaborate costumes of the ladies were severely crumpled, and in several cases torn off altogether. The surging mob picked many people off their feet and H. S. Holland related that he was thrown to the ground by the rush when the doors were opened, and believed he would have been trampled to death if a friendly giant had not held the crowd back and helped him up. On the dot of eight o'clock, Queen Victoria and Prince Albert, the Queen Dowager and the Duchess of Kent entered the royal boxes at the left of the stage. Mendelssohn and Mr. Grote sat together in the stalls, having surrendered their places in the Grote box to Fanny Kemble and Sir Charles Lemon, who had been unable to get tickets.

H. S. Holland recorded that when the curtain rose, "the excitement was indescribable." When Jenny made her entrance, being dragged onto the stage in her pilgrim's dress, the audience rose and applauded her. This was entirely contrary to continental custom and disconcerted her further. Her opening recitative could scarcely be heard. But quiet was restored by the time she had reached the passage in which Alice tells the Prince of his mother's death, and the audience decided then and there that its historic sufferings had been worthwhile.

In the second act, every verse of "When I Left Normandy" was applauded separately, and when she had finished the song, the audience thundered for more encores—for as long as twenty minutes, it was said—until people began crying "Shame" and the performance was allowed to continue. When Jenny came out for her first curtain call at the end, Queen Victoria with her own hand dropped at Jenny's feet the huge bouquet the theater management had presented to Her Majesty. This was as unprecedented at the British Court as the similar act of the Empress Dowager in Vienna had been at the Austrian Court. The Queen exclaimed her rapture to Mr. Lumley over and over when he visited the royal box.

Sick, suffering Louise Johansson did not get home until 2 A.M. and complained that there was no one there to help her but a footman. She could not get up the next morning. Jenny—Louise does not record the hour when *she* got home—arose fresh and exuberant and brought Louise's breakfast to her in bed.

From that night on, Her Majesty's Theatre was packed and Mr. Lumley's patience throughout his long travail was rewarded beyond his most opulent anticipations. The music critic for the *Times* of London wrote two whole columns about Jenny's Alice. It was full of such expressions as "The delicious quality of the voice, the rich, gushing tone, was something entirely new and fresh. The audience did not know what to make of it." The *Illustrated London News* called Jenny the first soprano of the day, and after praising her voice, her technique and her acting, remarked, "Were it even possible to detect a flaw in her voice, her singing would still be resistless, for it reaches the heart, and touches the deepest cords of human feeling."

Jenny's Amina in *La Sonnambula*, a very popular opera with the British, was received even more rapturously, if gradations are possible when Jenny's every appearance was met with wild enthusiasm. Queen Victoria wrote in her diary, after seeing Jenny's opening performance as Amina, "It was all *piano* and sweet, like the singing of the zephyr; yet all clear. Who could describe those long notes drawn out till they melt quite away; that shake which becomes softer and softer, and those flute-like notes, and those round fresh tones which are so youthful!"

Usually the perilous walk across the bridge by the heroine, the high point of this opera, was made by a substitute for the prima donna, but

Jenny would not permit anyone to take her place. Her courage appealed to the British, too. And then came *Daughter of the Regiment*, also played in Italian under the title of *La Figlia del Reggimento*, presenting an entirely different and gay and bewitching Jenny in the role of Maria. Her admirers were beside themselves.

During the whole of the three seasons that Jenny appeared in London, the magazine *Punch*, devoted ordinarily to humor and satire, carried on a continuous love affair with her. There was hardly an issue which did not contain something about her in either poetry or prose, in veins ranging from the whimsical to the unashamedly sentimental.

"Jenny Lind excites in the public mind an enthusiasm which now amounts to actual delirium, interrupted only by a few lucid intervals, when attention is awakened by some very urgent necessity of life. In pity to her admirers, she should exert her powers of fascination less powerfully, for she is beginning to cause people to neglect their affairs, and leave the most important business unattended to."

On one occasion *Punch* suggested that the scarcity of gold could be counteracted by issuing "Jenny Lind Script." This could be accomplished simply by using tickets to Her Majesty's Theatre as legal tender. "This script has already been circulated to a very great extent in the money market, and in every instance has realized large sums. The holder of four Opera Bonds for private boxes, with six coupons to each, cleared £100 last week."

On another occasion *Punch* advised the Queen's Ministers to "purchase heavily in the Lumley Funds, which is the great circulating medium at the present moment, and increases in value every day. If they do not do this rapidly, they may depend upon it that Emperor Nicholas will be before them in the market and will be sending £5,000,000, or some such Russian trifle, to buy up as much Jenny Lind Script as possible, as being the very best stock in Europe he can invest his money in."

Jenny's soubriquet of "Swedish Nightingale" provoked a spate of bird analogies in the press. Even the sophisticated *Punch* contributors could not resist this temptation.

"The Nightingale is the most celebrated of all warblers; but she is the one of which the least need be said, simply because nothing can describe her. In the first place, there is no mistaking this Nightingale, nothing in the world singing like her. She is the most graceful of all the warblers, being about five feet high, with an extent and strength of wing that carry her over continents and across seas, borne upon the breath of heartiest, deepest, gratitude and praise. Her shape is very succinct and her habits at once frank, graceful, shy and receding.

"Her nest is in the wide world's heart, even though the said nest is feathered with the finest bank paper, carrying the very heaviest figures. She sings equally well whether by day or night; and may often be heard in the vicinity of Hanover Square, about two in the afternoon; and as late as ten, somewhere in the Haymarket in the evening. . . .

"We cannot arrive at a certain knowledge of the food of this Nightingale. Some say she lives on roses steeped in moonbeams; some say, on melted amber. But certain it is, from the divine emanations of her music, most certain is 'she on honeydew hath fed and drunk the milk of Paradise.'"

Various biographers have ascribed to various times and places the origin of the "Jenny Lind Craze" or "Lindomania" which arose spontaneously in Europe without the benefit of modern advertising or high pressure sales methods, and reached almost psychopathic heights in the United States. But there can be no dispute that it came to full flower in England, among the supposedly stolid British. Souvenir manufacturers began reaping a harvest. Every shop that sold prints was advertising "authentic portraits" of Jenny as Maria, with soldiers in the background beating drums; as Amina crossing the bridge; as Alice clinging to the cross. There were dinner services with a Jenny Lind pattern. Her picture was placed on snuffboxes, matchboxes, candy boxes and even on pocket handkerchiefs. Horses, dogs, cats, pet birds and children were named for her. Young people danced to the tune of the "Jenny Lind Polka," or the "Jenny Lind Waltz," or the "Jenny Lind Galop." One William Barnes of Nottingham developed a Jenny Lind gooseberry and showed it at the fairs. Before her first London season had ended, so many products had been given the name "Jenny Lind" that, according to *Punch*, lady shoppers at Swan and Edgar's Yard Goods Emporium would ask "How much is that Jenny Lind a yard?" and a gentleman, presenting a bouquet to a lady, would beg her to accept "these Jenny Lind roses."

"Their Sufferings Have Become Historic"

"In the smoking rooms at the Clubs, men talk of a prime cigar as a Jenny Lind, and request the pleasure of a glass of Jenny Lind with you, or desire you to pass the Jenny Lind this way. At all conversations, her name is mingled with the discussions, and but the other day a lecturer at the Royal Institute, forgetting what he was about, said 'Jenny Lind' when he meant hydrogen."

On three different occasions, the House of Commons had to suspend sessions because so many of its members were at Her Majesty's Theatre hearing Jenny sing that they could not raise a quorum.

A stream of gifts poured upon Jenny from unknown admirers—parasols, gloves, fans, clocks, shawls, handkerchiefs, silverware, many of them embroidered or engraved with her name, or perhaps with a bird, singing.

And what was the effect upon Jenny of this tumultuous adulation? She kept herself as much apart from it as she could. The residence Mr. Lumley found for her and Louise Johansson was a pretty cottage on an estate called Clairville, at Old Brompton, on the north edge of London. Its garden boasted a fine plane tree and a beautiful magnolia, in whose branches nightingales perched and sang. Jenny told Mrs. Stanley, the wife of the Bishop of Norwich, that she thought the song of the English nightingale was the sweetest of any, and wondered that so much power could be contained in so small a body, measuring the length of the bird against her own palm. She must have wondered many times at the different kinds of power her own not very large body appeared to possess.

Jenny accepted few invitations to big affairs, and when she did, invariably regretted it. Her hostess at a party in one of London's great houses was so absorbed in Jenny that she paid no attention at all to the Duke of Wellington, waiting patiently to be greeted. The guests then tagged Jenny so closely from room to room, that she fled to the picture gallery to get away from them, and begged Mrs. Grote to take her home. Another time, when Mr. Lumley gave an outdoor fete in her honor, she was so distressed at the crowds pressing up to get a glimpse of her that she hid in one of the pavilions, and left after an hour. Mrs. Grote and her brother, Dr. Lewin, escorted Jenny back to Clairville Cottage, where she suddenly developed high spirits, insisted that they stay for supper, turned out all the resources of the kitchen to provide them with a gala meal.

Jenny Lind, the Swedish Nightingale

Sheltered by the walls of Clairville, Jenny tried to forget the crowds that lingered by the gate hoping to get a glimpse of her as she went in or out. Hans Christian Andersen visited her there and she sent him back to London in her carriage. The crowd surged forward to peer into the windows and Andersen was vastly amused when the cry went up, "It's only a strange man!"

The Grotes had a country seat not far away, at Burnham Beeches, and Jenny spent much of her free time there. She liked to walk in the woods with Mrs. Grote, and would study her roles while sitting on the roots of the ancient trees, singing along in a low voice.

Mrs. M. M. Simpson said in her *Many Memories of Many People* that her first sight of Jenny Lind was of the singer bounding up the walk at Burnham Beeches, singing the "Rataplan" from *Daughter of the Regiment*. Added Mrs. Simpson, "She would go out and sing to the nightingales, and mimic them. They would sing all the louder. She called them her 'little sisters.'"

There were of course command appearances at Buckingham Palace, where Victoria treated Jenny as a friend rather than as an entertainer. At one performance, where the Italian stars from Covent Garden were also taking part, Jenny was thrown off by the accompanist, Costa, and did not do herself justice. The Queen perceived Jenny's difficulty and recognized its cause. She walked over to Jenny and suggested that she sing something in which she could accompany herself. Jenny did—the Swedish songs for which she always played the piano—and drew bravos from Jenny's competitors. Before the season ended Jenny had received the usual jeweled bracelet at the hand of royalty—in this instance a particularly fine one—and many other favors, including the gift of a Pekinese from the Queen's own kennels. (These little dogs, bred in China for the rulers and their families, were very rare in the Western world at this time.)

The Duke of Wellington presented his compliments to Jenny while she was still staying with the Grotes in London, and was seen with her frequently thereafter. The hero of Waterloo, it seems, brightened his declining years by seeking the company of the popular stage stars. When Rachel had had her great triumph in London during the season Jenny studied in Paris, he had attached himself to her, and now he sought out Jenny. Though erect as ever, the Duke was of an age—seventy-eight at the time of Jenny's first London season—when one took it there was no harm in him, and Jenny had no scruples about accepting his chivalrous gestures.

He invited her to go horseback riding with him and Jenny had to confess that she did not know how to ride. So the Duke of Wellington taught her, on a gentle mount from his own stables. Thereafter they could be seen now and then jogging sedately together along Rotten Row or riding along the wooded roads of Wimbledon. The Duke seldom missed a performance of Jenny's, occupying a box just below that of the Queen, "like a loyal old watchdog, guarding his mistress," Chopin remarked. As soon as Jenny appeared on the stage he would rise, bow and ask her ceremoniously how she did. Jenny would bow in her turn, thank him and say she did very well, after which the performance would go on.

There were a few sour notes among the paeans of praise. The dour Carlyle pronounced her nothing more than a very true, clean, genuine little creature with a voice of extraordinary extent and little richness of tone; while Thackeray, who had sat next to her at dinner, found her dull and ordinary. He very much deplored the fact that to be accepted socially, it had become necessary to be able to say one had heard Jenny sing.

In Norma, a role which had always brought her the highest praise, the English critic, Mr. Chorley, felt that her delivery had been heavy and halting, and her interpretation inferior to that of Grisi. Though she had the usual ovation from the audience, Jenny performed Norma only three times in London. All her appearances in other roles, however, served only to increase the enthusiasm of the critics and the public.

When it became evident that Mendelssohn could not finish the music for *Die Lorelei* for the 1847 season, Lumley instead introduced Verdi's *I Masnadieri*, an opera based on Schiller's *Die Räuber*, which the composer had written with Jenny's voice in mind. Verdi himself conducted the first two performances and Jenny had another success, though the opera dropped out of sight after Jenny ceased to sing it. *I Masnadieri* was followed by *The Marriage of Figaro*. Jenny had a particular reverence for Mozart, and the tenderness with which she invested the role of Susanna made it one of her most moving ones. *La Sonnambula* closed the season, in a welter of encores and bouquets, and then Jenny started on a tour of the provinces, with a rumor abroad that Queen Victoria herself, incognita, had seen the Nightingale off at Liverpool Station.

In every town the singer entered—Brighton, Birmingham, Manchester, Liverpool—a holiday was declared. As Jenny's party stepped from the train, all the church bells would begin to ring, all the whistles to blow, crowds jammed the platform to greet her and still other crowds filled the streets to see her pass by. At Norwich, to the deep tones of the Cathedral bells was added the boom of the cannon at the Castle. And here a very special honor awaited Jenny. She had been invited to stay at the home of the Bishop of Norwich. Many stars of stage and opera had been asked to perform for royalty, but it was the first time a stage personality had ever been invited to stay at the home of a bishop.

Then a brief engagement in Berlin, on her way back to Stockholm, where Rellstab maintained that her singing and acting were better than ever, and the German audiences loved her more than ever, and King Frederick William IV appointed her his "Kammersängerin"—court singer—as the Emperor of Austria had done the preceding spring. But what affected Jenny particularly was that instead of the usual official notice from the Court Chamberlain, the honor was conveyed by King Frederick William himself, in an informal and kindly note written by his own hand.

And now the time has come to pause a bit and try to determine why this unglamorous and unassuming woman succeeded in appealing to the imaginations and emotions of the multitudes in country after country, to an extent that has never been equaled before or since. Hers was not the only marvelous voice of her era, and some claimed that the voices of Sontag and Alboni were better. Yet their names were scarcely heard after their careers had ended, while Jenny Lind's recurs over and over again even today. What was the magic that impressed "this Swede," as Chopin called her, indelibly on the hearts of men and women?

It must be realized, first, that Jenny was much more than a lovely voice. Fine musicians spoke always of her "talent." Berlioz declared when he heard her first at the gathering of crowned heads at King Frederick William's château near Bonn, "Her talent is far above anything one ever hears in the French and German theater." Mendelssohn told Hans Christian Andersen, "There will not be born, in a whole century, another being so gifted as she."

Besides her gift of voice, she had a gift for acting, for dancing, for playing the piano, for language; and a fine intelligence which enabled her to perform almost miraculous feats of learning, both of words and music, while studying a role and perfecting a performance, all in an incredibly short space of time.

Second, she was fortunate in having been born at exactly the right time for her type of voice and personality to be particularly valued. The romantic movement in music composition, with its sweet melodies and imagination-firing operatic themes, was just becoming well established, and most of its Olympians still lived and moved among men. Their music was of a type in which Jenny's voice showed to best advantage; their heroines, given added spiritual value by Jenny's interpretations, pulled at the heartstrings of the public. One exception was Richard Wagner. She did not like his music, considering it pretentious and ruinous to the voice, and wisely never sang it, for it seems unlikely that Jenny would ever have made her mark as a Wagnerian soprano. Another was Brahms, who wrote his great music after she had largely retired, though she knew him and recognized his talent.

But Jenny was Mendelssohn's favorite interpreter for his songs. She helped establish Schumann and Schubert, she was supremely fitted to portray the heroines of Weber, Bellini and Meyerbeer, Verdi, Rossini and Donizetti, and the critics agreed that Mozart's music and heroines had never before been given as felicitous a rendition as by Jenny Lind. (She spoke of Mozart always as "the divine Mozart." After she became acquainted with Bach's music, she called him "that blessed old man.")

Mendelssohn's one criticism of Jenny—that she wasted her great talent in singing inferior music, meaning by that the operas of Meyerbeer and others—stemmed from the fact that Jenny had not been exposed to the work of the truly great composers in her youth. When she heard Beethoven, she had no words to express her ecstasy, and she turned from opera to the great oratorios of Handel, Haydn and Mendelssohn as soon as she was able to do so. Her response to the best and highest was im-mediate, when once she met it.

Jenny Lind, the Swedish Nightingale

Yet it was the voice, after all, that moved the multitudes, and how is it possible to give or receive an adequate idea of a voice that has never been heard by anyone living today? After photography arrived, someone lamented that there was not a similar way to preserve for posterity the voices of great singers, Jenny's in particular. Eventually there was a way, but it came too late.

However, we are told that Jenny's range extended from B below the line to the G above high C, two and three-fourths octaves. It has already been mentioned that Mendelssohn particularly loved her high F sharp and used it repeatedly in the soprano solos for his *Elijah*, with the idea that Jenny should sing them. Otto Goldschmidt later employed the same famous note over and over in his oratorio "Ruth," also written for Jenny. Her high A was another note that was considered especially moving. Chopin, who declared that "this Swede does not show herself in the ordinary light of day but in the magic rays of the aurora borealis," noted that one of the most remarkable features of her singing was her pianissimo rendering of these very high notes. H. S. Holland enlarges on this. "Her pianissimo was as rich in power as her mezzo-forte. And though falling on the ear like a whisper, it reached the farthest corner of the theater or concert room.

"By nature her voice was not a flexible one, only perseverance and unremitting practice had made it so. Her breathing capacity also was not naturally great, but she renewed her breath so quickly and cleverly that the keenest observer could not detect her doing it, and the outside world credited her with abnormal lung capacity. Her messa di voce [the art of swelling or diminishing a sustained note from softest piano to full volume and vice versa] was unrivaled by any singer. In like manner in her shakes [trills we call them nowadays] her scales, her legato and staccato passages, she evoked astonishment and admiration no less from competent judges than from the general public. And be it noted, the singer made use of ornaments and cadenzas only insofar as they were in perfect keeping with the intentions of the composer and the meaning of the music."

That was Mendelssohn's gospel—that music should be sung and played as written by the composer—and it became Jenny's as well.

In 1846, Clara Schumann described Jenny's voice as follows: "The

Lind has a genius for song which might come to pass only once in many years. Her appearance is arresting at first glance and her face, although not exactly beautiful, appears so because of the expression in her wonderful eyes. Her singing comes from her inmost heart; it is no striving for effect, no passion which takes hold of the hearer, but a certain wistfulness, a melancholy, which reaches deeply into the heart, whether one will or no. At the first moment she might appear to one as cold, but this is not so at all; the impression is caused by the purity and simplicity which underlies her singing. There is no forcing, no sobbing, no tremolo in her voice, not one bad habit. Every tone she produces is sheer beauty. Her coloratura is the most consummate I have ever heard. Her voice is not large in itself, but would certainly fill any room, for it is all *soul*."

The great German critic, Ludwig Rellstab, also found her voice more pleasing than powerful, though not without fullness. "It moves with charming lightness and certainty, though the middle register is sometimes shaded by a soft veil which serves to bring out the upper notes in clearest and most silvery contrast. This beautiful natural gift is supplemented by a groundwork of most diligent study." Rellstab felt, however, that her voice improved and gained power as her slender body filled out in her late twenties.

H. S. Holland emphasized the effect of her remarkable articulation upon her listeners. "She never erred in the delivery of even the most difficult word in any language whatsoever. So perfect was the mastery she exercised over larynx, throat, lips, tongue, teeth, soft palate, that never a syllable was stifled at its birth, never a vowel sound corrupted in its passage through the longest group of mingled leap, arpeggio or scale. It was this high quality that lent so potent a charm to the complicated 'divisions,' the rapid passages of fioritura (flourishes such as trills), of which Lablache, in describing them to Madam Grisi, said 'Every note is a pearl.' The purity of the vowel sounds, by which the pearls were strung together, secured their perfect equality of tone and timbre; and whether the most rapid notes were sung legato or staccato, they either ran on velvet or rang out sharply and clearly as the touch of a mandolin."

Men like Chopin and Rellstab and Holland recognized the hard work that lay behind the fluid ease with which the lovely notes floated from

Jenny's lips in opera or concert, and the gift she had acquired for concentrated application perhaps stood her in as good stead as her natural talents. Frau Birch-Pfeiffer, who was Jenny's German teacher and helped her prepare for her role in *Camp in Silesia*, remembered that on one occasion she had left the house as Jenny was starting to practice the difficult word "zersplitter" on a high B flat. Returning to the house several hours later she found Jenny still practicing "zersplitter" and she kept on until the short "i" was open and perfect on the high note, something beyond the power of most German singers.

Jenny was well aware herself of the "veiled" quality of her middle register, mentioned by Rellstab. She never worked it out to her satisfaction until about ten years before her death, when, as she expressed it wryly, conquering it did her little good except to feel that she had conquered it. Nevertheless, during her singing years she turned this defect into an asset by means of her skill in transitions.

Both Chopin and Manuel Garcia dwelt on the trueness and purity of Jenny's voice. Jenny's old singing master at long last admitted he had underrated Jenny when she studied with him. "I remember hearing her sing the *Messiah* at Exeter Hall. The first notes of 'Come Unto Me, All Ye That Labor' were so full, pure and perfect in intonation that the refrain which preceded them sounded out of tune." John Addington Symonds also spoke at length of the pure timbre of the voice, "which so vibrated and thrilled my very soul that tears came into my eyes."

Many commentators mentioned the "flutelike" quality of her high notes, and at least one critic described her voice as "like a clarinet, penetrating and tearful and sweet." Mrs. Stanley, the wife of the Bishop of Norwich, said that what distinguished Jenny's voice from all others was that it was like the warbling of a bird, and a woman who as a schoolgirl had heard Jenny sing in Nashville, Tennessee, wrote many years later, "The dreamlike echoes of the notes still linger in my ear. It was something unearthly, far away; like the cry of a wildbird lost in the sunset." Henry Wadsworth Longfellow declared that she "sings like the morning star; clear, liquid, heavenly sounds."

One thinks of Galli-Curci's voice as possibly the nearest to Jenny's among twentieth-century sopranos. But Galli-Curci's voice did not possess the unconscious note of pathos which "went straight to the heart," the words, over and over, of critics and laymen who heard Jenny Lind. Few people could boast that they had heard Jenny Lind sing without at some time feeling their eyes fill with tears.

Finally, Jenny's character had a deep appeal for the masses who would never hear her sing. Mr. Lumley had prophesied correctly when he had said that her success in England would be transcedent because "independently of her genius she has that purity and chastity of manner which none but a really good person can possess and which, in England, will gain her partisans on all sides." It was her purity of life and her charities which most decisively set her apart from other stage personalities of her day.

Her personal records showed that every fourth or fifth time Jenny sang, it was for some charity or special cause. By her second season in Vienna, she had raised more money for these purposes than she had received in pay for herself. Writing to Judge Munthe from Berlin, when her salary first began to reach respectable proportions, she rejoiced because the houses were "always crowded, and I have got together quite a lot of money for the poor by my singing these last weeks, praise be to God!"

It was Jenny's character and modesty that made the profoundest impression on Bishop Stanley. He had many talks with her in Norwich and afterwards wrote down several points about her which were, briefly stated:

1. She regarded her talent as a gift from God; she said she never sang without reflecting that it might be for the last time.

2. So far as her profession was concerned, it was obvious that her greatest object was not only to keep herself unspotted, but also to elevate its whole tone and character.

3. She made it a principle never to represent such passion as would awaken bad feelings. And she felt that if she were to do otherwise, she would destroy her own character and all that was good in her.

4. Her attention to servants and inferiors was remarkable.

Jules Benedict expressed it more succinctly: "Jenny Lind makes a conscience of her art."

Jenny took particular pleasure in helping young people and children who were musically gifted but poor. Her first venture in this direction was the term of study abroad that she made possible for her composer friend, Jakob Axel Josephson. After that, Jenny hardly filled an engagement anywhere that she did not devote a portion of her receipts to helping a student in some branch of the musical arts. In Vienna, she gave a benefit for a six-year-old girl violinist, who had already played in concerts and needed money for more study. In Darmstadt, she gave one for the son of a member of the orchestra, when the father told Jenny proudly how well his boy could play the horn. She always gave one or more benefits for the members of the orchestra at theaters where she appeared, for the chorus and perhaps for dependents of orchestra members as well.

She also left behind her a trail of benefits for worthy institutions. In one place it might be an asylum for blind soldiers, in another a children's hospital or refuge. A benefit she gave for the Governesses' Benevolent Institution in 1848 enabled the organization to set up its first home for retired governesses. In 1960, this organization had three homes for governesses and schoolteachers, and still remembered the debt it owed to Jenny Lind.

And there were many individuals for whom Jenny gave private concerts. For sick people who could not leave their homes; for old women in almshouses; perhaps for an innkeeper's wife in the course of Jenny's travels, who would sigh that her one desire was to hear Jenny Lind. And Jenny would sing for her, and then say, "Now you have heard Jenny Lind."

Stories of this kind were legion and each contributed its bit to the Jenny Lind mania. Her own colleagues were as much affected as outsiders. Jenny was always receiving special tributes and accolades from the orchestras and choruses of the theaters where she sang. At rehearsals or performances, the actors not on stage would crowd the edges of the scenery to see and hear her.

Never before had a woman been worshiped so adoringly by so many. It seems one of the greatest paradoxes of romantic history that Jenny was twenty-seven years old the October following her personal conquest of Britain. Yet never once had she heard the words, "I love you," from a man she herself could love.

CHAPTER EIGHT

ℐ Book Is Closed

J ENNY had scarcely arrived back in Stockholm after her triumphal tour of England and Scotland, when she suffered the worst blow of her life. On November 4, 1847, Mendelssohn died. He had left England for Frankfurt the previous May 9, after seeing Jenny's fabulous launching in London. Before he had had a chance to recover from the strain of producing his *Elijah* in two English cities, and worrying over Jenny besides, he was told suddenly and brusquely of the death of his sister Fanny, of whom he was extremely fond. He fell to the ground in a faint, and never fully recovered. In June, he and Cecile went to Interlaken, Switzerland, so that he might have a complete rest. He took *Die Lorelie* and other unfinished work with him, but composed no music that summer. After their return to Leipzig in September he remained in seclusion, and suffered a stroke on November 3, dying the next day. He was only thirty-eight years old.

Jenny made no attempt to hide her grief. She dreaded opening letters from friends in Germany, lest they contain some reference to Mendelssohn. She wrote Frau Birch-Pfeiffer that "as soon as I am obliged to hear or read anything about him, I get almost incapable of carrying out the great duty which I have taken on my shoulders . . . I do not belong to this life, my heart seems ready to burst from my breast." She told Hans Christian Andersen that her very soul had been altered by Mendelssohn's death. She could not bear to sing his songs, and dropped them from her concert programs.

Her preoccupation with religion deepened perceptibly at this time. Louise Johansson's nerves and head could stand no more of the kind of rigors to which they had been subjected in Vienna and London, and she resigned as Jenny's companion and chaperon, her place being taken by Josephine Åhmansson, a cousin of Mrs. Izak Berg's and a devout Methodist. Jenny's religion, acquired first of all from Grandma Tengmark's stories and Bible readings, appears to have been Christian in an all-embracing sense, with little reference to denomination. She went to Swedish churches, which were usually Lutheran, when she could, but had felt at home with the ceremonies of the Church of England. Now, under Josephine Åhmansson's influence, she was going frequently to little, out-of-the-way chapels where the "pure gospel" might be found. Stockholm began to fear that Jenny was becoming a religious fanatic.

But there was always work to be done and Jenny sang once more at the Swedish Royal Theater, opposite Julius Günther. She gave a great many benefits for worthy causes and for fellow musicians, among them Jakob Axel Josephson; her girlhood friend, Mina Fundin; Herr Randel, the concert master, and others of the Royal Theater personnel.

Over in London, Mr. Bunn at last brought the legal action he had been threatening for several years. His attorney represented Jenny's actions with regard to the disastrous contract in the worst light he could, claiming she had turned traitor to Mr. Bunn because she had received a better offer from Mr. Lumley, and had "come to England with two contracts in her pocket." Jenny was pictured as being sly, tricky and greedy. In the end Mr. Bunn was awarded £2,500 damages—he had asked for £10,000—which Lumley paid. The case attracted a good deal of attention and a book Mr. Bunn published subsequently, reproducing all the papers in the case, was widely read. But it seemed to have no effect on the attitude of the British toward Jenny, and Mr. Bunn no longer had any power to demand and threaten.

That winter brought another notable development in Jenny's life. Since his two years of study with Manuel Garcia in Paris, Julius Günther no longer felt abashed in Jenny's presence and became her constant escort. One night he spoke the words Jenny had waited so long to hear. "I love you, Jenny. Would you, could you, marry me?"

A Book Is Closed

Jenny felt as though she had come home after weary wanderings. Günther was the first and only man she had ever considered in the light of a lover, and to know that he loved her too seemed the ultimate blessing from God, who had already given her so much. She understood now why Günther had not spoken before, and chided him gently for it. There was no hesitation in Jenny's mind; they became engaged that night.

Mendelssohn's death had intensified her yearning to retire from the stage and she would have retired then and there to become Günther's wife, except for two things. One was that on returning to Sweden, she had become concerned about a decline in morals she thought she detected among the young people. She recalled that Mendelssohn had spoken about a similar moral decline among the youth of Germany in this fourth decade of the nineteenth century. Jenny was mature enough now to realize how very fortunate she had been in escaping the degrading experiences which so often beset a young girl in a stage atmosphere. It became her goal to set up some kind of school which would not only give training to gifted young Swedes, but would watch over their souls and morals as well. She wrote a letter to the Stockholm *Aftonbladet*, setting forth her wish to leave behind her some "permanent contribution to my country's native art and prepare others to take my place, after my own efforts have ceased." It would take a great deal of money to achieve the goal she had in mind. That season she dedicated all of her own earnings, which consisted of one-third of the theater's receipts, with prices raised 50 per cent over the usual ones, to this purpose. The price raise had been made with Jenny's consent this time, so that she might get more money for her school.

(It should be said here that her great plan went through a number of mutations, ending in the form of scholarships in music and the various visual arts, administered by the Swedish Academy of Music.)

Meanwhile Jenny's countrymen were seizing what they thought might be their last opportunity to honor the young woman who had brought so much honor to them. The employees of the Royal Theater commissioned a portrait of Jenny by Södermark and presented it to the Theater. It was hung there with much ceremony in January, 1848. March 7, the tenth anniversary of Jenny's first major triumph in *Der Freischütz*, was

[133]

celebrated by all Stockholm. Jenny sang Agatha again, and there was a "birthday party" for her afterwards, with dancing until dawn, a present from Queen Desideria, and a song written by Prince Gustaf for the occasion.

On April 12, she sang Norma for her farewell appearance on the stage which had been a home to her since childhood, and then started for London, taking the Izak Bergs with her, as well as her new companion, Josephine Ahmansson. Günther accompanied the party to London, but had to return to Stockholm immediately.

Jenny had made no public announcement of her engagement, for she knew the turmoil that would ensue. But Belletti was not the public. He had gone to Paris from Stockholm, and had been well received. Learning of Jenny's affection for the baritone, Mr. Lumley had engaged him for Her Majesty's Theatre, solely upon his star's recommendation. When they met after their separation, Jenny threw her arms around Belletti and told him her happiness was now complete. She was to sing again with her dear Belletti, and she was to marry the other member of their old triumvirate!

Belletti tried his best to be happy for Jenny. He had seen something of Günther while the tenor was in Paris studying with Manuel Garcia, and knew that the former gay blade had settled down. He had also heard that the turning point in Günther's life had been the realization that he loved Jenny. In any event, Jenny was no longer a child, her feeling for Günther had persisted through the years. Belletti pondered on the way Fate had seen fit to manipulate the life threads of the old triumvirate, separating them, shifting them about, bringing them together again in different patterns, but with their original positions always unaltered. Günther still played the leading male role in their little romantic comedy, though now back in Stockholm. Belletti, though now on the scene, still played the yearner who never was to win the girl, on stage or off. Since plainly he had been ordained for this role, Belletti accepted it, and became an interested observer of Jenny in England, as he had been in Sweden.

Her second London season was a duplication of the first, except that the public's interest in her rose to a higher pitch, if such a thing were possible. In spite of her attempts to keep her engagement secret, word of it had spread, together with rumors that when married she planned to retire from the stage. The "Jenny Lind crush" which had signaled her first season was as bad or worse than ever at the theater. Black market prices for tickets shot higher still, as people became afraid that if they missed hearing her this season, they might never get a chance to do so.

Queen Victoria and Prince Albert attended nearly all of her performances, seeing her over and over in the roles that were their favorites. The Queen showered her with magnificent gifts, among them a nightingale made of precious stones, and Her Majesty was flattered when Jenny wore it in her hair that night in the opera. Equally gorgeous presents, and some very bizarre ones, came from other persons. The great actor William Macready heard Jenny and called on her to express his admiration and to invite her to see him in a play. Jenny accepted the invitation, but no one watched Macready that evening. Everyone in the audience was looking at Jenny Lind.

Her triumph this season was the more significant because these were troubled times politically all over Europe, and the unrest had extended even to stable England. Many wealthy persons were leaving London; several theaters had to close. Covent Garden, whose Italian stars had originally set Lumley on Jenny's trail by their defection from Her Majesty's, went through bankruptcy. Yet all the while, whenever Jenny Lind sang, Her Majesty's Theatre was packed.

Belletti was keenly aware of these evidences of the stature Jenny had attained. And there was a radiance about her now that came not from success, but from her knowledge that the man she had loved so long returned her love. In rehearsals, she was as full of fun as when she had been a coltish young star in Stockholm. This was the summer Jenny came to know Chopin, and each was enchanted by the other, Chopin finding Jenny as delightful a personality as she was an artist. Later Jenny added to her repertoire several of Chopin's mazurkas, to which she had words fitted in Italian.

But it was not very long before this new radiance of Jenny's began to dim. After Günther's return to Stockholm, matters went less well between them. In accepting Günther's proposal, Jenny had had no thought except to leave the stage forever as soon as she could discharge her self-imposed obligation to set up a school for gifted young Swedes. Jenny believed that Günther had understood her desire to do this, and that that was why he had made no objection to her signing for a second London season. But as they exchanged letters about their future plans, it began to seem that Günther did not want her to end her career at all.

Günther thought he was in a position, following his study with Garcia, to strike for the highest honors in the operatic world, and was counting on Jenny's popularity to help him. He had felt somewhat martyred when Jenny and Belletti went off and left him to carry the whole weight of the Swedish Royal Theater alone, according to his view of it. That had put him back by years, years that Jenny could wipe out with a single stroke if she were to go on singing operas in which they would star together.

Jenny, on the other hand, had been able to endure the crowds and the endless demands upon her only because the end was not far away. Besides, if she were to continue on the stage, what of her hopes for a family? Jenny would be twenty-eight in October of this year, 1848. If she were to have children—and she very much wanted children—she had better lose no time.

The misunderstanding deepened when Mr. Lumley began importuning Jenny to sign with him for the next season, pleading that only she could carry Her Majesty's Theatre through the difficulties created by political unrest. Jenny didn't know what to do, appealed to Günther for advice, and he refused to give it. He knew that Jenny had been responsible for getting Belletti to London. He could not understand why Jenny did not say she would accept a contract for the next season on the condition that Günther, too, should join Her Majesty's Theatre.

Probably Jenny would have done that if she had realized Günther wanted it, but the thought never entered her mind. She had told Julius over and over how weary she was of her life on the stage, both physically and spiritually. He had seen something of the strain she had labored under for ten years; he must have known she could not go on indefinitely. So Jenny never wrote the words that Günther waited for, and he sulked. This bewildered Jenny, who had always hung back from making decisions. After becoming engaged to Günther, she had looked to him to shoulder burdens of this kind.

The situation grew so bad that Izak Berg took it upon himself to write Günther, urging him to press for an early wedding date, but so far as is known, Günther did not. Jenny was being beleaguered also by pleas from her parents for extra money, to which as usual she yielded, with the usual warning that it was to be for the last time.

Partly in order to counteract the confusion and depression she was beginning to feel over her relationship with Julius Günther, Jenny threw herself into plans for a benefit for the Old Brompton Hospital for Consumptives, which was located near Clairville Cottage. Jenny had participated in a host of benefits, but she took full charge of this one, directing all the details from first to last, intent on making it memorable. The programs were printed on white satin; Jenny herself acted as mistress of ceremonies; and in addition to her own numbers, she enlisted Lablache, Belletti and several other prominent singers. A characteristically generous touch was her choice of accompanist for this galaxy of stars. Otto Goldschmidt, the lad—he was only nineteen that August—who had protested the dropping of the students' free list at Jenny's first Gewandhaus concert, had left the Leipzig Conservatory after Mendelssohn's death and had gone to Paris to study with Chopin. When the political upheavals caused Chopin to go on to London, Goldschmidt had followed him there. Jenny was introduced to Otto by Chopin, it is believed.

As soon as she learned of the young musician's connection with Mendelssohn and that he had been present when the musicians had serenaded her after the Gewandhaus concert, Jenny invited him to Clairvillage Cottage and had him play for her. She liked him, and found him talented. When she was planning the gala benefit for Old Brompton Hospital, she thought of him and gave him an opportunity rare for a musician so young and as yet completely unknown.

The benefit made possible a Jenny Lind Wing for the hospital, balancing the Queen Victoria Wing. When it was dedicated, Benjamin Disraeli was the speaker. "We hear of the Kings and Caesars of this world," he said. "But how great is the artist who can say, 'Any morning,

I can assemble the world together in the auditorium of a theater, and can support an institution, or reward an individual, ten thousand times more than any King or Emperor!' " He spoke also of the character of the young woman who "never for a moment has been the victim of the inebriation of vanity, but when the riches of the world are poured at her feet, and the plaudits of the millions ring in her ears, turns aside to feel the common sympathy of our common humanity and pays, as it were, her tithes to human nature."

With the end of the London season on August 24 came another tour of the provinces, a very grand one, with Lablache, Belletti and the French tenor, Roget, accompanying Jenny. This was Mr. Lumley's enterprise and because of the size of the payroll for his list of stars—Jenny alone was receiving £10,000—he himself did not make a great deal of money out of the tour. But he said it was worth the trouble to have the satisfaction of seeing his principal star make a "Queen's progress" through the countryside, with members of the nobility and high clergy vying for the privilege of entertaining the prima donna in their homes.

Yet Jenny could not overcome a growing depression over the rift that seemed to be deepening between herself and Günther. The engagement was still in force, after a fashion, and Jenny and Günther even considered renting an apartment in Stockholm which was to be their home after their marriage. However, the impasse continued on the matter of whether or not Jenny should sign with Mr. Lumley for the season of 1849. And Jenny took Günther's silence as an indication that he did not care very much about either their marriage or her peace of mind.

Belletti was the one person in addition to the Bergs and Josephine Åhmansson with whom she felt free to talk about her troubles with Günther. She told Belletti that she had thought she knew how to bring out the best in her fiancé, but lately she had seemed to bring out the worst. She realized that under the pressure of problems and demands, she wrote to Julius in an irritable fashion, which only made him angry. But didn't Julius know her well enough to understand how nervous she became at times, and shouldn't he discount her irritability?

In September, Jenny made one last attempt to reach through to Günther's love for her. She had a deguerreotype taken of herself, standing at the piano and striking the G note, which had had a special significance in her own life and in her love passages with Günther. She reminded Julius of what the note of G had meant to them both and assured him of her continuing love. But she had become so uncertain of his love for her that she asked him to send the daguerreotype on to Judge Munthe if he did not wish to keep it himself.

Jenny destroyed Günther's letters to her after their romance ended; and Günther left orders that all of Jenny's letters to him should be destroyed at his death, which was done. But from letters of Jenny to close friends, it was evident that his communications to her during the period of their engagement were hardly those of a lover, perceiving her problems and wanting to help her, but of a man entirely wrapped up in his own selfish ambitions. Or at least that was the way they appeared to Jenny. Perhaps to Günther, Jenny's appeared equally selfish.

Jenny wrote Judge Munthe on the twenty-sixth of September that all was over between herself and Günther, but she was apparently so deeply hurt that she could not speak of it even to the Bergs or Belletti. They sensed that she had broken the engagement, for she had lost all her former gaiety. She decided she would not accept the contract with Lumley for the next London season. After performing *La Figlia del Reggimento* in Brighton on November 3, 1848, she told Belletti she had promised herself this would be her last appearance in opera, though she would go on giving concerts until she had the money she needed to set up her school in Stockholm. She had ceased to speak of Günther.

Günther never made the break into the outside world that he had longed for so ardently. In 1850, the year Jenny started her brilliant American tour, he began to teach in the Royal Theater School in Stockholm and in 1862 became a teacher in the Conservatory in Stockholm. He trained some of the most notable Swedish singers in the generation following his and Jenny's at the Royal Theater, but this was the principal use he made of the techniques he acquired in his study with Manuel Garcia.

Soon, however, Jenny's behavior began to bewilder Belletti quite as much as Günther's had bewildered Jenny. The tour ended in early December, and after the last concert Jenny gave a party for the singers and orchestra, with an excellent supper and many toasts, and dancing until 3 A.M. Belletti grieved for Jenny, for he believed her gaiety that evening had been a fine piece of acting. What was Belletti's surprise when he heard, not long after he had returned to London, that Jenny was already engaged to an Englishman, and had set her wedding date for the following March 7!

This whirlwind affair, so foreign to Jenny's usual manner of doing things, appears to have started even before she had broken her engagement to Günther. When she had sung at Newcastle in September, she had stayed at the home of Joseph Grote, the brother-in-law of her great friend Mrs. George Grote. There she had met a twenty-three-year-old army officer, Captain Claudius Harris. He was well set up and good-looking, but Jenny had considered him dull at first, though she came to have a more favorable impression of him when she found he was very religious. For his part, Claudius had fallen in love with the singer at their first meeting, and had accompanied the Lumley group to Scotland and Dublin.

Undoubtedly at any other time Jenny would have been struck by the parallel between the handsome but weak and mother-dominated Claudius and her own father. She was even five years older than Claudius, the exact situation between Anna Marie and Niklas. But Jenny was feeling adrift emotionally and to have an admirer pop up immediately after the break with Günther was balm to her wounded pride. She clutched gratefully at what she considered a sincere love and accepted Claudius. The early wedding date was selected because March 7, her "second birthday," was the most sentimental anniversary in her calendar.

Meanwhile, she threw herself into another sentimental undertaking. Mendelssohn's friends had been wishing to set up a musical foundation of some kind to carry on his high ideals, and Jenny suggested a special performance of the *Elijah* which she had never sung, though the soprano solos had been written for her voice, to start the fund raising. Once more she spared no effort of her own to make the occasion an outstanding musical event.

(As in the case of Jenny's school for young Swedish artists, the plans for the Mendelssohn Foundation went through many changes, finally emerging in its turn as a Mendelssohn Scholarship. Arthur Sullivan was the first to receive it.)

A Book Is Closed

That was how it happened that Jenny appeared for the first time in oratorio in England in December, 1848, in Exeter Hall, London, and thereby began a second musical career. Everything was done in the way that Jenny felt Mendelssohn would have wished. Except for Jenny, all the other soloists had sung in Mendelssohn's own productions of the *Elijah*. Mendelssohn's place as conductor was filled by the well-known musician, Jules Benedict.

Now still another Jenny was presented to her British admirers, one who inspired reverence and awe rather than the frenzied adulation that had greeted her operatic triumphs. She laid aside the vocal pyrotechnics of trills and cadenzas which had enraptured her theater audiences, and sang the straight, clear, musical line with not a note and not a rest otherwise than Mendelssohn had written it. Though her spoken English had a strong Swedish accent, this was not apparent in her singing, and her perfect articulation brought home every word to her listeners. When Jenny came to the passage where the widow says to Elijah, "I go mourning all the day long, I lie down and weep at night," the natural pathos of Jenny's voice and the poignancy with which she delivered the words made them almost unbearably moving.

Jenny did not return to Stockholm that winter for obvious reasons—the strained relations with her parents and the break with Günther, plus the fact that she was engaged now to Claudius Harris—but stayed on in England. Her first activity after the *Elijah* was a series of concerts for charity, one of them in Norwich, and again she was a guest at the Bishop's Palace. Bishop Stanley and his wife found Jenny considerably changed from the young woman who had visited them a year before. She struck Lady Stanley as being somewhat more withdrawn and averse to meeting new people, though she charmed the Bishop's lady by coming back to the Palace as to a home, remembering every detail about it. Her concert in Norwich was to be for the benefit of the poor of the city, and Jenny had expressed a wish to the Bishop that the tickets should not be priced too high.

"What would you think of one pound apiece for the reserved seats?" the Bishop asked.

Jenny replied, "Why not make it ten shillings apiece? Then I can give two concerts! I have left the stage now; I can do what I please. I am

[141]

free, free!" And she lifted her arms high as though she were a bird about to launch into flight.

She spoke to the Stanleys of her marriage, which was to take place soon, and told them what a joy it was to her that her fiancé felt as she did about her singing, her charities and her retirement from the stage. She declared emphatically that if that had not been the case, she could not think of marrying at all. She went on to say that Claudius also shared her love of the country and of peace and quiet. Jenny's dream was to settle near trees and water and a cathedral. "I am tired, body and soul, but my soul more than my body."

In less than ten weeks, Jenny cleared £10,000 for a variety of charities, and in February began a round of concerts for herself. The *Elijah* was given several times more, and Otto Goldschmidt served as her accompanist for the latter part of her tour. Now, when Jenny's wedding day was only weeks off, disillusionment about young Claudius had set in. Jenny had been singing to him on one occasion and he had fallen asleep! She began to think a little more about what her life would be when she limited herself to an audience of one, who could not stay awake. She postponed the wedding, giving the need to complete her concert series as the reason, and sang *The Creation* on April 3 at Exeter Hall in London.

Mr. Lumley had accepted Jenny's decision to leave the stage and had engaged Alboni, the Italian contralto, who had had a successful debut. Nevertheless the public was staying away from the box office, waiting to hear when Jenny would appear. Queen Victoria refused to make any plans to attend, until she could be assured she would hear her favorite. Once more Mr. Lumley appealed to Jenny to save his theater, and she weakened to the extent of agreeing to six performances. They would be operas, but she compromised with her conscience by insisting there should be no scenery or stage props and the operas should not be acted, only sung, making them concerts in reality. Mr. Lumley was glad to get Jenny on any condition, and the first of the opera-concerts was given on April 12, Jenny singing but not acting *The Magic Flute*, with Lablache, Belletti and Coletti supporting her. In spite of the big names and the quality of the singing, the affair was poorly attended and the applause was half-hearted. There was no question but that the remaining five concerts should be canceled, and Jenny did not want her triumphant career to end on a note of failure. She therefore contracted with Lumley to appear in six more full-scale operatic performances.

This proved to have been one of the luckiest decisions of Jenny's life, because it led Claudius Harris and his mother to show their real colors. Egged on by Mrs. Harris, Claudius insisted that Jenny withdraw from her contract. The stage was Satan's playground, he declared, and he hated everything about it including actors and actresses. He added that his mother did, too.

Jenny was shocked and angry, but she had suffered guilt feelings over the part she felt her irritability had played in her break with Günther. She did not want to be guilty a second time of breaking an engagement through her own ill nature. A lawyer friend of Mrs. Grote, with the unusual name of Mr. Nassau Senior, was already engaged in working out the complicated details of Jenny's marriage settlement. Jenny asked Mr. Senior to come to Clairville cottage and poured out to him her perplexity, resentment and hurt at Claudius's harsh indictment of an art which everyone but the Harrises felt Jenny had greatly ennobled. Jenny was deathly tired of the demands made upon her as a great operatic star, she wanted to be free of the stage, but she loved the stage itself and would not have it maligned. Apparently the Harrises, Jenny told Mr. Senior indignantly, expected her, Jenny Lind, to retire to Bath as a reformed sinner, doing constant penance for her alleged wickedness. Jenny could not see herself playing this role.

Mr. Senior advised her that it was her duty to carry out her contract with Mr. Lumley. If Mrs. Harris—by now it was plain that Claudius had no will of his own—wished to break off the marriage on that account, Jenny should consider that she was well out of it. That was what Jenny had wanted to hear.

Confronted with Jenny's firm resolve, the Harrises reluctantly withdrew their objections to the six operas, and the wedding date was set again, this time for May 16, 1849. The controversial performances would be over with by then. Mr. Senior proceeded with the marriage contract. But now the Harrises demanded that Jenny guarantee in writing that she would never appear on the stage again. They also demanded that Jenny turn her whole personal fortune over to Claudius, Mrs. Harris quoting

Scripture to prove that it was contrary to God's wishes for a married woman to have any money of her own. Jenny refused both conditions, and once more the Harrises backed down; but by this time any pleasure Jenny might have found in believing she was truly loved had vanished.

Jenny's last operatic appearances topped everything that had gone before. She sang *La Sonnambula* and *Lucia di Lammermoor* twice, and *Daughter of the Regiment* once, saving her Alice in *Roberto il Diablo* for her farewell to the stage. At the end of *Roberto il Diablo* the audience rose in a body and cheered and wept and wept and cheered.

After that, a little ceremony was held backstage. The members of the chorus formed a circle around Jenny and their leader presented her with a bracelet engraved with an appropriate inscription. Jenny embraced several members of the chorus, Lablache and others who had been especially good to her, then ran weeping to her dressing room. Josephine Åhmansson found her there, her book in which she recorded engagements open before her, methodically adding the last entry, "May 10th, 1849, London—Roberto." Preceding that entry, and filling many pages, was the record showing that Jenny had given 677 performances of thirty different operas, in Swedish, German, Italian, French and English, since her debut as Agatha twelve years before.

It is presumed that neither Captain Claudius Harris nor his mother was a member of the audience at any of these six performances. Now that they were over, Claudius asked to have the wedding postponed again. Mrs. Grote was in Paris and Jenny decided to join her there, begging Judge Munthe to come to Paris also. She wrote: "I have been so terribly lonely and unhappy, that I hardly hang together." Jenny arrived in Paris on May 16, which was to have been her wedding day. She told Mrs. Grote that she was tired to death, but that she and Claudius had agreed finally to break off their engagement. Now at last she was really free, from the stage, from the importunities of Mr. Lumley and from the impossible Claudius and his mother. Judge Munthe arrived, together with Frau Arnemann, wife of the Swedish Consul at Frankfurt. Jenny attended Meyerbeer's new opera and was entertained by the English Ambassador. She struck up a warm friendship with the famous Angelica Catalani, now growing old, who had persuaded Jenny to sing at a party by saying,

"It is old Catalani, who wishes to hear Jenny Lind sing before she dies!"

Just two days later Catalani was dead of cholera which had appeared in Paris in epidemic form, and the Grote-Lind party made a speedy departure. At Coblenz, an eminent doctor whom Jenny consulted found her to be on the verge of a serious breakdown and forbade her to sing for at least six to eight months. Meanwhile Mr. Lumley had persuaded Henrietta Sontag to come out of retirement. Her name, added to that of Alboni, was drawing people to her Majesty's Theatre, and Jenny felt that a heavy weight had been lifted from her.

She spent the summer sampling the cures of which the Continent offered a great variety, and working out her own tangled emotions. From Schlangenbad she wrote to Cecile Mendelssohn for the first time since the composer's death, apologizing for her long silence and "for re-opening a wound which will never close." She described in detail the production of the *Elijah* which had taken place the previous winter. "In my opinion he never wrote anything finer, and assuredly could not have written anything loftier in the future. With what solemnity we all stood there to perform it, and with what love do people still speak of him! How the good English have understood and absorbed this particular music! As for myself, I sing it in quite a special mood. May I say that not many—no, only a few—have understood him as I did. I hope you will not think me presumptuous for saying this, for all that is best in me is rooted in this conviction." Jenny ended by saying that one day the three of them would meet together, "and then it will be well with us!"

As she gained perspective on the events of the past year, Jenny could poke fun at herself over the ridiculous affair with Captain Claudius Harris. She had thought the British would turn against her when she broke her engagement to an Englishman, only to find that everyone had been wishing she had never made it. It was sobering, however, to realize that she felt only joy and relief at being through with Claudius, and as she examined her emotions, she decided that even in the case of Julius Günther, it was her pride that had suffered, not her heart. She had wanted love and marriage and children. Julius had appealed to her romantic fancy when she was a young girl; it had appealed to her romantic fancy at twenty-eight to marry the only man she had ever cared for in that way. But she realized now that she had not loved Julius. She had seen in him a way to fill her need for companionship, for a home and children, for someone to take on the business of decisions and details that she found so burdensome. But she had not been willing to surrender any of her dreams and desires in order to have them fit with Julius's. The wall she had built about her emotions in order to avoid the mistakes of her parents had grown so strong and high that she would never be able to break out from behind it.

But she had no grounds for complaint. She thought how fortunate she had been in escaping other evils that might so easily have resulted from her peculiar family situation. If she must put her dreams of marriage and children from her firmly forever more, the memory of the blessings showered upon her would be ample compensation.

After Jenny had arrived at this conclusion and accepted it, she began to be herself again. She wrote freely to her friends about her folly in engaging herself to a young man who, aside from the age difference between them "was both without occupation and tied to his mother's apron strings." She regretted that she would never experience motherhood, which she considered the finest and most sacred role of all, but she was happy, now that she had resigned herself to being wedded wholly to doing good.

"The experience has passed over my soul like a beneficent storm which has broken through the hard shell of my being and freed many little green shoots to find their way to the sun. And I see quite clearly how infinitely much there is for me to do with my life. I have only one prayer, that I may be able to show a pure soul to God. . . . I am glad and grateful from morning to night! I do not feel lonely or bored, and my only complaint is that the days fly by too quickly. I have a brightness in my soul, which strains toward Heaven. I am like a bird!"

She decided to go back to Sweden and start the work of setting up her school, but she gave some concerts in Hamburg first. Young Otto Goldschmidt happened to be there. He called to pay his respects and at Jenny's request served as her accompanist at several of her concerts. She returned the favor by singing in a concert he gave. He came often to play for her, and they talked a great deal about Mendelssohn. It seemed to Otto a pity that the singer whose voice Mendelssohn had placed above all others should no longer sing his songs. Mendelssohn had written them to give joy and no one had given as much joy by singing them as Jenny Lind. But Jenny would shake her head and say, "I can't, Otto, I can't."

One evening Otto sat down at the piano and began to play "The Spring Song." He had always addressed the great singer hitherto in the manner of a young person speaking to someone older and very distinguished, but now he commanded. "Come Fräulein, sing! It is what Mendelssohn would want if he could speak." And Jenny came to the piano and began to sing "The Spring Song," haltingly at first, but soon with full, joyous voice.

Otto was present at a children's party Jenny gave subsequently, and she danced with him, the first time she had danced since Mendelssohn's death. At a concert in Göttingen, not long after this, she sang Mendelssohn's "Rheinisches Volkslied," with its many F sharps, so effectively that the audience went wild. From that time on, Mendelssohn's songs were restored to their old place in her programs, and this she owed to young Otto Goldschmidt.

As soon as the word got around that Jenny was once more appearing in public, her dream of a quiet winter in Stockholm evaporated. November 19, 1849, was the birthday of the Queen of Prussia. King Frederick William IV wanted Jenny to sing for the occasion and traced her to Hamburg where she received the royal invitation. Mendelssohn's friend, Herr Taubert, now conductor of the Court Orchestra, was sent by the King to escort Jenny to Berlin.

On her return to Hamburg, she found Herr Berg, her old singing master from the Swedish Royal Theater, waiting for her with a royal command from her own sovereign, King Oskar of Sweden. Crown Prince Charles was to be married in June, and his father, the King, desired Jenny to sing in several operas as part of the preliminary festivities. Jenny told Herr Berg that not even the request of her King could change her determination to sing in no more operas, but that she would be glad to go to Stockholm in the spring and would sing in as many concerts as the King and the Royal Theater might want. Herr Berg returned to Stockholm with Jenny's reply to King Oskar, Jenny and Josephine Åhmansson going as far as Lübeck with him. There Josephine came down with measles and was rather seriously ill. Jenny stayed with her in Lübeck for a month. Her plan was to go back to Berlin after Josephine had recovered, and perhaps after that to make a concert tour in Russia, where she would be able to garner a large sum of money in a short time, then retire to private life.

But at Lübeck she finally consented, after numerous refusals, to see a man named John Hall Wilton. He had been sent from America by Phineas T. Barnum to persuade her to undertake a concert tour in the United States.

CHAPTER NINE

"This Jenny Lind Business Will Ruin You!"

PHINEAS T. BARNUM would have been the first to admit that his was one of those success stories, from humble beginnings to fame and riches, in which the American public of the nineteenth century delighted. Son of an innkeeper and storekeeper in Bethel, Connecticut, Barnum had started his own career as a storekeeper, with a side interest in lotteries, and had had his first business failure, a necessary ingredient for any true blue success story, before he was nineteen. He had then started a weekly paper, *The Herald of Freedom,* in Danbury, Connecticut, where he developed the literary style which was to stand him in good stead in publicizing his later ventures. What he lacked in education he made up for in imagination, and while his prose was sprinkled with crudities, and frequently misspelled, it was fluent and never suffered from lack of vividness.

His first firm step up the ladder of fortune came in 1835, when after several experiences with traveling shows and circuses, he bought a wizened, crippled slave named Joice Heth and exhibited her about the country. Barnum's claim that she was a hundred and sixty years old and had been George Washington's nurse aroused considerable controversy in the newspapers, much of which Barnum himself instigated. Barnum, in fact, liked nothing better than to have the papers call him a humbug, so long as they spelled his name correctly. When Joice Heth died, and autopsy showed that she might be ninety years old but could not possibly be any older, Barnum made further publicity capital out of that.

In 1841, he purchased Scudder's American Museum in New York City, at once renaming it "Barnum's Great American Museum," and stocked it with a variety of freaks and hoaxes. The public obligingly flocked to see his "Feejee Maid" (her upper part a stuffed monkey, her lower part the tail of a big fish); his "Zip, the What Is It?"—another synthetic monster; his "cherry-colored cat" (a black alley cat, but as Barnum explained, "At night all cats are black"); and his "industrious fleas," which Barnum claimed could pull a vehicle a thousand times their weight with the precision of a cart horse.

Barnum's own description of his museum was "a vast National Gallery, a million things in every branch of Nature and Art, comprehending a Cyclopaedical Synopsis of everything worth seeing and knowing in this curious world's curious economy." When he started his circus, it was of course the "Greatest Show on Earth," and remained that until it was bought by Ringling Brothers in 1907. The hippopotamus was identified as "the Great Behemoth of the Scriptures," and his Happy Family a "community of Natural Enemies and a Convention of Antagonists, in which may be seen cats fondling with rats and mice, dogs playing with squirrels, owls on friendly terms with sparrows and hawks feeding young pigeons with motherly solicitude." Other ventures of his, ordinary traveling companies, were sent out under such labels as "Barnum's Grand Scientific and Musical Theater" and "Barnum's great Asiatic Caravan, Museum and Menagerie."

In 1842, he took his first step away from humbuggery by promoting a genuine, live midget, Charles Stratton. Promptly dubbing his find "General Tom Thumb," Barnum made this name a household word and exhibited the miniature man over America and Europe with great success, his triumphs including a command appearance before Queen Victoria at Buckingham Palace.

But Barnum's reputation was of a kind that brought guffaws at the recollection of his outrageous hoaxes, or headshaking over the gullibility of the people who thronged to see the collection of freaks in his American Museum. Thorough extrovert though he was, Barnum had a certain amount of sensitivity, and after he had made a good deal of money out of his hoaxes and oddities, he cast about for some undertaking that would lend dignity to his name.

"This Jenny Lind Business Will Ruin You"

A daguerreotype of Barnum appearing in the frontispiece of his auto-biography, first published in 1854, gives the impression of a statesman or professional man, rather than of the all-time master of wiliness and humbuggery. It shows a stocky man, clean-shaven, with a pugnacious nose and deeply cleft, determined chin, rather long curly hair swept back from a high forehead and eyes that looked out penetratingly from beneath heavy brows.

He was an ardent teetotaler and a good family man. A born showman and promoter, he saw nothing wrong in exaggerating or suppressing facts in order to gain his ends. He was esteemed by the solid citizens of the community who knew him, as well as admired by other shrewd operators. And it was true, as he himself maintained, that nothing was ever presented in his enterprises calculated "to offend the sensibilities of young or old." His hoaxes harmed no one, and were so obvious that they did not even deceive.

He seems to have had a genuine desire to offset his fooleries by something that would lend dignity to mankind, too, in some degree. He had even gone so far as to send out scouts to find a perfect specimen of man and woman in each country of the world, whom he would exhibit under the title of a "Congress of Nations." However, he had heard a great deal about Jenny Lind, though he had never heard her sing. He had left London with his famous midget shortly before she arrived there for her first season at Her Majesty's Theatre.

It occurred to him now that if only he could bring Jenny Lind to America, his name would be linked with culture forever more. For as yet no great European singer had visited America while at the peak of his or her fame and abilities. Several, including Malibran, had come before they had achieved renown, others when they were on the down slope. To bring the most conspicuous star of all at a time when the whole of Europe was clamoring for her would raise America's artistic status, as well as that of P. T. Barnum, in the eyes of the world.

He believed Jenny would draw great crowds and make money for him, but that was not his principal motive. He wrote in his memoirs, "Inasmuch as my name had long been associated with 'humbug' and the American public suspected my capacities did not extend beyond the power to exhibit a stuffed monkey, I could afford to lose $50,000 in bringing to this country, in the zenith of her life and celebrity, the greatest musical wonder in the world, provided the engagement was carried out with credit to the management."

For his emissary to Jenny, Barnum chose John Hall Wilton, one of his employees, because Wilton was an Englishman and also a musician, in Barnum's rather limited understanding of the term, having come to America some months before with the Sax-Horn Players. Wilton was to engage Jenny Lind on a "shares" basis if possible—equal sharing of profits or losses, as the case might be—but if she refused that, he was to engage her willy-nilly so long as the price did not exceed $1,000 a concert for any number of concerts up to a hundred and fifty. "Wiltons' compensation was arranged on a sliding scale," remarks the canny Barnum in his autobiography, "so that the farther he kept below my limits, the better he would be paid for making the arrangement."

On arriving in Europe, however, Mr. Wilton found Jenny apparently unimpressed both by his nationality and his claims to musicianship, for she refused even to give him an audience. After following her about over the Continent with no results, the horn player appealed to a friend of his, Mr. Hoffman, father of two very talented musicians—a daughter Helen, possessor of a fine voice, and a teen-age son Richard, then showing promise as a pianist. Hoffman was acquainted in London's musical circles. Could Mr. Hoffman suggest some way by which Wilton might obtain an appointment with the singer? Mr. Hoffman obligingly introduced Wilton to Sir George Smart, conductor of the Philharmonic Society, who had been Helen Hoffman's singing teacher and with whom Jenny herself had studied oratorio. Sir George gave Wilton a letter of introduction to take to the diva in Lübeck, which urged her at least to see the man and hear what he had to say. Jenny then consented to do so, but was very cool, at first, to the idea of appearing under Barnum's management, and especially cool to the suggestion about going shares.

She was already being importuned by Chevalier Wyckoff, an American who had managed a successful American tour for Fanny Elssler, the dancer, to undertake a concert tour of America on a shares basis, and there was also the Russian tour that she had been thinking about. Wilton, having in mind his employer's injunction that the main thing

was to get Jenny Lind to America, blurted out to her Barnum's top offer
—a guarantee of $150,000 for 150 concerts—with no further haggling.

Chevalier Wyckoff practically screamed when Jenny told him of this.
"Barnum! That uncouth American! A mere showman! Oh, what that
man would not do! Why, that trickster would stoop to anything for
cheap public display. He would not scruple, I assure you, to put you in a
cage and exhibit you throughout the United States at twenty-five cents
per head. Surely you cannot consider such a thing!"

Jenny considered it just the same, for $150,000 was a great deal of
money. However, she was no longer the naïve young woman who had
refused even to bring up the subject of payment with Alfred Lumley,
and she had gained a precise idea of her value. She wrote to Mr. Joshua
Bates, of the banking firm of Baring Brothers in England, asking whether
Mr. Barnum would be able to pay the sum he had offered her. Mr. Bates
replied that his firm considered Mr. P. T. Barnum to be thoroughly reliable in business matters. Her next step was to lay down some severe
conditions.

In his offer, Mr. Barnum had included salary and expenses for Jenny's
companion and a secretary, an accompanist who could double as orchestra
director, and a tenor. Jenny ran a line through the word "tenor" and
substituted "baritone," then told Wilton she would accept only if her
supporting artists were Jules Benedict, who had conducted the *Elijah* in
its first performance after Mendelssohn's death, and Giovanni Belletti.
So Wilton hurried back to London and got the consent of these two
gentlemen to make the tour, Benedict for a salary of £5,000 (about
$25,000), Belletti for £2,500.

Shuttling back to Lübeck, Wilton was met by some more conditions.
Jenny must have full control over the number of times she was to sing in
a week and over the number of pieces sung by her at a concert, so long
as they were not less than four. She was in no case to be required to sing
in opera. She was to have perfect freedom to sing for charity whenever
she felt inclined, though she would consult with Mr. Barnum first as to
his convenience, and would refrain from singing for charity in any city
until two concerts had been given there under her arrangement with him.

She was to have all travel and hotel expenses paid for herself, her companion and her secretary, and besides this was to have a maid and man-

servant at her disposal and a carriage and pair. Mr. Barnum was to pay all the expenses for the concerts given under his management. And finally, he was to deposit in a London bank, or banks, the full sum for the salaries and expenses of Jenny's entire party before they would sail from England. This sum, as Jenny and John Hall Wilton figured it out, came to £ 37,500, or $187,500 in American money. Mr. Wilton, with victory just within his grasp, did not so much as consult with his employer. "Oh yes, Miss Lind," he assured the singer. "This will all be done. You can count on it!" Whereupon Jenny signed her name to the memorandum that Wilton prepared. Wilton signed it in P. T. Barnum's behalf.

Jenny wrote Baroness French, "I know I shall never love the Americans as I love the English, oh no. But I fancy the country must in some parts be magnificent, and while I have the opportunity, I think it is a fine thing to see as much of God's creation as may be allowed me."

To her friend Frau Wichmann she wrote in much more jubilant vein. "I now wish to give you a clear idea of my future plans, so that you— and all yours—may know the truth and be able to distinguish the facts from mere reports.

"I have decided to go to America. The offer from there was very brilliant, and everything was arranged so nicely, that I would have been wrong in declining it; and since I have no greater wish than to make much money in order to found schools in Sweden, I cannot help but look upon this journey to America as a gracious answer to my prayers to Heaven!

"I shall be able to gain there in the course of one or two years a very large fortune, and, after three years, should not be required to sing a note unless I wish to do so. My heart resisted going to England at the present time; and indeed it is heavily weighted and I have often had a hard time of it. Now I need not think of England and I feel quite re- lieved, since I signed the contract three days ago. Herr Benedict (son of the M. Benedict you saw at Meran) comes with me and you could not meet with a more reliable musician. An old friend of mine, Signor Belletti, goes also. He is a distinguished singer, and we have known one another from old times in Sweden, for the last twelve years. In short, nothing could be arranged more admirably. I gave over at once any plans as to Russia and did so gladly, for Josephine could not have stood a Russian journey. . . .

"So now we remain—and more particularly Josephine—here in Lübeck until the first steamer leaving for Stockholm, which I hope will be in April. Then I go home to sing a few times in concerts (as I have promised my King to do), make arrangements in view of my long absence from Sweden, and leave Stockholm again the last of June or the beginning of July in order to go through a 'Milch Kür' somewhere, only not too far away. This I must have concluded by the middle of August in order to leave for Liverpool, there to take steamer for America for the first days of September!"

John Hall Wilton had accomplished his mission. Jenny had engaged herself to go to America. All that remained for Wilton now was to break to P. T. Barnum the news about the terms to which his agent had bound him.

Wilton returned to London, where he got the signatures of Benedict and Belletti to the memorandum, and in a few days was sailing back to America on the S. S. *Atlantic* with plenty of time to wonder how Mr. Barnum was going to react. As soon as the ship docked at the Canal Street pier in New York, Wilton hailed a cab and went to the American Museum. Finding that Barnum was in Philadelphia, Wilton decided to convey the good part of his news first. He sent Barnum a telegram which read:

HAVE CONCLUDED ARRANGEMENTS WITH JENNY LIND STOP COMING AUGUST STOP CONGRATULATIONS.

Barnum wired back: SAY NOTHING TO NEWSPAPERS. But already Wilton had run into two reporters for the New York *Tribune*, who knew that P. T. Barnum had sent Wilton to Europe to try to induce the Swedish Nightingale to undertake an American tour. Had he succeeded? Was she coming? Wilton had told the whole story, except the amount of money involved, and that Barnum must place it all in a London bank before Jenny would embark. This last undoubtedly was held back because Wilton did not want Barnum to get his first intimation of it from a newspaper.

Barnum took the early train for New York the next morning, his mind busily engaged with the publicity campaign which he would start late in the spring—it was now early February of 1850—and step up with increasing intensity as the date of the diva's arrival drew near. At Princeton he bought a New York *Tribune*. On the front page was the headline, "Another Barnum Enterprise!" with Wilton's news about Jenny Lind, somewhat embellished by the imaginations of the two reporters. The publicity campaign had started already! Now the problem would be to keep the interest of the public whetted for six months. He decided to see what effect the news would have on the train conductor, whom he knew well.

"Here is a story about a new project of mine," he said, showing the headline to the conductor. "I am bringing Jenny Lind to New York. She will positively appear here in late August or early fall."

"Who's Jenny Lind?" the conductor wanted to know. "Another one of those dancers?"

Barnum says in his memoirs that the conductor's words chilled him as though they had been made of ice. Jenny's name might be well known in Australia, as she had once been assured by the Bishop of Tasmania, but evidently it had not yet penetrated to darkest America. Barnum wrote that the conductor's reply made him realize, "If this is all that a man in the capacity of a railroad conductor between Philadelphia and New York knows of the greatest songstress in the world, I am not sure that six months will be too long a time for me to occupy in enlightening the public with regard to her merits."

He received a much severer blow at the American Museum, where John Hall Wilton was waiting for him with growing apprehension. Barnum took the news of the salaries and expenses he was to shoulder well enough, but when Wilton revealed that $187,500 must be deposited in advance, Barnum was staggered. It was a much more impressive sum than it is nowadays, and far exceeded Barnum's liquid resources.

Barnum had made his fabulous offer on the assumption that he would be paying the artists as proceeds came in from the concerts. Even so, it was a gamble, and he had been prepared to lose as much as $50,000 on it. But borrowing money in advance for a concert tour of America in 1850 and 1851 was like trying to finance a dream. No musical enterprise to date in the young country had made much more than bare expenses. Yet Barnum, in his grandiose way, had conceived of such a concert tour as had never been held in any country before, covering thousands of miles —including Havana, Cuba, in fact—taking nearly a year to complete and calling for a hundred and fifty appearances, if his star were to demand it. What had seemed a reasonable risk, with receipts from the big Eastern cities to tide him over, now threatened to wipe him out before Jenny had set foot in this country.

Nevertheless, he did not for one minute consider dropping the project. Instead, he decided that the sooner the publicity was started, the better it would be for money-raising purposes. His first act, therefore, was to write a letter to each of the New York papers, confirming that the Swedish Nightingale was indeed coming to America, and at a cost previously unheard of. He dwelt on her "vocal powers, which have never been approached by any other human being," and upon her character and her notable contributions to charity. Her visit would prove a blessing to America, as it had to every other country she had visited. It was on this account that he was resolved to bring her to America, Barnum concluded, even if he knew he would not make a penny on the venture.

Actually, Jenny was not as completely unknown in the United States as the remark of Barnum's conductor friend had indicated. Ditson of Boston had brought out "The Jenny Lind Quadrilles for Pianoforte" and "The Jenny Lind Polka" in 1847, and Firth, Hall and Pond of New York had published "The Jenny Lind Waltz" in the same year.

But these gave little idea of Jenny's abilities, and raising the $187,500 was the hardest task of Barnum's life. The moneyed men to whom Barnum applied as his next step did not share his eagerness to confer a blessing upon America, and from a business standpoint they considered the enterprise completely mad. His friends shook their heads sadly over the predicament Barnum had gotten himself into, but had no intention of sharing it.

Learning quickly that he could look for little or no help from outside, Barnum put in all his own cash, sold real estate, and placed heavy mortgages on the American Museum and his home at Bridgeport. Still he needed about $25,000. He held some second mortgages which he took to a New York bank where he had done business for years. The president of the bank looked at the proprietor of the American Museum with a total lack of enthusiasm.

"Nothing will satisfy me for another loan except first mortgages on New York or Brooklyn property," he said. Barnum then offered to make over his contract with Miss Lind to him, suggesting that the banker could appoint a receiver who would take all receipts above $3,000 per night toward payment of the loan.

"It is preposterous to think you will ever receive as much as $3,000 a night from any concert singer anywhere! Mr. Barnum, it is generally believed in Wall Street that this Jenny Lind business will ruin you!"

The banker did, however, give him a letter to Baring Brothers of London, and this firm, being well aware of Jenny's drawing power, advanced $20,000 against his second mortgages. Still there was a balance of $5,000 to raise. Coax and plead and exaggerate Jenny's attributes as he would, Barnum could not induce any banker, any business associate, to lend him a penny more.

By mere chance, Barnum was relating his troubles to an old friend, the Reverend Abel C. Thomas of Philadelphia. The minister said quietly, "Your enterprise is worthy. Jenny Lind can do good in America. I happen to have $5,000 saved up for old age. Would you take it off my hands?"

For once Barnum was speechless, and tears came to his eyes as he looked on while his preacher friend sat down and wrote out a check.

Throughout his campaign to raise the advance payment, Barnum was feeding a steady stream of stories about his star to the New York dailies and to Boston and Philadelphia papers. It was the first known example of a "made press" (Barnum called it "working" the press), and it soon became apparent that the papers would print anything they were given about the Swedish Nightingale, for the editors read the papers from London in order to learn what was going on in Europe. They knew of Jenny Lind's triumphs there and on the Continent. They recognized the cachet it would bestow on America's cultural reputation to entice this rare bird across the Atlantic.

By good luck, Barnum ran into an English journalist who had actually attended several of Jenny's performances. Barnum paid him for several rapturous columns about Jenny each week, in which the Englishman described her singing, her personality and character, and her successes. These appeared in different newspapers, under a London date line.

Before long, people began to talk about Jenny Lind and to look forward to her arrival in America simply because they had been assured it would be a great event. The interest was not confined to the big cities where

Barnum's artfully concocted "news releases" were appearing. Papers in the hinterland picked up the word from the metropolitan papers, and soon there were few places in the United States where the name of Jenny Lind had not been heard.

Nineteen-year-old Richard Hoffman returned to New York in August after a concert tour with the violinist Joseph Burke (billed in his precocious childhood as "Master Burke, the Boy Phenomenon") to find Jenny's picture in all the store windows, her coming the main topic of conversation. He was especially interested because of the part his father had played in bringing this about. He wrote later that it seemed to him a wonderful stroke of good fortune to receive a letter from P. T. Barnum requesting the young pianist to join the company of artists who were to assist Jenny, and to appear at the first New York concert, which Barnum believed would take place around the middle of September. Hoffman's friend Joseph Burke was also engaged, possibly at Richard's suggestion, as violinist and concert master, and was one of the few of the original group who remained with Jenny throughout her entire American tour.

Barnum's letter to Hoffman mentioned that Richard's sister Helen, a contralto, would come with Jenny, to sing with the prima donna in oratorios. What happened about the sister is a mystery. Jenny's later detractors maintained that in a concert given by the Lind group in Manchester, shortly before sailing, the audience was so insistent in its applause for Helen's singing in a duet with Jenny, that Jenny was forced to sit down while Helen repeated her number. A day or so after this, the story ran, the engagement for America, made with her father because Helen was still under age, was canceled, and her brother retained instead, to assuage the father's feelings. However, Richard Hoffman, who was to become a distinguished pianist and the father of the famous sculptress, Malvina Hoffman, did not refer to any such unhappy incident in his own story of his family's contacts with Jenny. And in any event, Helen Hoffman's promising career was terminated not long after this when she married a man who had the same opinion of the stage and performers as Claudius Harris, and would not permit her to sing in public. One hopes that he, at least, stayed awake when she sang for him!

While P. T. Barnum struggled with the problems created by Jenny's demands, the singer herself embarked on a whirlwind tour of north

Jenny Lind, the Swedish Nightingale

Germany. Stopping back in Hamburg on March 20, 1850, she found that Robert and Clara Schumann were giving a concert in nearby Altona the following night. Once more she begged to be allowed to take part, and the Altona audience was amazed and delighted to see Jenny Lind walk out onto the stage, all unheralded. She sang several of Robert's songs at sight, so beautifully that Robert declared they might have been sung from the depths of his own heart. Clara Schumann wrote of this concert, "There was tremendous and enthusiastic cheering—at her singing, at my own performance which was not so bad, and at Robert's beautiful trio. And how Jenny Lind sang! "The Rheinisches Volkslied" by Mendelssohn, the "Sonnenschein" by Robert—now that really cannot be described. Robert said to her, 'When you sing my sunshine song, it really makes the sun shine on one's back.' "

So it was May before she got back to Stockholm. At Lübeck, where she took ship for Sweden, she gave several concerts and Otto Goldschmidt came from Hamburg to accompany her in one of them. A great crowd waited for her in Stockholm and there was a good deal of grumbling when it was learned that she had given up opera for "hymn singing," as many Stockholm citizens referred to her venture into sacred music. Instead of the balls and high-society parties she had enjoyed in former years, Jenny went to church and prayer meetings. She was seen many times in the congregation of a famous revivalist, the Billy Sunday or Billy Graham of his day, whose exhortations were considered undignified by the more orthodox.

Nevertheless the concert she gave at the Royal Theater and the two special galas in honor of the royal wedding met the usual enthusiastic response, and the government struck a medal in her honor. Jenny sang in two churches, St. Klara's, in the parish where she had been born, and St. Jakob's, in the parish where she had sat in the window of the superintendent's cottage at the Widows' Home and sung to her cat.

In June, she sang once more at a private party in the apartment of the Queen Dowager, Desideria, and after she had finished, the Queen opened her jewel case, begging Jenny to choose whichever one of the jeweled bracelets she preferred. Fröken Von Stedingk, lady-in-waiting to the Queen Dowager, was present and wrote in her diary that tears came to Jenny's eyes. "She begged the Queen to be allowed the favor of singing once before Her Majesty without other reward than a little bunch of forget-me-nots which were in a vase on the table." Desideria granted this wish, and Fröken Von Stedingk said the little bouquet of flowers appeared to give Jenny greater happiness than if she had been showered with diamonds.

A huge crowd gathered at the dock to wave farewell when Jenny boarded ship on June 27, 1850. It would be her last visit to Sweden until she should return with enough American gold to build her schools, and spend the rest of her life in acts of charity and piety.

She went to Germany first, where there were dear friends to whom she wished to say good-bye. Many demands for concerts had come—Jenny wrote Frau Wichmann that one offer from Berlin was so large it was shameful—but Jenny sang only at benefits, one of them for a friend of Jules Benedict. Then on to Liverpool, where she was joined by Benedict and Belletti, stopping in London just long enough to say good-bye to friends, among whom was Queen Victoria. The three artists gave two concerts in Liverpool before sailing, benefits toward a new hall for the Liverpool Harmonic Society. The hotels filled up, crowds gathered outside the hall where rehearsals were held, hoping for a sight of Jenny. At the first of these concerts, Jenny sang favorite airs from opera, a new song by Benedict, "Take This Lute," and Herr Berg's "Herdsman's Song." She was to sing both these songs in many concerts in America.

Her second concert in Liverpool, however, was a distinct departure. She sang Handel's *Messiah* for the first of countless times and was considered incomparable in it. The critics particularly praised the simplicity with which she rendered "He Shall Feed His Flock," and the devotion with which she sang "How Beautiful Are the Feet" and "I Know That My Redeemer Liveth." Jenny always stressed the "know" in the latter theme, making it a personal declaration of faith.

P. T. Barnum, informed in advance of the concerts and programs, saw to it that detailed eyewitness descriptions of Jenny's concerts and the reactions of her audiences appeared in the New York papers, though the writer never left New York.

Jenny was to sail August 21 on the S. S. *Atlantic,* a paddle-wheel steamer that was the floating palace of its day, and arrive in New York September 1. Barnum had still another gimmick up his sleeve to sharpen the American public's anticipation of the great event. On August 14, he gave the New York *Tribune* a copy of a letter which he said he had just received from Jules Benedict. It was dated August 24, from Schlangenbad. On August 24, Jules Benedict was on the ocean, three days out from Liverpool, but this slight discrepancy seems to have escaped the attention of the editors. The letter read:

> My dear Sir: I have just heard Mlle. Jenny Lind, whose voice has acquired—*if that were possible*—even additional power and effect by a timely and well-chosen repose. Mr. Wilton will bring you the programme for the first concert, which cannot fail to produce the most thrilling sensation in your noble metropolis. You may depend on it, that such a performance as hers, in the finest pieces of her repertoire, must warrant an unprecedented excitement and justify all expectations. Mlle. Lind is very anxious to give a Welcome to America in a kind of National Song, which, if I can obtain the poetry of one of your first rate literary men, I shall set to music, and which she will sing IN ADDITION to the pieces originally fixed upon.

P. T. Barnum forthwith announced a prize of $100 to the lucky "first rate literary man [a Barnumism if there ever was one] who would best meet the wishes of Jenny Lind" with a poem written especially for her arrival. The Jenny Lind Prize Song Composition Contest was now launched. It had never occurred to Jenny to wish to have an American National Song composed in her honor, and P. T. Barnum had to use all his powers of persuasion to get her to consent to the scheme after her arrival. Nevertheless, the contest brought the added publicity Barnum was angling for, specially after he followed his opening volley with a still bigger one two days later, in a letter to the editors of the *Tribune*, this time signed with Barnum's own name.

> Messrs. Editors: Will you please to state that Jenny Lind, having expressed a strong desire to sing at her first concert in New York a "Welcome to America" and Mr. Jules Benedict, the eminent composer, having kindly volunteered to set such a composition to music, I hereby offer $200 for such song as may be accepted by the following committee: Messrs. George Ripley, Jules Benedict, Lewis Gaylord Clark, J. S. Redfield, and George P. Putnam. The songs to be addressed to The Committee, Box 2743, Post Office, New York, and to reach here by the 1st of September.

The names of the authors are to be sealed in separate envelopes and no one will be opened except that containing the name of the successful competitor. All the songs, except the one selected, will be returned to any address designated.

Barnum had gathered a distinguished group for his committee. George Ripley had been one of the leaders of "Brook Farm," had succeeded Margaret Fuller as literary critic of the New York *Tribune* in 1849, and had been among the founders of *Harper's New Monthly Magazine,* launched in 1850. Lewis Gaylord Clark was the editor of the *Knickerbocker Magazine,* which flourished through the 1840's and 1850's. He was considered indispensable as a speaker at public dinners and literary assemblages.

Julius Starr Redfield had been the publisher of the *Family Magazine,* and at the present time had a book store and was engaged in general publishing. (He was the first publisher of P. T. Barnum's autobiography. Later editions were brought out by several other publishers.) George Palmer Putnam was a publisher also, identified with the production of finely illustrated books. In 1852, he was to establish *Putnam's Magazine,* and in 1866 would found, in conjunction with his sons, the publishing house of G. P. Putnam's Sons.

Though the time was short, 753 poems, from all parts of the country, had found their way to Box 2743 by September 1. It would now be Barnum's task to break the news of what he had done in Benedict's name to that gentleman, when he arrived.

The night of August 20, before embarking on the S. S. *Atlantic* the next day, Jenny wrote a letter to her parents, apparently the only one she had sent them since leaving Sweden.

Along with Jenny's deeper absorption in religion, and the acceptance of her lot which she had attained after the break with Claudius Harris, she had become resigned to the situation with regard to Anna Marie and Niklas. She had realized that they would never change, that it must be her task to supply them with the comforts of life, simply because she wished them to be comfortable. She would not permit their ingratitude and lack of interest in her as a person, not to mention a daughter, to disturb her.

Before leaving Sweden, she had dutifully gone out to Pommern, where she had taken a small place for her parents, and danced around the Maypole with Niklas Lind. Her letter to them was obviously a duty letter, markedly different from the warm, often gushingly affectionate ones she was accustomed to write to older women among her dear friends, such as Frau Wichmann, whom she addressed as "Dearest Mother," and others. It indicated that she had no expectation of receiving a warm response, or any great faith that her parents would act upon the suggestions she made.

My dear Parents: May these lines find you in enjoyment of good health. I have been very well since I left Sweden, and am now starting for the New World. For we leave tomorrow morning at half-past ten.

I have been in England eight days, and have sung here in two concerts, both of which have been most successful, and the English public has greeted me as if I belonged to them. I am met everywhere with heartiness and love. Oh, may I succeed in deserving them more and more!

I have been to see the steamer which will take us over to America, and nothing grander of its kind, I should think, could be found in any country. The vessel is 300 feet by 80, and is decorated so magnificently that one can imagine oneself in a rich private house. I look forward to the sea—the ocean! When I have got across, I shall let you hear again.

As my mother wished to have a Daguerreotype of my poor features, I have sat for one in London. I hope it will have succeeded. Farewell, good Mama and Papa! Think of me with friendliness and give me now and then your blessing, for a parent's blessing is something good to travel with. Let me hear occasionally how you are at Pommern. Remember to look into the books which I gave you, while stopping with you there—and may the Lord enlighten and bless you! Thus prays most sincerely,

Your attached Daughter.

For secretarial duties, Jenny was taking with her a young Swede named Max Hjortzberg. Of course Josephine Åhmansson would go along, and there were two servants for Jenny besides. A valet for Benedict and Beletti completed the party.

Punch, reporting Jenny's imminent departure under the heading "The Nightingale Takes Flight," predicted that she would never return to Europe but on her arrival in New York would at once be crowned Queen of the United States, "the President politely withdrawing."

CHAPTER TEN

Departure and Arrival

THE CROWDS had started assembling long before daybreak. They packed the docks nearest the spot where the S. S. *Atlantic* lay at anchor, not far from shore, and the lines were rapidly extending up and down the banks of the Mersey. The river itself was filling with craft, large and small.

It was still early morning when the head of the Liverpool police roused John Hall Wilton, whom Barnum had sent back to England to help Jenny in the arrangements for her departure, to say that if the Lind party were to arrive at the quay between 9 and 10 A.M., as had been planned, the authorities could not guarantee to keep Jenny from injury in the crush that would inevitably ensue.

The plans were hastily changed, and at a quarter of eight, Jenny and her fellow artists slipped out of their hotel by a side door, where a police escort was waiting. To escape detection, the carriages took a devious route, through byways and alleys, to a dock where a river boat was moored. Even so, a group of idlers on the dock recognized Jenny, and were so delighted to have a close look at her that the police had difficulty in getting the men to stand back and let the party through. Though the intentions of the men could not have been friendlier, Jenny was white and trembling when she boarded the river boat, which carried them to the S. S. *Atlantic* without further incident.

Just before 10:30, the hour appointed for sailing, a carriage drove up to the S. S. *Atlantic*'s dock at a furious pace, a man in clergyman's garb leaped out and seizing a portmanteau in either hand, begged the crowd to make way for him as he ran to the tender which was about to take the last load of passengers to the ship. He had happened to be passing the side door of Jenny's hotel that morning when she was leaving, had realized that she was on her way to embark, and had been seized by a desire to sail on the S. S. *Atlantic* himself.

His chances were slim, for though the *Atlantic* was carrying the largest complement of passengers in her history, there had not been nearly enough accommodations for all the people who wanted to cross the ocean with Jenny. The clergyman had gone to the steamship office nonetheless, and had found that two reservations had not been claimed. He snapped up one of them and had just time to collect some hand luggage and get to the dock before the last tender pulled away.

Another passenger on the tender, an elderly man, had no luggage at all, only what appeared to be a change of "unmentionables," the Victorian euphemism for underwear, rolled up under his arm. He paced the deck of the tender in evident anxiety, and in spite of his advanced years leaped agilely up the S. S. *Atlantic's* gangway exclaiming, "Where's Jenny Lind? Can anybody tell me where Jenny Lind is to be seen? Where the *devil* is Jenny Lind?" It was said that even Jenny had to laugh when this incident was reported to her.

The crowd began to chant, "Oh Jenny, Jenny oh! Come out and wave good-bye to us!" The singer, who had stayed in her suite since boarding now came on deck, escorted by Captain West of the S. S. *Atlantic*. He helped her up onto the near paddle box—one of two, on either side of the ship, covering the great wheels that propelled the vessel. Captain West climbed up beside her.

After it was all over, the correspondent for the *Illustrated London News* staggered back to his lodgings

> with ears still so deafened by the booming of cannon, and the shouts of the thousands who were assembled on either side of the Mersey, and eyes so dazzled by the gay effect of innumerable craft, which were illuminated by the sunlight as they ran to and fro on the surface of the river or followed in the wake of the *Atlantic* that I can scarcely give you a sober description of this extraordinary scene. . . . [so began his dispatch to his paper].
>
> When at last the hundred and fifty passengers who had en-

gaged all the berths were received on board, with all their luggage, and had taken leave of all their friends, and when the sound of the gun booming across the water from the bows of the steamer announced that all was ready for departure, what was certainly a great 'scene' commenced. The immense floating mass began to move and as if by magic, all the craft that had been playing about on the surface of the river formed into lines, and made a sort of procession. As the *Atlantic* steamed up from her moorings, past the Albert Docks, she turned her head inshore, in the direction of the town, and slowly passed in front of the magnificent line of quays, amidst the enthusiastic shouts of thousands who lined the shore, not merely on the Liverpool side, but also all along the Cheshire coast, from Birkenhead onwards to the mouth of the great arm of the sea. Salutes were fired from the shore, and were returned from the *Atlantic*; and the whole scene—such an army of crafts of all sorts and kinds floating, with pennants flying, such shouting, such a roaring of cannon, such a bright sunlight which broke out suddenly, as if to afford presage of fair weather—was really one of the most extraordinary sights we ever witnessed. Every eye was strained to get a sight of Jenny Lind. There the little woman stood on the paddle-box, with her arm in that of Captain West, and waving her handkerchief enthusiastically in return for the greeting of the crowds who had assembled to witness her departure.

A passenger who stood next to the paddle box said that Jenny threw kisses from the tips of her fingers as well, and occasionally stopped to wipe away the tears that flowed down her cheeks. "There was such enthusiasm as I have never seen before," the passenger recorded in his diary. "None but the stupid stoic could boast of dry eyes in the excitement of that hour."

The sunshine, which had appeared a good augury to the correspondent for the *Illustrated London News* when the S. S. *Atlantic* drew away from her anchorage at Liverpool, did not last long. The wind rose that night and the next day there were rough seas; nearly everyone was seasick. On the third day out, a tremendous wave surged over the bow of the *Atlantic*, snapping off the uplifted arm of the Triton that served as her figurehead and severely injuring three sailors. The first officer would have been carried overboard if he had not grabbed hold of the anchor as he was swept past it. The passengers stayed in their staterooms until the winds had subsided and the sea had calmed.

As had been the case a number of times before when Jenny had been persuaded to embark on a new venture, in the beginning all was auspicious. She could find no fault with the arrangements Barnum had made. He had engaged the deluxe suite, had had a grand piano installed in its sitting room for her particular pleasure, and John Hall Wilton had seen that her rooms were filled with flowers.

Jenny was friendly and gay when she emerged on the fifth day out, and quickly became involved in shipboard activities. When the band started to play that night after dinner, she was the first to dance, and she danced every evening thereafter, with "any gentleman who was introduced to her properly." The passengers had worried lest the rough weather might interfere with the musical treats they had been looking forward to. But one evening after tea, Jenny went to the piano in the main salon and started playing and singing a Swedish folk song. Word spread throughout the ship that the Nightingale was singing, and the passengers gathered to hear her, along with all the ship's officers whose duties permitted them to do so.

The next day, Jenny and her fellow artists gave a benefit concert for the crew members who had brought them safely through the recent perils. They were crossing the Newfoundland Banks and it was raining, but the sea was quiet and Jenny, Benedict and Belletti, assisted by a passenger who proved to be a good enough pianist to play duets with Benedict, presented a full program of operatic selections and airs. At its close, Jenny sang Benedict's own composition, "Take This Lute," and the Norwegian "Echo Song." Three hundred dollars was raised for the sailors, which appeared an impressive sum to the numerous persons on the passenger list who recorded the event for posterity. However, because of the rain and fog, Captain West had had to stay on the bridge and had missed the concert. Jenny sent word to him that they would repeat it for him and his officers, and did so the next evening, Jenny adding a number of her livelier Swedish folk songs for the officers' benefit.

She had struck up a great friendship with Captain West. The Captain, very much aware of the honor that was his in having the world's most acclaimed woman under his care, lost no opportunity to be at her side.

They had a standing joke about sea serpents, and the Captain would lend Jenny his binoculars to aid in her search for the interesting monsters.

Jenny told him she would like to see an ocean sunrise, so on the first cloudless morning Captain West had her called just before dawn. She stood beside him silent and motionless, watching the changing colors in the sky repeated in the great expanse of water. Then, when the first rays of the sun appeared above the horizon, she began to sing "I Know That My Redeemer Liveth," her favorite aria from the *Messiah*, softly at first, then gradually swelling the notes to a paean of praise and faith. Captain West always claimed that never again would anyone hear this aria sung as he had heard it, standing beside Jenny on the bridge of his ship.

Jenny talked to the sailors a great deal, asking them about their work and their families, so that she became good friends with them as well. She went down into the bowels of the ship where men naked to the waist were stoking the furnaces. She was inspired to ask one of them, a big Irishman, whether he would change places with her if he could.

He thought it over for a minute, leaning on his shovel, then replied, "Faith, and I would, if I could sing as well as you."

"Why would you?"

"Because the wages are better!"

While Jenny made herself at home with the officers and crew, the other members of the party occupied themselves in various ways. John Hall Wilton kept an eye on Jenny's movements, writing down everything that he thought might be grist for P. T. Barnum's publicity mill. Jules Benedict and Giovanni Belletti spent much time going through the heaps of scores Benedict had brought, and consulting over the programs for their concerts. Jenny, of course, would make her own selections for her solos and would decide about her duets with Belletti. The audiences could be counted upon to listen rapturously to anything she might sing. But the instrumental numbers required much thought.

Jules Benedict, in his middle thirties, German-born but reared and educated in England, had won fame as a pianist, composer and conductor. Besides conducting the orchestra and officiating as piano accompanist, he would play piano solos. One consideration that had weighed heavily in his decision to make the tour was the opportunity it offered to bring the best in music to the American continent. But it would not do to have the music too far over the heads of the listeners.

There would be no such reservoir of people long accustomed to fine music, presented by the ablest performers, as artists could count on in England and on the Continent. Part of the task of the supporting artists would be to educate those who would be drawn by the lure of Jenny's name. He welcomed the assistance of Belletti, considered by some critics to be the greatest baritone of his century, and a musical scholar as well, in this undertaking.

Jenny's secretary, young Max Hjortzberg, had quickly managed to make himself disliked by the other men of the party. He had displayed an officiousness that grated on John Hall Wilton, and had developed a puppy-like infatuation for Jenny of which the two musicians disapproved. However, Hjortzberg found a kindred soul in one of the passengers, Charles Seyton, a civil engineer from Scotland. Hjortzberg had also been trained as a civil engineer, and the two became constant companions.

Belletti had not intruded upon Jenny during the passage. They had had little time for confidential talks since they had met again in Liverpool in August, after separating the previous fall, but he knew Jenny would send for him if she wanted to talk to him in private.

The tenth day out from Liverpool—they were to arrive in New York the next day—Belletti observed that Jenny did not exhibit the high spirits she seemed to have acquired with the calming of the waters. She was noticeably quiet at meals, and had little to say at the traditional farewell party Captain West gave his passengers that evening. She appeared even more embarrassed than usual by eulogies delivered in her presence, when Captain West launched into a little speech he had prepared in advance—he gave John Hall Wilton a copy of it—in reply to a toast.

"I thank you sincerely for the compliment just paid me. I have always endeavored to make my passengers aboard my ship comfortable and contented, and when they tell me that I have been successful, they simply reward my care. On this voyage, however, we have enjoyed a pleasure that I could not contribute—the talents of a lady whose name has long been familiar to us. The lady is about to visit America, where her fame has gone before her—not only her fame for the possession of one of the rarest gifts of nature, but her fame as a most kind and charitable woman. She is now among us, I may say on American soil, under the Star Spangled Banner. We who are citizens of the United States are the first of our countrymen who have had the chance to bid the stranger welcome, and I am sure that under the circumstances, you will honor the toast I now propose: Jenny Lind, the Nightingale! Jenny Lind, the kindhearted, unaffected Swedish girl—welcome to the United States of America!"

Jenny, appearing agitated, acknowledged with a strained little smile the cries of "Welcome to the United States of America!" from the American passengers, then after a murmured apology to Captain West, made her way toward the door of the salon. Belletti followed her. Outside the salon, she picked up her skirts and ran. He caught up with her as she emerged onto the now deserted deck. Tears were running down her cheeks.

"Why, Jenny, my dear, what is it?" Belletti fell into step beside her as she hurried along the deck.

"Belletti, I cannot do it! I cannot sing in America! Captain West is expecting so much of me, and so are the others, and I shall disappoint them! I shall disgrace myself and my country, too. Belletti, I am not going to get off the ship in New York. I am going to return to England with Captain West."

Never in his life had Belletti felt so at a loss. He had wondered a bit at first, along with everyone else who knew her, that Jenny had even considered going to a region as remote from her usual orbit as America, and had been somewhat surprised that up to the time of their departure she had exhibited none of the fears that had plagued her previously before every step into the unknown. Once they were aboard the S. S. *Atlantic*, however, all such thoughts had vanished from his mind. Who could have dreamed that after crossing the ocean, Jenny would refuse to leave the ship!

The silence had grown long. Jenny looked at Belletti anxiously. "You won't mind too much, will you, dear Belletti? I shall of course pay you and Benedict your salaries, and reimburse Mr. Barnum for the money he has spent in bringing us here. It is the only honorable thing to do."

Jenny Lind, the Swedish Nightingale

"But Jenny, you need the money for your schools and charities! You have said it was the reason why you signed the contract with Mr. Barnum."

"I shall only have to work a few years longer, that is all. I should never have left England. It was a mistake, a dreadful mistake."

"What of your contract with Mr. Barnum? Our friend Wilton has told me this man is counting very heavily on your tour."

"Mr. Barnum would not like it so well if I were to have a big failure. He will get back all the money he has put in the bank for us. This will be far better than if I were to go before American audiences and be hissed and booed off the stage!"

Jenny, Jenny! thought Belletti despairingly. After all the adulation and adoration she had received, still living under the dread that sometime, somewhere, an audience would hiss or boo her! The fact was that the very frenzy of the farewell given her at Liverpool had contributed to Jenny's self doubts. For it was part of her phobia that the greater the love shown her by those she had come to know, the surer she was that she would be rejected by those she did not know. Yet to argue with her when she was in the grip of one of her unreasoning panics would, Belletti realized, be fatal. What was the ruse Günther had used in persuading Jenny to go back to Berlin and carry out her promise to Meyerbeer to introduce his *Camp in Silesia*? He remembered now. Günther had told her flatly that someone had thought she was not an accomplished enough artist to sing in Berlin! What had worked with Jenny once might work with her again.

He clutched at the first pretext that came into his mind. "Perhaps you are right. Wilton has said that the Americans have heard very little good music. They probably would not understand or appreciate what we bring to them. Malibran herself attracted little attention there. I suppose it is idle to think we might succeed where Malibran failed."

"Belletti!" Jenny said reproachfully. "We have always been honest with each other. Do you think I am still a child, that you must play tricks with me?"

Jenny knew him too well; she had detected at once the insincerity of his approach. They had reached the prow of the ship, where Jenny had liked to seat herself beneath the Triton figurehead and read or perhaps

[172]

doze. Now by common consent they went to the rail and stood looking at the moon path running ahead of them over the gentle swells, pointing the way westward. Belletti knew of nothing else to do except to say what was in his mind. "Very well, Jenny, I will be honest. I think it *is* childish for you to run back to England without giving the Americans a chance to know whether they like your singing or do not like it. Everywhere, the public has loved you. I do not believe it will be otherwise in America.

"So far as I am concerned, I accepted Mr. Barnum's offer only because to be with—to sing with you is the greatest pleasure of my life. But Benedict will be frightfully disappointed. The American passengers have told me that nothing is spoken of in New York but you. *That* will bring people to our concerts, and give us all a chance to introduce the Americans to fine music.

"*That* is the reason why Benedict accepted Mr. Barnum's offer—you know how devoted he is to art. He has been especially pleased because we shall be bringing our music not only to cities on the coast, where I understand the people are somewhat more civilized, but to parts where, so Wilton says, they have never had a chance to hear good music by real artists. It is you alone who can make this come true."

Jenny stood in silence, looking down at the waves folding back before the thrust of the *Atlantic*'s prow. Belletti feared he had offended her beyond mending. But when she spoke, it was to say in a low voice, "Belletti, I am ashamed! I had not thought of the music, of the good we might do in America. I had thought only of the money. It is the first time I have ever let myself be guided by money alone, I suppose because Mr. Barnum offered me so much of it. How it blinds one to everything else!"

"No, Jenny, it was not the money you thought of, but of what the money would do for the young artists of your country. You were thinking of the good that would come out of the great sum Mr. Barnum offered you. You only let the money blind you to what you might do for the Americans themselves."

Jenny drew a deep breath. "So! Well, we shall see then how the Americans receive us. If they do not like our music, we can go back with Captain West the *next* time he returns to England!"

"Ah, that is my brave, sensible girl! Now I will confess that I myself have been looking forward quite eagerly to seeing something of this hemisphere which my countryman discovered. I have been saying to myself ever since we left Liverpool, 'Belletti, once again an Italian is sailing westward on a voyage of exploration, whither he knows not, but trusting to Providence that the natives will not boil him in their cooking pots and eat him for their dinner!' "

He said this so comically that Jenny laughed, partly at the absurdity of her own fears as Belletti had revealed them to her. It was fully agreed, before Belletti had left her at the door of her suite, that these latter day adventurers into the unknown would at least let the American natives declare their intentions, before beating a retreat to England.

It was long before Belletti got to sleep that night. He paced back and forth in his stateroom, keyed up by the narrowness of the escape from disaster, and stirred by the realization that the inner Jenny was so little altered from the girl he had known in Stockholm. Stopping presently he drew a folded, yellowed piece of newsprint from his wallet. It was a crude sketch, of the kind used for newspaper illustrations before the days of photography, and it showed the young Jenny, flanked on one side by Günther, on the other by Belletti, wearing the costumes from an extravaganza the Swedish Royal Opera Company had put on as part of the Jubilee for the Twenty-fifth Anniversary of King Karl Johann's accession to the throne. Jenny had sung folk songs in the colorful costume of a peasant girl from Värmland, and Belletti had played the part of an itinerant Italian singer. The sketch, done by some hack artist, made Jenny seem plainer than she had been in fact, but conveyed the dash and elan that she brought to her livelier roles. She looked like a frolicsome schoolgirl. And it was thus Belletti had still thought of her, that spring of 1844. When he began to view her with different eyes, she could think of no one but Günther. And when that affair had been broken off, the callow Claudius Harris had won her pledge of marriage under Belletti's very eyes.

But the Harris affair, too, was over now, Günther's name was never spoken in Jenny's presence, while fate was placing Belletti at Jenny's side throughout the long American tour. He had not been thinking of that when he risked Jenny's displeasure in order to persuade her to carry out her contract with Mr. Barnum. He had been thinking what a black mark would be against Jenny's name if she were to refuse, something she would never live down. But suddenly he felt a hope for the first time in his long acquaintance with Jenny. He had remained a bachelor, out of his unspoken love for her. No other person understood her as he did. Had it been intended that they two should come together at last, after Jenny had found her younger suitors unable to supply the needs of her heart?

Of one thing Belletti was very sure. It would not do to rush matters. From the time she was eighteen, he had been "Uncle Belletti" to her, the disinterested friend and confidant. Jenny must still feel able to turn to him freely, without self-consciousness, whenever she needed help or support. The change from friend to lover must be effected gradually. But there was no rival in the field, now, he was sure of that. And there was time. A whole year!

There would be periods later when Belletti would find himself wishing that the party had indeed gone back with Captain West, though he always tried to thrust such thoughts from him. However, when he rapped at the door of Jenny's sitting room the next morning, Jenny herself opened the door, her face bright, the megrims of the day before obviously put behind her. Her bags and Josephine's were being closed in anticipation of disembarking. Nothing more was said about returning with Captain West.

Everything about the arrival played into P. T. Barnum's hands. The storms had upset Captain West's schedule, and instead of coming in on Saturday night, as had been the plan, the S. S. *Atlantic* steamed through the Narrows on Sunday when working New Yorkers had a day of rest, a fact which greatly augmented the crowds Barnum had tried earnestly to lure to the dock. In order to be the first to greet Jenny in America, Barnum had gone to Staten Island and spent the night at the home of his friend, Dr. Sidney Doane, the health officer for the Port of New York. No ships could enter the harbor without first passing Dr. Doane's inspection.

It was about 1 P.M. when a two-gun salute was heard from the direction of Sandy Hook, and immediately after that a flag signalling that a ship was approaching went up at the Telegraph Station below Clifton.

Jenny Lind, the Swedish Nightingale

The watchers on Staten Island soon sighted the S. S. *Atlantic,* a huge, amorphous bulk in the mist that still hovered over the entire bay. The Quarantine Station boasted no Swedish flag, so Dr. Doane ordered the Prussian tricolor run up instead, in tribute to the distinguished passenger. On passing the Narrows, the S. S. *Atlantic* fired a second salute, and stopping her paddles, came slowly in with the tide.

Dr. Doane, Barnum and a reporter for the New York *Tribune* jumped quickly into the Quarantine boat and were rowed out to the ship, Barnum carrying a huge bouquet of red roses. It was something of a feat to climb the rope ladder to the deck, and Barnum kept his bouquet intact by thrusting it down his shirt front.

Alas, he had been outsmarted! When Captain West led the men from the Quarantine boat to where Jenny stood, flanked by Benedict and Belletti, they found Mr. Collins, owner of the steamship line, in the act of presenting a bouquet to Jenny that the *Tribune* reporter said was three times the size of Barnum's. Exercising his prerogatives as owner, Mr. Collins had had himself put aboard at Sandy Hook. However, Jenny saluted Barnum cordially, and gave him a present in return for his roses. It was a fan that Queen Victoria had had made expressly for Jenny, of rare point lace with mother-of-pearl sticks. Woven in the lace was a delicate pattern of roses with two nightingales hovering over them, and on one of the end sticks was engraved "Jenny Lind." It was encased in a rosewood box with a glass top.

(Captain West also received a gorgeous gift from Jenny as soon as it could be made up to her order. It was a silver tankard, in the shape of a ship's capstan, surrounded by massive cables. On the front was an engraving of the S. S. *Atlantic* at sea, surmounted by clearing clouds and a horizon spanned by a rainbow, commemorating the rainbow Captain West had called Jenny to the bridge to see after the big storm. An eagle on the back was a copy of one on the stern of Captain West's vessel and a Triton on the lid represented the figurehead of the ship. The handle of the tankard was a sea serpent, as a reminder of their joke, with a spyglass in its mouth. A bundle of harpoons, with which to catch the serpent when sighted, formed the base of the handle. There was also a wreath of laurel, to which Jenny considered Captain West was entitled. The inscription read: "To Captain West in remembrance of his greatest friends, Jenny Lind, J. Benedict and G. Belletti.")

Departure and Arrival

Jenny was wearing a short coat called a "visite," of black cashmere, over a dress of silver-gray silk, a pale-blue silk hat and black veil. At her feet lay the Pekinese Queen Victoria had given her. The reporter had never seen a dog like it and, while describing it in detail, admitted that he had no idea what breed it was.

Jenny, he concluded, was rather more robust in face and person than her pictures would indicate. "Her forehead is finely formed, shaded by waves of pale brown hair, her eyes light blue and joyous, her nose and mouth, though moulded on the large Swedish type, convey the impression of benevolence and sound goodness of heart which is thoroughly in keeping with the many stories we have heard of her charitable doings. Her manners are very engaging and there is an expression of good humor in her eyes, which would win her the heart of a crowd by a single glance.

"Mr. Benedict, who is a German by birth, has a vigorous face with that expressive breadth of forehead which always marks a composer, and wears a thick brown moustache, as is becoming a musician. Signor Belletti, who is a Genoese, is a man of medium size, with rather thin but expressive features, dark hair and moustache."

As the S. S. *Atlantic* got under way again, Captain West invited the artists to take a station on the starboard paddle box, where, the *Tribune*'s account proceeded, they "could observe the beauties of our harbor without being inconvenienced by the crowd on the deck." (When *Punch* learned that Jenny had arrived in New York standing on the paddle box, having left Liverpool on the same vantage point, it concluded whimsically that she had spent the entire passage on the paddle box.) Jenny surveyed the shore through Captain West's spyglass. There were no tall buildings in that day to impress visitors from abroad, but Jenny declared that the New York City "bay" was the finest she had ever seen. The reporter said that Signor Belletti reiterated his joy at beholding the continent a countryman of his had discovered. Passing the Swedish vessel *Marea* in the harbor, Jenny waved vigorously to the sailors who crowded the rails, and the S. S. *Atlantic* fired a salute to the Swedish flag.

The Canal Street pier was covered with people and there were thirty thousand on West Street. "The spars and rigging of the vessels, the bulkheads along the wharves, and every other spot was crowded, while every tender at the Hoboken Street Ferry House was topped with a piece of

[177]

living statuary," said the *Tribune*. "Mademoiselle Lind, struck by the air of respectability which marked the thousands of people assembled, turned to Mr. Barnum and asked, 'Have you no poor people in your country? Everyone here appears to be so well dressed!' "

Conspicuous among the crowd were all of Barnum's employees, each dressed in black broadcloth and carrying a large bouquet of red roses. Barnum's men had also erected the bower of green branches on the dock, on one arch of which were the words "Welcome Jenny Lind," and on the other, "Welcome to America," adorned with the painting of an eagle. The whole pier, from landing area to the gates at the street, was decorated with American flags and red, white and blue bunting overhead, with the flags of other nations ranged on either side.

As soon as Jenny, her Pekinese under her arm, appeared at the top of the gangplank, escorted by Captain West, with Josephine Åhmansson, Benedict and Belletti following, the forward rush commenced. Several persons were pushed off the dock into the water, getting a "cold duck," as Barnum expressed it, "instead of a look at the Nightingale." The harbor police were kept busy fishing them out, but no one drowned. Farewells were said to Captain West and Jenny, Josephine, Benedict and Belletti got into Barnum's carriage which was waiting at the foot of the gangway. Barnum mounted to the driver's seat. He wrote in his memoirs, "I took that seat as a legitimate advertisement, and my presence on the outside of the carriage aided those who filled the windows and sidewalks along the whole route, in coming to the conclusion that Jenny Lind had arrived."

The crowd inside the gates immediately surrounded the carriage, "edging to the wheels and crowding around the windows," the *Tribune* said, "cheering all the while with an enthusiasm we never saw surpassed. The multitude outside began to press against the gates which were unbolted in all haste, to prevent being forced in. Scarcely had one gate been thrown back, however, before the torrent burst in with an energy frightful to witness. The other half of the gate instantly gave way, the planks snapping like reeds before the pressure. The foremast ranks were forced down upon the floor and those behind, urged on from without, were piled upon them until a serious loss of life seemed almost inevitable. The spectacle was most alarming; some forty or fifty persons lay crushed by the inexorable crowd, stretching out their hands and crying out for help." One man, on the bottom of the pile and hardly able to breathe, afforded a touch of comic relief by holding out his new hat at arm's length, imploring someone to take it and save it from being crushed.

The police, aided by civilian volunteers, succeeded in driving back the crowd and rescuing the victims. A good many bruises and bloody noses were sustained, and two twelve-year-old boys were hurt rather seriously, but recovered. Thanks to the prompt action of the police, there were no deaths or permanent injuries.

At last, Barnum was able to start his matched bays, and the crowd made way for the carriage, but filled it with flowers as Jenny passed by. More than two hundred bouquets were tossed through the windows. The rest of Jenny's party, with the luggage, followed in rented hacks.

The Irving House, where they were to stay, was America's most luxurious hotel, filling a whole block on Broadway from Chambers Street to Reade Street. Its bed chambers were adorned with carved woodwork, gold leaf, chandeliers decked with crystal pendants, and massive, carved, four-poster beds. Its bridal suite, which Barnum had reserved for Jenny, was the first of its kind in America. Five thousand people jammed the streets around the hotel, waiting for a glimpse of Jenny. But the police, alerted by the near riot at the dock, were already on hand and cleared a way to the entrance. Then the crowds stood with necks craned upward, speculating as to which of the windows might be Jenny's. They cheered and called her name until she appeared at one of the parlor windows and waved.

It was estimated that a good ten thousand people remained massed along Broadway and Ann Street throughout the afternoon and evening. The New York *Herald* reported that about dusk, several ladies appeared on the balcony, but it was too dark to tell whether Jenny was among them. "The crowd, however, imagined she was there, and that was sufficient for them. One of the ladies, after eating a peach, threw the stone over the balcony, when a tremendous rush took place to secure what was presumed to be a precious memento of the fair songstress, and a regular street fight nearly ensued."

At midnight, two hundred members of the Musical Fund Society marched up, escorted by three hundred firemen in red flannel shirts, gray helmets, black pants and boots, carrying torches. They called for Jenny so insistently that Barnum led her out onto the balcony. She was given a serenade which began with "Hail Columbia" and ended with "Yankee Doodle." Barnum recorded that Jenny kept time to the music, clapping at the end of each number.

"Is this your American folk music?" she asked Barnum, after "Yankee Doodle."

"I presume it is," he replied. The truth was that the man who had brought the Swedish Nightingale across the ocean, was tone-deaf, could not tell one tune from another, and had not the least idea what Jenny meant by folk music.

When Belletti said goodnight to Jenny, she was exhausted but still in the gay mood with which she had started the day. "Do you believe now that the Americans will like you?"

Jenny threw her arms about the Italian's neck and danced him around the room. "It has been like Liverpool!" she exclaimed. "I did not think that ever again there could be anything like Liverpool!"

It was late when P. T. Barnum got to bed that night, if indeed he made it at all. The papers had to be given full accounts of the voyage over, and of the leave-taking in Liverpool, to run with their stories of the arrival. The New York *Sun* published the entire program of the shipboard concerts, and the New York *Herald*'s description of the performance could hardly have been more realistic if the writer had been there and heard it.

There was another matter demanding immediate attention. It had been decided that the first concert would be held September 11, and the prize song had to be selected quickly from the 753 entries, so that Benedict could set it to music. That very night Barnum got off a letter to Mr. Redfield, the committee's chairman, calling attention to the urgency of the situation and imploring the committee to get to work at once. There was a postscript: "Mr. Benedict says, go ahead and make your selections, then let him read ten or twenty of the best and he will join you in deciding. He is busy every moment."

The postscript hinted at an uncomfortable session when Barnum had tackled his task of telling Benedict about the project which had been set in motion in the composer's name. Faced with a *fait accompli*, Benedict obviously had decided he must go along, but as obviously had balked at reading 753 pieces of alleged poetry.

Barnum pointed out to reporters the magnitude of the task facing the committee, and this alone ensured daily stories recording the progress of the committee as the members made their way through the mass of drivel. Could they possibly finish in less than a week? By superhuman efforts they could and did, and on September 5 the papers carried a triumphant announcement, signed by all the members of the committee, to the effect that the choice had been made, and that when the sealed envelope accompanying the prize song was opened, it was found to contain the name of Bayard Taylor.

In 1850, that name had as yet acquired faint luster. Bayard Taylor was then twenty-five years old and a reporter on the staff of the New York *Tribune*. An aspiring poet, he had a single slim volume of poems to his credit, *Ximena*, or *the Battle of the Sierra Morena* which had been published in 1844 and had attracted little attention. He and his great friend, Richard Henry Stoddard, had entered the contest solely because they needed the prize money rather desperately. When his poem won, Taylor worried lest its mediocre quality might hurt such small literary reputation as *Ximena* had brought him, remarking to Stoddard two months later, "Is that damned song to be the only thing that will save my name from oblivion?"

He may well have worried, for the song, plentifully sprinkled with capital letters in the style of the day, read as follows:

GREETING TO AMERICA

'Tis said that in silence the heart must reveal
    What the faltering lip to its pleading denies,
When the warmth of its beating we may not conceal
    And grateful emotion is soft in the eyes.
But silence itself, in the region of Song,
    Is Music made sweeter and purer in tone,
And the minstrel whose hopes to that region belong,
    Must *feel* in its beautiful language alone.

I greet, with full heart, the Land of the West,
    Whose Banner of Stars o'er a world is unrolled;
Whose empire o'ershadows Atlantic's wide breast,

And opes to the sunset its gateway of gold!
The land of the mountain, the land of the lake,
And rivers that roll in magnificent tide—
Where the souls of the mighty from slumber awake,
And hallow the soil for whose freedom they died!

Thou Cradle of Empire! though wide be the foam
That severs the land of my fathers and thee,
I hear, from thy bosom, the welcome of home,
For Song has a home in the hearts of the Free!
And long as thy waters shall gleam in the sun,
And long as thy heroes remember their scars,
Be the hands of thy children united as one,
And Peace shed her light on thy Banner of Stars!

It was Jenny, in fact, who had made the final selection, out of the
"ten or twenty best" requested by Benedict, and she had chosen Bayard
Taylor's poem because it was the shortest. At that, she sang only two
of the three stanzas.

And this was not the end of the Prize Song Contest. As soon as the
winner was announced, the losers cried "foul" because one of the judges,
G. P. Putnam, had published Bayard Taylor's book of poems and another,
George Ripley, was a fellow staff member with Taylor on the *Tribune*.
D. Appleton and Company, the book publishers, quickly brought out a
pamphlet by William Allen Butler, author of the poem "Nothing to
Wear," entitled *Barnum's Parnassus—Confidential Disclosures of the
Jenny Lind Prize Committee*, which consisted of more or less witty
parodies of the song.

The *Evening Mirror* poked fun throughout the whole affair. It printed
daily a chapter of what it called "Barnum's Jenny-sis," the one on September 5 beginning, "Today we commence the 5th Chapter of the New
Book of Jenny-sis. . . . The Song Committee have awarded the prize of
200 dollars to Bayard Taylor who deserves, in addition to the money,
which is a mere bagatelle, to be called 'The Chevalier Bayard.' " Chapter
VI of the New Jenny-sis read, "We understand that the actual number
of songs sent to Mr. Barnum's Committee-men was 753, and that seven
hundred and fifty-two persons have been heard to express great indignation at the decision of the Committee."

Jules Benedict grudgingly provided some music for Bayard's effusion,
wondering the while what his hastily composed setting to a hastily writ-

ten hack poem would do to his reputation in Europe. (It is pleasant to record that both the poet and the composer survived this incident, the Prize Song constituting no blot upon their subsequent careers and fame.)

P. T. Barnum was gleeful. His $200 prize money had brought him many thousands of dollars' worth of publicity and the publicity would go on as long as the protests and controversy and parodies continued. He chuckled at the memory of one parody, which tickled him particularly:

> So, Jenny, come along! You're just the card for me.
>   If you'll quit these kings and queens for the country of the free,
> They'll welcome you with speeches, and serenades and rockets,
>   And you will touch their hearts, and I will tap their pockets;
> And if, between us both the public isn't skinned,
>   Why, my name isn't Barnum, nor your name Jenny Lind!

Barnum bought thousands of copies of *Parnassus* and had his agents distribute them free of charge.

CHAPTER ELEVEN

"Barnum Is Nowhere"

THE MORNING following Jenny's arrival, she was waited upon by Caleb Woodhull, the Mayor of New York, and other notables, after which Jenny and Barnum had some business to transact. Maunsell Field, a New York attorney, had scarcely reached his office that morning when a messenger arrived with a letter for Mr. Field's partner, John Jay, asking him to call on Jenny at the Irving House. He had been recommended by Baring Brothers of London. Since Mr. Jay was abroad, Mr. Field went instead. Barnum met him in the lobby, which was so crowded with the curious that the guests and employes could hardly get through it. The showman led the way to Jenny's drawing room, exclaiming en route, "I am going to introduce you to an angel, sir, to an angel!" When the singer appeared, wearing a short-sleeved summer dress with low neck, Mr. Field thought she looked pretty substantial for an angel. Indeed, both the daguerreotype Jenny had had taken for Anna Marie in England and one made of her in Philadelphia that fall, show her as almost buxom.

It developed that Jenny had come to America without a formal contract, only the memorandum drawn up in Europe. The three sat down together and had no difficulty in arriving at terms satisfactory to both principals. Thereafter Maunsell Field and his partner, John Jay, were Jenny's legal representatives in the United States.

On Tuesday, Jenny and Barnum, accompanied by Benedict, Belletti, and Josephine Åhmansson, set out in Barnum's carriage to select a hall for the concerts. Whatever doubts Barnum might have entertained originally about the success of his enterprise had been dispelled by Jenny's reception. The only thing remaining was to find a suitable auditorium that at the same time would be big enough to hold all the people who would want to hear her sing. In spite of a drizzle, crowds pressed about the carriage and half a dozen vehicles followed it, forming what one paper called a "royal procession" from one amusement hall to another.

The first stop was at Tripler's Hall, on the west side of Broadway, opposite Bond Street. A. B. Tripler had begun the building in late summer, hoping to have it ready for Jenny's concerts, but there had been delays and the party learned that the hall would not be finished for several weeks.

Some of the larger theaters were visited next, and finally they reached Castle Garden, the huge auditorium set out in the water 200 feet beyond Battery Park, at the foot of Broadway.

The park had been the site of the first fort built for the protection of New Amsterdam. Dutch burghers had played bowls on the greensward, which had been a common then. Now it was planted thickly with elms and poplars, laid out with many shady walks and surrounded on the land side by a handsome iron fence. A sea wall extended along the water front, from which was presented a beautiful view of the harbor.

Battery Park contained the City Hall, built early in the century at a cost of $538,734, considered the finest building in New York and one of the finest in the country. Other public buildings were the Hall of Records and the Rotunda, formerly the Post Office, but now occupied by the Department of Alms Houses. The park's most spectacular feature, however, was a fountain which had a basin 100 feet in diameter, and a variety of jets which allowed constant changes in the fountain's play. When thrown upward in a single stream, the water rose to a height of 70 feet. The favorite promenade of all New York was from Trinity Church, around the Battery and back on the east side of Broadway. The neighboring streets, Chatham, Chambers and Centre, were entirely residential.

Castle Garden, connected with Battery Park by a bridge, was the largest amusement place in the city. Jenny, Benedict and Belletti went up onto the stage, took turns at speaking and singing a bit, and were pleased both with the size of the auditorium and its acoustics. It was agreed that Castle Garden would be the best place for the concerts.

The next day was given over to sightseeing. As their carriage swung up Broadway, which was the principal street, Barnum explained to the musicians that the Irving House was on the "fifty-cent" side of the street, where the fashionable and more expensive shops were located, while the opposite side was the "shilling" side for the more common trade. However, in 1848, A. T. Stewart had raised the status of the shilling side considerably by erecting a magnificent marble building at Chambers Street and Broadway, and opening the largest department store in the world. The fifty-cent side now depended largely for its prestige on a wide walk, which was a favorite evening promenade for the beaux and belles of the town.

The party's first stop was at Barnum's Great American Museum, at the corner of Broadway and Ann Street. The three Europeans were introduced to the famous "Feejee Maid," the "cherry-colored cat," and similar oddities, and saw the "lecture room," where an aging actor named Levy Lyman, under the name of "Dr. Griffin," discoursed on many subjects, and moral lessons were driven home through plays such as *The Drunkard* and dramas based on Bible stories. And there was the famous door bearing the sign, "This Way to the Egress." Barnum explained, chuckling, that it was another of his little ideas, a device for clearing the museum to let another group in. The customers would go through the door, expecting still another marvel, and instead find themselves in the street.

It was perhaps as well that the contract had been signed the day before, for this was a far cry from Buckingham Palace and the sort of entertainment Jenny had been used to. She must have wondered whether Chevalier Wyckoff had been right in forecasting that she would be classed with these fakes.

The carriage went past the Astor House, the swank hotel on Broadway between Barclay and Vesey Streets; Brady's Gallery, advertised as the best deguerreotype studio in town, where "miniatures," as deguerreotypes were called in 1850, might be had for $1 to $5. But Brady advised in his advertisements that "none that are really good can be obtained for less than three or four dollars." Barnum pulled the horses to a halt near Pearl Street, where the great fire of 1835 had started. He described how the fire, the worst in America up to that time, had burned out a wide circle around Hanover Square. The flames had consumed hundreds of residences, along with shops and the warehouses of importers, with their bales of costly silks, laces and other fine merchandise. The damage had been estimated at $20,000,000. But it proved to be a blessing in disguise, for the old two- and three-story buildings had been replaced by substantial ones four and five stories high. There was even talk nowadays of carrying office and store buildings and the like up considerably higher than that, since the granite rock of which the island was made afforded firm footing for the most ambitious architectural schemes.

Barnum continued with a tour of the choice residence districts, at that time clustering about the Battery. On State Street were the fine houses of Moses Rogers and Archibald Gracie, while Greenwich Street, for two or three blocks north of the park, was known as "Millionaires' Row." Here were the town residences of Brockholst Livingston, John Johnston, Robert Lenox, Adam Norris and others of the city's leading merchants. On the east side of the city, along Wall, Pine, Hanover Square, Pearl and Cherry Streets, were the homes of many other well-known families. The Walton house on Pearl Street was considered the most luxurious and handsome residence in the United States. But New York City now had a population of a little more than half a million, and society was moving uptown a bit. Union Square and 14th Street had become a fashionable district, and Henry C. de Rham had recently paid $57,000 for the Brevoort mansion at Fifth Avenue and Ninth Street.

Jenny was impressed more by the air of growth and progress in the city than by its buildings, for she had seen far finer ones, but she viewed everything with interest. Presently she asked, "Where are the alms-houses?"

"Why should you want to go to those places?"

"To help, of course."

Tuesday was the end of idling. Benedict had to audition the musicians for the sixty-piece orchestra he was to conduct at the first concert eight days away. It was said that Jenny often listened in too, and gave her opinion. Nearly all the orchestra members were chosen, in the end, from the New York Philharmonic Society.

It appeared that the to-do over the prize song might have been super-fluous, for scarcely had Jenny walked down the gangplank of the S. S. *Atlantic* than tradesmen were paying their own good money to get her name in the papers, in advertisements of their wares. Such as, "Jenny Lind's here! Eat at our famous dining-salon!" "She's arrived! So have our new umbrellas!" Delmonico's began at once to feature Jenny Lind dishes. The Jenny Lind pancake, first served at this "famous food empo-rium" as Barnum called it, survived on the menus of a number of New York restaurants for many years. Women started parting their hair in the middle and rolling it smoothly over their ears, in the style Jenny had worked out for controlling her own very fine, ash-blond hair.

Maunsell Field accompanied Jenny to her first rehearsal at Castle Garden and found that Battery Park, all eleven acres of it, was one dense mass of humanity, gathered to see Jenny go into the Garden and come out again. After the rehearsal, Jenny took Field's arm to return to the carriage, which had been left standing opposite the Bowling Green. "Immediately after we had made our exit from Castle Garden, the crowd pressed upon us so wildly that the police had difficulty in forcing a passage for us," said Field. "Some endeavored to press petitions for charity into her hand, and the only object of others was to satisfy their curiosity by gazing into her face. Never before or since has New York witnessed such a furor as the advent of Jenny Lind produced."

The rehearsals, too, were reported in the press. The *Tribune's* critic, in what would be called nowadays a sneak preview, said, "We went there by no means prejudiced in her favor. We have returned another man. . . . She completely disarmed us of criticism. . . . In the trio concertante with two flutes and voice (the famous trio from *Camp in Silesia*), the orchestra *came to a dead stop.* They had been listening to the vocalist and forgot their parts."

Still Barnum was not satisfied. He had realized early that the fabulous sum he was paying Jenny would in itself arouse great interest, but would also set people wondering if it would not send the price of tickets beyond their reach. A week before Jenny was to arrive, Barnum announced that in order to give all who wanted to hear Jenny an equal chance, the tickets would be sold at public auction, starting at the nominal price of $3.00 per ticket.

From that moment, the newspapers speculated as to what price the tickets would command. "It is every man's business to exercise the greatest possible foresight whereby his calling can, in an honest way, be made most profitable," Barnum wrote with engaging frankness in an article in the October, 1887, issue of *Cosmopolitan Magazine*. "I clearly foresaw what effect this auction sale of Jenny Lind tickets would necessarily have in the existing excited state of the public minds; and that the higher the prices obtained, the more would the frenzy be increased."

The auction was to be held at Castle Garden the Saturday preceding the first concert on Wednesday. In his article in *Cosmopolitan*, Barnum revealed that he was responsible for the fact that John N. Genin, who had a hat store at 214 Broadway, only two doors away from the American Museum, won undying fame by buying the first ticket to Jenny Lind's first concert in America.

Barnum went to see Genin the Hatter and suggested to him under promise of secrecy that if he were to bid up the first Jenny Lind ticket, it would give him thousands of dollars' worth of advertising. "And the higher the price paid, the greater renown it will give you all over the country within twenty-four hours after the purchase!"

Genin, who according to Barnum was a "good advertiser," seized the idea and Barnum's hand simultaneously, "You have made my future! This is one chance in a lifetime. I will send my bookkeeper to buy the first Jenny Lind ticket, but I will not mention it, even to my wife, till I have secured it."

Since Genin, good advertiser though he was, had not seen for himself the great opportunities for publicity offered by winning the auction, Barnum feared that the other New York businessmen would miss the point, too, and the bidding would not be very high. So he called on Dr. Brandreth, reputed to be a quack but described in Barnum's article as "the great pill maker and a tremendous advertiser," and asked for a private interview.

"The doctor invited me into his office, and, locking the door, pointed to an easy arm-chair and then said in a low voice, 'Friend Barnum, what is up?'

" 'A mighty big thing for *you*,' I replied, 'If you will keep it a profound secret for three days.'

"The doctor's eyes sparkled with delight as he squeezed my hand and said: 'My dear Barnum, I pledge my honor not to divulge it to a living being till you say the word.'

" 'Buy the first Jenny Lind ticket at auction, even if you have to pay high for it,' I replied, 'and let every newspaper in America and Europe announce that Dr. Brandreth, Jr., the maker of the celebrated Brandreth Pills, secured the first Jenny Lind ticket at fifty or one hundred dollars, as the case may be.' "

At first, all Brandreth could see in this suggestion was a trick on the part of Barnum to run up the price of the tickets for his own advantage. After arguing for several minutes, Barnum remarked prophetically, "Doctor Brandreth, I have long admired your ingenious methods of advertising Brandreth Pills. But if you can't see the value to your business of my suggestion, I beg to say you will surely regret it when that first Jenny Lind ticket falls into other hands."

Eventually he led Brandreth to realize that there could be no better boost for his pills than a link with Jenny Lind, and the pill maker said, "I thank you for the hint, Mr. Barnum. Perhaps twenty or thirty dollars expended for the first ticket would not be a bad investment. I will send my cashier to the auction, with instructions to make a liberal bid."

More than three thousand people attended the auction, each one paying the lessees of Castle Garden the usual charge of a shilling (twelve and one-half cents) for the privilege of crossing the bridge from Battery Park. Genin was represented by his bookkeeper, Brandreth by his cashier, neither being aware that Barnum had confided his suggestion to anyone else. Brandreth's cashier started the bidding at $25, which was answered by a bid of $50 from Genin's bookkeeper. From then on the auction was entirely a contest between the two, the audience cheering every time a new, higher bid was announced. But when Genin's agent awed audience and auctioneer alike by calling out the undreamed of sum of $225, there was silence from the Brandreth sector. After the auctioneer had recited his "Going, going, gone," he asked "Who was the lucky purchaser?"

"John N. Genin the Hatter!" cried the bookkeeper in stentorian tones.

"The multitude seemed thunderstruck at first," Barnum recalled, "but in an instant there went up 'Three cheers for Genin the Hatter!' which were distinctly heard on the mainland and reverberated around the world."

Genin told Barnum later that he had instructed his bookkeeper to bid as high as $1,000, if necessary. "After that, I told him he might use his own discretion, knowing as he did how my bank account stood."

All befell as Barnum had predicted. Brandreth mourned that he had told his cashier to stop at $200, not dreaming that anyone else would bid half that. "I had better have paid $5,000 than to have missed securing the first Jenny Lind ticket. Such a splendid chance for notoriety will never offer itself again."

The next day the name of John N. Genin the Hatter appeared all over America wherever a daily was printed. In Dubuque, Iowa, twenty or thirty men were waiting in the Post Office for the arrival of the newspaper which would tell who had won the auction for the first Jenny Lind ticket. When the paper came, one of the men read aloud to the others, "The first Jenny Lind ticket sold for $225 to Genin the Hatter."

"Genin the Hatter!" the name was chorused after him. Somebody called out, "Say, anyone here got a Genin hat?" The men pulled off their hats to look for the maker's label, and sure enough, the stamp of J. N. Genin was found in a battered old felt not worth fifty cents. The others solemnly shook hands with the owner, congratulating him. Someone had another idea. "Let's auction it off!" The owner being willing, this was done, and it was knocked down for $7.50.

The *Times* of London gave nearly two columns to the auction and the other Jenny Lind excitement in America and suggested that Mr. Genin's seat at the first concert should have a huge hat suspended over it so that the hero of the hour might be recognized by the audience. As a matter of fact, the night of the concert the ushers were asked by nearly every ticket holder, "Which is Genin's seat?"

Genin was acquiring so much kudos through his $225 investment that a rival hatter, Charles Knox, whose store was located at 128 Fulton Street, evidently felt he had better put out some counter propaganda.

He inserted an ad in the newspapers which stated, "There is no truth in the assertion that Knox the Hatter paid $225 for the choice seat at Jenny Lind's first concert. Knox can't afford it; and it must have been done by some Broadway Hatter, who sells a poor article at a high price, as Knox is contented with very small profits. His Fall style of Hats is the admiration of Everybody."

A Genin hat became the prestige symbol for the American male. Every New Yorker wanted one, and visitors to the city made it a point to take Genin hats back home with them. Winning the auction made John N. Genin a rich man. And the glory lingered on. Twenty years after the first Jenny Lind concert, a friend of Barnum's, George Augustus Sala, the famous correspondent for the London *Daily Telegraph*, came to New York. Barnum called on him at the Brevoort House and took him for a ride through Central Park in his sleigh. "On the way, I called at the house of Mr. Genin in Fourteenth Street, and invited him to join us. As we rode through the park, engaged in pleasant conversation on numerous topics, Mr. Sala said: 'By the way, Mr. Barnum, what became of that man Geenin the Hatter, who bought the first Jenny Lind ticket at auction?' "

Genin and Barnum were convulsed with laughter, Barnum exclaiming to his friend, "You can see how immense the value was of that ticket purchase when a leading London newspaper man remembers you after twenty years, simply missing the usual pronounciation of your name." Genin replied that he was quite satisfied.

"And well he might be," Barnum ended his article in that 1887 issue of *Cosmopolitan*, "for it made his fortune and identified him with the history of a musical enterprise, the unparalled receipts of which were seven hundred and twelve thousand one hundred and sixty one dollars and thirty-four cents, for ninety-five concerts given within a period of eight months." Barnum was still publicizing Jenny Lind, thirty-seven years after her trip to America.

By the morning of the concert, every ticket has been sold, either at the auction or at the regular prices, ranging from five dollars to ten dollars for seats, and three dollars to five dollars for standees or "promenaders," as they were called.

Barnum was equally foresighted and thorough in his arrangements for the concert itself. He had used tricks and dodges to stir up public interest, but Jenny need not have worried about being personally cheapened. Her impresario was determined that his prize should be presented with the dignity her fame and character called for. Though an immense crowd filled Battery Park and clustered around the gates of the bridge leading over to Castle Garden, there was no disorder. The chief of police in person arrived at five o'clock with sixty of his force, who formed a double row extending from the gates of the bridge to the Battery grounds. (In that day, all New York City policemen wore civilian clothes. For some years to come, attempts of the authorities to get them into uniform were met with an indignant, "No self-respecting American would wear livery!") Other policemen directed traffic, and a system of one-way streets was instituted. Carriages could go only one way on Whitehall, to the gates of the bridge. On discharging their passengers they had to turn off into Battery Park. When Jenny's carriage arrived few people knew of it, and she got to her dressing room without creating any great excitement, though by dusk the line of carriages extended up State Street and into Broadway.

There was no hint of the "Jenny Lind crush" which had been a feature at Her Majesty's Theatre in London throughout Jenny's three seasons there. The doors were opened at five o'clock, though the concert did not begin until eight. The brilliantly lighted bridge, over which Barnum had an awning extended, restricted the number of men in Prince Albert coats and white ties, and the scattering of elaborately gowned ladies, who could approach the doors at one time. The great auditorium was divided into four sections, each designated by a lamp of different color. The tickets and even the seat numbers were printed in the color of the particular section, and the twenty-five ushers assigned to each section wore rosettes and carried wands in their section color. Thus the vast audience was seated with a minimum of confusion, and, we are told, behaved itself very well.

The only discordant note came from a gang of hoodlums in boats on the water behind the Garden, who yelled and shouted, to the accompaniment of drums and fifes, and at one point tried to force their way into the auditorium. The police had no way of getting at them, and the *Tribune* pointed out that the incident illustrated the city's need for river police. "If such a force had been in existence, this attempt could not have been made." Before long, New York City had river police.

John Sullivan Dwight, America's most scholarly music critic, whom the New York *Tribune* had brought down from Boston to cover the first concert, thought that P. T. Barnum had done very well with the arrangements and decorations, considering the brief time he had had to work in. In place of the usual drop curtain at the back of the stage, there were painted replicas of the flags of America and Sweden, above arabesque ornaments in white and gold to match the piano, of San Domingo mahogany enameled in ivory touched with gold. Barnum announced that the instrument had been made especially for Jenny Lind's use by Chickering of Boston, and had cost $5,000. It was to accompany Jenny on all her tours, and "the makers have agreed that no duplicate of it will be turned out while it is in use by Jenny Lind."

The only evidence of bad taste observed by Mr. Dwight was a large sign, "Welcome, Sweet Warbler!" worked in flowers and suspended over the pillars of the balcony directly facing the stage. Mr. Dwight did not consider this quite fitting.

The program was an impressive booklet of twenty-eight pages, full of advertisements, which the ushers sold for twenty-five cents a copy, so that it probably brought in some revenue too. The front cover carried pictures of Jenny, Benedict, Belletti and Barnum, and inside were biographical sketches of the four. The back cover was given over to an ad for Hutchings Vegetable Dyspepsia Bitters—"the most popular family medicine of the age! These bitters remove all morbid secretions, purify the system against all future diesease. . . . Also cure liver complaints, jaundice, costiveness, heartburn, faintness, disorders of the skin, liver and kidneys; loss of appetite, low spirits, nervous headaches, giddiness, palpitation of the heart. . . . Especially recommended for females who suffer from a morbid and unnatural condition." Just *what* morbid and unnatural condition was left to the imagination of the reader.

The musical program was substantial and interesting as well. It began with the Overture to Weber's *Oberon*, played by the sixty-piece orchestra with Benedict conducting. Belletti next sang the Sorgete from *Mahomet the Prophet*, one of Rossini's most elaborate and difficult arias. There was a hush, then Benedict appeared, leading Jenny by the hand. Dressed in white, except for a blue belt adorned with small flowers, she came down the stage with her graceful, gliding walk.

"It is impossible to describe the spontaneous burst of welcome which greeted her," wrote the New York *Tribune*'s guest critic. "The vast assembly rose as one man. [Mr. Dwight had previously commented on the remarkable fact that not more than an eighth of the audience were ladies. "They must stay at home, it seems, when the tickets are high, but the gentlemen go nevertheless."] For some minutes nothing could be seen but the waving of hands and handkerchiefs, nothing heard but a storm of tumultuous cheers."

For her first number Jenny had chosen to sing "Casta diva," the challenging Chaste Goddess solo from *Norma*. Her voice seemed to tremble a bit at first, but soon was under complete mastery. Mr. Dwight commented that "every soprano lady has sung it ["Casta diva] to us; but nearly everyone has seemed only trying to make something of it, while Jenny Lind *was* the very music of it for the time being." He went on to say that Americans had never heard tones of such consummate sweetness and a voice so pure, so sweet, so fine, so whole and all-pervading that it was impossible to describe.

After the "Casta diva," Benedict and Richard Hoffman played a duet by Thalberg on two pianos. Young Hoffman thought the applause given them at the end was chiefly because they had quit playing. "If we had essayed an encore in response, I feel sure a mobbing or a lynching would have followed," he wrote in describing the memorable affair. The audience wanted Jenny and clapped its approval when she came on next with Belletti to sing the duet from Rossini's "Il Turco in Italia," "How Shall I Please the Lady Fair?"

It was during the intermission following that the hoodlums on the water side of the Garden tried to force an entrance, the police beating them off with a good deal of noise and shouting on both sides.

Calm was restored as the orchestra played the overture to Benedict's own opera *The Crusader*. And now Jenny sang the famous trio with two flutes from *Camp in Silesia*, which could always be counted on to dazzle an audience, for it required an expert ear indeed to tell which of the flutelike sounds was Jenny's. Then Belletti sang "Largo al Factotum," the rollicking Figaro song from the *Barber of Seville*, a role in which Belletti was supreme among baritones of the day.

After that a lengthy pause, with the rustlings and whisperings of the audience subsiding as it waited for what had been rumored would be the supreme event of the evening—Jenny's Scandinavian folk songs, in which she always accompanied herself, and which were unique with her.

Jenny Lind, the Swedish Nightingale

At length Jenny came on again, seated herself at the ornate piano and began to sing the words so familiar to her, "Fjerran i skog," (Far in the woods") the opening phase of "The Herdsman's Song" composed by her old music master, Izak Berg. It was a simple and plaintive air, and the words were equally simple, the English translation being:

> Far in the woods,
>   Parted from thee,
> Thy image fair
>   Still dwells with me.
>
> So let the horn breathe
>   My secret to thee:
> Death for my love
>   Hath no terror for me.

The feature of this song was a high note in the last stanza which became gradually pianissimo until it could no longer be heard. In the complete quiet, the audience would sit motionless, scarcely breathing. Then the soft note would be heard again, swelling in volume until the walls would seem to vibrate with it. Jenny would repeat the stanza, and the song always brought a tremendous response.

Next came the "Norwegian Echo Song, Kom hyra, kom hyra, kom alla di unerli dyra" ("Come hither, come hither, my pretty herd"), a quaint wild melody that swung from high to low and depended on an odd musical interval, a sharp seventh, for the echo effect.

> Come hither, come hither, come hither!
>   Hoah, hoah, hoah!
> Come cow, come calf and weanling brood
>   Come all my cattle dear!
> And the smith come forth
>   With hammer tongs
> To put the brand on the animal
>   For so will the sheriff have it done.
> Hoah, hoah, hoah!
>   Come all ye my poor dear!
>
> The sun is setting behind the hills
>   And shadows are lengthening;
> The night will soon close in
>   And hold us in its lap.
> The pot is on the fire
>   And to the Alp I wend my way.

The herdsman's calls and the leaping melody gave opportunity for all manner of variations, and Jenny never sang it twice the same way. The coda, with the echo, was unaccompanied. At this point Jenny would turn from the piano, facing the audience, so that the echo would play back and forth across the hall, with what Richard Hoffman described as an effect of ventriloquism. At the end she would turn slowly back to the piano and strike a final D chord as the echo faded away on the D below the line. At the close of this part of the program, the audience clapped and cheered until Jenny repeated the charming folk songs.

Then she returned for her last number, the much publicized "Greeting to America." It was listed on the program as "The Celebrated Prize National Song as sung by Mademoiselle Jenny Lind at her first concert in America. The poem written by Bayard Taylor, Esq." Another tumult of applause, and Jenny stepped forward for a final curtsy, then left the stage and did not appear again in spite of the continued clapping.

Now it was Barnum's turn. When a lull came in the demonstration, the ushers, as previously instructed, began calling "Barnum! Barnum! where's Mr. Barnum?" The cry was taken up by the audience, and Barnum stepped to the front of the stage, perspiration streaming down his face, his collar wilted.

"My friends, you have heard it asked, 'Where's Barnum?' Henceforth you might say, 'Barnum's nowhere!'"

Just what Barnum meant by this remark is not quite clear, but it was received by the audience with laughter and applause. He went on to say that even though Mademoiselle Lind had asked him not to do so, he could not refrain from letting the audience know that she had promised to give her entire share of the earnings of this concert to charity, and that her share amounted to $10,000. There was wild applause and cheering.

Barnum says in his memoirs that the next day there were one hundred businessmen in New York City who would have given him $200,000 for Jenny's contract. He was importuned to part with a fourth, an eighth, a sixteenth part in this miraculous new source of wealth, but he refused all offers. Barnum stated flatly that he had assumed the whole risk; he was going to take all the rewards.

Nothing less than a commemorative medal would satisfy him as a memento of the tremendous success of his daring venture, and he had one struck at once. One side showed Jenny's head in profile, with her name underneath—borrowed from the medal made in Jenny's honor in

Vienna, without a by-your-leave. On the reverse side were the words: "First concert in America. Proceeds $35,000. At Castle Garden, New York, September 11, 1850. Attended by 7,000 people. Twelve thousand five hundred dollars given by Miss Lind to charitable institutions."

The medals, with their somewhat inflated statistics, were sold by the hundreds in hotel lobbies and by sidewalk vendors. But Barnum made it a point to present a medal, in person, to every banker and businessman who had refused to lend him money when he was trying to scrape up the $187,500.

CHAPTER TWELVE

Benevolent Lady

BARNUM'S announcement signalized a change in his arrangement with Jenny. The auction on Saturday had alone brought in more than $10,000, and the complete sellout indicated that the profit on the first concert, after expenses, would come to $20,000. (This did not include the profit, never divulged, made by ticket speculators, who appeared on the New York City scene for the first time when it became obvious that people would pay any price to hear Jenny Lind. They flourished throughout Jenny's New York run, and ticket speculators have been a fixture in the city ever since.)

As soon as Jenny heard this, she asked that her arrangement with Barnum be reconsidered, though she said she realized that her contract was legally binding, and that she would hold to it if Barnum insisted. He listened attentively, then told her to tear up that contract and have her lawyer draw up another according to her dictation, naming for her services whatever she thought fair. "I will sign it without hesitation." Maunsell Field was sent for and a new contract was drawn up on the spot.

Jenny and Maunsell Field agreed that the move to change the contract came from her. In his memoirs, Barnum says he volunteered the change, and his biographer, M. R. Werner, ponders on the childish vanity Barnum revealed in so doing. The promoter had in fact acted most magnanimously, and when it was found that the profits only amounted to some $17,000, a number of bidders at the auction having failed to pick up their expensive tickets, Barnum gave Jenny $10,000, taking the loss himself. At the same time, in his memoirs he distinctly disclaimed any noble impulses for his actions. "Let it not be supposed that the increase in her compensation was wholly an act of generosity on my part. I had become convinced that there was money enough in the enterprise for all of us."

Under the new contract, Jenny was not only to receive $1,000 per concert and all her expenses, regardless of the receipts, as had been previously agreed, but after Barnum had taken out $5,000 per concert for his expenses and services, any profit remaining was to be divided between them equally.

Barnum made just one condition. He asked that Jenny hire someone to look after her interests at the box office, and to be present when Le-Grand Smith, Barnum's right-hand man, counted the receipts, now that she was a partner in the enterprise. Jenny demurred at first at the idea of checking up on Barnum, but he would have it no other way. Charles Seyton, the young Scot who had become friendly on shipboard with Jenny's secretary, Max Hjortzberg, was given the job. (Eventually, Seyton became a well-known businessman in New York, a member of the brokerage firm of Seyton and Wainwright.) After the new arrangement was completed, Jenny said to Barnum, with emotion, "You are so good to me, I will sing for you anywhere, at any time."

Barnum had the twelve-page contract, written by hand on both sides of the paper, placed in a heavy gilt frame, but in such a way that he could take it out whenever he wanted to prove that his behavior toward Jenny had been open-handed to an extreme.

However, the rewards were by no means financial only. Barnum had attained his original aim of having his name associated with the highest in art and culture. Next day the New York *Herald* cited Jenny Lind as proof that "the wand of civilization" had passed to the hardy northern races, adding that to have Jenny in America was "as significant an event as it would to be to have Dante, Tasso, Raphael, Shakespeare, Goethe, or Michael Angelo appear among us."

The other critics vied with each other in producing high-flown, extravagant tributes to her voice, artistry and character. Even the prize song was described as "having a soul in it, coming from those lips," and the *Tribune* declared that the "national songs"—the folk songs and "Greeting to America"—had been the favorites of the evening.

The *Evening Mirror*, whose attitude toward Jenny Lind, Barnum, and the prize song in particular had been conspicuously irreverent up to this point, said of the concert, "It would be useless to attempt to convey any idea of the effect, and therefore we shall not do so; nor will we venture to offer anything like a criticism of the performance, we can only subscribe to the opinions that have been expressed of her in Europe, that she is the most extraordinary vocalist that has been heard, in the present age at least. . . . Her last effort was the Prize Song, which has been set to pretty though rather commonplace music; but she sang it with so much spirit and feeling that even had it possessed no merit, she would have insured its success and popularity."

Holden's Magazine exhorted its readers to "Sell your old clothes, dispose of your antiquated boots, hypothecate your jewelry, come on the canal, work your passage, walk, take up a collection to pay expenses, raise money on a mortgage, sell 'Tom' into perpetual slavery, dispose of 'Bose' to the highest bidder, stop smoking for a year, give up tea, coffee and sugar, dispense with bread, meat, garden sass and such like luxuries— whatever you must to get the needful change—and then come and hear Jenny Lind!"

Among those who took the advice was Washington Irving. Sixty-seven now, and with a dislike of crowds as great as Jenny's own, he nevertheless came down to New York from his home up the Hudson to hear Jenny, and wrote a friend that he was at once enrolled among her admirers. "I cannot say, however, how much of my admiration goes to her singing, how much to herself. As a singer, she appears to me of the very first order; as a specimen of womankind, a little more. She is enough to counterbalance, of herself, all the evil that the world is threatened with by the great convention of women. So God save Jenny Lind!"

This opinion of Jenny was not shared by everyone, however. Nathaniel Hawthorne also heard Jenny, and was not greatly impressed. And when Niles Wadsworth, a Connecticut blacksmith, expressed his desire to go to New York to hear the remarkable lady, his wife declared that if he did such a godless thing she would never speak to him again. The blacksmith went anyway and Mrs. Wadsworth kept her promise, never addressing a word to him afterwards, even when he lay dying. Perhaps the blacksmith considered that he had come off very well—to have heard Jenny Lind sing, and then to have enjoyed peace and quiet at home until he died.

After a day or so Jenny moved from the Irving House to the New

York Hotel, farther up Broadway. Barnum announced that it was to get some privacy from the crowds that continued to haunt the vicinity of Irving House, but the proprietor of the New York Hotel let it out that he was paying Barnum $1,000 a day for the privilege of entertaining Jenny and her entourage. This plan was followed by many hotels during Jenny's tour, considerably cutting down Barnum's bill for her personal expenses.

The second New York concert brought in $14,203.03, and this time the audience was less orderly, though the percentage of ladies was higher. The "promenaders" made a concerted rush for gallery seats not yet occupied. When the ticket holders arrived, the "squatters" refused to vacate and there were several fights. Thereafter Police Chief Matsell deputized police to patrol the gallery and parterre. Once again a happy, perspiring Barnum appeared onstage after Jenny had refused any more curtain calls, and announced that for a second time Jenny was giving her share of the proceeds, in this case "nearly" $10,000 (in fact a little more than $7,000) to charity.

From then on, Barnum saw to it that the papers each day were given details of Jenny's donations to charities of the previous day, which were large enough to be legitimate news. But publicity of this kind was a double-edged sword. The *Herald*, edited by James Gordon Bennett, soon began to attack Barnum because he did not turn over an equal proportion of his own share to charity. Mr. Bennett did not take into account that when Jenny sang for charity she contributed her voice, but Barnum paid all the expenses out of his pocket. Jenny urged him repeatedly to deduct these costs before turning the gross over to her to give away, but he always refused.

"The more liberal the public considers you to be, the better for our joint enterprise," he would say, never replying to the charges of niggardliness brought against him.

For Jenny, too, the publicity accorded her benevolence became a two-edged sword. She was besieged by begging letters. At this time, Henry Wadsworth Longfellow had not had the slightest connection with Jenny. But the evening before her first New York concert, he received a visit at his home in Cambridge, Massachusetts, from a man he described as a "vendor of essences." Would Mr. Longfellow please write Jenny Lind a "poetic" begging letter for him to sign?—the man requested, offering a dollar's worth of his essences in payment.

"An ignoble Yankee is probably the most ignoble of all God's creatures," the scandalized poet wrote in his diary that night.

Nor did the recipients display much gratitude as a rule. Maunsell Field had made up the list of organizations which were to receive the $10,000 from the first concert. It started with $3,000 to the New York City firemen, $2,000 to the Musical Fund Society and $500 each to a number of orphanages, homes for the aged, and similar philanthropic organizations, including a home for aged colored persons and an asylum for colored orphans.

At Jenny's request, Field distributed the largess in person. "I started on my mission of mercy. Before I got through with it, I almost regretted that I had consented to be her almoner. Scarcely anybody—there were a few praiseworthy exceptions—was satisfied. At almost every establishment at which I called, they tried to persuade me that a larger allotment should have been made to their particular institution, and that its needs and deserts were much greater than those of such and such a sister one."

Among the praiseworthy exceptions were the New York Volunteer Fireman, some three thousand business and professional men who, as in smaller communities today, would drop their work at the sound of the alarm, seize helmets and jackets and rush to man the hand-operated pumps. There were many casualties, and money was badly needed to take care of the wives and children of men who were killed or disabled. The firemen could not do enough to show their appreciation of Jenny's generous gift. (Maunsell Field said she had scarcely looked at the list he had made out, but the firemen did not know this!)

They serenaded her again and presented her with a rosewood bookcase containing a handsome set of Audubon's *Birds and Quadrupeds of America,* bound in morocco and beautifully illustrated. Jenny told the men that she prized the gift particularly because she loved birds and animals. "If I have any fixed manner of singing, it is to imitate the birds as nearly as I can."

But she had small pleasure from perhaps the balance of her gifts. Throughout her stay in New York, she was beseiged by people who demanded money from her as though she owed it to them. Maunsell Field wrote, "I am ashamed to be compelled to say that many American ladies urged their pleas in behalf of objects, some of them undoubtedly meritorious, with an importunity which overstepped the bounds of propriety." One lady spurned a twenty-dollar gold piece that Jenny offered her with the indignant statement that she had come for a contribution, not for alms. Swedes seemed to feel they had a special claim on the bounty of their countrywoman, and they came from far and near. The one occasion on which Jenny was known to exhibit indignation at the attitude of the money-seekers was when a Swede became downright insolent in his demands. Maunsell Field, who happened to be present, said that Jenny ordered the man from her suite in a way that would have done credit to the actress Rachel. She probably felt as Longfellow had in the case of the vendor of essences, that the ignobility of one's own kind is more deplorable than that of other people.

However, she made a great fuss over the Reverend Gustavus Uonius, who was starting his Protestant Episcopal Church of St. Ansgarius in Chicago, and had come East to raise funds. She gave him $1,000 for his Swedish congregation. Later she learned that a Norwegian Lutheran Church in Chicago had befriended some Swedish immigrants to that city who had been swindled out of their savings. She sent a silver communion service, valued at $1,500, to the Norwegian pastor, the Reverend Paul Anderson, to express her appreciation of the kindness his church had shown to her own countrymen. When the Norwegian Church, now located in Lake View, Illinois, and called the Lake View Lutheran Church, celebrated its one hundred and tenth anniversary in 1958, the Jenny Lind communion service was the chief exhibit at the ceremonies.

Except with insolent Swedes, Jenny kept her temper. Time and again, when Benedict and Belletti visited Jenny's suite to consult with her about musical matters, they found the sittingroom filled with strangers, well dressed and in all degrees of ill dress, waiting to get money from Jenny. She would go patiently from one to the next, listening to the plea for the worthy charity or the hard luck story, supplying each demand insofar as she was able to do so.

Benedict, and others who witnessed the bad manners of so many of the suppliants, could not understand why Jenny continued to put up with them. She wrote Judge Munthe that she felt compelled to give money away freely in America because of the enormous prices paid for tickets at the auction. She also felt it incumbent upon her to ignore insolence and ingratitude when she encountered them, because she herself had been guilty at first of thinking only of the money she would make from her American engagement, rather than of the good she might accomplish. She had felt no compunction in asking Barnum for a larger share of the profits because he was making so much money himself, and she thought she would use it for better purposes than he would.

Barnum was right in his prediction that publicizing her gifts of money would be good business. The six concerts she gave in New York in September, 1850, brought in $87,055.89 and the American Jenny Lind craze became countrywide, its extravagances exceeding even those of the Jenny Lind Mania in Britain.

Jenny expressed a liking for a certain kind of cake served to her in New York. Immediately, the "Jenny Lind Cake" appeared on hotel menus everywhere, and remained on many until well into the twentieth century. In Alaska, where the first gold rush was going on, an enterprising baker had a sign on his shanty announcing that he made Jenny Lind cakes.

Just as in England, the most inappropriate commercial articles were named after her. Cigars, which she abhorred, servants' caps, flies for trout fishing, poker chips, snuffboxes, a pipe, a tropical fish of the amber-fish family, and a number of barrooms. A teakettle was called the "Jenny Lind" on the excuse that when placed over a fire, it began to sing. A new kind of buggy manufactured in Pennsylvania in 1850 was named the "Jenny Lind." As late as 1939 the "Jenny Lind Buggy," very little altered from the original, was in use among the Pennsylvania Dutch, especially among the Amish in Lancaster County.

Theaters used Jenny to advertise other attractions, often without even mentioning her name, there being only one "she" so far as America was concerned. A sketch entitled merely "She's Come!" was added to *The School for Scandal*, being played at Burton's Theater in New York, and people were urged to come and see "Her Great Reception, Procession and Everything Else. A chunk of fun!" The Walhalla Theater on Canal Street hastily offered "The Jenny Lind Female Opera Troupe, consisting of some of the best female musicians in the world!"

Leonidas Westervelt, the American collector of Lindiana, at one time made up a list of objects inspired by or named after Jenny Lind that he came upon as he collected newspapers and other publications of her day, and followed her path across America, many years later, visiting antique shops in each place where she had been. A large number are represented in his collection in the New York Historical Society, either by a specimen of the article or by a photograph, but there must have been many more between 1850 and 1852 of which no trace was left.

Mr. Westervelt's list included, besides the things already mentioned, a dahlia; a pudding; a wooden figure to advertise Jenny Lind cigar stores; a stove and a flatiron stand. There were Jenny Lind paper dolls, and a Jenny Lind chewing gum with her picture on the wrapper. The Jenny Lind bedstead was very popular and examples still exist. A clipper ship, built at Portsmouth, New Hampshire, in 1851 by Samuel Hanscomb, Jr., was christened *The Nightingale*; her figurehead was a bust of Jenny, and the stern carried a wooden statue of the singer in a reclining position, with a nightingale perched on her finger. The name, *Nightingale*, was painted in blue and gold—the colors of Sweden—on the stern, on the bow and on the quarter.

The list continues through sewing machines, a muskmelon, a gooseberry, combs, needle boxes, pin boxes, and mirrors. Mr. W. H. Slingerland of Norman Kills, New York, somewhat indelicately renamed his prize milch cow for the prima donna. There were Jenny Lind coats, gloves, bonnets, shawls, mantillas, robes, pianos, card-receivers, sofas and chairs, and Jenny Lind fabrics for upholstering the two last-named items. Alphabet plates for children, dance-program cases, purses, needle books, handkerchiefs, not to mention several theaters, all carried the magic name.

Out in mushrooming San Francisco, the citizens took stock of their buildings and realized that these did not include a hall suitable for Jenny Lind to appear in. Thereupon a hall was built for her use, though Jenny never went west of the Mississippi in her American travels, and never had any intention of doing so.

Presents of all sorts were showered upon her by milliners, mantuamakers, shopkeepers of every variety. They felt amply repaid if they received a letter from her acknowledging the gift, which they could exhibit as proof that they were "purveyors" to the uncrowned sovereign in their midst.

Godey's Lady's Book for December, 1850, felt called upon to take a

cold analytical look at this propensity for associating with Jenny practically every commodity offered to the public. It stated that the Jenny
Lind "bandeau," by which was meant Jenny's distinctive way of doing
her hair, had been the only thing copied extensively in America until she
had actually arrived, but "then the furor commenced." To be sure, such
dignified establishments as Stewart's, Beck's and Levy's had held aloof.

But in the Bowery, Canal Street, or Eighth and Second Streets,
in Philadelphia, Jenny Lind plaids, combs, silks, earrings, work bas-
kets, bonnets, and even hair pins were advertised and recommended.
Now, these had no legitimate claim to the title, inasmuch as we do
not believe Mademoiselle Lind had ever seen, much less worn,
the articles in question. It was a bare-faced shopkeeping ruse, but
nevertheless it succeeded; and half the American public are now
wiping their heated brows with Jenny Lind pocket handkerchiefs,
or dressing their hair with Jenny Lind combs.

But there is one article that has more legitimate claim to the
title—the riding hat. The first one of the style was presented to
Mademoiselle Lind by Genin, the celebrated Broadway Hatter,
who, as everyone knows, did not stop at compliments but paid a
good round sum to hear her sing. Moreover, it was worn by the fair
lady in her morning rides, and is thus fairly entitled to the appella-
tion of *The Jenny Lind Riding Hat.* We have before us an exact
duplicate, and will try to give our lady readers some idea of its
style. It is a black beaver, has a low crown and a brim of moderate
width, turned up slightly on each side. The principal beauty of the
hat is a broad band of velvet and satin ribbon encircling the crown,
ending in an oval rosette a little to the left, which confines a
heavy black plume, made to float backwards. Nothing could be
more tastefully arranged, or have a better effect in a rapid canter.
The side rosettes are of corded white satin ribbon, the strings of the
same to be knotted a little on one side of the chin.

Mademoiselle Lind usually wears a habit of dark blue cloth, and
looks very well in the saddle. Cloth is now generally in favor of
habits, and is more suitable for winter especially; the heavy folds of
the skirt keep in place better. One of the new styles has a small
peak or flap, lined with silk, behind the corsage, but this is not
graceful, and approaches too much to the masculine air, that is so
disagreeable in a riding costume.

The magazine maintained that the rolled-under coiffure, seen in so
many daguerreotypes of the Civil War period and copied from Jenny,

was a very bad imitation of the "soft, child-like curl or ripple that distinguishes the hair of the cantatrice." Its readers were instructed in the way to get the true Jenny Lind effect. "The front hair is divided into three parts, and the upper one is put back, while the two beneath are frizzed close to the head. The upper portion is then rolled smoothly over, or rather, over and under these divisions, and twisted around the ends that are left. The entire hair thus makes a smooth roll, filled or stuffed with the frizzed portion."

It was hardly necessary now for Barnum to give out items to the papers about his star. They kept a watch outside Jenny's hotel, and journalists fought to get an "in" with Barnum for exclusive stories. A reporter for the New York *Post* was privileged to accompany Jenny and Mr. and Mrs. John Jay on a visit to the city's Institute for the Blind. (Mr. Jay, returned from Europe, had taken over from Maunsell Field as Jenny's lawyer.) The Superintendent had not known they were coming and was thrown into confusion on learning that Jenny Lind was in his anteroom. Jenny brushed his apologies aside, saying that she had come to sing for the children. The *Post* reporter gave a touching description of the scene as the children gathered in their tiny hall, with its battered, out of tune piano, and heard Jenny sing "The Small Bird" and other Scandanavian folk songs that she thought the children would enjoy. Afterwards they crowded around her, seeking to touch her and "see" her with their fingers. Jenny was greatly moved. Taking the hand of a sixteen-year-old blind girl, who had listened to the music with a special expression of rapture, Jenny exclaimed, "My dear, how I wish I could make it possible for you to see the sky!"

"But I shall see it in heaven," the girl replied, "And I shall see you there too."

A reporter from the *Herald* was present when Jenny, Josephine Åhmansson and Barnum set out for Jenny's first horseback ride in New York. Barnum hired the horses at Distrow's Riding Academy at 20 Fourth Avenue, and had them delivered to the New York Hotel and tied to the hitching posts in front of the hotel. When the little party came out and mounted, the reporter was able to announce triumphantly that at last a flaw had been discovered in the otherwise perfect Jenny. *She could not mount a horse without using a chair!* "She may be able to fly," the reporter wrote, "for that comes naturally to birds and angels. But she is no horsewoman." This evidence of a human weakness in their goddess appeared to endear her more to the American public than her whole catalogue of virtues.

The largest crowd thus far tried to buy tickets, or jam into the Garden as standees, for the third concert. Jenny gave an almost entirely different program this time with the aria, "I Know That My Redeemer Liveth," as the featured number. After a reverent silence at the close, it was applauded more vehemently than the operatic numbers. Jenny learned that America would accept the best she had to offer.

Among the musical critics at this concert was Nathaniel Parker Willis of the *Home Journal*, who had heard Jenny sing in Europe. He praised "the liquid purity of her voice as it slid gracefully through its labyrinthine passages," in the current flowery fashion, but in his later writings probed deeper, trying to determine what it was about Jenny that moved the public to such hysterical heights of adoration. He did not believe that her talent and art, great as these were, could account for the phenomenon. In fact, he felt that her very innocence of life, in its fullest implications, rendered her incapable of singing the second half of "Casta diva" with the earthy passion demanded when the priestess begs her Roman lover "to return and sin again." His decision finally was that the secret lay in what Willis called her "six-barreled greatness."

That God has not made her a wonderful singer *and there left her,* is the curious exception she forms to common human allotment. To give away more money in charity than any other mortal —and still be the first of prima donnas! To be an irreproachably modest girl—and still be the first of prima donnas! To be humble, simple, genial and unassuming—and still be the first of prima donnas! To have begun as a beggar child and risen to receive more adulation than any queen—and still be the first of prima donnas! To be unquestionably the most admired and distinguished woman on earth, doing the most good and exercising the most power— and still be a prima donna that can be applauded and encored! It is the combination of superiorities that makes the wonder, it is the concentrating of the stuff of half a dozen heroines in one simple girl, and that girl a candidate for applause, that so vehemently stimulates the curiosity.

It was evident that Jenny could have drawn crowds in New York for months to come, but Castle Garden was promised for the annual Industrial Exhibition. Also, Barnum knew that it was good business to stop while the excitement was at its height. So only three more concerts in New York, making six in all, were given at this time. To forestall any possibility of clashes between seat holders and desperate "promenaders" at the last concert, Barnum ordained that standee tickets should not be sold before 7:45 on the night of the concert, and then only at a certain entrance. When the ticket sellers arived, they found the entrance and vestibule jammed so tightly they could not get through. It was suggested that the ticket sellers be hoisted up and walk on the shoulders of the crowd, and this was done.

More than a thousand standee tickets were sold in the next fifteen minutes, and the promenade area was packed and overflowed up the stairs to the very top of the gallery. Some young men who couldn't get inside climbed up the outside of the building to the top of the dome, and peered down at Jenny through the ventilators.

CHAPTER THIRTEEN

In the Citadel of American Culture

T HEY were to appear next in Boston, and LeGrand Smith had gone on ahead to hire a hall and make other advance arangements. Barnum had to cope unaided with the hundreds of letters, telegrams and business propositions regarding Jenny, which were pouring in every day. Fortunately, he had spent a week or two in the White Mountains in August, gathering strength for the ordeal ahead. He wrote afterwards that for nine months following Jenny's arrival, he had not a minute free of anxiety and strain.

The party sailed on the *Empire State*, Jenny going aboard early to avoid the crowds, which had gathered densely by sailing time. In his memoirs, Barnum said that Jenny never could understand why hordes of people were always on hand for her arrivals and departures, in spite of her efforts to keep these secret. She knew that Barnum knew how much it distressed her to be the center of a press of struggling humanity, and her impresario carefully kept from her the fact that he was disseminating information of this kind, telegraphing her expected arrival time to the newspapers of the next city. Jenny was easy to deceive, inasmuch as she had never had dealings before with a man of P. T. Barnum's type, and could not imagine that he would go against her wishes deliberately, when he had acted so generously toward her. Barnum maintained that he felt fully justified in his actions, because the demonstrations intensified interest in the concerts.

People were waiting all along the shore to get a glimpse of the vessel, even where it was too far away for them to be able to distinguish Jenny

Lind. At dinner that night, the centerpiece of the Captain's table, where Jenny of course was seated, was a spun-sugar replica of Castle Garden, at the top of which was a doll representing Jenny wearing her famous costume for *Daughter of the Regiment,* and holding an American flag.

In Boston, again, a crowd popped up as if by magic to greet her, and no sooner was Jenny installed in the Revere House than the Mayor hurried over to pay his respects. The Boston papers had been full of her gifts to charity, and the Mayor complimented her so fulsomely on her fine character that Jenny said with some asperity, "What do you know of my character? How can you possibly know anything about my private character? I am no better than other people, I assure you, no better at all."

The coachman who had driven Jenny to the Revere House remained outside, offering to let onlookers kiss the hand that had been honored in helping the diva out of the coach, at $5 per kiss for adults, $2.50 for children. Though it was raining, the crowds continued to mill around the hotel until the Mayor demanded that they go away, so that Jenny could get some rest. The next night, the Germania Society held a torchlight parade in her honor and serenaded her. Boston's official welcome to Jenny closed with a huge display of fireworks on the Common.

The Hub City was acknowledged to be the cultural center of the United States. Nevertheless, even here, the public in general was indifferent to good music. Serious attempts had been made to establish the classics, in what John Sullivan Dwight has described as two major waves, but they had met with failure. The Germania Society, a group of musicians who had come over from Germany in 1848, had held some successful concerts, but continuing support had not been forthcoming. Tremont Temple, Boston's largest and finest hall, was pitifully small, its acoustics poor. For entertainment, Bostonians, at the time of Jenny's arrival, were being invited to "make a tour of 2000 miles" in Burr's "Seven-Mile Mirror" at the Melodeon, and to visit the new gallery of wax statuary, containing nearly two hundred figures, which had just been opened at the Boston Museum. The papers were also announcing the arrival of another chapter of *David Copperfield.* (Dickens's novels were published serially in an English magazine as he wrote them, and as quickly as possible pirated by various journals in America.)

It was upon its literary and intellectual lights that Boston's fame for culture depended, and these strove to make up for the lack in the musical field. Next morning Jenny received calls not only from the Governor and Lieutenant Governor of Massachusetts, but also from Edward Everett, Henry Wadsworth Longfellow and Daniel Webster, at this time Secretary of State in President Fillmore's Cabinet. Everett, scholar, writer, teacher, and president of Harvard for several years following the death of Josiah Quincy, had already filled important posts in the Massachusetts and Federal governments, and was to become Secretary of State on the death of Daniel Webster two years later.

Today, however, his name probably means less to the average American than that of the gentle Harvard professor and poet, Longfellow, whose major work, *Evangeline: a Tale of Acadie*, had been published just three years before. As for Daniel Webster, many considered this orator and statesman the greatest living American. Nathaniel Parker Willis thought it was as tremendous an honor in the United States for Jenny Lind to have Daniel Webster call on her, as it would be in England to have the Duke of Wellington call on her. (Willis may or may not have known that the Duke had done this very thing.) Jenny was particularly impressed by Webster, because of his manners and conversation. Barnum said that after he had left, Jenny walked up and down the room exclaiming excitedly, "Ah, Mr. Barnum, there is a man! I have never before seen such a man!"

Longfellow found Jenny intriguing as a personality, before he heard her sing. "She is very feminine and lovely. Her power is in her presence, which is magnetic, and takes one captive before she opens her lips." Edward Everett said she must come over to Cambridge and see Harvard College, and the following week a reception was held for her there. She drank tea with professors in Prince Albert coats and their modestly dressed wives. Her tour of the handful of college buildings then existing included the Observatory. Just as Jenny was looking through the telescope, trying to find Saturn, a brilliant meteor flashed across the sky. This was not a rare phenomenon, nevertheless the astronomy professor and his colleagues maintained gallantly that it was a heavenly display in honor of Jenny.

The ticket auction, which had been held on the Saturday preceding their arrival, had been even more spirited than the one in New York. A daguerreotypist, Luther Hale, started the bidding at $250—$25 more than the price Genin had paid. William Fetteridge, the manufacturer of "Russian Salve" and "Balm of 1,000 Flowers," came back with $275. The publisher of *The Flag of Our Union* jumped the bid to $450. Thus it went until the first ticket was knocked down for $625 to Ossian E. Dodge, an entertainer who sang comic songs, accompanying himself on the guitar.

The Boston papers crowed mightily over the fact that the center of culture had outbid New York City, center of finance, for the first ticket. In no time at all, lithographs were on display, showing Dodge with his guitar in his hand and bearing the legend, "Ossian F. Dodge, the man who gave $625 for the first choice of seats to hear the great Diva, Jenny Lind." A butcher in Lynn, Massachusetts, was already selling Jenny Lind sausages when these works of art appeared, and Thaddeus W. Meighan, under the pseudonym of "Asmodeus," quickly brought out a sequel to New York City's *Parnassus*, entitled *The Jenny Lind Mania in Boston*.

There were several incidents of the kind Barnum particularly loved, because they made excellent newspaper copy, though Jenny never found out how it was that the newspapers managed to get wind of them. Max Hjortzberg happened to overhear a girl remark, in the line queued up for the $3 tickets, "Well, here goes a week's salary, but I've got to hear Jenny Lind no matter what!" Max told Jenny and she exclaimed, "Would you know the girl again if you saw her? Oh, do try to find her and give her this as a present for me!" The secretary located the girl in her gallery seat just before the curtain went up and gave her the present from Jenny —a twenty-dollar gold piece.

The day of the first concert, September 27, a Swedish servant girl called on Jenny. The diva kept her several hours, talking about Sweden, and in the evening took her to the concert in her carriage, gave her a good seat and, at the close of the performance, sent her in a carriage back to Roxbury, where she was employed.

Also on this day, Jenny wrote to her parents for the first time since her arrival in America, nearly a month before. After describing the voyage, she went on to say:

> I have met with quite an astonishing reception and have given already six concerts in New York, in a hall that holds 11,000 people. It has been crowded each time, and we shall be able, most likely, to give forty or fifty concerts in New York alone. Here

everything is done on a large scale. The first ticket for today's concert was sold by auction for $625! It is amazing what heaps of money they seem to have here. My health, thank God, is excellent and my voice fresh and strong, and I am looking forward, when this tournée is over, to a time of peace and rest. For indeed, in these two matters so precious to human beings, I seem to be given little share, torn and bothered as I am from morning to night. Still it is touching to see how much good will and kindness I receive. People do not seem to know how, enough, to show their favor and genuine interest. I wish I could send home to you some of the lovely fruit and flowers I continually receive.

We have lovely warm weather, still, and even a divinely blue sky. Time does pass—I shall soon be thirty years of age. How happy I am to become an "auld hag"! Every day I see round me numbers of new faces and I am finding it rather a bore, but I am trying to terminate my engagement perhaps in a year.

When we meet I shall have heaps to relate which I now have no time for. It is already more than three months since I was dancing round the Maypole at home. Now pray take care of yourselves, and remember with tenderness your far off daughter.

Tremont Temple, hired by LeGrand Smith for the concerts, could not begin to hold all those who wanted to hear Jenny. The night of the first concert a huge crowd stood outside, hoping to catch at least some stray notes; and the owner of a stable which backed up to the Temple tethered his horses outside, filled the stalls with chairs and rented them out at fifty cents apiece.

Jenny's first programs were very like the ones in New York City, except that she added "The Bird Song" (its German title was "Ich Muss Singen"), by Mendelssohn's great friend Herr Taubert. Taubert had written it for Jenny to sing at her last concert in Berlin. It was greatly applauded, and Jenny sang it frequently thereafter. She had to repeat both the trio with flutes from *Camp in Silesia*, and the "Echo Song."

The Boston audiences responded so sympathetically that for her fourth concert Jenny dared to give a program made up principally of sacred music, arias from the great oratorios of Handel and Haydn and from Rossini's "Stabat Mater." After her favorite aria, "I Know That My Redeemer Liveth," the audience would not leave off applauding until she repeated it. In the opinion of Benedict and Belletti, her singing of the passage "And Now the Christ is Risen" was one of the most perfect things she had ever done. A newspaper critic said that emotion shone so strongly from her face, one could almost see it as a halo around her head. At the conclusion, a tall, impressive man rose from his seat in the center of the balcony and bowed profoundly. It was Daniel Webster.

Jenny dared something else in Boston, as well. Interested as she was in folk music, she had been learning several of the simpler songs in English, helped in her pronunciation by Joseph Burke. She had remembered "Comin' Through the Rye," which she had heard in Scotland, and had been practicing the words of "Annie Laurie," "The Last Rose of Summer," "Auld Robin Gray" and "John Anderson, My Jo." Jenny had sung "The Last Rose of Summer" as an encore in New York, but Barnum had advised against the dialect songs, as long as she was in the more sophisticated North, and particularly as long as she was in ultra-sophisticated Boston. When they were touring south of the Mason-Dixon line, novelties of this type would be more appreciated. But Jenny sang "Comin' Through the Rye" in Boston, and Boston loved it. Is there a soprano since her time who has not used this song as an encore?

On October 7, Jenny went over to Providence, Rhode Island, for one concert, and here her reception was nothing less than delirious. It also was marked by a feature that had been lacking hitherto in the United States. For George Upton, a student at Brown University who later became a noted musician, said that while the entire population of Providence, men, women and children, had "Jenny Lind Fever," the students at Brown had it the worst of all. "Alma Mater finally had to throw up her ancient hands in despair, and let her children have their way."

In Europe, whenever Jenny had sung in a university town or city, she had received especially enthusiastic acclaim from the students. Time and again the young men—young women did not attend college in those days—had unhitched her horses and themselves pulled her carriage though the streets, the ultimate accolade. They would serenade her with their student songs. When she had left Göttingen the previous February, a student corps had escorted her as far as Nordheim, a four-hour drive. There they had taken possession of the inn, serenaded Jenny again, toasted her in champagne and appointed her an honorary sister of their corps. Jenny had made a rosette for each lad from green and white ribbons, procured at a nearby shop, and had declared that the date, February 5, 1850, would be stamped on her mind indelibly, in letters of gold.

She always enjoyed thoroughly these marks of appreciation from the young.

It was perhaps because American college students had never before been exposed to a reigning prima donna that those in New York and Boston lagged behind their European fellows. No mention at all is made of Columbia in connection with the attentions heaped upon Jenny in New York City; and in Boston it was the Harvard faculty, not the pupils, who paid her special honor.

So far as can be determined today, the students at Brown alone displayed, as a body, a proper sense of the honor being paid their city, but in a manner of their own. Several hundred attended the ticket auction, not to bid, for that was a luxury beyond them, but as champions of Colonel William Ross, the manager of a delivery service, who was popular with the students because he was generous in extending them credit.

Colonel Ross, locally famous for his eccentricities, had determined to become the John Genin of Providence by buying the first ticket, whatever it might cost. Since other merchants had come with the same idea, the bidding was so fiercely competitive that several times contenders had to be separated to prevent fist fights. Protected from bodily injury by solid ranks of Brown students, and cheered on by them, Colonel Ross captured the prize for $653—the highest price paid yet in the ticket auctions, and the highest ever paid.

When Jenny heard of Colonel Ross's exploit, she exclaimed, "What a fool!" But this was not the whole story. Captain Ross's seat, Number 650, was empty the night of the concert, though Barnum had presented the delivery-service magnate with a special ticket, twenty-one inches long and seventeen wide, printed in blue and gold, the colors of Sweden, and autographed by Jenny. The Colonel explained to Barnum that he cared nothing about music and had bought the ticket for the precise reason Barnum had auctioned it off. His apparent eccentricity in refusing to avail himself of its use had brought him even more "notoriety." Colonel Ross, however, made up for the implied slight to Jenny by attending all her concerts in Havana—at the regular prices.

The night of the concert, students squeezed into every cranny left in Howard Hall by such prosperous citizens as the Iveses, Browns, Goddards and Hopkinsons, who were there in full force, and cheered the Nightingale so lustily that she repeated their favorite encores several times.

The authorities of Brown University had declared a half holiday and suspended the rules which barred students from entertainments on week nights, so that all could attend who had the means. Nothing would have delighted Jenny more than to have been serenaded by the Brown students, and to have heard their American college songs. But they could not know this, and possibly were too shy to impose their own singing on the famous diva. In America, the serenades for Jenny were from groups either of adults or of children.

George Upton recorded that his roommate, "a wild Hoosier, who knew no more about music than a hen," had a particularly virulent attack of the Jenny Lind Fever. "He invested all of his scanty pocket money in hairs supplied by one of the hotel chambermaids, who declared she took them from Jenny Lind's brush. He reluctantly allowed me to have one or two, and I kept them as precious relics, until it was ascertained later that this commercial genius had been doing a lucrative business, disposing of her own combings and those of other chambermaids and guests."

Back in Boston, Jenny found a polite note from Henry Wadsworth Longfellow inviting her to his home in Cambridge on Brattle Street near Harvard College. Barnum knew little more about literature than he did about music, but he understood that Professor Longfellow was considered a "first-rate poet," and advised Jenny to accept. The poet's home, which was called "Craigie" for a previous owner, long dead, was a large, rambling structure, built early in the eighteenth century, set in a large garden and shaded by ancient elms. From his study windows, the poet could look across the Brighton meadows to the hills of Brookline.

Jenny felt more at home at Craigie than at any time since coming to the United States, for Harvard was the nearest thing to Uppsala that America could offer, and Longfellow reminded her of the scholars and men of letters who had been her good friends there. Moreover, Longfellow had spent a considerable time in Sweden and the other North Cape countries before starting his lecturing at Harvard, and having a great aptitude for languages, had familiarized himself with Scandinavian literature. His *Song of Hiawatha*, published in 1855, was in fact an edda of the American Indian, an imitation of the Finnish epic, *The Kalevala*.

Besides being able to talk about home with Longfellow, Jenny absorbed from him much fascinating lore about the Indians and the early history of the American Colonies. Longfellow was a descendant, on his mother's side, of John and Priscilla Alden—his *Courtship of Miles Standish* was to appear in 1858. George Washington had stayed at Craigie in 1776. Jenny was excited to learn that Boston had been the cradle of the movement toward freedom and democracy which to date had been the young country's main contribution to the world. The Longfellows became Jenny's very good friends, and during her later stay in Boston she was to be at Craigie frequently.

The concert Jenny gave for charity brought in $10,000, which was distributed among Boston's hospitals, poorhouses and orphanages. At this concert, Jenny sang Mendelssohn's "If With All Your Hearts" for the first time on her American tour.

The odd combination of highly spiritual songstress and wily promoter seemed to be working out perfectly. The Reverend John Peabody wrote of Jenny in the *Christian Register* in lyrical terms. "It is hard to describe her. She looked as if she had just stepped down out of a poem. Our readers may have seen some young girl whose approach seemed always to awaken pleasant and kindly feeling in the whole circle about her. . . . Jenny Lind has, beyond almost anyone that we ever saw, a countenance which possesses this indefinable charm."

There seems no doubt that in spite of her ampler proportions and approaching thirtieth birthday, Jenny still conveyed an impression of youthful innocence. Richard Hoffman related that nothing could have been more naïve and charming than her manner on the stage. "She would trip on and off, as if in an ecstasy of delight at the opportunity of seeing, bowing and smiling to her audience, giving everyone present a flattering sense of contributing in a measure toward the success of the evening."

Hoffman, however, described her voice as being not so much brilliant as full and rounded and with a great reserve power. Herr Rellstab, the Berlin critic, had also noted the greater fullness of her voice which seemed to have come as her slender figure fleshed out more in the late 1840's.

Hoffman said that Belletti sang beautifully, with a pure vibrant Italian voice, but with a way of pronouncing English that Americans found very amusing. "His 'Wy do ze nazzions so fooriosely raage ze gedar?' always provoked a smile from the audience."

Benedict had been an inspired choice for orchestra conductor and accompanist. In addition to his superb musicianship, he was a fine-looking man with great dignity, and his protective attitude toward Jenny enhanced her own air of youthfulness and of being something rarely precious. Whenever Jenny came on stage to sing, Benedict would escort her from the wings to her position in the center of the stage, then bow and hand her her music sheets. Sometimes she would make her appearance on his arm, sometimes he would lead her forward by the hand.

Many invitations came to Jenny from Boston ministers to attend their services. Barnum did not venture to dictate. or even to suggest, what Jenny should do about church attendance, but was secretly delighted when she chose to go to the Seaman's Bethel, where sailors from many lands went to worship under the guidance of a rough-and-ready evangelist known as Brother Taylor. Jenny went because she thought she might find some Swedish sailors there, but Barnum realized what good copy her visit to the humble mission for seafaring men would make. And it did. A rough-looking fellow in the front row broke into the sermon to inquire, "If a person was to die while he was listening to Jenny Lind sing, would he go straight to heaven?" The minister replied acidly, "A fool will still be a fool wherever he is, whether it be at a Jenny Lind concert or at the foot of a pulpit!"

Before long, Barnum had the best local story yet to give out. Jenny Lind was going to furnish the money to enable a Massachusetts girl to study in Europe! Mr. and Mrs. Phillips of Marshfield had brought their daughter, Adelaide, to Jenny at Revere House. Jenny had given the girl two auditions and, prophesizing that Adelaide would become a great singer if properly trained, had offered to pay for Adelaide's training under European masters. In 1856, Adelaide Phillips made her debut in opera in Boston, and went on to become the greatest American contralto of her day.

Tremont Temple had proved woefully inadequate, and the musicians were delighted when Barnum told them he had hired a big hall over the new Fitchburg Depot for the last two concerts in Boston. Jenny suggested that inasmuch as this hall was larger, the price of tickets could be reduced. Then more of the less affluent citizens could hear her. Barnum promptly acceded to her request, announcing tickets "at popular and unheard of prices."

Richard Hoffman wrote, "I think this was the first time a concert was given in a railway station, and undoubtedly it will be the last." The depot had barely been finished, and this was the first tryout of the hall on the second floor. One third of the floor was used for offices, which were on either side of the hall, blocked off only by big panes of glass. The hall held around fifteen hundred seats, and it was estimated that there was room for about three hundred standees in the wide passageway leading to it and around the ends of the seats. The only means of reaching the concert room was by two steep, winding staircases at either corner of the front of the building.

The depot was a considerable distance from the center of the city and in a not very desirable section, so that not too many people found their way to the first concert there, which went off fairly well. But the lowered price of tickets—one dollar for standees—plus the fact that this would be the last opportunity for Boston citizens to hear Jenny, proved catastrophic for the second one. Agents in outlying districts were selling tickets, and through some error, anywhere from five hundred to a thousand more tickets were sold than the hall could accommodate.

The miraculously warm weather Jenny had mentioned in her letter to her parents still held, and by seven o'clock that evening the roofs of buildings and coal sheds adjoining the Depot were covered by spectators, the streets around it were jammed.

The holders of reserved seats were allowed to enter the building first, then the signal was given to let the standees in. A tremendous rush ensued. The "promenade" space was filled in no time, and a continual cry of "Move up in front! Move up in front!" from the people packed on the stairways brought no results, for there was no room in front to move up to. Clothing was torn, tempers grew short.

Richard Hoffman, arriving at one of the front entrances a little late, found himself confronting a solid wall of humanity which constituted "the most enraged crowd I ever saw." Hoffman explained to the policemen who were hovering around helplessly that the concert could not begin until he got to the stage, and they succeeded in pushing a way for him into the building, and up the stairs. But the aisles were so densely blocked that he had to be lifted up and passed over the heads of the crowd in a horizontal position. "It was not unlike being tossed in a blanket, but I was a youth of slim proportions and finally reached the footlights rather more dead than alive, and very much disordered in my general appearance."

When the concert began, there was so much noise in the hall and on the crowded staircases behind it that the orchestra's opening number could hardly be heard. Belletti's solo, which followed, might as well have been in pantomime. Benedict brought Jenny on next, out of turn, in the hope that her appearance would quiet the crowd. She sang "On Mighty Pens," from *The Creation*, and there was comparative quiet for awhile. But it was suffocatingly hot in the hall, and the people who were packed in the passageways suffered from the heat and lack of air. Men began smashing the glass partitions to the offices, climbing through to open the outside windows. Women fainted, and were passed over the heads of the crowd to the orchestra room. Soon it was full and the victims overflowed into Jenny's dressing room.

An effort was made to go on with the program, but it proved hopeless. The orchestra members put their instruments in their cases and the artists got out by a steep, winding staircase at the stage end, the steps of which were still covered with mortar, pieces of lath and other debris. The audience also departed, but it was a slow and perilous process. When the indignant crowd had finally gained the street outside, a mob rushed to the Revere House, the members shouting that they wanted either their money back, or Barnum. There was talk of tarring and feathering— a good old New England custom that would have startled Jenny considerably.

But Barnum this time was literally "nowhere." He had slipped off to Brighton, after assuring himself that Jenny was all right, and spent the night with friends. The next day he took the train for his home at Bridgeport, leaving LeGrand Smith behind to refund the money of ticket holders who had not been able to get inside the hall.

Richard Hoffman said that the entire troupe was thoroughly disgusted with Barnum, and there was much muttering among them. One Boston paper accused Barnum of fraud. The editor of another wrote the impresario asking for a loan of $100 for a few days in return for suppressing an article unfavorable to Barnum's actions with regard to the Fitchburg concerts. Barnum replied: "I hope you will by no means curtail the privilege of correspondents or editors on my account. Publish what you please, so far as I am concerned. I have no money to lend, and never yet paid a farthing of blackmail, *and so help me God, I never will.* Signed P. T. Barnum." Barnum then released the two letters to the other Boston papers, though omitting the name of the editor.

The troupe joined Barnum at Iranistan, and the visit to their impresario's home must have been another fascinating experience for the artists from abroad. Mrs. Barnum proved to be as shy and retiring as her husband was gregarious and self-confident. She kept in the background, their daughter Caroline acted as hostess. Caroline also, rather than her mother, accompanied the troupe on their subsequent travels, taking with her a Bridgeport friend, Mrs. Lyman.

Iranistan itself, once seen, could never be forgotten. Barnum had received the inspiration for it from the Pavilion at Brighton, the first building of Oriental type to be erected in England, and the dream child of King George IV, of unsavory memory. Its prototype in America combined Byzantine, Moorish and Turkish architecture, and had minarets and spires sticking up all over it. A conservatory formed a big bulge at either end of the edifice. The extensive and beautifully landscaped grounds were dotted with fountains, and stocked with iron deer and elk, in the current Victorian tradition. The inside was reputed to be as "elegant as a steamboat."

As usual, Barnum had a double motive in planting a mixture of mosque and Oriental palace in the peaceful Connecticut countryside. "I thought a pile of buildings of novel order might serve indirectly as an advertisement of my various enterprises."

It is significant that Barnum makes no mention at all of the unhappy Fitchburg Depot incident in his memoirs, but dwells at considerable length on Jenny's reaction to Iranistan. He said she expressed surprise that he would leave so beautiful a place for the wear and tear of taking her about the country, then confessed that it was a picture of Iranistan, on the first letter John Hall Wilton wrote her asking for an appointment, which had induced her to see Barnum's agent. "I said to myself that a gentleman who has been so successful in his business as to be able to build and reside in such a palace cannot be a mere adventurer," he quotes her, and says he replied, "That fully repays me for building it, for I intend and expect to make more by this musical enterprise than Iranistan cost me."

This hardly squares with the known facts that Jenny refused to see John Hall Wilton until he had procured an introductory letter from Sir George Smart, and had not considered Barnum's offer seriously until she had checked on his financial responsibility with Baring Brothers. Considering the feelings of the troupe toward their impresario at this time, one might conclude that there had been some bitter words on their arrival, and that Jenny and Barnum had exerted themselves to get things back on a friendly basis afterwards. But it is hard to believe that Jenny expressed her reactions to Iranistan in just those terms.

That all was not actually as harmonious as the amiable exchanges reported by Barnum would indicate was evidenced by the fact that a very short time later, Barnum was complaining that he was "beset by petty annoyances" arising out of the fact that the very success of the first New York concert had opened Jenny's mind to "evil advisers." He wrote in his memoirs, "It would seem that the terms of our revised contract were sufficiently liberal to her and sufficiently hazardous to myself, to justify the expectations of perfectly honorable treatment; but certain envious intermeddlers appeared to think differently. 'Do you not see, Miss Lind, that Mr. Barnum is coining money out of your genius!' said they."

The only names Barnum ever mentioned in relation to "evil advisers" were those of Max Hjortzberg, Jenny's Swedish secretary, and John Jay, her American lawyer. He said specifically that Benedict and Belletti both "behaved like men." And he added that the "high-minded Swede," though of course she saw that Barnum was coining money, "despised and spurned the advisers who recommended her to repudiate her contract with me at all hazards, and take the enterprise into her own hands— possibly to put it into theirs."

Nevertheless, on October 23, 1850, not long after the supposedly pleasant interlude at Iranistan, Barnum wrote to Joshua Bates of Baring Brothers of London—the bankers who had assured Jenny of his integrity in business and had loaned him $20,000 on his second mortgages—asking him to intercede in the situation.

Mr. Bates was well aware, Barnum said, that in the United States, "the rapid accumulation of wealth always creates much envy, and envy soon augments to malice." Every day, he declared, persons, some of whom "moved in the first classes of society," were approaching Jenny and Benedict and spending hours in traducing Jenny's impresario. "Even her attorney, John Jay, has been so blind to her interests as to aid in poisoning her mind against me, by pouring into her ears the most silly twaddle, all of which amounts to nothing and less than nothing. Such as the regret that I was a 'showman,' exhibitor of Tom Thumb, etc., etc."

Barnum said that such men as Edward Everett and others would testify there was no charlatanism or lack of dignity in Barnum's management of Jenny's concerts, and that "without the elements I possess for business, as well as my knowledge of human nature, acquired in catering for the public," Jenny's concerts would not have been one-half as successful from a pecuniary standpoint.

Jenny's mind, he insisted, "ought to be as free as air, and she herself as free as a bird, and, being satisfied of my probity and ability, she should turn a deaf ear to all envious and malevolent attacks on me." Barnum suggested that Mr. Bates write letters to Benedict and John Jay to this effect.

"I have risked much money on the issue of this speculation—it has proved successful. I am full of perplexity and anxiety, and labor continually for success, and I cannot allow ignorance or envy to rob me of the fruits of my enterprise."

The concerts had indeed been tremendously profitable, and had been conducted with dignity—with the exception of the last one at the Fitchburg Depot. Reading between the lines, and knowing as we do Barnum's propensity for withholding or altering facts for his own advantage, we may conclude that Jenny had come close to breaking with Barnum after the Fitchburg Depot debacle. John Jay would hardly have been deploring Barnum's previous activities at this point unless the Fitchburg Depot had revived suspicions that he was not the man for a high class enterprise. Barnum would not have been filled with perplexity and anxiety lest he be robbed of the fruits of his enterprise unless Jenny had been much displeased, and the mention of Benedict would indicate that the conductor shared her indignation. Barnum, being Barnum, could not admit to Mr. Bates that he had been remiss in the affair of the Fitchburg Depot. He had to put the whole blame for the trouble on the envy and malice of unnamed persons.

Whether Mr. Bates ever wrote to Benedict and John Jay is not known, but evidently Barnum succeeded in patching matters up, for the tour continued as planned. The incident, however, left some scars.

The next engagements were in Philadelphia and they went there from New York by steamer, principally to avoid the crowds that swarmed wherever rumors said the Swedish singer would appear. Nevertheless, the throng waiting for them at the Philadelphia dock was so dense that Barnum had difficulty opening a way for Jenny and the members of her party to enter the carriage. Thousands followed them to the Jones Hotel, where thousands more were waiting. Jenny had a severe headache, and Barnum begged the crowd to disperse, but they said they would not leave until Jenny appeared on the balcony.

Barnum had Josephine Åhmansson put on Jenny's bonnet and shawl, and led her out onto the balcony. Josephine bowed gracefully to the multitude, which gave her three big cheers and then departed. "Miss Lind was so utterly averse to anything like deception, that we never ventured to tell her the part which her bonnet and shawl had played, in the absence of their owner," Barnum said. However, Jenny lent herself to a similar deception later on during their tour.

The ticket auction in Philadelphia rivaled the one in Boston. M. H. Root, a daguerreotypist, bought the first one for $625, the exact amount paid by Ossian Dodge. The Chestnut Street Theater was quickly sold out for the three concerts. But there the resemblance to New York and Boston ended.

Aristocratic Philadelphia had read with disdain about the frenzies of its sister cities over Jenny. The first Philadelphia audience came with the firm determination not to be swept overboard, and for the first time in America the troupe faced listeners who had come not to worship, but to challenge.

There was not the usual ripple of applause when Benedict appeared to conduct the opening orchestral number. Only a faint spattering of handclaps was accorded Belletti's first solo. Jenny too was received in silence and as she surveyed the cold, indrawn faces before her, she realized that she was being dared to prove her qualities. There was a stir as she sang an aria from *La Sonnambula,* "Come per me sereno." The audience began to respond in spite of itself. Her next duet with Belletti was applauded enthusiastically, and Jenny's singing of Benedict's composition "Take This Lute," with which the first half of the program concluded, was met with cheers. From then on, Philadelphia was as abject a slave as New York and Boston.

The total receipts for the three concerts came to nearly $20,000, and the distaste many Philadelphians had felt for the auction was softened by the announcement that a considerable proportion of the proceeds was to be given to the Philadelphia Volunteer Firemen and various charities.

Jenny had conquered the most critical audience she was likely to encounter in the United States, and Barnum took this as an excellent augury for the rest of the tour.

There was one jarring note. At the close of the last concert, Barnum asked Jenny to come to the front of the stage, then handing her a daguerreotype of herself to display, announced that it was to be auctioned off for charity, since there had not been time to give the usual concert for this purpose.

Taken by surprise, and being in full view of the audience, Jenny held up the daguerreotype as Barnum suggested, smiling pleasantly the while. But she ordered Barnum *sotto voce* never to ask her to do a thing of that kind again.

He never did. However, a second scar had been added to the first.

CHAPTER FOURTEEN

The Grand Tour Begins

BACK to New York, after the Philadelphia concerts, where the brand new Tripler Hall was now finished. (Tripler Hall was one American project during this period that was not named for Jenny Lind. Mr. Tripler had planned to call it the Jenny Lind Hall, then evidently decided it would be good business to be different from the rest of New York.) At the first rehearsal, Jenny pronounced the acoustics perfect, and the stage and seating arrangements all to her liking. The troupe settled down for a run of ten concerts and five oratorios, the longest of the tour.

Jenny suggested to Barnum that inasmuch as all the wealthy people in New York who wanted to hear her undoubtedly had done so during the first six concerts, it was time to lower the prices so that everyone else might hear her. Barnum scented a possibility both of good publicity and good business in this proposal and at once acceded, asking Jenny to write him a letter which he could show to the other members of the troupe. Jenny's letter, written October 24, read as follows: "You know I have always been in favor of having lower prices to make the tickets available to the masses, and at the same time prevent speculators from taking advantage of the reduction. Will you permit me to suggest that Tripler Hall is immensely large and that with proper precaution, you might avoid selling tickets to speculators, and at the same time put the prices within reach of the people at large. You will greatly oblige me, my Dear Sir."

Barnum replied that very afternoon: "I hasten with much pleasure to

[228]

say in reply to your letter of this morning that the great capacity of Tripler Hall will enable me to comply with your suggestions, and that accordingly I shall fix the prices to the entire first floor and second circle at $3 each, the front row in the first circle at $5, and all other seats in the same circle at $4 each. I shall give immediate directions that these prices apply to the concert tomorrow and all future concerts during your brief stay in New York." He at once gave both letters to the newspapers. Barnum had hoped that this exchange might pack the patrons in for several concerts, at least. It packed them in for all fifteen appearances, the demand for tickets increasing with every performance.

Daniel Webster attended one of the concerts in New York. It was reported to Jenny that he had complained to a companion, "Why doesn't she give us one of her simple mountain songs from her native country?" Before long the piano was moved to the front of the stage and Jenny sang the "Echo Song." For a second time Daniel Webster rose from his seat in the first balcony and made her a deep bow.

The first oratorio, Handel's *Messiah*, was given on Friday, November 15. Jenny was dressed all in white with a wreath of white roses around her head. The music editor of the *Tribune* pronounced the performance to be "by far the grandest musical event that has yet transpired in New York, and so, we suppose, with Boston's permission, in America. . . ."

Actually, the *Messiah* had been a fizzle except for the imported artists. The local singers hired to supplement the principals in solos and chorus were not sufficiently trained and the organ was out of tune. The tenor soloist broke down in one of his arias and was unable to finish it. Jenny's singing alone redeemed the inadequacies of the native artists.

The *Evening Journal*, the *Post* and the *Sun* went along with Horace Greeley's *Tribune* in singing Jenny's praises, but there was a change of attitude at the *Herald*. James Gordon Bennett, owner of this paper, was experimenting with the idea that one newspaper in a city should be in opposition to the others, and finding it profitable. He issued orders to his reporters that there should be no more glorifying of Jenny Lind. So far as Barnum was concerned, from now on he was to be designated as a fake and an impostor.

Jenny was mystified and hurt at the unfriendly comments which at once began appearing in the *Herald*, and Barnum was at first nonplused. LeGrand Smith wanted to bring a suit for libel, and another of Barnum's employees, Henry Bennett—not related to James Gordon—threatened to horsewhip the editor. But by this time Barnum had figured out his strategy.

He issued an order to his staff, "Let Bennett alone. Every attack is an advertisement. If he wants to say something good about us, that's first-rate. If something bad, that's all right too. But for heaven's sake, let's hope he says something!"

To counterbalance the *Herald*, stacks of eulogies of Jenny were coming out in weekly and monthly magazines. Barnum knew that these articles would be read all over the country and would add to the clamor to get Jenny to come to this or the other city on her grand tour. Even the *Herald*, while criticizing Jenny's singing in its news and editorial columns, was running such advertisements as the following:

> Jenny Lind Sewing Stands: Here is a brief outline for a man of family to commence a good course of life, if he has not already done so. Suppose on Sunday mornings he intends going to church, but when getting ready he finds several items of sewing necessary to his apparel, he would not speak to his wife on the subject, but on Monday go to one of the furniture or fancy-goods stores and purchase one of Blackwell's Jenny Lind sewing stands, send it home and go about his business avocations. Soon after, his dear wife may be seen by the side of the stand, sewing every article of clothing that requires it. On Tuesday, they are in the wash, on Wednesday, ironed. And all the week there will be such affectionate smiles from the wife as to prepare the husband's mind in the best manner to go to church the following Sunday, where he will not forget in his prayers to mention Jenny Lind!

Ballads about Jenny Lind were coming out by the dozens. One of the most popular was a rollicking piece entitled,

THE JENNY LIND MANIA

> Of Manias we've had many,
>   And some have raised the wind,
> But the most absurd of any
>   Is that of Jenny Lind.
> Causing quite a revolution,
>   To compliment her fame,
> From a toothpick to an omnibus,
>   All are called by her name.
>   Of Manias, etc.

My wife has a Jenny Lind bonnet,
    And a Jenny Lind *visite*;
With Jenny's portrait on it,
    My handkerchief looks neat.
My wife's a slave to fashion,
    Against it never sinned;
Our baby and the kitten
    Are named for Jenny Lind.
        Of, etc.

Oh Jenny when you leave us,
    What shall we ever do
To catch another Nightingale
    To sing as sweet as you?
You are but a bird of passage,
    You'll leave us with the rest;
But you, I think, may plume yourself
    You've feathered well your nest!
        Of, etc.

The general election of November, 1850, occurred during this second series of New York concerts, and many citizens, disgusted by the ceaseless bickering between the Whigs and Democrats in Congress, which the recently enacted Missouri Compromise had only intensified, and at outs with the candidates of their own parties, relieved their feelings by casting their votes for Jenny for many offices in various parts of the country. At a political convention in Rensselaer County, New York, she was nominated for the state assembly. She received a tidy vote for mayor of New York City and votes for governor and lesser offices in a number of states.

(Jenny even entered into the American monetary system. In 1852, as her stay in the United States was drawing to a close, the Pequonnock Bank in Bridgeport, Connecticut, issued three- and five-dollar bills which had medallion portraits of Barnum and Jenny on either side of a vignette of Barnum's Bridgeport home, Iranistan. These were snapped up quickly for souvenirs. By a strange coincidence, P. T. Barnum was president of the bank.)

There was one redeeming feature of her second stay in New York City. Barnum no longer had time to act as her escort and thus call the public's attention to the fact that here was Jenny Lind. The pictures of her shown everywhere were for the most part so bad that Jenny was able to walk about New York City with Josephine Åhmansson without being recognized. (Parker Willis had complained that she allowed "with careless willingness, painters and daguerreotypists to make what they will of her.") It was her only escape from the petitioners who haunted her at the New York Hotel.

Willis described one of Jenny's days in an article in the *Home Journal.* She had given a concert the night before and as always was tired the next morning. Finishing breakfast at half past nine, she found her sitting room already half filled with people who had forced their way past the five guards—three hotel employees and two men employed by Jenny— who were supposed to keep intruders out.

First there was an argument over a music box which had been sent to her by a man she had never heard of. Now the man was demanding payment for it and refusing even to take it away with him. Next was a group of beggarwomen. To each of these she usally offered twenty or thirty dollars, but Willis said that in almost every case it was returned to her with some disparaging comment. "We must have been mistaken in your character, Miss Lind; we had heard that you were generous," was the general tenor of these remarks.

Besides these persons were applicants for places with the troupe, female fans expressing their passionate admiration, a dozen or so ladies with albums for Jenny to sign, one or two with things they had made for Jenny and for which they clearly expected to "get nothing less than diamond rings in return." Still another was there to demand an explanation as to why Jenny had not acknowledged a poem the visitor had sent her. Letters and notes were coming in at the rate of one every other minute and there were constant messages from Benedict or Barnum or others which required attention. It was no wonder that she was "torn in pieces." Moreover, the personal handouts were in addition to the some thirty-five thousand dollars she had given to various New York charities.

A French newspaperman had just criticized Jenny for being unsociable at a party and unwilling to dance, the writer reporting that her replies to him had been all of one syllable, though he tried to converse with her in three different languages. After he had seen Jenny dealing patiently all day long with the kind of persons he described, Parker Willis thought there might have been other reasons than dullness for Jenny's failure to be bright and sparkling in the evening.

At the party where the French editor had complained of her social deficiency, Jenny was too tired to take supper with the rest of the guests, and it was served to her in an alcove where she sat alone. Willis wrote that "she sat in a posture of careless and graceful repose, her head wearily bent on one side, her eyes drooped, her hands crossed before her, in the characteristic habit which has been seized by painters who have drawn her. There was an expression of dismissed care, which had been replaced by a kind of child-like and innocent sadness. This struck us as inexpressibly sweet, and we treasure it mentally as another of those phases of excessive beauty of which that strong face is capable."

Jenny never found another hall in America that pleased her as much as Tripler's, and the New York concerts could have continued indefinitely. But Barnum told his artists they must follow the rule, "Stop while the interest is high." Besides, the grand tour was already arranged. Some dates were yet to be agreed upon, but with the exception of a few Midwest towns which Barnum included later, the cities where Jenny and her supporting artists were to appear had been selected. There was to be a return engagement in Philadelphia. Then on to Baltimore, a city of growing industry, followed by Washington, the still unfinished, sprawling national capital, to Richmond, metropolis of the Old Dominion, and Charleston, the social capital of the South. From there to exotic Havana, capital of Spanish Cuba; next, to New Orleans and up the great rivers of the Midwest, stopping to sing at the cities along the way.

It was the longest musical tour that had ever been arranged in America, lasting from November, 1850, until late the following May, and covering around twelve thousand miles. It was also the most ambitious and costly, calling for transporting, along with the star, her supporting artists and retinue, Barnum and his assistants, and Benedict and his orchestra. Out of the sixty-man orchestra employed in New York City, twelve of the best musicians were selected for the trip. (In the different cities, the number was raised to thirty-five, forty or fifty from among local musicians.) The party was to leave New York on November 25. The first part of the trip, from New York as far as Wilmington, North Carolina, was to be made by train, and Barnum had leased a coach for his party's exclusive use. He took Jenny and Josephine to see the long bare car, with its coal stove in the corner and its rows of hard, straight-backed wooden seats. Jenny looked at the seats ruefully.

"Mr. Barnum," she suggested, "why not take out most of the seats and equip the car with comfortable armchairs and tables for books and papers? It could be like a parlor."

Barnum seized upon the idea and trumpeted to the press, "Miss Lind's railway car will be like a parlor!" Railway officials took note. This was the origin of parlor cars on American railroads.

Now was to begin the real challenge for Jenny—to take good music to the American masses. In the new, raw land of the North American continent, from colonial days to the Revolution, music in the English-speaking areas had been drawn principally from three sources: the classics, which only the performers understood; religious songs and psalms; and the folk ballads from Old England (these continued to be sung in pure form in the Kentucky mountains for many decades longer), modified and added to, imitated and expanded, by American popular composers. Beginning with the patriotic awakening inspired by the War of 1812, some distinctly American music began to be produced, but little was done to bridge the gap between the "high-class" music of the artists, and the "common" music of the evangelical churches and the folk ballads and jingles people sang on lay occasions.

Classical music was limited largely to the big cities of the Eastern seaboard. In the center of the country, where states were just being cut out of territories and many of the inhabitants lived in log houses or sod houses, it was practically unheard of. Even in the larger cities, the "high-class" performer found it very hard to make a living. Bands of the day played jig-time dances, or marches or waltzes. Minstrels, white and Negro, sprang up with the Andrew Jackson era, but the music of their banjos was as cheap as their jokes.

Now there was a new composer named Stephen Foster, a Pittsburgh musician in love with the South, who was producing songs of a type new in America. Tuneful and appealing, they were being sung with increasing enjoyment by the common people. Jenny bought copies of all Stephen Foster's songs that she could find and began mastering their English words with Joseph Burke's help.

What a wonderful thing it would be to bring the great music of the masters to these people! And it would be quite as gratifying to prove that good "popular" music could be enjoyed along with the classical works. How fine it would be to stimulate people everywhere to sing songs in which they could take real pleasure!

In the two concerts of her return engagement in Philadelphia, Jenny proved that this was possible. "I Know That My Redeemer Liveth" drew the usual ovation of mingled enthusiasm and reverence. As an encore she sang for the first time Stephen Foster's "My Old Kentucky Home." When she came to the chorus, she signaled to the audience to join in, and the whole hall took up the refrain, "Weep no more, my lady. . . ."

In Baltimore, Mayor Jerome called on Jenny, accompanied by the superintendent of schools and the director of education for the parochial schools, to ask Jenny what she would charge to sing for the school children on Saturday morning.

"Nothing," Jenny said. "It will be a great pleasure for me."

Accompanied by Belletti and Benedict and orchestra, Jenny arrived at the theater at ten o'clock Saturday to find it jammed—with girls only.

"But where are the boys?" Jenny asked. The Mayor explained that the boys would be there at eleven o'clock. In Baltimore schools, the sexes were kept carefully apart during youth. Jenny was expected to give two concerts!

She took it good-naturedly, and used the occasion to introduce "Hail Columbia." After she had sung the first stanza she invited the girls to sing with her. They were timid and did not respond as she had hoped. But when she tried the same thing with the boys they sang lustily, while Jenny beat time for them.

The next day, Barnum was shown an example of the power of publicity that he chuckled over to his dying day. Jenny always attended church on Sunday, and during her American tour she attended a Swedish church whenever one could be found in the locality. There was a Swedish church in Baltimore, and Jenny and Josephine Åhmansson slipped into it quietly, without attracting attention. Barnum took his daughter, her friend Mrs. Lyman and still another friend, a Baltimore woman, to a different church, Barnum driving the three there in an open carriage. The Baltimore woman sang in the choir of the pretentious church, and insisted that Caroline Barnum join her in singing with the choir. The congregation had seen Barnum escort the ladies into the church and took it for granted that Caroline was Jenny Lind.

Barnum wrote merrily in his memoirs: "It was soon whispered through the church that Jenny Lind was in the choir! The excitement was worked to its highest pitch when my daughter rose as one of the musical group.

Every ear was on the alert to catch the first notes of her voice, and as she sang, glances of satisfaction passed through the assembly. Caroline, quite unconscious of the attention she attracted, continued to sing to the end of the hymn. Not a note was lost upon the ears of the attentive congregation. 'What an exquisite singer' 'Heavenly sounds!' 'I never heard the like!' and similar expressions were whispered through the church.

"At the conclusion of the services, my daughter and her friend found the passageway to their carriage blocked by a crowd who were anxious to obtain a nearer view of the 'Swedish Nightingale,' and many persons boasted, in good faith, that they had listened to the extraordinary singing of the great songstress." The marvel was the greater to Caroline's father because, as he remarked dryly, "We have never discovered that my daughter has any extraordinary claim as a vocalist."

It might be maintained from this that Jenny's success in America stemmed from Barnum's humbuggery, were it not that her previous triumphs in Europe had been attained without a hint of such manipulation. And later on in the tour she was to meet still another situation in which her reputation was of no help. She would have to win over an actively hostile audience through supreme ability alone.

By this time, Jenny had sung for enough American audiences to know what selections would best serve her aims. As a rule, her program for the tour consisted of famous arias from *Norma, La Sonnambula,* and *I Puritani;* airs by Mozart, Weber and Meyerbeer; duets with Signor Belletti, and nearly always the famous trio with two flutes, from *Camp in Silesia.* Jenny wrote Judge Munthe in November, "The bird song, "I Know Not Why I Am Singing," and Herr Berg's song with the long-sustained notes, and the Norwegian echo-song—these are the standing pieces I must sing at every concert." In addition, Jenny made a point of introducing English and Scottish songs such "Comin' Through the Rye," "Annie Laurie," "The Last Rose of Summer," "Auld Robin Grey," "John Anderson, My Jo," and the newer American songs. All of these have remained firmly implanted in America's musical mores.

It was only a step from Baltimore to Washington, D.C., at this time called "The City of Magnificent Distances." To one acquainted with European capitals, however, the distances must have been more striking than the magnificence. They were filled for the most part with low, squat, business establishments, rooming houses for government employes, and a few scattered residential districts, separated from each other by mosquito-infested marshlands.

Stakes had been set out on either side of the Capitol marking the places where two wings were to be built, one for the Senate and one for the House. It was also proposed to raise the Capitol dome to twice its height. These improvements were going forward under the supervision of the able and energetic Senator Jefferson Davis of Mississippi, but funds must be found, and it was unlikely that they would be completed in much less than eight years.

On a hill overlooking a swamp, with the Potomac River beyond, a stone obelisk had been carried about 100 feet into the air. It had been intended as a monument to George Washington, and was supposed to soar high into the sky. But the members of Congress had learned that at least $100,000 more was required to finish the job, and ordered the work stopped. There was much complaint about the cost of the federal government. The day of Jenny's arrival, Editor William Seaton was pointing out in his paper, the *National Intelligencer*, that appropriations for the Interior Department had passed the $5 million mark, and that the country was "wasting" about $2 million a year on its Indian wards alone.

Fortunately, the huge statue of Andrew Jackson, which was to stand near the center of the park in front of the Executive Mansion, had been completed before the economy wave struck. Already the base was in place, and workmen were preparing to hoist the statue onto it. The Treasury Building, with its Greek columns, which Jackson had located to the right of the Mansion, and which housed the offices of Secretary of State Daniel Webster and his aides, was beautiful enough to make up for the scarcity of fine public buildings. Barnum, an "Andy Jackson Democrat," was delighted to see the impression his hero had left on the nation's capitol.

Southern leaders were reaching for more and more power, drawn together by the struggle for seats in the Senate and House as new territory was opened in the Southwest and West, from which new states would eventually be carved. The Whig party was declining, as its leaders failed to find a satisfactory way to deal with the slavery problem. Would the gold rush to California disturb the delicate balance between slave and antislave states? Would Hamilton Fish, just elected to the Senate from

New York, become the dominant Whig? Would the still immensely popular, though aging, Henry Clay try for the Presidency again? Or would Daniel Webster, who would be President now if he had not refused to run as Zachary Taylor's Vice President, yet attain the highest office? Would South Carolina keep up its threat of secession because of the abolitionist movement?

These were the questions agitating Washington when Jenny arrived there in early December of 1850. It is doubtful if Jenny ever heard the name of Abraham Lincoln. The backwoods lawyer from Illinois had returned home in 1848 after serving one term in Congress. He had displeased his constituency by questioning the basis on which President Polk had declared war on Mexico, and was now devoting himself to his neglected law business. The waters of oblivion had closed over him, as far as Washington, D.C., was concerned.

The party took rooms at the Willard Hotel, one of the few establishments provided for higher government officials and visiting notables. LeGrand Smith, serving as advance man, had bad news for his employer. Washington was sadly lacking in places of public entertainment, as in so many other things, and had no hall large enough for Jenny's concerts. Barnum had had a brilliant idea and had written at once to the Hon. C. F. Cleveland, the congressman from his Connecticut district, about it. It would really put the United States Congress on the map, he pointed out, if the world-famous Jenny Lind, who had enchanted the crowned heads of Europe, were to give her concerts in the Capitol Building! He feared that the Senate chamber would be too small, and he understood that, most unfortunately, the space beneath the dome was taken up by hucksters selling eggs, vegetables and other farm produce. But he believed that the House of Representatives, though a bit cramped, could be made to do.

Representative Cleveland had reported regretfully to LeGrand Smith that while the idea was certainly splendid, Congressional rules forbade holding concerts or other forms of public entertainment in the Capitol Building. So rigid were these rules, he emphasized, that not even the heavenly choir, accompanied by Gabriel on his trumpet, would be allowed to sing there. Otherwise he would have been only too happy to accommodate as valued a constituent as P. T. Barnum. LeGrand Smith had taken the matter to Daniel Webster, already enlisted firmly among Jenny's admirers, and he had confirmed Cleveland's statement.

However, a fine new theater was being built across from Pennsylvania Avenue on E Street, on the site of the National Theater, which had burned down in 1845. It was to be called the New National Hall, and the builder was rushing the work in order to have the hall finished in time for Jenny's first concert. The architect had furnished LeGrand Smith with a written certification that its two-foot-thick brick walls, reinforced by iron straps and bolts, would be sufficient to "secure comfort and safety for any audience which may congregate within the walls of the building."

The first concert was set for the night of December 16. Editors Seaton of the *Intelligencer* and Thomas Richie of the *Washington Union*, both friends of Barnum, urged everyone to come and hear the "Sweet Ambassadress of Song," a new designation for Jenny which Barnum considered appropriate in the nation's capital. Barnum's advertisement, which ran in all the city's papers, announced that he had employed the whole of the Germanic Musical Society's Orchestra for the concerts. An adjoining advertisement stated that "Jenny Lind Opera Glasses, from Munich and Vienna," could be bought at an optical company on the corner of 10th and Pennsylvania, and would add much to the pleasure of the concert-goers.

As soon as President Millard Fillmore, brought into office by the death of Zachary Taylor the preceding July, saw in the paper that Jenny Lind was in town, he put on his hat and, accompanied by Mrs. Fillmore, strolled through the woods back of the Executive Mansion and the Treasury Building to the Willard Hotel. Jenny was out sightseeing, so the President left his card.

When Jenny returned and found it, she was greatly distressed because she had not been there to receive the visitors. "Come," she exclaimed to Barnum, "we must call on the President and his lady immediately!"

"What's the hurry?"

"Why, etiquette requires that if one receives a visit from the head of a state, it must be returned at once!"

Barnum explained that the etiquette of a democracy was very different from that of a royal court and that it would be more suitable to postpone their visit until the next day. The next morning Jenny, accompanied by Josephine Åhmansson, Barnum, Benedict, Belletti, Caroline Barnum and her friend Mrs. Lyman, spent an hour chatting with the President and Mrs. Fillmore. Jenny was shy at first, fearing that her English was not good enough, but was soon put at ease by Mrs. Fillmore's questions about Sweden and the President's suggestions about places she should see while in Washington. Presently she summoned courage to ask the President, "How are the American people governed? I have heard much about your democracy but I know little about the way it is performed."

Fillmore replied, smiling, "Our people govern themselves, mostly, which does not leave much for the President to do."

The President said that of course he and his wife were looking forward to hearing Jenny sing at her first concert. The affair rapidly turned into a state occasion; everyone in Washington who was anybody—high officials of the American government, foreign diplomats—was buying tickets. The members of the President's Cabinet and their wives would attend in a body, being led to their seats at the front of the auditorium by Daniel Webster himself.

The informality of the President and his wife, greatly as it contrasted with the rigid etiquette of the European courts, still had not prepared Jenny for the difference between a gala performance there and one in the American capital. On Queen Victoria's birthday, for instance, the outside of the royal box at Her Majesty's Theatre had been draped with crimson velvet, gold-fringed, and blue velvet trimmed with silver. The inside of the box was lined with blue tulle over white satin, ornamented with more gold, and the antechamber with white tulle over pink silk, and quantities of priceless lace. Victoria came to the theater in a procession of state carriages, escorted by yeomen of the guard. Throughout the performance two yeomen stood on scarlet-covered platforms that had been especially erected for them on the stage side of the box.

In Washington, the New National Hall was not even finished. No seats had been installed, let alone boxes. Barnum had had plush armchairs placed at the front for the President, Vice President, the members of the Cabinet and their wives, but the hall still smelled of wet plaster and the only attempt at decoration were the masses of flowers and greenery which banked the ornate Chickering piano on the stage. Nevertheless the distinguished audience, dressed in its best, seemed to see nothing improper in being required to sit on the crude benches provided for them.

Even more amazing to Jenny was the lack of ceremony with which the President and Vice President entered the hall with their families, and were shown to their easy chairs in front. They were greeted with only a light patter of applause, for President Fillmore had told Jenny quite truthfully that at the present time, at least, the American people mainly governed themselves. Not since Andrew Jackson had there been a strong personality in the Presidency to provoke worship or hatred. (At the end of his term of office, President Fillmore is reported to have remarked that Jenny Lind's visit to Washington was the most exciting thing that happened to him while he was in the White House.) Similar little ripples of applause were accorded the various foreign diplomats as they entered and were recognized.

Then, one by one, the real celebrities came in. Tumultuous clapping greeted General Winfield Scott, the hero of the recent war with Mexico. The leading politicians took care not to arrive until the house was nearly full. Popular idols like Senators Thomas Hart Benton of Missouri, Henry Foote of Mississippi and Lewis Cass of Michigan would pause at the back of the hall until the audience, craning to see who was next, signified recognition by a spate of clapping. Then each would advance grandly down the aisle to his seat, bowing to right and left.

It was time for the concert to begin. Jenny, after peering out at the scene in wonder, had retired to her dressing room to await the call for her first number. Still the armchairs that had been reserved for the seven Cabinet members and their wives were vacant. Barnum had Benedict hold up the overture for five minutes. When there was still no Cabinet, Barnum gave the signal to start. Benedict held his baton aloft, but at that moment a great cheer began at the back of the hall. This must mean that the Cabinet was arriving. Once more Barnum signaled Benedict to wait. But at the door of the auditorium a frail, white-haired man, dressed in a dark suit, was standing all alone. He made no move to advance, so Benedict brought his baton down, the musicians began the overture to *Oberon*. When it ended, the whole audience rose and broke into loud cheers. Benedict started to take his accustomed bow, then realized that the people were looking toward the back. Their homage was for the thin man in the dark suit who now started down the aisle to the accompaniment of "Three cheers for Henry Clay!"

The concert went on, with the audience in a holiday mood. It gave the Nightingale as much applause as the revered senator from Kentucky, which was all it had to give. Throughout the first part, the fourteen armchairs in the front row remained conspicuously empty. During her numbers, Jenny kept looking toward the back expecting any moment to see the distinguished figure of Daniel Webster come through the doors with the Cabinet trailing behind him, and make the occasion complete. But the intermission arrived and there was no sign of the Secretary of State or his colleagues.

The truth was that the truants were enjoying the dinner the Russian Minister, Count Bodiscov, gave each year to the President's official family. Hospitality at the Russian Embassy included, as Washington society knew well, the rarest wines and the most potent spirits served anywhere in the capital city. When Jenny's concert began, the gentlemen were still toasting the President of the United States, the Czar of all the Russias and other world dignitaries, while their ladies, in the Bodiscov drawing room, could do nothing but await their husbands' pleasure.

The program called for Jenny to open the second part with "Hail Columbia." She had barely started it when in walked the Cabinet members and their wives. Instead of waiting at the back for the conclusion of the number, as Henry Clay had done, they trooped down the aisle to their armchairs with majestic dignity and seated themselves. When Jenny reached the chorus, Mr. Webster rose unsteadily to his feet. Striking a grand pose, he joined in the song. Mrs. Webster pulled at her husband's long coattails, but he paid no attention, his deep, melodious bass voice rolling out the melody.

Titters rose to laughter. Jenny smiled and kept on singing. A burst of applause greeted the end of the chorus. Webster waited while Jenny sang the second stanza and again joined in the refrain, more lustily than ever. Then while applause mingled with cheers and laughter broke over the hall, he advanced toward the stage and made a gallant, if wobbly, bow. Jenny curtsied low, Webster bowed again and Jenny curtsied back, while the audience went wild with enjoyment of this unrehearsed scene. A tug from the hand of Mrs. Webster, too imperious this time to be ignored, finally pulled the great statesman down into his seat.

Throughout the rest of the concert, political differences and dignity alike were forgotten. "Comin' Through the Rye" brought the loudest cheers of all, with many laughing glances toward the happily oblivious Secretary of State, tapping time to the music with his foot. Jenny obligingly sang it again.

Then she stepped forward for the finale which on this occasion was to be an American song instead of a Scandinavian melody that usually ended her concerts. It was not a new song. It had been first presented at Covent Garden in 1823, part of an opera, *Clari,* for which Boston-born John Howard Payne had written the words and Henry R. Bishop the music and then had sold, along with two other operas, for $250. *Clari* had long been forgotten, but this one song, "Home, Sweet Home," had caught the public fancy. Since 1823 it had been sung in many languages and played in a great variety of instrumental arrangements, but the composers had never received a penny more for it than the original $250. John Howard Payne once remarked how ironical it had been to hear the strains of the song he and Bishop had written coming from a cafe in a strange city, where he was walking the streets penniless and with no place to stay.

Barnum had learned that Payne was in Washington and was to attend Jenny's first concert. He had thought it would be a "good piece of business" for Jenny to sing "Home, Sweet Home" even though its popularity had diminished after so many years, and Payne's connection with it was on the way to being forgotten. (The playwright's name was not even on the copy of the song that Barnum had procured.) Jenny's eyes ran first over the simple melody, then went to the words. She said, "I will sing this song." Before the concert began, Barnum had showed Jenny where Payne was sitting, at the left of the stage, a slight man, wan and gray-haired.

The orchestra held the chord softly while Jenny began the words, directing them to the gray-haired man.

> Mid pleasures and palaces, though we may roam,
> Be it ever so humble, there's no place like home.

Many great singers have included "Home, Sweet Home" in their repertoires since Jenny sang it in Washington, but one doubts that it has ever since been sung as Jenny Lind sang it that night. The unconscious pathos that had always been a feature of Jenny's voice was intensified as the singer, who longed for a home she had never had, expressed the yearning for home that the poet and playwright had felt in his wanderings. Howard Payne sat with bowed head, a hand over his eyes. Everywhere in the audience, handkerchiefs appeared. When Jenny finished there was no applause. Men and women were too busy wiping their eyes and blowing their noses. Finally Mr. Payne stood up and bowed, and Jenny curtsied to him. Then the entire audience rose to its feet with a great outburst of cheering.

The next morning's event was always considered by Barnum to have been the crowning point of his career, perhaps because it was one occasion he himself had had nothing to do with inspiring. A delegation comprising all the real powers in Washington came to the Willard to pay their respects to the Swedish Nightingale. It included Henry Clay, General Winfield Scott, Senators Benton, Foote and Cass, besides the grateful John Howard Payne and the editor of the *Intelligencer*. As they left, they all shook hands with Barnum and thanked him for bringing Jenny Lind to Washington. Nearly all requested that tickets be reserved for them for the next concert.

The success of the second concert assured, Jenny asked Barnum to reduce the prices so that more of the common people could hear her. This time Barnum did not consent. He knew that the new National Hall could be filled a second time no matter how high the price of the tickets. His argument to Jenny was that there were no common people in Washington. "Everybody here is a celebrity of some kind."

Jenny was attended by a court of her own when she went off that noon to Mount Vernon, then the home of Colonel John A. Washington, a great great-nephew of the first President. Barnum chartered a river steamboat for the trip, and took along not only Jenny's fellow artists and the orchestra members, but Editor Seaton of the *Intelligencer* and his wife, and the members of Congress from the various states where Jenny would be singing on her tour. History has not recorded whether this was the origin of Congressional junkets, but it may well have been another Barnum-Jenny Lind first.

They disembarked a short distance from the tomb, which they visited. Jenny looked at the stone sepulchres of the first President and his wife with the same reverence she had felt when, with Hans Christian Andersen, she visited the burial vault in Weimar where Goethe and Schiller lay. Jenny had an almost superstitious respect for creative genius. The Austrian poet, Hermann Rollet, chancing to visit the vault while Andersen and Jenny were there, sat down and composed, on the spot, a poem about the Nightingale mourning the dead poets. Andersen included it in his autobiography.

Jenny Lind, the Swedish Nightingale

From Longfellow Jenny learned to what extent George Washington had been responsible for creating a new country, with a new philosophy and way of life. When the party went on to the house, Jenny was impressed by the graciousness of the Washington home, and was fascinated by the mementos of the great man. Colonel Washington's wife served what Barnum described as a "beautiful collation, arranged in fine taste." Then, before the party left, she gave Jenny a book from the Mount Vernon library, in which George Washington had written his name. Barnum said that she was much overcome; calling him aside, Jenny expressed a desire to give the Washingtons something in return.

" 'I have nothing with me,' she said, 'except this watch and chain, and I will give that if you think it will be acceptable.' I knew the watch was very valuable, and told her that so costly a present would not be accepted, nor would it be proper. 'The expense is nothing, compared to the value of that book,' she replied, with deep emotion. 'But as the watch was a present from a dear friend, perhaps I should not give it away.' Jenny Lind, I am sure, never forgot the pleasurable emotion of that day."

Colonel Washington also presented Jenny with a book, a history of Sweden, written in French, with marginal notes and comments in George Washington's hand. Jenny took the book, and tears came to her eyes. Mrs. Seaton remarked, "You are not an American, yet you reverence Washington so much!"

"Whoever loves mankind must love the name of Washington," Jenny answered. Mrs. Seaton remembered that Jenny's pronunciation of "mankind," with a "t" instead of the final "d," brought smiles from the party.

Jenny visited both houses of Congress and was escorted on a tour of the Capitol and its grounds by the Hon. C. F. Cleveland. She pleased Mr. Cleveland very much by her tactful compliments. They went to the Treasury Building where Jenny was welcomed by Secretary of State Webster in his red-carpeted, walnut-paneled office, with its framed portraits of former Secretaries of State, its outsize desk and bookcases and equally impressive brass spittoons.

There was a single threat to Jenny's brilliant success in Washington, and Barnum moved quickly to counteract it. Editor Richie of the Washington *Union* came to Barnum with an ugly rumor. There was talk, Richie said, that Jenny Lind had made a donation to some abolitionist organization in the North. Was this true? Realizing what a rumor of this kind could do to his singer in Richmond, Charleston and other Southern cities, Barnum at once wrote a letter to Editor Richie for publication in the *Union*, for some reason dating it from Baltimore:

> In reply to your letter of yesterday, inquiring whether there is any truth in the report that Mlle. Jenny Lind has given a donation to an association of Abolitionists, I beg to state most emphatically that *there is not the slightest foundation for such a statement.* I feel no hesitation in saying that this lady never gave a farthing for any such purpose, and that her often expressed admiration for our noble system of government convinces me that she prizes too dearly the glorious institutions of our country to lend the slightest sanction to any attack upon the Union of these states. I have the honor to remain. Yr. Very Obed. Servant P. T. Barnum.

The ugly rumor was squelched.

For the second concert also, the President and Mrs. Fillmore, all the members of the Cabinet—completely sober, including Daniel Webster—and their wives; diplomats; Supreme Court Justices; members of Congress and other assorted celebrities were in their places when the overture began. Again the crowd gave Jenny and her accompanying artists a rousing response. John Howard Payne was not there this time, but Jenny again sang "Home, Sweet Home." As soon as the first notes were heard, applause drowned out her voice. She stopped, waited for silence, smiled and started the song again.

"Home, Sweet Home" became America's most popular song. The publishers could not print copies fast enough to supply the demand. As the American tour progressed, it gradually displaced Jenny's Scandinavian folk songs as the prime favorite. She could not give a concert without singing "Home, Sweet Home" at least once, and it became her hallmark with the American public. When her admirers in one city after another serenaded her with the song, one wonders what thoughts went through her mind.

John Howard Payne, alas, received none of the financial profits that resulted from the rebirth of the song. He died two years later, far from home, in Tunis, Morocco. But Jenny's gestures in Washington attached his name to it firmly for all time, and gave poet and song immortality.

And once more, Barnum's luck was in. The hastily completed New

National Hall did hold together, as the architect had promised, on the two occasions when nearly all the top people in the federal government were gathered to hear Jenny. The next time its doors were opened for an entertainment, a few weeks afterwards, the walls collapsed. That was the end of the New National Hall until a third building was erected on the site in 1852.

CHAPTER FIFTEEN

South to Havana

RICHMOND turned out so enthusiastically for the ticket auction that the newspapers and the citizens felt they were entitled to have two concerts instead of the single one that had been scheduled. But arrangements had already been made to go on to Charleston and Barnum had to refuse. The one concert, however, brought in $12,385, the most receipts for a single concert since the first Boston appearance. It was given in the Marshall Theater, at the corner of Seventh and Broad Streets. The Richmond *Republican and General Advertiser* declared that the Nightingale "looked majestic and beautiful, yet simple and gentle as a child," and the music critic for the Richmond *Whig* said that Jenny "glided into the intricate beauties of an Italian song with as much ease as a bird into its native elements. . . . We have no apology for the intensity of our admiration."

(An editorial in the same paper denounced as rank folly the talk of secession in Mississippi and South Carolina; and an attorney advertised for soldiers, and widows and orphans of soldiers, who had claims against the United States growing out of the Revolutionary War, the War of 1812 and the Indian Wars.)

Jenny sat for her picture at the gallery of Montgomery Pike Simmons, Richmond's well-known daguerreotypist. Mr. Simmons proudly exhibited his daybook with her signature and the one other word she had written —"Sweden."

The members of the state legislature, which was in session at the time, adjourned in honor of Jenny and walked in a body from the state capitol to her hotel to pay their respects. Jenny shook the hand of each person as he was presented by the Speaker of the House.

Just before the party was to leave Richmond, so many people crowded into the hotel to get a glimpse of Jenny that Barnum told her it would be almost impossible to get out of the building.

"How much time is there before we must start?" she asked.

When Barnum replied "About half an hour," she said smiling, "Oh, I will clear the passages before that time!" She went into the upper hall and called out that she would like to shake hands with every person present, but on one condition. They must pass by her in single file, and as soon as they had shaken hands go downstairs and out, not blocking the passages. The crowd accepted the condition joyously and within fifteen minutes the exits were free.

The parlor car trundled along toward Wilmington, North Carolina, on the way to Charleston. But the track had been newly laid and petered out at Weldon, a town in the northern part of the state. As the party started to eat supper at a hotel, the room filled with spectators, who surrounded the table where Jenny was seated and followed the course of every bite of food from her plate to her mouth. Jenny fled to a private parlor, most of the waiters trailing after her. The other passengers from the train were left without service.

They went the rest of the way to Wilmington in carriages, and there boarded the steamer *Gladiator* for Charleston. The usual time for this coastal voyage was seventeen hours, but about midway, a severe storm blew up. The ship was badly tossed about and most of the passengers, including Barnum, Benedict and Belletti, were violently seasick. Max Hjortzberg and Jenny were not. The secretary prowled around the salon, lighting one cigar from another, while Jenny went about doing what she could for the sick, praying to herself the while. When the ship was fifteen hours overdue in Charleston, an enterprising reporter for the Charleston *Courier* sent out wires to papers over the country. "A ship bearing Mlle. Jenny Lind, the Swedish singer, Mr. P. T. Barnum, her manager, and a great collection of distinguished musicians and many other passengers, is presumed lost in today's storm off the North Carolina coast."

About the time the headlines were being set up in morning papers in many parts of the country, the *Gladiator* limped into Charleston Harbor, nineteen hours late. As Barnum sat in the lobby of their hotel recovering from seasickness and fright, he muttered to LeGrand Smith and the *Courier* reporter, "This is one hoax they can't blame on me!"

They spent ten days in Charleston, and enjoyed a quiet, peaceful time after the frenzies in the Northern cities and the eventful stay in Washington. There was a good audience for the first concert, on December 21; but the second one, on December 23, ran into the traditional Southern firecracker celebration of the Yule season, and the receipts were only $3,653. The third and last concert, on December 28, was somewhat better, and Jenny left behind her $3,500 for local charities. More important to her than concert receipts was that she was personally bothered very little in this easy going city. She and the other members of the troupe rested, basked in the mild winter sunshine and enjoyed the "deep South" atmosphere of flower-filled, languid Charleston. Her favorite walk was on the Battery which looked out over the bay toward Fort Sumter. She could stroll there and through the residence districts with no more than a curious glance from occasional passers-by. A pleasanter setting could not have been found for her first Christmas in America.

The traditional Swedish Christmas observances had always been very dear to Jenny. In Paris, during the Christmas season, she had mourned that her mother "had no child to light the Christmas tree." Her second Christmas in Berlin, learning that Hans Christian Andersen had spent the day there alone—he had come to Berlin expressly to be with Jenny at Christmas, but she, supposing he would be "surrounded by princes and princesses," had not thought to invite him to her little party of Scandinavian friends—Jenny had made another feast, for Andersen's benefit. He was the sole guest, and all the gifts on the tree were for him.

Jenny had long since sent Christmas packages of articles bought in America to relatives and close friends, and had provided Judge Munthe with a long list of presents he was to buy for her numerous protégés. Now, as Christmas drew near, she told the troupe she would like to celebrate it in true Swedish fashion. She sent several of the men to buy the most stately Christmas tree they could find, and install it in her parlor at the hotel. At that point, Jenny took over.

On Christmas Eve, there was a bountiful dinner, served by white-jacketed Negro servants. Then the doors were thrown open to Jenny's parlor where the Christmas tree stood, covered with decorations, glowing with candles and loaded with presents. More candles shone in the chandeliers, and the walls were decorated with holly, and with mistletoe cut from the great live oaks in the nearby swamps. Jenny rose for a speech. In her gay moods, she often teased Barnum by mimicking his pompous manner and characteristic phrases and now she did her P. T. Barnum imitation, her Swedish accent making the performance more hilarious.

"Mine friends, I haff here a list of first-rate Christmas presents. I can guarantee that all will be amazed, entertained and—what is that word?—humbugged!" Barnum's hearty "ha-ha" could be heard above all the others.

For each member of the troupe there was a mirth-provoking present from Jenny. Benedict was handed a huge package, from which he removed wrapping upon wrapping until he came to a can of tobacco—Cavendish, his favorite brand. Barnum's "fun" present was a statue of Bacchus, a rib on his strict temperance principles. Belletti received a bottle of tonic for his thin moustache, and so around the group. But there was a genuine present for each as well. Benedict's, a baton, was later bought by Edward, Prince of Wales, as a present for his wife.

New Year's Eve, Jenny again entertained in her apartments. There was music, singing, story telling, then the rugs were rolled back for dancing. Jenny asked Barnum to dance with her. He replied that he would like to, but that he had never danced in his life.

"That is all the better," she said gaily. "Now I can teach you!"—and they started with a cotillion. Barnum said he had never heard Jenny laugh more heartily than she did at his awkwardness. "She said she would give me credit for being the poorest dancer she had ever seen!"

But just before midnight, Jenny stopped the merry making. "Let us be quiet. In fifteen minutes, this year will be gone for ever." She sat down, resting her head upon her hand, and the others joined her in contemplation of the year just past. At midnight, they wished each other happy New Year and went quietly to their rooms, for they saw that Jenny was weeping.

The stay in Charleston offered little relaxation for Barnum, aside from these frolics, for every day the mailman brought huge bundles of letters. Not all were concerned with the concert tour. Many asked where the songs Jenny was singing could be obtained. Those most in demand were "Home, Sweet Home," "Hail Columbia," "My Old Kentucky Home," and "I Know That My Redeemer Liveth." America was coming alive with a new kind of song.

What might be called Belletti's campaign to win Jenny's hand, though he himself gave it no such pretentious title, had not progressed very far. In the Northern cities, Jenny's days had been filled by visitors and petitioners when she was not rehearsing or sightseeing. Usually the sightseeing trips were a group affair, with Barnum turning them into public parades insofar as he was able to. When Barnum was not present, Benedict, with his paternal attitude toward their star, took it upon himself to look after Jenny's welfare.

Charleston afforded the first opportunity for Belletti to have any quiet talks with Jenny. Sometimes he would take Josephine Åhmansson's place as companion on her walks, and now at last Jenny confessed to him the sadly ridiculous and ridiculously sad affair of Claudius Harris.

"I was such a fool! But at least it taught me something. I shall never be such a fool again. He was a child; my fancy built him into a man." She had restored Belletti to his old position of confidant, and surely that was something.

On the steamer *Isabella*, which took them to Havana from Charleston, there was time for more walks about the deck. Even though they had been a good deal together after Belletti joined Her Majesty's Theatre, they both exclaimed that there had been little time for intimate talks since Jenny had left the Royal Theater in Stockholm. Moreover, Jenny could talk to Belletti in Swedish, a language he had learned during his stay in Stockholm, and with his help she improved her Italian accent, for she had had to learn Italian quickly, to sing in it in London. It was exactly the kind of slowly developing intimacy that Belletti had envisioned, as a prelude to that moment when it would be appropriate for him to declare his love. This was perhaps the happiest time for Belletti on the entire trip.

Barnum had had every intention of providing the troupe with comfortable and pleasant accommodations in Havana. Before he left New York on the grand tour, he had arranged with an agent in Havana to rent a house and furnish it tastefully. It was to be all ready for them to step into when they reached Cuba. But the agent had let Barnum down. Seeing a way to make a further profit for himself, he had rented out parts of the house to other persons. The furniture he had installed was far from the kind Barnum had ordered. Jenny walked through the depressing rooms, took one look at the curious heads poked out of the adjoining windows and asked to have a carriage brought. As soon as it came she commandeered the interpreter Barnum had hired for their stay and disappeared. Four hours went by and the rest of the party was beginning to be anxious about her, for they had not the slightest idea where she had gone. But she reappeared triumphantly with the announcement that she had found a house and rented furniture for it. She invited Barnum, his daughter and Mrs. Lyman to stay there with herself and Josephine Åhmansson. Quarters were found for the rest of the party at a hotel.

Jenny's find was on the Paseo, at that time a drive encircling the city but now a broad street in the center of Havana's newer downtown district. In 1851 the Paseo was lined by charming villas with walled gardens. Though it was January, the sun was hot at midday. The bougainvillea that wreathed houses and fences were covered with flowers, and the poinsettias, reaching as high as the second stories of the houses, were in bloom. Wild orchids could be found by those who knew where to look for them. Everywhere were stately palm trees, the first Jenny had ever seen. And not far from the villa was the incredibly blue Caribbean, edged with coral or with beaches of gleaming white sand, the picturesque Morro Castle jutting into the sky across the bay. It was a tropical paradise, but without the oppressive heat of the true tropics. Jenny luxuriated both in the privacy of her walled garden, and in the beauty that met her eyes whenever she ventured from it.

Barnum, however, did not take much pleasure in his surroundings. The ticket prices he announced in his newspaper advertisements appeared wickedly high to the people of Havana; meanwhile an Italian opera company was playing to good houses. Barnum, knowing no Spanish, could not exert his usual charm over the editors of the papers. They decried the prices for the Lind concerts and gave all the publicity to the Italian company. Barnum was told that he must reduce his price to $3 per ticket if he were to attract an audience, but he refused. He had increased his orchestra to a hundred for the Havana concerts and was paying $1,000 a night for the opera house. He declared he would give no concerts at all in Havana rather than lose money on Jenny's appearances there. There was great wealth in Havana, but the citizens resented Barnum's attitude. A fair number of tickets was bought for the first concert, but the holders came in much the same spirit in which these people of Spanish descent would have attended a bullfight. The insolent Yankee was the target of their hostility, but they would get at him by hissing and booing his Nightingale off the stage.

Barnum had not dared to tell Jenny about the resentment he had encountered. He had learned how nervous she was at appearing before a new audience under the best of circumstances, and he feared she would refuse to appear at all if she knew the facts. So Jenny came to the opera house that night with no preparation at all for what was to happen.

The hall filled quickly enough, mostly with men, though some escorted exquisitely dressed ladies. They paid scant attention to the programs which Barnum had had printed in Spanish and bound in bright yellow, the principal color in the flag of Spain, Cuba's mother country. When the time for the concert came, Barnum took a seat in the dress circle, leaving Jenny to her fate.

The applause for the overture was perfunctory, as was that for Belletti's first solo. Jenny was to sing next, and this time Belletti led her forward. There was a little spatter of hand-clapping, but it was immediately drowned out by a mounting crescendo of hisses. Jenny stopped near the center of the stage, frozen. Now, at last, in beautiful, romantic Havana, the fear that had haunted her all of her professional life had come true. She was being hissed! Belletti saw the look of horror on her face and suffered as much as she did.

But after the first shock, Jenny's mind began to operate. She was not being hissed because she had sung badly; no one in Havana had yet heard her sing. Why they should be hissing her she did not know, but she did know she had done nothing to deserve it. Before Belletti or Benedict could make any move to help her, Jenny drew herself up to her full height. Her wide mouth tightened, her gray-blue eyes flashed, her cheeks reddened. She was no longer afraid, she was furious! A correspondent for the New York *Tribune* who was present reported: "When she witnessed the kind of reception in store for her—so different from anything she had reason to expect . . . she stood there perfectly calm and beautiful. She was satisfied that she now had an ordeal to pass and a victory to gain worthy of her powers."

The orchestra began the first notes of "Come per me sereno," the love melody from *La Sonnambula* with which Jenny had enchanted so many thousands in Europe and America. The *Tribune* correspondent wrote: "Then followed—how can I describe it?—such heavenly strains as I verily believe mortal never heard except from her lips. Some of the oldest Castilians kept a frown upon their brow and a curling sneer upon their lips. Their ladies, however, and most of the audience, began to look surprised."

The reporter said that as the melody flowed on, in increasing beauty and glory, the members of the audience began to exchange glances, but nearly all "kept their teeth clenched, their lips closed, evidently determined to resist to the last." When someone gave vent to an involuntary "Brava!", it too was hissed. There was silence for a moment or two after Jenny finished, and she continued to stand there statue-like, her face that of an offended goddess. Then there went up such a tremendous shout of applause as, the *Tribune* correspondent said, he had never heard before.

"And how was Jenny Lind affected? She who had stood a few moments previous like adamant, now trembled like a leaf in the wind. . . . Trembling, slowly, and bowing almost to the ground, she withdrew. The roar and applause of victory increased. 'Encore! Encore! Encore!' came from every lip."

After the encore, she was called back to the footlights five times more, bowing to the madly cheering audience. Tears of joy were running down Barnum's cheeks. He was in the wings to greet her after the fifth encore with "God bless you, Jenny, you have settled them!"

Jenny threw her arms around his neck. She was crying too. "Are you satisfied?" she asked him. Barnum wrote in his memoirs that "never before did she look so beautiful in my eyes as on that evening." And though Barnum might have spared her at least the surprise element of her ordeal, by his somewhat cowardly handling of the situation he had enabled her to learn that she was equal to any situation she might encounter.

Twelve concerts had been scheduled for Havana. But several of the newspapers were still calling for lower prices, and people were holding off from buying tickets, hoping to get them at a lower rate. After the fourth concert, which was for charity and netted $4,500—Jenny gave most of it to Havana's two hospitals and a convent—no more were announced. The public, which had received Jenny so ungraciously at first, began to grow uneasy. Increasingly anxious inquiries were coming as to when the concerts would resume. For once, Barnum refused comment. Finally a group of leading Cubans offered to post a guarantee of $25,000 for three more concerts, but Barnum had become disgusted with the newspapers and the pressure to push down the price of tickets. He told the dons that there was not enough money in Cuba to induce him to give another concert and he did not.

For ten whole days after the charity concert, the troupe had nothing to do except explore Havana and its vicinity and enjoy itself. A croquet set was put up on the lawn of the villa, and now Barnum had no business responsibilities to excuse him from joining in games with Jenny. He says in his memoirs, "She would romp and run, sing and laugh. 'Now, Mr. Barnum, for another game of ball,' she would say, half a dozen times a day. Whereupon she would commence a game of throwing and catching"—Jenny always carried several light rubber balls with her—"which would be kept up until, being completely tired out, I would say, 'I give it up.' Then her rich, musical laugh would be heard ringing through the house and she would exclaim, 'Oh, Mr. Barnum, you are too fat and lazy, you cannot stand it to play ball with me!' "

One of P. T. Barnum's countless friends was Mr. Brinckerhoff, an American who lived at Matanzas, a coastal town near which the resort of Varadero is now located. He invited the artists to his home, a trip of about a hundred miles through the beautiful Cuban countryside. Mr. Brinckerhoff took them to see sugar and coffee plantations. Jenny was so impressed that after they had returned to Havana she insisted that Benedict, who had been too ill to go with them, must make the same tour.

Barnum had also found in Havana an old employee, a man he had billed years before as "Signor Vivalla, the World's Greatest Juggler." When Barnum hired him, the man had been performing in cheap shows in England and Canada for many years. Barnum raised his price to $150 a week by advertising that Signor Vivalla had just arrived from Italy and having the man pretend that he could speak no English. Signor Vivalla from Italy had put on his juggling and dancing act in the best theaters in New York, Boston and other Eastern cities. But he had suffered a stroke that had paralyzed the left side of his body. He could no longer dance or juggle, but made a precarious living with a trained dog, which turned a spinning wheel and performed other curious tricks. Vivalla called on Barnum frequently and one day Jenny asked who the man was. Barnum gave her Vivalla's history briefly. Jenny asked that $500 be set aside for Vivalla from the proceeds of the charity concert, so that he could realize his dream of returning to Italy and his brothers and sisters there.

After the concert was held and arrangements were in progress for Vivalla's return to Italy, the Italian called on Jenny with a basket of the most luscious fruit he could find. She had gone out for a drive. Vivalla, weeping with joy and gratitude, asked Barnum to thank "the very good lady" for him and give her the fruit. As he was leaving, Vivalla hesitated a moment, then said, "Mr. Barnum, I should like so much to have the good lady see my dog turn a wheel. It is very nice, he can spin very good. Shall I bring the dog and wheel for her? She is such a good lady, I wish very much to please her."

Barnum replied that Jenny would not care for the dog and that she never accepted thanks in person. That very morning a large delegation of children, all dressed in their colorful best, carrying banners and accompanied by a dozen or more priests, had called to thank Jenny for the donation she had made to their convent. She had refused to see them because, she said, "They have nothing to thank me for. If I have done good, it is no more than my duty, and it is also my pleasure." Barnum assured Vivalla that he was most welcome to the money and that was all that was necessary.

When Jenny came back from her drive, Barnum gave her the basket of fruit and told her laughingly of Vivalla's desire to show her how his performing dog could turn a spinning wheel. Barnum wrote in his memoirs that the tears flowed thick and fast down Jenny's cheeks. "Poor man, poor man, do let him come, it is all the good creature can do for me," she exclaimed. "I like it that he wants his dog to perform for me. Do let the poor creature come and bring his dog. It will make him so happy."

When Barnum hunted up Vivalla that same evening and told him that Jenny would see his dog perform the next afternoon at four o'clock, the man promised to be punctual, in a voice trembling with emotion. "I was *sure* she would like to see my dog perform," he said.

Barnum said that for a full half hour before the time appointed, Jenny sat in her window on the second floor on the lookout for Vivalla and his dog. A few minutes before the appointed hour she exclaimed, "Ah, here he comes! Here he comes!" and ran downstairs and opened the door for him herself. A Negro boy was carrying the spinning wheel, while Vivalla led the dog. Jenny gave the boy a coin and, taking the wheel, said to Vivalla, "It is so very kind of you to come with your dog. Follow me," and led the way upstairs to her private rooms.

Barnum recorded: "Her servant offered to take the wheel, but no, she would let no one carry it but herself. She called us all up to her parlor, and for one full hour devoted herself to the happy Italian. She went down on her knees to pet the dog and asked Vivalla all sorts of questions about his performances, his former course of life, his friends in Italy and his present hopes and plans. Then she sang and played for him, gave him some refreshments, finally insisted on carrying his wheel to the door, and her servant carried it to Vivalla's boardinghouse."

Barnum remarked, rather piously, "That scene alone would have paid me for all my labor during the entire musical campaign." Poor Vivalla had probably never been so happy before, Barnum said, but his enjoyment had not exceeded Jenny's. The scene took on added poignancy when, a few months later, the New York *Herald* announced that Vivalla had died and said that the Italian's last words had been about Jenny Lind and Mr. Barnum. A fine bit of publicity indeed, but one for which Jenny's instinctive kindness rather than P. T. Barnum's genius should have received the whole credit.

Fredrika Bremer arrived in Havana a few days before the Lind party left. As soon as Jenny received Miss Bremer's note telling of her presence, she hurried to the house where the famous writer was staying. Miss Bremer wrote that Jenny's face had "that radiant, healthy, happy expression which no one who had ever seen it could forget. All the Swedish spring burst through in it."

The two had not met since Fredrika Bremer had been so upset lest the composer Lindblad's mooning over Jenny should hurt her reputation. Jenny had rather resented this. But now all she thought of was her long friendship with Fredrika and the struggles, inner and outer, that she had passed through in the intervening years. It made her long for her native country, and in the few days she had to spend with the writer, all she would talk about was the old days in Sweden and the many people there whom they both knew. Fredrika Bremer wrote that she could not get Jenny to discuss any of her experiences and overwhelming triumphs since leaving the Swedish Royal Theater. "They seemed not to have taken the slightest root in her soul."

When Fredrika Bremer saw Jenny off on the *Falcon* for New Orleans, the singer was depressed. The sight of this friend from home had made Jenny realize how tired she was of her wandering life and how glad she would be when she could put an end to it. She wrote Judge Munthe a little later that she hoped to be through with Barnum by the middle of June. "I cannot deny that I long quite terribly to have America behind me. It is tiresome in many ways though interesting to see. I wonder why I long so much for Sweden, when I was never happy there?"

When the *Falcon* docked at New Orleans, it appeared that everyone in the city had come down to the waterfront to see Jenny Lind arrive. The crowd was so thick it was difficult for the sailors to make room for the gangplank. Jenny, who had been free of curious, encroaching crowds ever since her experience in the little hotel in Weldon, North Carolina, felt the old shrinking when she saw the densely packed multitude. Barnum reassured her. "You stay out of sight for about ten minutes and I'll guarantee that you won't have any trouble getting through the crowd." He had his daughter Caroline put a veil over her hat and face, and escorted her with exaggerated courtesy to the gangplank.

"Make way for Mr. Barnum and Miss Lind!" LeGrand shouted from the deck railing. As usual, the crowd pressed around; everywhere hands were thrust out to touch Barnum's coat or the dress that was thought to be Jenny Lind's. But at length they reached the carriage and were driven to the huge Pontalba Apartment Row on Jackson Square. As soon as they had departed, LeGrand Smith led Jenny unnoticed to another carriage. She did have to appear several times on the balcony of her apartment, to wave her greeting to the shouting crowd, but she had escaped the jostling so disconcerting to her.

They were to spend the entire month of February in New Orleans and Madam Pontalba had turned over the central building of her row of apartments on Jackson Square for the party's use. Jenny's own apartment was on the third floor front. It was gorgeously furnished. Further to increase Jenny's pleasure during her stay in New Orleans, Madam

Jenny Lind, the Swedish Nightingale

Pontalba had engaged Boudro, the most famous *chef de cuisine* in Louisiana, which boasted the best food in the whole United States, to preside over Jenny's meals. When Jenny was leaving New Orleans, she declared that the two persons there whom she would always remember with warmest gratitude were her landlady and her cook.

Barnum made the rounds of the newspaper offices, meeting the editors and reporters, passing out cigars and complimenting each and all on the first-rate newspapers they got out. The *Picayune* for February 8 gave big space to the arrival of the Lind party. All the papers for Sunday, February 9, publicized the auction of tickets for the first concert. An admission of twelve and one half cents was charged—"to keep out the curious," Barnum said—nevertheless a thousand people crowded into Armory Hall.

Barnum paid the editors well to sprinkle among their news items and ads assorted references to Jenny Lind, "The famous Swedish Nightingale," or "The Divine Enchantress." In the columns of the *Picayune*, following an account of the bitter fight over the Missouri Compromise in various state legislatures, a news item reported that the Shakespearean actress Charlotte Cushman was staying over in New Orleans to hear Jenny Lind sing. "Mlle. Lind's first performance will positively take place in St. Louis Theater on Monday Night."

If Jenny had read the papers herself, which she probably did not, she would have seen the proclamation of her friend President Fillmore calling for the punishment of a mob that had entered the U. S. Court House in Boston and freed a Negro slave about to be returned to his owners in Maryland. She would have seen, next to a story about her concert in the *Evening Crescent*, the advertisement for the sale of "a choice gang of 140 slaves," listing the name, age and description of each, and signed by the South's celebrated auctioneer, J. A. Beard.

Sol Smith, the proprietor of the St. Charles Theater, was a former comedian who had performed many times in New York City and was another of Barnum's friends. Everyone in show business knew "Uncle Sol." He lent an expert hand to Barnum's by no means feeble ballyhoo of the Divine Enchantress. The first concert was a whirl of color and enthusiasm. So many bouquets were thrown on the stage that Jenny was barely able to get through them, and the final "Home, Sweet Home" had the whole audience wiping tears away. The receipts were all that could be desired—$12,500.

Barnum rushed to the stage at the close and announced that Jenny Lind had especially requested that $1,000 be given to "the brave protectors of the city's homes, the firemen." The New Orleans *Delta* recorded that "the splendid donation naturally aroused the gratitude and kindly feeling of that noble body of men," and they decided to honor their benefactress in the course of a grand celebration and parade they were holding.

The line of march was diverted in order to pass Jenny's lodgings, and as the parade approached the center of Pontalba Row, the brass band struck up "Home, Sweet Home." Jenny, Josephine Åhmansson, Belletti, Benedict and Max Hjortzberg stood on the balcony, and the *Delta* reporter said he had never seen Jenny look better. "Her eyes were full of brilliancy and enjoyment of the scene, and her face expressed great pleasure and happiness."

When the grand marshal of the parade, on horseback, extended to her "a splendid bouquet, made of the choicest and richest flowers of our clime," attached to a long staff ornamented with ribbons and rosettes, Jenny received it in the most charming manner—"Without any ostentations, display or parade but in a real frank hearty, unpretending style such as went to the hearts, and won the warmest regards, of our stalwart firemen."

The *Picayune* noted many delegations "of the loveliest of Alabama and Mississippi," at the second concert. Twelve concerts were given in New Orleans, with receipts averaging $7,000 a concert, and listeners coming from many parts of the deep South. Numerous "Jenny Lind Balls" were arranged. Jenny attended as many of these as she could, but when she declined, the soirees were held in her honor anyway. At one party, a visitor from Columbus, Ohio, bore such a striking resemblance to Jenny that many persons mistook her for the singer. Jenny seized the chance to remain in the background and let the American girl deal with the compliments and flattery intended for Miss Lind. At the end of the ball, Jenny gave the girl a gold handkerchief ring that she was wearing, in gratitude, and the Ohio girl gave Jenny her large bouquet.

CHAPTER SIXTEEN

Up the Mississippi

THE way to travel in the Mississippi
River basin was by boat, wherever this was possible. Up until 1849, not
a mile of railroad existed in Wisconsin, Iowa, Missouri, Arkansas, Tennessee or Texas. Even on the Eastern seaboard, such railroads as there
were usually extended only from one city to another. A passenger traveling
from Washington, D.C., to New York had to alight at Baltimore, transfer himself and baggage to the station of another railroad that would take
him to Philadelphia, then transfer to still another station and railroad to
get to New York.

With 1849 had begun a great fever for railroad building, so that there
were continuous tracks for Jenny's parlor car as far as North Carolina.
But the fever had not reached the central portion of the country until
1850. In early 1851, where one could not go by water it was necessary to
use stagecoaches or private conveyance.

At this time, the population of the United States was a little more than
23,000,000, of whom 19,500,000 were whites, and a considerable proportion of the white population was moving westward. Pittsburgh, Columbus, Louisville and St. Louis, all had more than doubled their popula-
tions since 1840, and many adventurous souls were heading still farther
west. Hence the decade between 1850 and 1860 was one of great expansion of river travel, at the same time that the railroads, being built at a
phenomenal rate, were starting the trend toward travel by land. Steam-
boats had multiplied on the Mississippi, the Ohio and the Missouri, and

a number of them represented the last word in elegance, so far as Americans were concerned.

Barnum chartered the *Magnolia,* one of the most magnificent of all the river steamers, for the trip as far as Cairo, Illinois, with stops for concerts at Natchez and Memphis. From Cairo the party would take another steamer to St. Louis, then turn back to the mouth of the Ohio, go up that river to the Cumberland and thence to Nashville. From there they would go overland by stagecoach to Louisville, then up the Ohio again, with concerts already booked for Cincinnati and Pittsburgh. The journey back to Baltimore would be by stagecoach, and they would go on to New York by train. Jenny would have sung in every American city of importance at that time except Chicago, and used every kind of conveyance except oxcart.

During the closing days of the New Orleans stay, Barnum frequently got into his rented open carriage, with two spirited horses and a Negro driver and footman, and dashed down to the wharf to oversee the preparations on the *Magnolia.* It was indeed a splendid vessel, freshly painted in gleaming white, with two decks; a spacious salon; one dining room for the captain and passengers and another for the crew and the passengers' servants; comfortable sleeping quarters with built-in beds, porcelain water pitchers, basins and slop jars; and a barbershop and bar for the gentlemen. A huge paddle wheel at the rear, powered by a steam engine, propelled it through the swirling, muddy waters of the Mississippi.

Barnum had some elegant furniture moved in for the salon, and closed the bar. The bartender was disconsolate until Barnum told him he could come along for the ride, and would be paid his salary just the same.

The original plan had been to leave New Orleans on Sunday, March 9, but Jenny flatly refused to begin the journey on Sunday. (The New Orleans *Crescent* ran an editorial commending in glowing terms the Nightingale's "strong religious nature.") So it was on Monday, March 10, 1851, that the party went aboard the *Magnolia.* Uncle Sol, the old comedian who owned the hall in New Orleans where Jenny sang, had announced that he was going along as far as St. Louis, and Barnum had hired him as advance man. Otherwise the party was the same as on the trip from New York—Jenny, Josephine Åhmansson, Caroline Barnum and her friend Mrs. Lyman; Benedict and Belletti with their valet; violinist Joseph Burke, Messers Ryan and Kyle, the flutists, and on this occasion thirteen other orchestra members; Barnum and his assistants, LeGrand Smith and Henry Bennett; and Jenny's personal maid and two male employes, Max Hjortzberg and Charles Seyton. All hands waved good-bye to thousands of cheering spectators on the wharf, and they were off on their journey through the heartland of America.

For Jenny and her fellow artists from abroad, the trip completed their education in the America of that day, except for the frontier and wilderness portions. They saw the deep South, before war ravaged it and changed forever its way of life. They saw what was later to be known as the Middle West, before the railroads opened up the country and made communities more interdependent. They observed the rich life of the Mississippi itself, and heard the calls the steamboat men used in sounding for the ever changing channel of the mighty river. One of these soundings, mark twain, was later to be adopted as the pen name of Samuel Clemens, the writer who would start his apprenticeship as Mississippi River pilot two years after Jenny's visit.

Just north of New Orleans they entered plantation country. As they drew up to wharves in tiny settlements, the Negroes gathered, and Jenny loved to hear their melodious voices and chants. Several times she gave impromptu concerts to audiences made up largely of slaves and freed men. She sang her best for them, and they spoke of her as "that good and lubly creature." At Natchez, the wealthy planters, in from their wide acres in Mississippi and Louisiana, were elegant in the long coats and lace-frilled shirts of the eighteenth and early nineteenth centuries. The women folk who clung to their arms wore white kerchiefs, dainty slippers, and skirts that billowed out over many petticoats from incredibly slim, tightly corseted waists.

Gradually the plantations gave way to farms, and at St. Louis the party moved into the area of tremendous expansion which the slavery system had made impossible for the deep South. St. Louis was one of the principal gathering places for emigrants headed farther west, for they could change to steamers which would carry them up the Missouri River, entering the Mississippi about twenty miles north of the city. From here on the party would encounter, in the cities where they stopped, all gradations of reaction to the burning questions then before the American public —slavery and secession.

Up the Mississippi

The state of Missouri was on the border between North and South, and the Missouri Compromise had excepted it from the rule that all states in the Louisiana Purchase, north of latitude 36° 30', should be free. Senator Benton, foreseeing that compromise would lead eventually to secession, was back home at the time of Jenny's visit, fighting to keep his state's proslavery general assembly from directing its delegation in Congress to support measures of this kind. His battle to preserve the Union was to cost him his seat in the U. S. Senate in the election of 1852, just as Abraham Lincoln's scruples about the Mexican War had cost him his seat in the House of Representatives in 1848. In St. Louis, however, where the chief slave market stood opposite the handsome, semiclassic stone County Court House, the new, emerging crop of business leaders were too busy taking advantage of the trade opportunities offered by the constant influx of transients and the doubled population—it stood at nearly 80,000, making St. Louis the seventh city in size in the United States—to bother about politics.

Nashville had been the scene of the Southern, or Nashville, Convention, which met to consider problems between the North and South. At an adjourned meeting in November, 1850, the body had expressed dissatisfaction with the compromise measures Congress had enacted and asserted the right of the South to secede. The American National Convention, held in Louisville at the time of Zachary Taylor's election, had declared for both the Dred Scott Decision, which permitted slaveowners to take their slaves into free states, and the upholding of the Union.

At Cincinnati, the Lind party would arrive in the North of this middle section with its rapidly developing industries. Ohioans had never wanted slavery within their own borders, but Taylor Atwater expressed the pious hope, in the first history of Ohio which appeared in 1837, that the institution would continue in the South for a century, so that "the broad, deep streams of wealth, numbers, enterprise, youth, vigor and the very life-blood of the slave-holding states" might continue to flow into the state. Cincinnati was the gateway through which much of this flow entered Ohio and had taken the lead in the whole section in manufacturing. The city had come a long way, in fact, since Frances Trollope had conducted her bazaar there in the late 1820's, in what she considered a futile effort to raise the city's cultural level. Her *Domestic Manners of the Americans*, published in 1831, was based upon her observations of Cincinnatians, and makes lively reading even today. But in the intervening years Cincinnati, like St. Louis, had received many German immigrants, and where there were Germans there was a love of good music. The first American Sängerfest had been held there in 1849, and Cincinnati's literary club, also organized in 1849, was believed to be the first in the United States.

In 1851, the city was much torn by dissension over slavery. It was an important center for the "Underground Railroad," the home of Harriet Beecher Stowe, who had lived there until 1850, having been one of the stations. She had collected much of the material for *Uncle Tom's Cabin* from slaves passing through. But slavery had its strong advocates, too. Here, perhaps better than anywhere else, the visitors from abroad could get an idea of the passions aroused by the slavery issue in the decade before the war.

But politics were laid aside when Jenny visited the cities in this agitated middle section. Even Senator Benton, busy as he was, took time off from the political wars to come and hear Jenny again when she sang in St. Louis.

Barnum's methods of getting publicity for his star formed a model for the press agents who, ever since Barnum's success with Jenny, have been indispensable to artists. First of all, he "would prepare the public mind in advance," as he called it. That is to say, he would send stories to the newspapers of cities ahead in the tour, telling of Jenny's marvelous reception in the city where she was then singing, extolling her virtues, and often containing some sly plug for the Barnum side of the combination. Usually the stories were labeled, "By Special Correspondence." Thus the Memphis *Eagle* ran an item from its "special correspondent" in New Orleans to the effect that "Mlle. Lind is beyond doubt the greatest woman of her age. . . . The ladies accompanying Mlle. Lind are highly accomplished and pretty. One of them, Miss Barnum, has attracted considerable attention during her stay in this city."

From Memphis, the St. Louis *Republican* received a two-column woodcut of the "fair Swede," and ran it in its March 16th issue with a long story of Jenny's life, signed by "Brother Jonathan"—one of Barnum's many journalistic pseudonyms. Nashville readers were informed by telegraph that when the *Magnolia* docked at Cairo, "the people were in the greatest excitement. . . . Mr. Barnum, and in fact all the suite, appeared in excellent health and spirits. The concert at Memphis turned out to be the most brilliant held yet, taking all things into consideration."

To one paper after another Barnum sent ahead the heart-warming news that the many admirers of Thomas Moore's exquisite song, "The Last Rose of Summer," would have an opportunity of hearing it from the lips of the Swedish Nightingale, followed the next day by the news that Miss Lind had consented to sing several popular American favorites, ending with the prime favorite of all, "Home, Sweet Home."

Newspaper readers were enthralled by an incident which was reported as having taken place in city after city where Jenny sang. It was attributed first to Boston, where, according to busy Brother Jonathan Barnum, Jenny had had her first chance to get out into the country. She had started to sing, out of sheer happiness and exuberance, and a small bird, hearing her, had taken up the song. Exactly the same thing was reported to have happened in nearly every other city, the variety of bird involved depending upon the songbirds of the region. In one instance, there was an added touch. The little bird, inspired by Jenny's music, sang and sang until its little heart burst, and it fell dead at the human songstress's feet.

The Buffalo *Times* revived the story in its edition of March 18, 1923, with an embellishment. "In the United States, no program of Jenny Lind's was complete unless it had at least one bird song, with flute accompaniment. It is on record that frequently on her travels she would cause her carriage to be stopped along the road, near the woods, to hear the flutings and warblings of the birds. Often she charmed the birds with her own warblings and on more than one occasion had her coach filled with feathered visitors who had flocked to hear her."

Presently Uncle Sol would appear, to hire the hall and plant advertisements and more free publicity in the papers. He spread all over the Middle West the pun that had started in New York City—about Jenny being for-giving, Barnum being for-getting. The famous minstrel, G. N. Christy, picked it up, and used it in his show for many years.

Then the party would arrive, and Barnum in person would make the rounds of the newspaper offices, distributing cigars, exuding camaraderie and placing more and bigger advertisements, which would nearly always be flanked by advertisements of local merchants, also invoking Jenny's name.

Jenny Lind, the Swedish Nightingale

St. Louis numbered more German immigrants than native-born residents, so the artists were assured of a warm reception. Sol had run into some trouble, however, about the hall. Charlotte Cushman was appearing in Bate's Theater, the largest and finest hall in the city, and Sol thought the owner of the theater asked an exorbitant price for rent, and that the $250 requested to compensate Miss Cushman for giving up the theater on the concert nights was pretty high. Besides, Sol did not believe that Bate's Theater was built strongly enough to stand up under the jamming he knew it would be subjected to. He chose a smaller but safer hall, and the owner of Bate's took his case to the newspapers, proving Barnum's thesis that any kind of publicity is good publicity. Though it was raining the night of the first concert, the hall where Jenny sang was filled to overflowing and thousands stood outside, under a forest of umbrellas.

The racing season had begun at St. Louis when the party got there, and four trotters, hastily renamed Jenny Lind, Barnum, Benedict and Belletti, competed against each other. Benedict won, Belletti came in second; whereupon Barnum commented lugubriously to Uncle Sol, "Jenny and I must be losing our speed!" But there was never any let-up in Barnum's efforts, and he was always ready to step into the limelight himself.

He was far too smart to get involved in the slavery issue, but at every city where more than one concert was given, he would deliver an address on temperance. It would come about in this way. A letter signed "Several Gentlemen" would appear in a local paper, asking Barnum to speak on his favorite topic and to name a time and place. The papers would then announce that Mr. Barnum had very graciously consented to comply with the request. "His experience as a man of the world, and one who has seen much of all varieties of life, will doubtless render his remarks highly interesting." At the close of his address, Barnum would call for members of the audience to come forward and sign the temperance pledge. Uncle Sol would then advance solemnly, in the role of a convert to temperance, and others in the audience would follow.

St. Louis was already the center of a thriving liquor trade, and the beer made by German immigrants had become celebrated all over the frontier. Barnum aroused considerable newspaper comment when he announced that he would speak against strong drink in Wyman's Hall, admission ten cents, and would turn over the proceeds to any charity the mayor might name. The mayor diplomatically declined the honor, but Wyman's Hall was crowded that night. Barnum never failed to extol Jenny's virtues, as well as temperance, on these occasions.

As the tour progressed, the ticket auction tended to lose a good deal of its news value. Barnum contrived to keep interest in it alive by retaining the leading mule or slave auctioneer of the section to conduct it. No one appeared to see any incongruity in this.

Whatever the means used to lure people to the concerts, Jenny enchanted them once they were there. The mysterious quality which had caused half of Europe and the inhabitants of the eastern United States to idolize her operated as strongly in this newer, more primitive region.

She rotated her gowns from pure white, with light blue belt and accessories, through pink and light blue to a greenish tint, with low-heeled slippers and a small fan to match each gown. Frequently the newspapers would describe her toilette in detail, the comments tending to be somewhat more frank than Jenny was accustomed to. In Nashville, a reporter wrote that "she is not remarkable for beauty," though conceding that she was bewitchingly graceful and simple in her manners.

Jenny enlarged her knowledge of American Presidents by visiting The Hermitage, Andrew Jackson's home and farm, not far outside Nashville. "Old Hickory" had been dead only six years, and the party was shown about by the old Negro who had been his servant. Here Jenny first heard mockingbirds singing in the trees, and the Nashville *Daily American* described her enchantment. This was the one authenticated bird story of Jenny's entire American stay.

The Adelphi Theatre in Nashville, built by order of the state legislature at a cost of $25,000, and opened only the previous July, boasted the second largest stage in the United States. However, when reports began coming in of Jenny's reception in the Mississippi cities, it was decided that the seating capacity was inadequate. The management had made frantic efforts to enlarge it before Jenny's arrival, but there were delays and much was still unfinished. In the new parts, rough planks served as seats, some of the doors had not been rehung and the wind blew through holes in the walls and ceilings. It was late March, however, the weather was pleasant and nobody minded. The songs applauded most were Taubert's "Ich Muss Singen," "The Last Rose of Summer," the Norwegian "Echo Song," and "Home, Sweet Home." The last two proved so popular on Jenny's Midwestern tour that when Adelina Patti, the child singing phenomenon, followed her in 1853, she added these songs to her repertoire.

The first Nashville concert brought in $8,000, which provoked a complaint from the Nashville *Gazette* because "the people of a town that pays for much of its household goods in wool, ginseng and brown beans" had spent $2,380 to buy Jenny Lind tickets at auction, adding that she was only successful "because she was in the hands of a master humbugger."

There was a sour note, too, among the paeans of praise in the St. Louis papers, the St. Louis *Republican* chiding those who had paid as much as $5, "more than the wages for two days' work," to hear the singer. "Take from Jenny Lind a certain prepossession of person and manner with which she is endowed; divest her of the reputation she has for benevolences and more than all, *separate her from Mr. Barnum,* and you would find not one, but twenty vocalists, probably, to compete successfully with her for public favor."

Despite such comments, the people who worked for less than $2.50 a day took Jenny to their hearts. The river men blew their steam whistles in salute to her when their boats passed hers. Policemen fought for the honor of escorting her carriage. The firemen, always included in her charities, serenaded her in all but the smallest of the cities and towns where she sang. Ministers came in delegations to thank her for her religious influence. And many working men who could not afford the price of a ticket stood outside the opera houses where her concerts were given.

During the previous Christmas season, the first steam railway engine ever seen in Tennessee had been brought to Nashville from Cincinnati, and, by the combined efforts of many mules and men, in four days had been pulled and pushed a mile through the city to the track that was being laid by the newly formed Nashville, Chattanooga and St. Louis Railroad. During Jenny's stay there, Tennessee's first train pulled out of Nashville and went as far as Antioch, nine miles away. Jenny had been invited to take part in the historic ride, but declined. Barnum volunteered to go in her place and shared the cowcatcher with the president of the railroad, waving his hat to the cheering onlookers who lined the tracks, as though he were personally responsible for this mark of progress.

Up the Mississippi

The stagecoach ride from Nashville to Louisville afforded the artists an idea of the country's natural wonders. The party stopped at "Benton's famous spring in Robertson County," according to a Nashville paper, (the "Mint Spring," where there was a resort for many years) to drink of the water, and spent two days at Mammoth Cave. The Elizabethtown *Reporter* stated, "Miss Lind declared that such a magnificent temple was beyond any similar wonder in Europe. She sat in a curious rock formation called the 'arm chair,' and good-naturedly warbled an aria."

Louisville and its sister city, Lexington, shared the distinction of being the capitals of the Kentucky Blue Grass aristocracy, justifiably proud of its fine Bourbon whisky, fast horses and beautiful women. Lexington could claim Henry Clay as a resident, but Louisville was called "the mistress of commerce of the South." Its citizens also maintained that Southern tradition came to fuller flower there than elsewhere. The tradition for hospitality was the easier to maintain because, at the time of Jenny's visit, the choicest beef cuts were six cents a pound, turkeys cost fifty cents apiece, eggs were four cents a dozen and chickens seventy-five cents a dozen.

Kentuckians also believed they had solved the vexing problems connected with slavery, priding themselves on their treatment of slaves, so that the loyalty of Kentucky slaves to their masters was another cherished tradition. Slaves were plentiful. Households of any size maintained two cooks, one to be on hand in case the other should be temporarily out of commission. Every white child of good family had his or her own small Negro body servant.

Fundamentalist religious sects, which did not believe in dancing, were beginning to get a foothold in the region, and had somewhat affected the social customs of Louisville. Often, instead of balls, there were "promenades," where beaux and belles merely strolled about, chatting with each other. However, Louisville fathers were fiercely protective of their beautiful daughters, and no young man could chat with a young lady at a promenade, or see her if he called at her home, without first undergoing paternal inspection. There was a story that one father had forbidden his house to an otherwise eligible suitor, because the young man had appeared in trousers that buttoned in front, in accordance with the latest style in the East, instead of on the side where the trousers of Kentucky gentlemen were supposed to button.

The most delicate nuances of courtship could be conveyed through the "language of flowers"—and every well-conducted Louisville household exhibited an illustrated album, explaining the language. Thus a young man could express his admiration by sending a bouquet of acacia, or of apricot blossoms if he yearned for reassurance, while asphodels were a gentle hint that a romance was ended.

Louisville, with its high regard for female virtue, went all out to do Jenny honor. A coachload of civic leaders met her ten miles outside the city, took the stage horses out of the traces and replaced them with four superb white Kentucky horses. The buildings were draped with flags and the streets lined with welcoming crowds as Jenny entered the city. At the house where she was to stay, a group of children waited for her with bouquets. She sang "Home, Sweet Home" for them—her favorite song, according to a local chronicler. Only two concerts had been planned for Louisville, but the demand for a third was so great that she and Barnum yielded. Jenny's visit was recorded as the outstanding Louisville event of the 1850's.

Signor Salvi, a famous European tenor who had been the chief attraction of the Italian Opera in Havana, joined the company in Louisville. A fine artist, with a fine voice, Salvi strengthened the group and provided a fresh focus of public attention. By the time the party arrived in Cincinnati, interest, instead of diminishing, had reached such a pitch that a huge crowd waited at the quay to greet them, even though the steamer docked at six in the morning. Jenny took one look at the densely packed throng and ran back to her stateroom. Barnum did not dare to repeat the ruse he had used in New Orleans to throw the crowd off the scent, for it had been too good a joke to keep and people all over the Midwest had laughed over it. He determined to take advantage of this very fact. Assuring Jenny that she had nothing to fear, he took her arm and led her boldly up to the gangplank. LeGrand Smith again called from the deck railing, this time exclaiming, "It's no go, Barnum. You can't pass your daughter off as Jenny Lind this time!"

A great shout of laughter arose. "You can't fool us, Old Barnum!" the Ohioans chorused, "You could fool New Orleans folks, but you can't come it over us Buckeyes. We're going to stay here till Jenny Lind comes out!"

Jenny had been in her suite in the Burnet House for some time before it dawned on the crowd that it had indeed been Jenny whom Barnum had shepherded off the boat so solicitously, and not his daughter Caroline. They took it good-naturedly, many remarking as they left the wharf, "Well, I guess Barnum did humbug us Buckeyes after all."

The Cincinnati *Enquirer* declared that April 12, 1851, would be forever distinguished by the installation of the first Democratic mayor the city had ever had, and by the arrival of Jenny Lind. A dog and pony show temporarily became the "Jenny Lind Circus," and the papers were filled with advertisements for Jenny Lind silks, Jenny Lind hats, Jenny Lind buskins and gaiters and "Jenny Lind everything else," as one advertiser expressed it. A pharmacy advertisement compared Jenny's influence on the community with Dr. Bull's Latest Improved Sarsaparilla. "The one feeds the soul with the inspiring melodies of ten dollar notes, whilst the other, for just half the amount, gives six quart bottles of precious health restoration."

Only one Midwestern concert failed to make money. While they were in Louisville, a citizen of Madison, Indiana, came to see Barnum to ask him to give a concert in his town. Barnum replied that Madison was too small to support a concert, whereupon the man offered to take over the management of the concert himself, guaranteeing Barnum $5,000. When they reached Madison, Barnum was informed that less than $4,000 worth of tickets had been sold. Moreover, to Barnum's even greater consternation, the concert was to be held in a "pork" shed, customarily used to auction off farm produce. Rather than disappoint the people who had bought tickets, Barnum held the concert and pocketed the loss. Several concerts in other places, however, managed by local citizens, brought the promoters a nice return as well as paying Barnum his $5,000 in full.

Eight charity concerts were given on the tour. Besides the usual donations for volunteer firemen, homes for widows and orphans and similar standard causes, Jenny always set aside some money to help local musical societies buy instruments and musical scores. She encouraged their efforts in other ways as well. In St. Louis, when the members of the Polyhymnia Society gathered under the windows of Jenny's hotel suite and serenaded her, she came down, thanked the singers and asked them to give a concert while she was in town. They did so, and Jenny and nearly all the troupe were guests of honor. Their presence brought many St. Louis people to the concert who would otherwise never have thought of attending it. At the end of the concert, Jenny went up on the stage and shook hands with each singer.

A blind boy from a poor white family, who played the flute, was enabled to hear Jenny because his friends took up a collection to send him to the city where she was appearing. Flutist Kyle heard the blind boy play and reported to Jenny that he had unusual talent. Jenny had the boy seated in a chair on the stage behind the scenery at the concert, the better to hear, and next day had him brought to her suite. She urged him to keep on practicing, and placed in his hand an envelope containing three hundred-dollar banknotes.

At the end of the Cincinnati engagement, the party boarded the steamer *Pittsburgh* for the trip to the city of that name, and Jenny was treated to the excitement of a race between the *Pittsburgh* and a rival boat, the *Messenger*. Captain Thornburg of the *Pittsburgh* issued the challenge when he saw the *Messenger* pulling away from the dock at the same time as his own boat. It was accepted, and the smokestacks of both vessels sent out showers of sparks as the furnaces were crammed with all the firewood they could possibly hold. The fact that the boilers of a racing steamboat occasionally blew up in no way dampened the enthusiasm of the river men for this type of sport. The contest continued for three hours, and ended in a dead heat.

Nevertheless, it gave Captain Thornburg and his steamboat a tiny niche in history. When he died in 1921, the New York *Evening World* headlined the story "Death of Noted Captain," and recalled that his "famous steamer, the *Pittsburgh*," had carried Jenny Lind and her party and had raced with the *Messenger*, seventy years before.

Pittsburgh was an interesting combination of burgeoning city and frontier town. It had had gaslight since 1837, but its concert and lecture rooms were mainly built above stores and saloons. The New Masonic Hall, on Fifth Avenue, had been completed in time for Jenny's concert, but the streets outside were paved with cobblestones, and the hoofs of horses and the wheels of vehicles made a tremendous racket.

There were cultured people in Pittsburgh, and the auction sale had gone well enough. But Pittsburgh was a mining community, and someone should have warned Barnum that Friday, the day set for the first concert, was also payday for the miners. According to immemorial custom, a considerable proportion of the men made immediately for the saloons, and by evening were going from one tavern to another in uproarious spirits.

As the time for the concert approached, the well-dressed people making their way toward the hall drew the miners' attention, and they too converged on the hall, filling the streets around it. This was one occasion when music appeared to arouse savagery, instead of quelling it. The men yelled and jeered throughout the overture and Belletti's first solo. Jenny herself could barely be heard over the noise and turmoil outside, and when police tried to turn away the mob, the miners responded with louder noise and any missiles that were handy. The sound of stones thumping against the outside walls was frightening, and the artists dared not leave the hall when the concert was over. The lights were turned out in the hall; the musicians waited hours for the noise to subside. Finally they slipped out through a back door and made their way to the hotel through alleys. The second concert that had been planned for Pittsburgh was canceled, and the party left the next day for Baltimore.

It was the one blot on the young country's record of receiving the foreign artist with kindness and acclaim.

CHAPTER SEVENTEEN

The Break with Barnum

J ENNY'S welcome back to the East-
ern seaboard, however, more than made up for the rudeness of the Pittsburgh miners. Her concerts in Baltimore, Philadelphia and New York
were as successful as her first appearances in these cities. The one given
for charity in Baltimore cleared more than $37,000. Jenny asked that
$2,400 of this be distributed among the orchestra members who had
accompanied her on the tour.

In New York, reporters again followed her every move, and the newspapers were filled with compliments for her singing. All but the New
York *Herald.* James Gordon Bennett continued his caustic comments,
and Walt Whitman, too, sided with the opposition, writing in one of
his "Letters from Paumanok," in the New York *Evening Post,* "The
Swedish Swan, with all her blandishments, never touched my heart in
the least. I wondered at so much vocal dexterity; and indeed, they were
all very pretty, these leaps and double somersaults. But even in the grandest religious airs, genuine masterpieces as they are, of the German composers, executed by this strangely overpraised woman in perfect scientific
style, let critics say what they like, it was a failure, for there was a vacuum
in the head of the performance. Beauty pervaded it, no doubt, and of a
high order, but it was the beauty of Adam before God breathed life into
his nostrils." He mentioned Jenny again in his "Good-bye My Fancy."
"The canary and several other sweet birds are wondrous fine, but there
is something that goes deeper—isn't there?"

[276]

The Break with Barnum

Nevertheless, the public remained solidly on Jenny's side. Barnum was able to cut his advertising appropriation to a bare minimum, manufacturers and storekeepers had so largely taken over the job of publicizing Jenny. Articles named for her were more numerous than ever, filling the shelves of stores all over town. Everybody wanted a Jenny Lind souvenir, and shops stocked small porcelain statuettes of her, in her concert dress or as one of the heroines she had portrayed in opera; woodcut prints; or glass bottles shaped at the top in imitation of Jenny's head and shoulders, and filled with schnapps.

What was much more pleasing to Jenny was the evidence on every hand that she had aroused the interest of countless thousands of Americans in music for its own sake. Numerous "singing societies" had been formed, on the pattern of those in the settlements of immigrants from Germany. Publishers of music were expanding their businesses under the demand for copies of "John Anderson, My Jo," "Home, Sweet Home," and "I know That My Redeemer Liveth." Even some of the easier operatic airs were being called for.

Vocal instructors in colleges and academies and in private studios were enrolling many more students, makers of pianos were selling their products to the comfortably situated as rapidly as they could turn them out. These were luxury items, beyond the reach of the usual farmer or worker. But coincident with the Lind tour, manufacturers of cottage organs, who were located for the most part in New York, Philadelphia, Cincinnati and Chicago, began to enjoy a boom. By saving for a year or so, many farmers and workers could acquire a cottage organ. Sales rose steadily, and for five decades afterwards, organ salesmen went into every town, village and farm community in the United States. Their carriages, pulled by two-horse teams, were built to hold at least two organs, and they sold the instruments by the tens of thosuands. For many years, salesmen would offer to throw in a book of songs Jenny Lind had sung, as an added inducement.

One morning, a man came up to LeGrand Smith in the lobby of the Irving House, where Jenny and her party were staying. He would like very much to meet Jenny Lind, he explained diffidently. He had planned to attend her second concert in his home city of Pittsburgh, and since there had been no second concert there, he had come to New York to hear her.

The man's name, Stephen Collins Foster, meant nothing to LeGrand Smith, even when the composer explained that Jenny had been singing some of his songs. It meant nothing to Barnum, either, who came in just then. Barnum's first thought was to turn the man away. Then it occurred to him that here might be a chance for a human-interest story, and suggested that the visitor wait until Jenny had time to see him.

As soon as Jenny heard Foster was there, she cried delightedly, "Stephen Collins Foster! Why, he wrote that beautiful 'Mein Old Kentucky Home!' Where is he?" Jenny gave Foster tea and had a long talk with him. The newspapers carried the story of the meeting between the singer and the man who was fast becoming the most popular song writer in America. There was an immediate increase in the sale of Foster's songs, and Foster's publisher expressed his appreciation by giving Jenny a leather case containing all of Foster's published work.

Fourteen concerts were held in New York this time, the first four in Castle Garden, the rest in Tripler's Hall, now renamed Metropolitan Hall. The last one was Jenny's ninety-second concert in the United States, and the American public was still as eager to hear her as on her arrival. There had never been anything like it.

But the party had traveled together thousands of miles in the meantime; with wear and tear on bodies and nerves, irritations had been inevitable. On the steamboat trips up the great Midwestern rivers, there had been a good deal of horseplay and practical joking, which Barnum describes at length in his memoirs. He himself had revived sleight-of-hand and magic tricks he had learned in his young days with traveling shows, and had so frightened the *Magnolia's* Negro barber with a threat to turn him into a black cat that the man had had to be restrained from jumping overboard.

The troupe was in Nashville on April 1, and several mild April Fool jokes were played on Barnum. He retaliated by sending telegrams to all the American members, with fabulous offers of employment, or tales of catastrophe at home, which the recipients took seriously. LeGrand Smith exacted vengeance for his telegram—that his home town in Connecticut, including his own dwelling, had been burned to ashes—by having Barnum warned of a plot to hold up their stagecoaches as the party went through the mountains between Pittsburgh and Baltimore. Barnum, believing the story, had sent all his money ahead except for the bare minimum needed to pay expenses en route, had furnished every man in the party with a firearm and had kept a tense watch until they were safely through the mountains.

Barnum remarked in his memoirs that Jenny enjoyed a joke, and she did, but this frontier type of humor was probably a little strong and cruel for her tastes. (She had asked Barnum to stop teasing the Negro hands on the *Magnolia* with his tricks.) Barnum for his part was aggrieved because Jenny did not close her ears to complaints of his management by Max Hjortzberg, and possibly by Charles Seyton as well. He says in his memoirs that he was approached in St. Louis by Hjortzberg, who reminded the impresario of a provision in Jenny's contract which permitted her to terminate her arrangement with Barnum after sixty concerts, if she wished to do so. The first St. Louis concert would be the sixtieth, and Hjortzberg said that Jenny wished to cancel her contract immediately after it.

It was also in the contract that if Jenny were to withdraw before the one hundredth concert, she would be obliged to pay back all she had received to date above $1,000 per concert. Doing some quick figuring, Barnum saw that he had already paid her $137,000; she thus would owe him $77,000 if she canceled at this time. He asked Hjortzberg if Jenny had authorized him to give notice in her behalf, and Hjortzberg replied that "that was his understanding."

Barnum said he would think it over. Hjortzberg was to return for his answer in about an hour. The promoter hunted up Uncle Sol, showed him the contract and described the annoyance he had been caused by Jenny's "selfish and greedy hangers-on, and advisers, legal and otherwise." Uncle Sol confirmed him in his own opinion as to what he should do.

When Hjortzberg returned, Barnum said quietly that he was ready to settle with Jenny and terminate the engagement. The secretary was very much taken aback.

"But you have already advertised concerts in Louisville and Cincinnati!"

"Yes, but you may take my contracts for halls and printing off my hands at cost." He added that Hjortzberg was welcome to the help of the agent who had made these arrangements and that Barnum would be glad to do what he could to get them through these concerts, thus giving them a good start "on their own hook."

Emboldened by this show of liberality, the secretary started bargaining. "Suppose Miss Lind should wish to give some fifty concerts in this country, what would you charge as manager, per concert?"

"A million dollars and not one cent less," Barnum says he replied. He thought he knew now what was back of Hjortzberg's maneuver, and went on, "We might as well understand each other. I don't believe Miss Lind has authorized you to propose to me to cancel our contract. But if she has, just bring me a line to that effect over her signature and her check for the amount due me by the terms of that contract, some $77,000, and we will close our business connections at once."

"But why not make a new arrangement for fifty concerts more," Hjortzberg protested, "by which Miss Lind will pay you, say, $1,000 per concert?"

"Because I hired Miss Lind, and not she me," Barnum retorted, "and because I ought not take a farthing less for my risk and trouble than the contract gives me. I have voluntarily paid Miss Lind more than twice as much as I originally contracted to pay her, or than she expected to receive when she first engaged with me. If she is not satisfied, I wish to settle instantly and finally. And if you do not bring me her decision, I shall go to her for it tomorrow morning."

The next morning, Hjortzberg sought out Barnum to tell him that the whole thing had been a joke, and begged him not to say anything to Jenny about it. It was Barnum's firm belief that Jenny never knew about this attempt on the part of her secretary to terminate the contract.

This is Barnum's version, to be sure, but it is corroborated by Uncle Sol, who published his own memoirs in 1854, and had a good deal to say about the time when he had acted as Barnum's "legal adviser" in St. Louis. In the dedication, he reminded Barnum how the latter's "great star had sunk like a rocket-stem" after her engagement with him had been terminated. Uncle Sol apparently did not hold Jenny blameless in the affair and continued indignantly, still addressing Barnum, "Of all your speculations, from the Negro centenarian, who *didn't* nurse George Washington, down to the Bearded Woman of Genoa, there was not one which required the exercise of so much humbuggery as the Jenny Lind concerts; and I verily believe there is no man living, other than yourself, who could, or would, have risked the enormous expenditure of money necessary to carry them through successfully. Traveling with sixty artists, four thousand miles, and giving ninety-three concerts, at an actual average cost of $4,500 each, is what no other man would have undertaken."

In New York, according to Barnum, Jenny was back in the periphery of her other "evil advisers," John Jay chiefly, one may assume. After the eighty-fifth concert, Jenny herself notified Barnum that she had decided to end her arrangement with him at the one hundredth concert, paying a forfeit of $25,000, as specified in their contract. Barnum says in his memoirs that he was delighted to hear it, for he was weary of the constant excitement and unremitting exertions, and had made enough money to satisfy any reasonable man. He thought it would be good for Jenny to give the rest of her concerts without his assistance, for she would find out then how much he had done for her.

However, Jenny did not wait for the hundredth concert. In 1849, Barnum had organized "Barnum's Great Asiatic Caravan Museum and Menagerie," in association with Sherwood E. Stratton, the father of General Tom Thumb. They had chartered a ship and sent it to Ceylon for wild animals, leaving five hundred tons of hay on the Island of St. Helena on the way out, in order to feed the animals on the voyage back, and casks to hold water for them—a typical example of Barnum's enterprise and foresightedness. Now, two years later, the ship had returned, bringing a number of elephants among other examples of Asiatic animal life. Barnum had arranged a grand parade of his elephants up Broadway from the ship to the quarters set up for them, with ten of them hitched in pairs to a chariot, and had asked Jenny to review them from the Irving House. Jenny had complied.

But when she found that the next concerts Barnum had arranged, in Philadelphia, were to be held in a hall that had housed exhibitions of horsemanship, she evidently thought he was involving her too deeply in the animal world. Barnum's story was that the National Theater on Chestnut Street in Philadelphia had indeed been used for "equestrian and theatrical entertainments," but since had been thoroughly cleansed and fitted up by Max Maretzek for Italian opera. "It was a convenient place for our purpose. But one of her 'advisers,' a subordinate in her employ, who was always itching for the position of manager, made the selection of this building a pretext for creating dissatisfaction in the mind of Miss Lind.

"I saw the influences which were at work, and not caring enough for the profits of the remaining seven concerts to continue the engagement at the risk of disturbing the friendly feelings which had hitherto uninterruptedly existed between that lady and myself, I wrote her a letter offering to relinquish the engagement if she desired it, at the termination of the concert which was to take place that evening, upon her simply allowing me a thousand dollars per concert for the seven which would yet remain to make up the hundred, besides paying me the sum stipulated as a forfeiture for closing the engagement at the one hundredth concert.

"Towards evening I received the following reply: 'My dear Sir: I accept your proposition to close our contract tonight, at the end of the ninety-third concert, on condition of my paying you seven thousand dollars, in addition to the sum I forfeit under the condition of finishing the engagement at the end of one hundred concerts. I am, dear Sir, yours truly, Jenny Lind.'" This letter was dated June 9, 1851.

The financial report Barnum submitted to Jenny showed that the total receipts—they had agreed not to count the first two New York concerts in their arrangement—had been $712,161.34. Jenny's net share of this had been $176,675, leaving $535,486.34 as Barnum's gross receipts after paying Jenny. He never disclosed his own net profit, but his good friend Sol Smith put this at $200,000 in his preface to his book of reminiscences, indicating that Barnum had paid out more than $300,000 in expenses; and Uncle Sol probably knew. Receipts for twenty concerts given for charity were not included in Barnum's reckoning, though he had paid the expenses for them. Barnum clearly felt that these figures should have counterbalanced whatever faint horsey aroma may have lingered in the National Theater.

But Max Maretzek, a well-known manager and conductor of operas in the United States during this period, whom Barnum had cited as having cleaned the National Theater after its equestrian uses, viewed the matter of the National Theater somewhat differently. As soon as Barnum's version came out in his autobiography, first published in 1854, Maretzek wrote an indignant letter to Lablache, the great tenor with whom Jenny had sung in England.

He maintained that he had *not* cleaned out and fitted up the National

Theater before it was hired by Barnum, since he had not played there until three months after Jenny's appearances, and suggested that it was the elephant parade which had soured Jenny against her manager. Maretzek said she must have remarked the same faces in the crowd which had greeted her own arrival, the same enthusiastic crowds which had followed her carriage, when the elephants, ostriches and monkeys paraded through Broadway, "preceded by bands of music, tawdry inscriptions traced upon banners, and other mummeries" designed to excite the curiosity of passers-by.

"Is it not possible that, upon this occasion, Jenny found out that in Barnum's eyes she was no more than his wooly horse or one of his monkeys? Would it be astonishing that the Swedish Nightingale felt hurt in her womanly pride? Can it be marveled at that she should become entirely disgusted with the 'Prince of Humbugs' and preferred paying $7,000 additional forfeit to staying another moment under his guidance?"

Maretzek, of course, was only guessing at the thoughts going through Jenny's mind when she reviewed the wild-animal parade, and she could have consoled herself that while curious crowds had gathered to look at the elephants, as they had to look at her, at least the elephants had not been greeted at the dock by a crowd of thirty to forty thousand people, and that the public's interest in them subsided as soon as they had passed out of sight. It seems probable that Barnum had engaged the National Theater in Philadelphia, as he had engaged rather unsuitable halls in many places, simply because it had seemed the best building available at the time; and that he had fitted it up as well as he could, as he had also done in so many other places. Jenny had not objected before, even at being asked to sing in the "pork" shed in Madison, Indiana.

It is recorded that when she first returned to Europe, Jenny said many disparaging things about the American people, and many harsh things about Barnum and his management of her concert tour. She is quoted as saying that Barnum had forced her to sing in a hall "where wild animals had been exhibited," thus combining the parade down Broadway and the National Theater in one complaint. On another occasion she charged that Barnum "exhibited me just as he did the big giant or any other of his monstrosities!"

Actually, the wonder is that the strange alliance lasted as long as it did. It is unlikely, to be sure, that Jenny ever knew a tenth part of the tricks and stratagems Barnum constantly employed. In Europe, a "made" press, in the way Barnum manipulated it, was unknown. The unprecedented demonstration at Liverpool, like many previous demonstrations in Europe and England, had been completely spontaneous. The only puzzle about America was how the news of all her doings could have leaked out, and this Barnum carefully kept from her.

But Barnum's lack of taste and his crudities of expression, which he reveals relentlessly throughout his autobiography—above all, his way of reducing everything to dollars and "advertising"—must have grated on her time and again during their months together. Whether it was the wild-animal parade, or because the National Theater had previously been used for horses, that tipped the scale, the partnership probably had been teetering precariously for a considerable time.

Yet when Jenny took the management of her concerts away from Barnum, she was overwhelmed with troubles of a different nature. Barnum had already advertised two more concerts in Philadelphia, and Jenny proposed to carry them out under her own management. Barnum says that during the intermission in the first concert, the evening of the day she and Barnum had agreed to terminate their engagement, he took General Welch, the lessee of the National Theater, back to her dressing room and introduced him. Jenny was as polite and friendly with Barnum as ever, and when General Welch said he was willing to release Jenny from Barnum's sublease of the building if she wished, she replied that she had found it much better than she had expected and that she would retain it for the remainder of the concerts.

However, her "evil advisers" having already broadcast that Jenny had severed relations with Barnum because he had forced her to sing in inappropriate surroundings, they thought it would not look well if Jenny continued to sing at the National Theater of her own volition. Jenny yielded to their persuasions and moved to a smaller hall.

That brought about another difficulty. As part of his publicity routine, Barnum had sent complimentary tickets for the concerts to the editors of newspapers within a hundred miles of Philadelphia. But there was hardly room in the smaller hall for all those who had bought tickets. The night of the second concert, one of Jenny's representatives (probably

Charles Seyton), whom Barnum accused of having played an indirect part in causing Jenny's break with him, refused to honor the editors' tickets. Barnum stepped in at this point, urging the man to reconsider, but he refused. Barnum then took the case to Jenny, who immediately gave orders that her agents should accept the tickets.

But on the night of the third concert, the unnamed representative again refused to honor the complimentary tickets, and Barnum had returned to Iranistan. The editors, many of whom had come a considerable distance and had brought their wives, had to pay for their tickets before they could get in. As soon as Barnum learned of this, he sent the editors the money they had paid out, from his own pocket. Thus Barnum ended his great enterprise with the same scrupulous honor on the financial side that he had exhibited from the first.

And it would be hardly fair to blame him too much for the flamboyant and sometimes deceitful devices he had used to make the enterprise the great success it became. Barnum had a genius for making the public think and do what he wanted it to. He could no more have forborne to give this highly worthy project the full benefit of his ingenious and wily mind, than Jenny could have forborne to sing her best whenever she faced an audience. In a way, perhaps, he represented the very genius of the still young America of that time, bursting with energy and ideas and ingenuity, and untrammeled by nice considerations of taste.

In fact, William Roscoe Thayer remarked, in the second volume of his *Life and Letters of John Hay*, "If the question had been asked during the third quarter of the nineteenth century. 'Who is the typical American of this period?', a perspicacious observer might have replied, 'Phineas T. Barnum.' " Barnum's unique contribution, Thayer added, was his discovery of the immense potentiality of advertising. "He not only assumed that people liked to be fooled—that was an ancient discovery. He demonstrated in his Great Moral Show that it made little difference what the object was, so long as it was effectively advertised."

Yet Barnum had done more than advertise Jenny Lind. He had taken on his own shoulders the entire burden of dealing with the multitudinous details involved by travel, the booking of concerts and putting them on. He had done everything he could to allow Jenny's mind "to be free as air and herself as free as a bird." He had used all the arts he possessed to present to the public the picture of an almost supernaturally flawless being.

He said in his memoirs that LeGrand Smith often remarked to him, "Well, Mr. Barnum, you have managed wonderfully in always keeping Jenny's 'angel side' outside with the public." Barnum's own comment was, "With all her excellent and even extraordinarily good qualities, Jenny Lind was human, though the reputation she bore in Europe for her many charitable acts led me to believe, *until I knew her* [Italics ours], that she was nearly perfect. I think now that her natural impulses were more simple, childlike, pure and generous than those of almost any other person I ever met. But she had been petted, almost worshipped, so long, that it would have been strange indeed if her unbounded popularity had not in some degree affected her to her hurt, and it must not be thought extraordinary if she now and then exhibited some phase of human weakness.

"Like most persons of uncommon talent, she had a strong will which, at times, she found ungovernable. But if she was ever betrayed into a display of ill-temper she was sure to apologize and express her regret afterwards."

Jenny would have been the first to admit that she had her share of human weaknesses and she had struggled all her adult life to control her temper. She was well aware of the danger that she would be spoiled by the worship she had had, even though she was never able to understand why she received it, and had striven mightily to avoid being affected by it. But she had never been able to overcome the suspiciousness inculcated by her experience with Alfred Bunn—a fault Barnum did not mention, and which she probably did not recognize herself as a fault. That was what had made her susceptible, finally, to the faultfinding of the evil advisers Barnum alludes to, to her own sorrow, as events were to show.

Jenny now continued her tour in more leisurely fashion, giving in all forty more concerts in seventeen towns and cities, including Columbus, Buffalo and Toronto. At first, things seemed to go well, aside from the little contretemps in Philadelphia regarding honorary tickets for newspaper editors. There were no more ticket auctions, and prices for tickets were fixed on a scale of $3 and $7, as against Barnum's system of charging as much as he thought the traffic would bear. Jenny benefited now from Barnum's strategy of allowing himself to be pictured as wily, greedy and grasping, in order to throw Jenny's generous nature into stronger relief. She wrote Judge Munthe, "The pleasure on the part of the public that I have parted with Mr. Barnum is so great that it is as pleasing for me personally to see such confidence and sympathy, as it is horribly little flattering for Mr. Barnum to see himself so little trusted and liked." Jenny had not yet begun to realize that Barnum had made himself a scapegoat for a definite purpose; and that without him, *she* would be blamed for whatever did not suit the public's taste.

For a while, the magic of Jenny's name drew many requests for concerts and brought people clamoring to hear her. However, she never attracted the same crowds and receipts as before. She made Charles Seyton her manager, with an agreement that he should receive one-fourth of the receipts for his pay. Seyton cut expenses all around, in order to increase his share. Instead of the lavishly decorated booklets Barnum had always provided, Seyton had the programs printed on double sheets, eliminating the biographical material and the decorative borders with nightingales at the corners which had turned Barnum's programs into souvenirs.

Benedict was no longer with the party. His health had suffered as a result of the heavy work of having to hire and train an orchestra in every place they visited. He had returned to England as soon as the party arrived back in New York, and Joseph Burke was made orchestra conductor. To replace Benedict as her accompanist, Jenny had sent to Hamburg for Otto Goldschmidt, continuing Richard Hoffman as second pianist. She had been very pleased with Otto's playing when he was her accompanist in Europe, and thought this would be another way to further his career. Because he was so young, only twenty-one, she had carried on the financial negotiations with his father.

There had been an embarrassing incident when young Otto arrived in America. Jenny had gone to Niagara Falls for a little rest, and he followed her there. When she received him in her sitting room—Josephine for once was not present—he had rushed to her, seized both her hands and kissed them over and over, stammering his joy to be with her again. Jenny was fond of Otto and considered him talented. The connection with Mendelssohn had been a special bond between them. But thought of romance with any of the young men in her entourage was completely out of bounds so far as Jenny was concerned, and displeasing to her. "I will forget that this has happened, Otto. But it must never happen again!" she told him firmly. Then she started talking about his voyage and her plans for the concerts. Otto did not offend in this way a second time.

The changes, however, proved detrimental before long. After a few concerts, it became clear that with reduced receipts, their standing orchestra would be too expensive, so it was disbanded. Now Joseph Burke had no core of experienced instrumentalists to work with. In each city, he had to audition and train a completely strange group, except when he was so fortunate as to find an adequate local orchestra. For one of her New England tours, Jenny was able to engage the Germania Society of Boston. Such luck as this seldom came Joseph Burke's way, however, and in time the orchestra was dispensed with entirely, to save money.

Another handicap was that Goldschmidt did not find favor with the audiences. His youth counted against him, for one thing, and he looked even younger than he was. He lacked Benedict's commanding presence— he was scarcely taller than Jenny herself, and weighed less. His stiff German manner did nothing to woo the audience. Otto persisted in playing long classical solos, while the audience stirred restlessly, began to chatter, and gave him only token applause when he had finished.

Barnum undoubtedly would have corrected this situation quickly by a spate of publicity which would have made young Otto appear to be the instrumental prodigy of the age, causing the audiences to feel there was something wrong with *them* if they did not detect genius in his playing.

The showman could have pointed out quite honestly, in fact, that the young German had not only been a pupil of the great Mendelssohn at the Leipzig Conservatory, but had also taken private piano lessons from the hardly less eminent Clara Schumann and had studied counterpoint under Moritz Hauptmann. What further distinctions the showman would have invented for Otto out of his own fertile imagination is anybody's guess.

But once again Barnum was nowhere, so far as the Lind party was concerned, and Charles Seyton and Max Hjortzberg, in whose hands now lay the responsibility for publicity as for other matters, were no Barnums. Nor were they capable of handling the mass of business detail. Jenny admitted to Barnum later, when she stopped for a brief visit at Iranistan, that from the time she parted with him, she had been sadly harassed. "People cheat me and swindle me very much, and I find it very annoying to give concerts on my own account."

Now at last Belletti's time had come. With Benedict's kindly aid no longer at her disposal, beset with problems and irritations on every side, Jenny had need of Uncle Belletti, and she turned to him increasingly for comfort in her bewilderment. More and more she was opening her heart to him. He waited only for just the right moment.

Concerts in New York State and New England filled June and part of July of 1851, followed at less frequent intervals by appearances in those areas and in Pennsylvania, Ohio and Canada during the summer and early fall. Generally, churches were used rather than theaters, Jenny's youthful managers explaining that this meant "less financial risk." In Buffalo, a considerable city, two concerts were given in the North Presbyterian Church, which was on Main Street, between Huron and Chippewa Streets. The tickets were numbered according to the pews.

Jenny, however, appeared to produce the same effect on her listeners as before, and was dressing more elaborately, perhaps to make up for the miserly arrangements of her managers. A journalist in Buffalo noted that "she wore a rich dress of white lace and satin, with a rose-wreath on her brow, a small brilliant on her neck, white kid gloves and a crimson bracelet, or bandeau, on her bare arm, and held a silver fan."

At Toronto, there was a touch of the kind of attention Jenny had been accustomed to receive so bountifully in Europe, and in America while Barnum was in charge. The 71st Regiment of Scotch Highlanders, from Dundee, was stationed there, and the regimental band attended the concert in a body. As Jenny and her party made ready to leave the hotel for the railway station, she found the musicians waiting for her. They lined up and marched ahead of her carriage, to their own martial music. When they reached the station Jenny thanked them and assured them she would never forget them. (Nor did she. Five years later, Jenny was giving a concert in Perth, Scotland, and learned that the 71st Regiment was there. She sent tickets for her concert to all the members of the band.)

This attention meant much to Jenny, for in a number of places reaction was beginning to set in against her. With Benedict out of the picture, there seems to have been an end to the introduction of new songs. Jenny sang the same programs, over and over, and people began to get a little bored. With concert receipts falling off, she had to cut down her gifts to local charities. A number of newspapers now began to accuse *her* of being greedy and stingy.

The word spread that she was "against Negroes"—a rumor as damaging to her in the North as the rumor that she had contributed to an abolitionist society would have been in the South. This probably arose from a remark she may or may not have made to Maunsell Field during her first weeks in New York, but quoted by him, that she thought Negroes ugly. Actually, she had made her decision about the question she had heard argued so much through the Mississippi Valley. In the spring of 1852, she wrote a letter to Harriet Beecher Stowe in her quaint English, praising *Uncle Tom's Cabin*. "Forgive me, my dear Madam, it is a great liberty I take in thus addressing you, but I have so wished to find an opportunity to pour out to you my thankfulness in a few words to you that I cannot help thus intruding. I have the feeling about *Uncle Tom's Cabin* that great changes will take place by and by, from the impression people receive out of it, and that the writer of that book can fall asleep today or tomorrow with the bright, sweet conscience of having been a strong means in the Creator's hand of operating essential good in one of the most important questions for the welfare of our black brethren."

Jenny was often worried to distraction by the inadequacies of her business staff, and angered by the public's refusal to put the same estimate that she did on Otto Goldschmidt's ability. Stubbornly, she determined to make the people accept him. She had his name printed on the programs in the same large type as her own. And when the audiences still declined to applaud him as much as they did the other performers, she remained in the wings during his solos, instead of going to her dressing room as usual, where Otto could not see her but the audience could. When he had finished, she clapped vigorously, and the audience would obediently follow suit, though with some resentment.

Otto, probably wrapped in his own miseries, had not been aware of Jenny's efforts to stir up applause for him until a concert in Philadelphia, during which the audience broke into his solo with boisterous applause that was a clear indication for him to stop. This time Jenny came forward and shook his hand warmly, throwing a defiant look at the audience.

The next day Otto asked to see Jenny. Coming into the sitting room of her suite at the hotel, his face pale and set, he made a formal little bow and said stiffly, "With your permission, Fräulein Lind, I would like to resign and return to Germany."

Jenny looked at him incredulously. "Are you deserting me, Otto? I thought that I could count on *you*, at least."

"I do not wish to desert you, Fräulein. I shall remain until you have found someone to take my place. But I cannot impose any longer on your kindness. I have failed. My presence does not help you, it makes things worse for you. This must not be."

Jenny argued and pleaded, shed tears, but Otto could not be moved. After he had left the suite, she sent for Belletti. The baritone found her walking up and down the room in a state of agitation.

"Now it is Otto, who says he must leave us!" she exclaimed as soon as Belletti entered. "He says he has failed, because the audiences do not like him. I have tried to make them see what a brilliant pianist he is. What more can I do?"

"You have hurt his pride, Jenny," Belletti told her gently.

"How can it be that I have hurt his pride? I was only trying to help! The audiences here do not know good playing when they hear it. Otto is not to blame."

"It hurts his pride that the audience will not applaud him unless you force them to. And I think it hurts him more, because he is a little in love with you." Belletti smiled indulgently.

Jenny reddened. "But that is ridiculous! He is much too young! Oh, there was a little nonsense when he first arrived, but I spoke to him about it and there has been nothing of that kind since."

"Haven't you noticed the way he looks at you, Jenny? And when a man cares for a woman in that way, even so young a man as Otto, it hurts his pride for her to fight his battles as though he were a child."

Jenny sat down abruptly on a sofa. "You mean that I have been making him appear ridiculous?"

"I believe he may think so."

After this, Jenny forced herself to go to her dressing room and stay there while Otto played his solos, but she found herself straining for the applause, suffering when it was scanty. She wondered if what Belletti had said could be true—that Otto felt his humiliation more keenly because he was in love with her. She thought what a fine person Otto was, of his selflessness in helping her to find joy again in singing Mendelssohn's songs, and how lonely he must feel in this foreign country which rejected his playing. She determined that he should not go back to Germany under a burden of failure. She must establish him in his own esteem at least.

Jenny began asking him for frequent rehearsals of her songs, when no rehearsal was needed, on the ground that she required his help to work out difficult phrases. She let no opportunity go by to praise him on his excellence as a pianist. She laid her business problems before him, insisting that she could not get along without his advice. She gave little parties for the greatly reduced troupe, during which she paid special attention to Otto. She invented pretexts to bring him often to her suite, or to accompany her when she left the hotel. Whenever she was to see Otto, she amazed Josephine Åhmansson by being fussier about her appearance than if she had been going to a ball. It was all, she told herself, to make Otto happy, to make him feel his presence was necessary. And she did nothing about finding a pianist to replace Otto.

Jenny made Boston more or less her headquarters, returning there after her tours. Henry W. Longfellow wrote in his diary for June 26, 1851, "Jenny Lind called this morning with Mr. Goldschmidt, a young pianist from Hamburg. We had a pleasant half-hour chat. There is something very fascinating about her, a kind of soft wildness of manner, and sudden pauses in her speaking, and floating shadows over her face. Goldschmidt, we like extremely." As the visitors were leaving, the poet made a pretext to get Jenny aside and said to her warmly, "He is a *good* man!"

Jenny took great comfort from this.

Otto received Jenny's attentions with the same respectful courtesy he had shown her ever since she had rebuked his display of emotion on his arrival. Had she only imagined, she began to wonder, that his expression of joy at that time had been more than pleasure at reunion with a friend? Jenny found, to her consternation, that the idea hurt.

"Why, I have been pursuing him!" she acknowledged to herself. "Can it be that I am in love with him?"

This thought gave her greater distress than all her business problems and vexations. She had accepted so firmly the idea that she was done with love. And above all, she had had such a bitter lesson with Claudius Harris, only five years younger than herself. Otto was nine years younger than she, less two months. He had barely reached manhood. Yet she could think of nothing but Otto.

She turned to Belletti—she had been too ashamed to speak of her dilemma to Josephine Åhmansson. "I do not know myself any more, Belletti. How can I be in love with Otto? Yet if it is not love, what is it that has taken possession of me?"

"Of course it is not love," Belletti assured her with sincerity. "How could you be entirely yourself, when you have so many troubles? You are sorry for young Goldschmidt. It is this that you have confused with love."

"I suppose you are right," Jenny said wryly. "Oh, Belletti, what would I do without you? You are the only one to whom I can confess how very stupid and silly I can be!"

Belletti was tempted to say then the words that had been formulated in his mind for so long. But it did not seem quite the moment. And already, he thought, he may have had said too much. Had it been his own comment that Otto was in love with her, that had put the idea of love in Jenny's mind? Since it was there, it might be better to wait until she had recognized the folly of it for herself, as she had recognized her folly in the Claudius Harris affair. That would be the time to speak of his own mature and seasoned love.

All through the late summer and fall of 1851, Jenny wrestled with the obsession she felt for Otto. She kept reminding herself of the foolish predicament with Claudius Harris. But she would then turn around and remind herself that the similarity ceased with the fact that both men were younger than herself. She could find no fault with Otto's character —it shone all the more in comparison with Claudius's and Günther's. Otto was a sober, serious person, a member of that "Church" of which Mendelssohn had spoken so often, and to which Mendelssohn had at once admitted Jenny—a dedication to the highest and finest in music and art. Otto was a Jew, it was true, but so had Mendelssohn been a Jew, and like Mendelssohn, Otto was embracing Christianity. She had learned by accident, for Otto had said nothing to her about it, that he was taking instruction in her own Lutheran faith. But always she came up against the great difference in their ages. Otto was twenty-two in August of 1851, but Jenny was thirty-one on October 6. On October 8, she wrote to Judge Munthe, confessing her mixed feelings about Otto, begging him to advise her.

"He is a great pianist, second only to Mendelssohn, and the noblest man I have ever met. He has all Lindblad's refinement and genius, together with Günther's, only more reliable and cultured, and with a character above reproach. What is still more remarkable, he exceeds Lindblad, Mendelssohn and Günther, all three, in being fond of me, and believing good of me and allowing me to influence his soul in the most uplifting way I can. He is like Günther, only small and much younger. He is the first person I could confidently and with inner conviction swear before God that I could make happy in every way and am really made for. But he is so young—seven years younger than I am [even to her guardian Jenny could not tell the whole truth]—though only outwardly. Goldschmidt can fulfill all the needs of my soul. . . . He heard me in Leipzig six years ago, and since then has been my warmest friend. Isn't this cruel! Isn't this absolutely desperate! . . . . No one ever has existed or can exist with whom I can live so as one soul and one heart as with Goldschmidt, but age, age!"

CHAPTER EIGHTEEN

Jenny Makes Up Her Mind

AT LEAST ONE of Jenny's doubts had apparently been dissolved by the time she confessed her dilemma to Judge Munthe. There was a peaceful, happy interlude in early July of 1851, when the little troupe, now consisting only of Jenny, Belletti, Salvi, Joseph Burke and Otto Goldschmidt, went to Springfield, Massachusetts, to give a concert. Jenny stayed at the Warriner home on Howard Street, which had been redecorated for the occasion, and fell so in love with Springfield, and was so comfortable at the Warriners', that she made the house her headquarters for a week.

The concert was held on July 1 in the old First Congregational Church, which was jammed with as many people as it could possibly hold while "a great throng, unable to enter, heard what they could of the concert through the open windows."

The next morning five hundred school children gathered beneath the balcony of Jenny's room to serenade her, and she tossed carnations down to them. Two days later, by unanimous request of the townspeople, she reviewed the Fourth of July parade from the same balcony. As long as the Warriner house stood, many people used to visit the second-floor rooms Jenny had occupied. And when the house was torn down, the balcony from which she had reviewed the parade and dropped carnations to the school children was preserved in a local museum.

The Springfield *Post* commented, "The best musical performances here rarely draw over 300 or 400 people at 25 cents a ticket. In this case, the merited fame of one young woman of marvelous gifts, crowds the most spacious edifices with people who eagerly pay three and four dollars a ticket for such music." (The foregoing was quoted on the program for the Jenny Lind concert which Frieda Hempel gave in Springfield on April 7, 1923.)

There was even greater excitement in nearby Northampton, over the concert she gave in the Congregational Church there on July 3. A platform for the performers was erected in front of the pulpit, and a private room constructed for their use in a corner of the auditorium, with a special entrance made for it through a window. A heavy rainstorm, beginning at six on the evening of the concert and continuing through the night, kept no one away. A local account records that "the aristocratic and wealthiest people entered heart and soul into the spirit of the occasion. It was without doubt the 'toniest' assemblage ever gathered in this town. The enthusiasm spread far and near and drew people from a radius of twenty miles, some coming from as far as Brattleboro." Jenny repeated Taubert's bird song and "Home, Sweet Home" by urgent request of the audience, but refused to repeat them yet again, though the audience kept clapping and cheering. Jenny also gave a concert in Hartford during this week.

She had lingered on in Springfield because of the comfort of the Warriner home and the hospitable atmosphere created by the townspeople. But she fell in love with Northampton because of the beauty of the New England town and the Berkshire hills around it. She promptly dubbed it the "Switzerland of America" and visited it several times, being driven back and forth from Springfield in a barouche drawn by four white horses, a touch reminiscent of her reception in Louisville. On one visit she and her entourage climbed to the top of Mount Tom. Jenny singled out Otto to walk with her around the crest, and stood with him, apart from the others, looking out over the hills.

Exactly what was said in the low-voiced, earnest conversation between the two is not known, but there are indications that Jenny deliberately opened the way for Otto to tell her that he had loved her ever since, as a lad of sixteen, he had first heard her sing in Leipzig. She was a different Jenny when they rejoined the others. She told them gaily that she and Otto had been bestowing names upon the various features of the landscape. She pointed to a beautiful wooded section a short distance west of Northampton. "That shall be called 'The Paradise of America,' and the lake there at the foot of Mount Tom must be 'Paradise Lake.' " And thus these spots were known henceforth, according to local legend.

Before the party started down, Jenny took a last look at the sweep of mountains and valleys in the midst of which nestled Northampton, with its village green and the spire of the old church rising above the elms. Later she confessed that she had said to herself, "If I marry Otto, it is here that I would like to spend my honeymoon."

On July 7, 1851, Jenny visited Prospect House, on the top of Mount Holyoke, at the invitation of the proprietor. The legend lingers on that she also dubbed this area, "The Paradise of America." A facsimile of the page in the hotel register bearing her signature was hung on the wall of Prospect House, and was joined later by a facsimile of the page for August 31, 1860, containing the signature of Abraham Lincoln, then the Republican candidate for President. When the property was given to the Commonwealth of Massachussetts in 1940 and converted into the Joseph Alden Skinner State Park, Prospect House became Summit House, and the registers bearing the actual signatures were presented to the Northampton Historical Society. However, photostatic copies of the two pages may be seen today on the walls of Summit House.

A letter to her old friend, Jakob Axel Josephson, in 1853, is revealing of the thoughts that were going through Jenny's mind in this summer of 1851. Jenny could not help but know that she was not an ordinary person, that she had more to lose than most people if she were to make a bad marriage, and she wrote of this frankly. "But it was hard for me to be alone and be so torn to pieces by people and the world as I was, and the desire for a home had always been strong in my heart, so far back as I can remember. It had never been in my mind that I might some day marry Goldschmidt. I have always been afraid of marrying a man younger than myself. But I got to know him well in America, saw his gentle and kind disposition, had the opportunity to watch his behavior under so many different and difficult situations, found so much unselfishness and so moving and unusual a fondness for me, that after long and careful consideration and the killing of all illusions, with nothing but the hard, naked truth in front of me, I determined not to turn from me the one who had proved himself the noblest and most selfless of them all."

However, nothing more had been said since the conversation at the top of Mount Tom. The decision had to be Jenny's. Otto felt honor bound not to try to influence her, since he had so little to offer her. It became evident that she would also have to be the one to speak, and it took her some time to summon the courage. One day they were alone in her sitting room, going over some scores. Jenny put down the music and said to him, her face flushing with embarrassment, "Otto, I have thought a great deal since we talked together at Northampton. I am much older than you, and you are young, even to consider marriage to anyone. The world may think that I have wronged you, taken advantage of your youth. This I would not mind for myself, but I would mind it for you."

Otto's eyes grew bright, his usually pallid face flooded with color. Once again he seized her hands and kissed them, and this time Jenny did not draw them away.

"Fräulein, in comparison with you I am nothing. The world would think I was taking advantage of *you*, you are so far above me. But you have given me the courage to say what I have longed to say, and never before have dared to. Will you marry a poor student of music?"

And Jenny, smiling, answered, "If you will promise to love, protect and support me!" Or so she always declared afterwards that she had replied to Otto's proposal. And she added, "Now that we are engaged, I think you should call me Jenny."

They had planned to keep the engagement secret, but soon everyone in the little troupe knew that something decisive had happened between the two. Belletti came to Jenny. "I am sorry to leave you, but I have received an offer from Europe which I cannot refuse. Will you permit me to withdraw?"

Tears came to Jenny's eyes. She threw her arms around his neck. "How I shall miss you, Belletti!" But she did not urge him to stay on. There was so much trouble over financial and management matters that they were giving very few concerts; she felt she could not stand in Belletti's way.

Belletti never did speak of his love. Once again he had delayed too long. For already Jenny and Otto were planning their wedding, to be "sometime after Christmas." They would honeymoon in Northampton,

as Jenny had promised herself that day on Mount Tom. They would stay
at the Round Hill Hotel. And though this was to be only a temporary
home, still it would be the first real home that Jenny had ever had, and
she wanted some things of her own about her. The newsmen in Boston
had somewhat relaxed their watch on Jenny, and she was much freer
to come and go than formerly. However, a reporter for the *Daily Courier*
trailed her carriage to Waterman's, and told the paper's readers that she
had bought several pieces of kitchenware. A little later he followed this
up with the news that she had ordered jewelry and a whole set of plate
from Jones's.

Nevertheless, no one outside the handful of people who had to be let
in on the secret guessed what was in the wind. Jones's did not divulge
that she had directed her new silver to be marked with a "J," encircled
by an "O"—explaining gaily to the engraver, "I am a cipher!" It aroused
no comment that Otto was often with her on her excursions. The public
was accustomed to the fact that some gentleman or gentlemen of her
party nearly always accompanied her when she went about the city, and
the number of gentlemen had shrunk so markedly that it seemed natural
for her young accompanist to hold the post of honor.

The wedding day had been set for early February, and seven rooms
were engaged at Round Hill, with the utmost secrecy. Jenny had taken an
apartment for Josephine Åhmansson and herself in Boston; Otto had
rooms in a private home near the Common, for the short time remaining.
Jenny had written a prenuptial contract with her own hand, modeled on
the one Mr. Senior had drawn up for her when she was engaged to
Claudius Harris. Jenny's fortune had been amassed for a definite purpose—to assure the future of her philanthropies, as well as her own.
Much as she loved him and believed in his good intentions, Otto was
young to be given such a responsibility. The contract, which Otto willingly
signed, gave her exclusive control of her money while she lived, but
named Otto as administrator of her estate after her death.

Then one day Jenny and Otto returned to her apartment from a walk,
to find the post waiting for her on the table of her sitting room. Otto
picked up some music and occupied himself with it, while Jenny tore
open the letters and scanned them quickly. He heard her exclaim. Looking up, he saw that she had gone to the window, and was standing, her
back toward him, her head bowed.

"Have you had bad news?"

"A letter from Judge Munthe," she replied, in a low, strangled voice, "My mother is dead. I had not even known that she was ill." The fact was that two previous letters from Judge Munthe had failed to reach Jenny. She had had no intimation that anything was wrong at home.

Otto started toward her, his arms outstretched, "Oh my darling, I am so very sorry!"

But before he could reach her, she turned, and he faced a Jenny he had never seen before. The eyes were large and dark and completely dry, though Jenny's eyes were quick to fill with tears over small tragedies, or anything that moved her. On her white face there was an expression of horror. Her hands came up to fend him off.

"Don't touch me, Otto! I am not worthy!" He would never have imagined that tones so harsh and ragged could have come from Jenny Lind. "My mother has died, and I feel nothing! Otto, I feel nothing!"

"It is the shock, Jenny. It is because the news is so unexpected."

Jenny paid no attention. "Go back to Hamburg, Otto, save yourself! I cannot marry you. I am a lie, my whole life has been a lie. There is no love or goodness in me. You did not know that I was born out of wedlock, but that is the truth. My mother had so little thought for me that she did not marry my father until I was a big girl, nearly fifteen, and then it was not for my sake, oh no. She sent me away as soon as I was born; she did not have me with her until she was forced to. She never let me know she *was* my mother until she was forced to. She never wanted me until I began to bring in money. Then she wanted only the money I brought in.

"You did not know that my father is nothing but a drunkard, who spends all his time in taverns until he gets so drunk someone must take him home. But that is the truth, about the father of the so respectable Jenny Lind.

"Can you think what it means to have been rejected by one's own mother, to have for a father a drunken ne'er-do-well? No, Otto, you cannot. So I must tell you that it is a canker that eats at the heart. I have no heart. I am not a woman but a monster, who feels nothing when her mother dies." On and on Jenny went, pouring out the hurts and wonderings and shames of her childhood and girlhood.

"You should have told me, Jenny," Otto said at last. "You should not have kept this shut up so long within yourself."

"How could I have told, how could I have made you understand?" Jenny said bitterly. "I have seen the look on your face, on Mendelssohn's too, when you spoke of your homes, of your mothers, so sweet and loving, the light and warmth in your eyes when you remembered things from childhood. How could I tell you that I had never known love from my mother, that her home was never a home for me, that I ran from it twice, because I could not bear it any longer! I can see it in your face now, how you shrink from me!"

"Stop, Jenny, stop!" There was a new authority in Otto's voice. "I do not shrink from you. I love you, Jenny, I love you!" In spite of her protestations he led her to the sofa and cradled her in his arms, rocking her gently back and forth and soothing her, as though she had been a child.

"The only wrong you ever did, dearest, was not to share this trouble with me. What is love for, if not to share the burdens and troubles of those we love? Jenny, what you have told me only makes more wonderful what you are, and what you have done." He repeated this over and over, rocking her back and forth. Gradually Jenny grew calmer. She raised her head once to say earnestly, "Papa was not always the way he is," and to tell Otto how she had adored the young Niklas when he came to see them at No. 4 Mäster Samuelsgrand, and held her on his knee while he sang Bellman's songs.

She began to remember happier incidents about her mother, too. "We did have a nice time the summer we went to the country together, after the law court had made me go back to them. And the last time I was in Sweden, she seemed fonder. Otto, I truly wanted to make her old age comfortable and happy. Perhaps if she had been happier, she would not have been so cross with me." Until at last the tears came, and, still cradled in Otto's arms, her head against his shoulders, Jenny was able to grieve for Anna Marie as she would have wished to do.

Now the last barrier was down, and from that time on, Otto was in Jenny's fullest confidence in matters relating to her parents. She was able to express to Judge Munthe in all sincerity her regret that his previous letters had miscarried, for had she known her mother was ill, she would have gone at once to her bedside. She described to Judge Munthe the simple stone that she wished to have erected over her mother's grave, and made provision for Niklas's future. It would not do to entrust him with more than pocket money, for he would spend everything in the taverns. Judge Munthe found a pleasant place for Niklas in a home on the outskirts of Stockholm, where he was made comfortable, and the bills for his keep were sent to Judge Munthe to pay.

For the first time since she could remember, Jenny felt at peace within herself. The canker that had eaten at her heart so long had been healed, through Otto's love and understanding. She who had grown up feeling unwanted at last was wanted for precisely what she was, with all her faults and failings. Now she could pity Anna Marie, and pity washed away the uncertainties and suspicions that had caused her to waver and shrink from life so many times before.

Jenny did not even mind too much when their last concert in Philadelphia, shortly before Christmas, provoked an almost vicious blast from the Philadelphia *Guardian*, which had heaped praise upon her in her earlier appearances there.

> Jenny Lind has resolved to give no more concerts in Philadelphia. Few persons will regret her determination, unless she should be able to better suppress the evidences of ill temper and vexation than she did on Tuesday evening last. She looked as stingy as a hive of wasps, and as black as a thunder-cloud, and all because the house was not crowded. The fact is that Jenny's attractions are not strong enough to counteract the dullness of Goldschmidt's piano playing, or the merely mediocre ability of Burke on the violin. The absence too of orchestra was a disgusting exhibition of parsimony, and a determination to make the most money she possibly could. Miss Lind has never succeeded since she left the guardianship of Mr. Barnum; and then she has had poor advisers, and has been in ill humor when the homage paid to her talent was not manifested with the greatest enthusiasm. The Nightingale has feathered her nest well in our country, and she can go back to her Swedish home where we wish her long health, a better disposition and a good husband to cheer her declining years.

Jenny knew now very well how ill advised she had been to turn over the management of her concerts to Max Hjortzberg and Charles Seyton —they were the ones who had forced the economies, not Jenny. She dismissed them. In a letter to Joseph Burke in 1853, Jenny speaks of Hjortzberg as "poor my Max." "I knew he would have dark days ahead of him, but it will come right again I hope, as he has the gift of throwing off many trials with the wave of a hand. He is to a very high degree violent in his temper, and only hard circumstance will put him down."

So far as Otto was concerned, *she* knew how brilliantly he played, how steeped he was in the finest musical tradition. There was no end to the excitement and pleasure the two of them found in exploring music together, there never would be an end. It no longer mattered that a country which had heard so few good performers before she came, failed to recognize Otto's worth.

Otto, Jenny and Josephine Åhmansson celebrated Christmas Eve in Jenny's apartment, with the traditional candle-lit tree, heaped about with presents. A week or two before their marriage, Jenny and Otto went to the celebrated daguerreotype studio of Southworth and Hawes, at 5½ Tremont Row, Boston, to sit for a wedding picture. This daguerreotype, with Jenny nestling against her accompanist, his left arm holding her close, his right hand over both of hers, would have filled the press with speculation about their intentions. But the daguerreotypist kept their secret too.

The evening of February 4, 1852, also, Jenny and Otto spent together quietly in her apartment, talking, and playing and singing some of Mendelssohn's songs. Jenny's great friend and Otto's teacher was much in their thoughts. The next morning Otto appeared at the Boston marriage bureau and took out a license to marry Jenny Lind. On the registry he gave Jenny's age as thirty-one, his own as twenty-nine—a gallant and forgivable prevarication. Then the two met at the home of Dr. Samuel Gray Ward on Louisburg Square in Boston. Dr. Ward was the brother of Julia Ward Howe, the poet, and was Boston agent for Baring Brothers of London.

Jenny was dressed in white with a red rose in her hair, almost the identical costume in which she had appeared in her first concert in Castle Garden, except that she had a short wedding veil over her head. Otto wore a Prince Albert coat, which Queen Victoria's consort had made the fashionable attire for gentlemen. At noon the couple took their places under a bower of lilies and roses, and two ministers stepped forward, the Reverend Charles Mason, and Dr. John Wainwright, who later became bishop of the Episcopal diocese of New York. (According to Richard Hoffman, Charles Seyton married Dr. Wainwright's daughter.) Standing near them were their hosts, Dr. and Mrs. Ward, and the handful of guests: Mr. and Mrs. T. W. Ward; Edward Everett; N. I. Bowditch, who had acted as Jenny's legal adviser in Boston; and the Swedish consul, Karl Habicht.

As their present to the bride, Dr. and Mrs. Ward gave Jenny a gold locket containing a daguereotype of Daniel Webster and a miniature of George Washington, the two Americans Jenny had often declared she most admired. Jenny called it her "good luck locket," and always wore it thereafter when she sang in a concert. (The locket, bequeathed to Jenny's daughter, and given by her to Leonidas Westervelt, is in the Westervelt-Jenny Lind collection at the New York Historical Society.)

Hardly was the ceremony over when the square filled with newsmen, alerted to what was going on after one of their number came upon the marriage license. "Miss Lind, Mr. Goldschmidt!" they shouted. "Why did you not tell us? Come to the door!"

At length the bride and groom did appear at the door, arm in arm. "Say something for us, Miss Lind—I mean Madame Goldschmidt!" a reporter for the *Traveller* implored.

"I have found in this man all that my heart ever wanted," Jenny said.

As soon as the members of the Germania Society heard the news, they hastily gathered up their instruments and marched to the Ward home to serenade the newlyweds, but found they had already departed for Northampton, leaving a great clamor behind them.

The wedding of the Swedish Nightingale and her accompanist, Otto Goldschmidt, was the principal news event of February 5, 1852. The Boston *Evening Transcript* declared that "it was rushed to the telegraph offices and flashed off to the east, the west, the north and the south, and it was known in Halifax, in New Orleans, at Quebec and St. Louis before nightfall!" The *Transcript* seemed to find a kind of morbid pleasure in revealing how the papers had been caught napping. "She bought her parlor furnishings at Hovey & Co. in Cambridge, her family stores at Pierce, her kitchen utensils at Waterman's, her jewelry and plate at Jones, Ball and Poor's. . . . All were bought openly, audaciously, and the fact was announced to the public through the papers. . . . Yet the itemizers of the press were unable to fathom her movements, and were unable to find straw to make a paragraph of."

The Boston *Courier* agreed that the match had taken everyone by surprise, "though we must say we were struck by something confoundedly arch and roguish in the twinkle of the Nightingale's eye when she sang 'John Anderson, My Jo' the last time she appeared in public in this city."

The Goldschmidts spent three months in Northampton, the first few weeks at Round Hill, the remainder of the time in a modest rented house. Josephine Åhmansson stayed on, taking over the management of household affairs, now that she was no longer needed as companion and chaperon. Presents poured into the Ward home in Boston until the Goldschmidts' whereabouts became known, then descended on them in Northampton in a steady stream. Jewelry, silverware, trinkets of great value and of no value at all, and books without number filled the tables and spilled over onto the floors of their rooms.

The presence of the Goldschmidts brought a romantic glow to the whole area. They were much sought after by the "aristocrats and wealthiest," and Jenny made a point of seeking out the plainer folk. She would stop in at the house of some hard-pressed family when out riding or driving, and, after chatting awhile with the occupants, leave a purse of money behind her. Driving by a farmhouse one day, she saw a herd of cows in the barnyard. She went to the house and asked if she might have a glass of fresh milk. Every day thereafter she would stop by for a glass of milk. Northampton's piano tuner, William K. Wright, with whom the Goldschmidts became well acquainted through his attentions to their piano, said that she often called at his house, sometimes coming in without stopping to knock or ring the doorbell.

Considerably more than half a century afterwards, Leonidas Westervelt found, in an antique shop in Northampton, a round metal ornament from the valance board of a canopied four-poster bed. On it was engraved the head of Jenny Lind, crowned with a laurel wreath on which is perched a nightingale. (Also to be seen in the Westervelt-Jenny Lind collection at the New York Historical Society.) All that was known about it was that it had come from some farmhouse in the vicinity. It was the only example of this particular bit of Lindomania that ever turned up, perhaps the only one ever made. Could it have been that some Berkshire swain, romantically inspired at having the Swedish Nightingale choose his native hills for her honeymoon, had had this ornament made to bless his own nuptial bed?

However, in spite of the excitement and the flood of presents and attentions, Jenny's marriage to the unknown and not very impressive young musician tarnished her luster a bit in the eyes of many Americans who had not been affected by the grumbling about the later concerts. Otto had not sold himself to the public, as today's spiritual descendants of P. T. Barnum would say, and it was generally felt that Jenny Lind should have been able to do much better. Barnum's estimate of Otto, who had arrived in this country in time to take part in a few concerts while Jenny was still under the showman's management, was that he was a "very quiet, inoffensive young man" and an accomplished musician. From Barnum, this was damning with faint praise. Even as a musician, Otto apparently did not merit the Barnum accolade of "first rate." Surely if the "Queen of Song" had wanted to marry a musician, rather than a member of royalty, or of the nobility, or a captain of industry, she could have chosen from among the great in her art—or at least someone whose playing did not actively annoy his audiences!

Rumors to this effect reached Jenny even in Northampton, and she went to considerable pains to counteract them. She wrote Dr. Robert Baird of Yonkers, New York, that she had gained the best and most disinterested friend in her beloved husband. "We are both musical souls and we feel on all matters the greatest, the most perfect sympathy I can imagine." There was the difference in age, she acknowledged, and it would have been better had it not been so. "But his youth exists more in his face than in his soul, for really he is as steady as an old man, that is to say, as a *steady* old man!" Jenny wrote many letters while she was in Northampton, and every one stressed Otto's virtues.

When the weather grew milder, Jenny and Otto climbed Mount Tom again. They so enjoyed their drives through the hills and woods surrounding Northampton, and their walks about Paradise Lake, that they toyed with the idea of making their permanent home in America. However, a letter to Otto from the directors of the Dresden Conservatory in Germany changed that. He was offered the position of Professor of Music, with the privilege of taking private students as well. This was recognition of Otto as a musician in his own right, and Jenny felt as Otto did that it should be accepted.

Out of the many concert offers Jenny had received, she selected a handful before leaving America—two in Boston, single concerts in several other New England cities, and three in New York City. Joseph Burke,

Jenny Makes Up Her Mind

Richard Hoffman and Signor Salvi, who had gone to New York when Jenny had ended the concert tour, were summoned back. Jenny and Otto yielded to the pleas of their new friends in Northampton for another concert in the "Switzerland of America," and Jenny for once realized to the full her ambition to bring her music to everyone. The tickets were all priced at $1.00 and $2.00 and everything remaining after expenses was given to the Northampton Young Men's Institute and the local charities.

The net of $937 was small when compared with the sums Barnum had brought in for Jenny's concerts, and with the sums Jenny had left behind for philanthropies in many cities. But perhaps nowhere in America was her contribution received as gratefully, and remembered as long, as in Northampton.

It might have been better if Jenny had stopped with the smaller New England concerts, for those in Boston and New York, while not failures, were far from being the brilliant successes Jenny had enjoyed before. Proudly, even defiantly, Jenny chose to stress her new status as the wife of her unpopular accompanist. The programs, containing no decorations or advertisements, proclaimed "MADAME OTTO GOLDSCHMIDT—GRAND CONCERT" in big black type, with a parenthesized "late Jenny Lind" in small type. This did not matter so much in Boston, which after all had been the scene of the songstress's wedding, and whose citizens recalled with relish how Jenny had stolen a march on the city's press. But in New York it was a different story.

Jenny was her own manager now, Otto assisting, and it is evident that she had taken the very broad hint conveyed in the Philadelphia *Guardian*'s criticism. The two followed Barnum's pattern as closely as they knew how, except that they stayed at Delmonico's Hotel, then located on Broadway at the corner of Morris Street, instead of the ones Barnum had chosen. Two concerts were scheduled for Metropolitan Hall (formerly Tripler's Hall), which Jenny had found so much to her liking, but the last one, on May 24, was to be at Castle Garden, where Jenny had made her American debut. An orchestra of eighty members was hired, with Theodore Eisfeld as conductor, Joseph Burke dropping back into his old place as leader. A rather pitiful touch was that Jenny even had a "Farewell to America" composed for the last concert, to balance the "Greeting to America" of the first one, which she and Benedict had gone through with only because they felt they had to. But there was no Prize Song Contest this time. Jenny simply asked a New York musician to find a poet to write the words, and Christopher P. Cranch, the poet selected, supplied three stanzas, which Otto put to music.

In New York, however, the full effects of Jenny's marriage were felt. The goddess had lowered herself by choosing a mortal for her mate, and a not very distinguished or appealing mortal at that. She had thereby lost her news value to a great extent, so far as the New York press was concerned. The concerts received little advanced publicity, and only short notices afterwards, though Harriet Beecher Stowe, who attended one of the concerts at the earnest urging of her brother, Dr. Henry Ward Beecher, wrote a friend that it had been to her "a bewildering dream of sweetness and beauty."

Most of the notices were mildly favorable, but the New York *Herald* reached for its old cudgels and returned to the attack with: "She has been principally engaged in singing pieces of operas and catches of all kinds, which were considerably more of the claptrap style than in accordance with the rigid rules of classical music. When she returns to London and makes her reappearance in opera, she will have to prune away a great deal of her ad libitum redundancies in which she indulged during her career in this land."

The farewell concert in Castle Garden brought in $7,000, but the hall was not filled, and there was no need, this time, for the elaborate precautions the city police had taken on the occasion of the first concerts. True, it was a rainy night, but when had rain ever kept people away while Barnum was in charge? There had never been any break in Jenny's friendly relationship with her former manager. She sent him complimentary tickets for the New York concerts and he attended the last one, going to her dressing room afterwards to bid her and her husband good-bye. His mind must have been full of thoughts of what *he* would have made of Jenny Lind's positively last appearance in America, but he kept them to himself.

Jenny accepted his good wishes warmly and returned them, telling him, however, that she did not propose to sing much in public any more, perhaps indeed this would be her last public appearance.

Barnum says in his memoirs that he reminded her how much enjoyment the voice with which Providence had endowed her had brought to her fellow beings, and that if she no longer needed "the large sums of money which they were willing to pay for this elevating and delightful entertainment, she knew by experience what a genuine pleasure she would receive by devoting the money to the alleviation of the wants and sorrows of those who needed it."

He says that Jenny replied, "Ah, Mr. Barnum, that is very true, and it would be ungrateful of me not to continue to use for the benefit of the poor and lowly, that gift which our Heavenly Father has so graciously bestowed on me. Yes, I will continue to sing as long as my voice lasts, but it will be mostly for charitable objects, for I am thankful to say I have all the money which I shall ever need." It is unlikely that Jenny used just these words, for they have been strained through P. T. Barnum's own involved, flamboyant literary style, but undoubtedly the sentiment was hers, for it was just what she did.

It may be added parenthetically that Barnum was so pleased with the results of his initial raid on the culture and art of Europe that he made several other forays into England. He succeeded in bringing back a group of Lancashire Bell Ringers, whom he persuaded to grow long mustaches, wear Tyrolean peasant costumes and appear as Swiss Bell Ringers. Such little deceits as this, he commented in his memoirs, hurt no one and were a great help at the box office. The "Swiss" Bell Ringers, in fact, proved very popular in America.

But when he proposed to remove the house Shakespeare was born in to his museum in New York, British pride rose in protest. A Shakespearean Association was hastily formed, the forerunner of the present memorial to Shakespeare at Stratford-on-Avon; the premises were bought and thus snatched from Barnum's clutches only just in time. Barnum declared that if the British had remained asleep a few days longer, "I should have made a rare speculation, for I was subsequently assured that the British people, rather than suffer the house to be removed to America, would have bought me off with twenty thousand pounds."

A few hundred people gathered outside Jenny's hotel to serenade her in the early morning of May 29, before she and Otto were to sail on the S. S. *Atlantic,* for Jenny refused to cross the ocean with anyone but her friend, Captain West. Some two thousand gathered at the foot of Canal Street to wish her bon voyage. The Musical Fund Society did not show up, but three hundred Volunteer Firemen, faithful to the last, came marching to the ship in their red shirts, and presented her with a gold box seven inches long and three inches wide, a truly royal gift.

Jenny's own last benefactions had not been publicized at all. They included several thousand dollars to New York hospitals, orphanages and churches, and $100 to an abolitionist society in Boston. There had been handsome presents for the artists who had accompanied her on the tour, the choicest being an expensive violin for Joseph Burke, typical Jenny Lind gesture, to counteract the searing Philadelphia *Guardian* notice. According to Richard Hoffman, this violin remined Burke's most treasured possession all his life.

The two thousand people at the dock were a far cry from the uncounted multitude who had come to see her off in Liverpool, and the thirty to forty thousand who had greeted her in New York. There was no need to mount the paddle box this time, and Jenny stood at the rail, her hand in the crook of Otto's arm. She had made some mistakes in America and had paid rather dearly for them. Yet it was through these very mistakes that she had come to appreciate Otto's character, had learned the selflessness of his devotion to her. Already Jenny was very sure that in accepting the happiness offered her by her young husband's love, she had made no mistake.

Whatever harsh thoughts about America and Barnum may have found expression after Jenny's return to Europe, the predominating one was certainly appreciation of the kindnesses and affection she had received. When she reached Europe, she wrote the wife of William Macready, deploring the fact that an illness had prevented the actor from taking his family to America. "It is a great country, and my travellings there have brought many serious reflections upon me. . . . It is the country for a peaceful and hopeful future. If at any moment Mr. Macready should feel disposed to live in America, he would now be appreciated more than ever, this I feel convinced of."

Both Jenny and Benedict kept up a correspondence with the American artists who had been in the troupe. Jenny wrote Joseph Burke a year after her departure, "I often think of America. It is the new world that is *true. There* is active life and room to take breath, while Europe is old, quite a grandmother to the rest of the world." She added that though she was surrounded by many kind people in Germany—she was then living in

Dresden—she felt that if she were to live there the rest of her life "my soul and faculties would remain undeveloped for want of such examples of moral activity, and understanding of life's objects and aims, as I have seen in England and in America. Yet how many good qualities do the Germans possess, but—their *Pride* makes them blind, and Pride is our greatest and most dangerous foe." An utterance with a hint of prophecy in it.

When Jenny heard, in the middle 1850's, that Barnum had over-extended his enterprises and was in financial difficulty, any resentment she may have felt toward him previously was forgotten. The man who had appeared to be made of money now needed money, and Jenny at once offered to lend him some. She wrote to a friend in Philadelphia: "That Mr. Barnum should fail in business is indeed painful for me to contemplate. I believe a good man should never fall, nor shall Barnum do so for want of a friend. His pride would not permit him to write to me under the circumstances; mine compels me to write to him. Neither he nor his shall ever know want while I have it in my power, owing to the goodness of Heaven I now enjoy, to keep it away."

Barnum replied to Jenny that he was more obliged than words could express, "but I have health and ambition, and I expect, with energetic purpose and Divine guidance, to be on my feet again."—an expectation that was soon fully realized. Later on, Barnum visited the Goldschmidts in England, and Jenny gave him a marble bust which the fashionable sculptor, Durham, had made of her. This he kept at Iranistan.

That Jenny's affection for America and Americans was real and lasting is evident in the fact that when she knew she had not long to live, she asked to have two articles placed in her coffin with her. One was the first of several magnificent shawls Queen Victoria had given her. The other was a patchwork quilt American school children had made for her.

And the effect Jenny had on America is embedded in our musical history. Encouraged by her success in what had been considered a country without any interest in art and culture, others of Europe's greatest singing stars, including Grisi and Mario, planned American tours. Le-Grand Smith became a concert manager himself, and had brought Henriette Sontag to New York before Jenny had left. Alboni followed soon after. Neither of these beautiful, gifted women created anything like the furor Jenny did, however. M. R. Werner, whose widely read biography of P. T. Barnum was published in 1923, explained that "aside from any difference in the quality of their voices, it was well known that young men in Europe drank champagne from Henriette Sontag's slipper, and Alboni's lovers were almost as many as Jenny's charities."

But then, no one since Jenny has ever created quite the furor she did. In 1855, Rachel, whom Jenny had so admired and envied when she was studying in Paris, toured America, and it was very nearly a debacle. The sad fact is that, though she was a year younger than Jenny, already Rachel's powers had waned and her health had been ruined by her excesses and profligacies.

Nevertheless, with Jenny's coming, the era had passed when not more than three or four hundred Americans would come to a concert, even though the tickets were only twenty-five cents each. The singers named were the vanguard of a host of writers and artists of all kinds, who brought the art and beauty and poetry of "Grandmother Europe," to use Jenny's phrase, to her lusty young offshoot across the sea.

Jenny Lind's programs taught professional musicians that their concerts would not be cheapened by including what the New York *Herald* had called "catches of all kinds," but which were in fact such songs of the people as "Home, Sweet Home," "Comin' Through the Rye," "John Anderson, My Jo," and Stephen Foster's "Old Black Joe," "Old Kentucky Home," "Jeanie with the Light Brown Hair," and others of their genre— the kind of songs that could be played and sung and enjoyed by anyone with the slightest musical ability.

Many musical organizations, still in existence, had their beginning during Jenny's tours. Some of the orchestra members who had played under Jules Benedict or Joseph Burke organized orchestras or bands of their own, a few became concert artists. John Hall Wilton started a new profession, filling a long-felt need, by taking over the management of individual artists.

Jenny's impress on Boston is felt to this day. John Sullivan Dwight gave her all the credit for setting in motion a third wave of interest in good music in that city, which was lasting. "We have no difficulty in recalling the wonderful impression which her song produced and the new interest and faith in music as a divine art, which she inspired," he said in his *Musical History of Boston*. According to Dwight, the instrument through which Jenny's influence operated was the Harvard Musical

Association, formed by a handful of Harvard graduates after her first
Boston appearances. Immediate outgrowths of their efforts were the
Journal of Music, edited by John Sullivan Dwight for many years, and
the Boston Music Hall, the latter, "opening a new chance for great music
in our city," in Dwight's words.

American girls who possessed talent for music or acting, for the first
time could hope to foster and make use of their abilities, without facing
social ostracism. The prejudice against the stage died slowly, but Jenny
Lind had shown that a woman could act and sing in public and still be
of the highest character and reputation. From her visit dates the development of native female talent in the performing arts.

The slight diminution in the regard of the public that Jenny suffered
after her marriage soon was forgotten. Americans remembered her as a
shining and beneficient presence, which it had been their great privilege
to have among them for a time. For many years, visitors to Niagara Falls
were shown a little mound on the Canadian side, which had been carefully preserved, because Jenny Lind had stood there in 1851 and sung her
rapture at the spectacle of the mighty waters. A large elm in Northampton, in front of the Samuel T. Billings house and opposite the home-
stead of Sophia Smith, the founder of Smith College, was called the
"Jenny Lind Elm" until it was blown down in 1904 in a storm. Northampton remembered that Jenny had stood beneath that elm and sung
while she was on her honeymoon.

The New York Times for July 24, 1927, ran a story about a movement
on the part of residents of Yonkers, New York, to preserve the "Jenny
Lind Rock" at the rear of the Saunders Trade School Building on South
Broadway, as a permanent memorial to the singer. She had stood on the
rock in order to get a better view of the Hudson when she had visited
Dr. Robert Baird and his family seventy-six years before. "She is also said
to have sung from it when requested to do so," *The New York Times*
article recalled.

Many events of historical importance took place in Castle Garden
before it was turned into an immigrant depot in 1855, and an aquarium
in 1896. Lafayette had been received there when he revisited the United
States in 1824. Also received there, in great public demonstrations, were
Presidents Jackson and Tyler, the Hungarian hero Louis Kossuth, and
the Prince of Wales. Daniel Webster delivered orations there, and it was

there that Professor Samuel F. B. Morse first demonstrated publicly the use of the Morse telegraph code. Malibran, Sontag, Grisi and other operatic stars sang there; the notorious Lola Montez even danced there. Yet these incidents have long been forgotten. To this day, whenever Castle Garden or old Battery Park are referred to in magazines or newspapers, it is nearly always with the added comment that "Jenny Lind sang there when she visited America."

In countless diaries, any contact with Jenny Lind was fully recorded. Many of these records, carefully preserved, were turned over to Leonidas Westervelt by their owners' descendants. Memoir-writing Americans included passages about Jenny Lind in hundreds of books. For many more Americans, she became a part of family legend. During an exhibition of his Jenny Lind collection at the New York Historical Society, Leonidas Westervelt came upon an old gentleman moving slowly from one exhibit to another, examining each one with great care. "This is the most nostalgic moment of my life," the visitor told Mr. Westervelt. "My mother heard Jenny Lind sing at Castle Garden, and she described it to us so often that it is almost as if I had been there myself."

CHAPTER NINETEEN

After America

WITH P. T. BARNUM no longer dedicated to supplying the newspapers with accounts of her doings, American knowledge of Jenny's later life remained sketchy and was considerably distorted. Barnum, however, did correct a widely circulated rumor in 1890, three years after her death, to the effect that Otto had never loved her and was neglecting her grave. The showman told reporters, when he returned from a trip to England, that Jenny had been very happy with her husband, and that Otto sent fresh flowers to her grave every day. He concluded lyrically, "Her whole life was a song!"

Even Barnum's biographer, M. R. Werner, seems to have been strangely misinformed about Jenny's life after her marriage. He states that her retirement was practically complete, except for a few oratorios in England and a few concerts on the Continent, finding it significant that she "could still her voice as soon as she changed her name to Madame Goldschmidt." He blamed the religious influences to which she had been subjected, naming in particular Josephine Åhmansson and the Bishop of Norwich, for what he considered a defect in her character. "There must have been moments in those later years of uninterrupted existence along family lines when Jenny was restless—for what, she did not know; but unfortunately for the development of her talents, in such moments she could always take quick refuge in God. Some pagan influences might have made her a great woman, for the God she adored had done all He could in the way of native gifts." Werner concludes his section on the Jenny Lind episode in Barnum's life with this paragraph:

"In her existence and triumph lies a tale wherein is contained the extraordinary circumstances by which a *Mädchen* who wanted most to be a *Hausfrau* attained, by means of a sweet, charitable disposition and a superb voice, to celebrity as well, and failed to become a great artist because she succeeded so well in becoming a *Hausfrau*."

The facts are very different. It is true that Jenny was a woman, as well as a greatly gifted artist. She had longed for love and a home, and she felt a completion she had never known before when at last these were given her. But her voice was never stilled until the very last, and she never was a *Hausfrau*, in Werner's meaning of the term. Josephine Åhmansson continued to supervise the housekeeping; Jenny was as free in that respect as before her marriage.

Her first concern after her return from America was to start her long-planned project for helping talented young Swedes. She set up two scholarships at once, one at Uppsala in honor of her old friend Geijer, who had "kicked her out into the world," the other at Lund University in honor of another old friend, Bishop Tegner. In 1862 she added a traveling scholarship, called the "Jenny Lind Stipendium," which gave her a special kind of satisfaction, as she thought of what it would have meant if she had had such help as this when she was trying to get the money together to study under Garcia. She wrote Herr Horsberg, who had watched over her paternally when she was a pupil in the Royal Theater School in Stockholm, that she was sure she would have flown across the sea, without any need for wings. Jenny always took a strong personal interest in the recipients of her various scholarships, sending them long letters of advice, rejoicing in their successes, and giving them motherly scoldings when she thought they did not work as hard as they should.

There were the bustle of getting settled in Dresden, trips to Stockholm in connection with her scholarships and to see old friends, visits to Otto's parents in Hamburg. It is true, consequently, that for some months after the return to Europe, Jenny did nothing with music except for her own enjoyment, and that of Otto and their friends. Meanwhile, her love and respect and admiration for Otto, and her dependence on him, were growing continually.

Undoubtedly there had been a strong maternal element in Jenny's original feeling for Otto. But in their marriage, it was Otto who looked after Jenny with tender solicitude. While Josephine Åhmansson ordered the household affairs, he lifted from Jenny's shoulders every other burden concerned with daily living. He was far more prudent about money than Jenny, and shielded her from annoyance. Jenny wrote Jakob Axel Josephson in 1853, of Otto, "Now that we have been together a little over a year, he has been everything that a woman could ask of a man, and grows more lovable and devoted every day, in a most touching way. I, who was ill-schooled in many respects, benefit from his magnificent schooling. In music, I hear nothing from him but the finest and greatest."

Jenny was experiencing such undreamed-of joy in her new estate that, when she learned, the first winter in Dresden, that she was pregnant, she could not believe she would survive childbirth. It was not so much that she was thirty-two, considered in those days a little old to bear a first child. She did not think it possible that she, who had already received so much more than most mortals, could be granted the additional boon of motherhood. The prospect caused her no dismay, for if her Lord now required her life, she would go to Him with every dream and wish fulfilled. She canceled a trip she had planned to Sweden, writing to Judge Munthe that she dreaded the strain of looking for the last time on faces and streets so familiar and so well loved. "I am preparing for my death, which seems more probable than that I shall continue to live, and I shall with deepest contentment leave this life for the prospect of one better and free from sin."

She made her will, appealing to the King of Sweden to help Otto acquire Swedish citizenship quickly, if the need should arise. For she had found that unless this were done, her father would be able to claim one-third of her estate. She wrote Judge Munthe, "I shall die in agony if I have the burden on my conscience of having placed so much money in unworthy hands, instead of using it to help my Fatherland and the cause of humanity."

A letter to Judge Munthe in July, 1853—the baby was expected in September—conveyed her last wishes, which she said she was anxious to get to him before her "hour should strike." She wanted to be buried at Ed-Sollentuna, beside Anna Marie, with only the simplest stone to mark her grave. She asked her dear old friend and guardian to come to Dresden as soon as he got word of her death, to help Otto with the sad task of taking her back to Sweden and burying her. "After that, I beg of you to go to Adolf and Sophie Lindblad. Tell them I have loved them to the last, and have never ceased to regard them as closest to my heart, except for my child. . . . If this is really my last letter, a thousand thanks for all your friendship. . . . Death, when it comes, is a return to our Father's house. Praise be to God! He knows what is best."

When the birth pangs began, Jenny lay down on her bed, expecting never to get up from it. She was astonished, though most happily so, to find herself very much alive, after a delivery so easy she declared she would scarcely have known that anything had happened. The baby, a boy, was named Walter Otto, and from that time on Judge Munthe was "Grandfather." Jenny's first letter to the Judge after her accouchement said that the poor little chap had inherited her nose, "otherwise he looks remarkably sweet, and so sensible and intelligent." Jenny's pet name for her son was "Little Broad Nose," but in letters to friends she could not help rhapsodizing about the looks and remarkable accomplishments of her baby. "Perhaps I shouldn't praise my own child this way," she once wrote to Judge Munthe. "Yet truly I cannot see why we should fail to notice the things the Lord has given us for nosebags when we travel life's thorny path." Jules Benedict, asked to be godfather, accepted promptly and went to Dresden for the christening. Belletti, who would presumably have been Jenny's first choice for this honor, had had a breakdown soon after his return to England and had retired temporarily to his native Italy.

Jakob Axel Josephson, who had been enabled to study in Germany and Italy through Jenny's generosity, visited the Goldschmidts later that fall. He found the new mother the same Jenny Lind, "only a little older and much calmer. . . . She looked very happy and was completely absorbed in her little boy. She asked after all the old friends and sent greetings to all. Her husband is a nice little man, a good musician and a decent, serious, somewhat blasé young man." In the evening Jenny sang for Josephson the songs of Lindblad and Geijer, which she had sung on her first concert tours in Sweden.

A little girl, whom they named Jenny, was born on March 31, 1857. Mrs. Stanley, the widow of the Bishop of Norwich, stood godmother to this baby. At the christening, Jenny told the minister, "I thought my heart had all it could desire, but now I must repeat it with fuller meaning." A third child, given the imposing cognomen of Ernst Svend David

—"to please all nations, and especially the Germans, Swedes and English," Jenny explained—was born in January of 1861, completing the Goldschmidts' family.

Soon after little Walter's birth, Jenny was making as full use of her voice as even M. R. Werner could have wished. She started with a series of concerts in Dresden, Berlin, Leipzig, Vienna and Pest. Otto, of course, was her accompanist, and also played piano solos. The next year she made a brilliant tour of Holland, after concerts in Hamburg and Bremen, and in June of that year she was again the star of the Lower Rhine Festival at Düsseldorf, just ten years after the one in which she had appeared with Mendelssohn. Such brilliant ornaments of the musical world as Liszt, Brahms, Joachim and Gounod also took part, but Jenny shone above all the others.

Some critics maintained that her voice had lost something it never regained during the year and a half she was away from the concert stage before and after little Walter's birth. But the Norwegian composer, Halfdan Kjerulf, who heard her at Düsseldorf, wrote that he had had to hide his face, "for I wept from her first note to her last in Gabriel's aria in *The Creation*. It was, for one thing, completely natural, sincerely simple, a wonderful beauty of sound. . . . It was remarkable to see so overfêted and world-weary a celebrity so unaffected and delightful. She took part in all the rehearsals, sang every note she had to sing, went over passages again and again for the sake of others without a sign of impatience, singing always as beautifully and indefatigably as ever. . . . More beautiful voices I may have heard, but never more beautiful singing." Brahms said years later, "Whenever I open the score of *The Creation*, the parts that were sung by Jenny Lind shine out as though printed in gold."

Carl Schurz, the eminent German-American, heard Jenny sing in 1854 and wrote his impression of her in *McClure's Magazine*. "She was no longer young when I heard her. Her appearance, though still exceedingly pleasing, had become somewhat matronly. Her voice might perhaps not have retained all of its original birdsong-like lightness of warble. But there was still that half-veiled tone, as if there were something mysterious behind it; that velvety timbre, that strange magnetic vibration, the mere sound of which could draw tears to the eyes of the listener. Of all the great voices I have heard, and I have heard many, none was so angelic and went so entrancingly, so caressingly, to the heart as Jenny Lind's."

Jenny Lind, the Swedish Nightingale

The committee in charge of the Lower Rhine Festival at Aachen, in 1857, had planned to ask Jenny to sing again, but was balked by Liszt. He had been engaged to conduct the festival, and declared he would not attend if Jenny took part. He wrote to the committee frankly, "With this great magnet there, everything else becomes superfluous. For just as Louis XIV was the State, so Jenny Lind is the Music Festival."

But Jenny did sing at Halle, Germany, the birthplace of Handel, so beautifully and movingly that Robert Franz, who was conducting, lost his place and the chorus and orchestra had to conduct itself until he got his emotions under control. Jenny gave this concert to raise funds for a statue his townspeople wished to erect in Handel's honor. In gratitude for Jenny's contribution, the committee at Halle had the face of one of the angels supporting Handel's music desk carved in Jenny's likeness.

There was a prolonged visit, with Otto and little Walter, to Jenny's good friends and ardent admirers, the King and Queen of Hanover, Niklas Lind joining them there. The Queen made long entries in her diary about what a privilege the royal pair had considered it to have Jenny with them again, and to hear her sing. The Queen was "not a little proud" at having sung duets with Jenny. There was a reunion with another good friend, Queen Victoria, and a private concert at Buckingham Palace, when Jenny went to England to sing *The Creation* and Mendelssohn's *Elijah*, with Benedict conducting.

In 1856, Jenny had a triumphal tour of England, Scotland and Wales, in which she was supported by Lablache and a number of other important artists. Benedict wrote Joseph Burke in America, "Their success is even greater than in 1847 and 1848. The receipts for the concerts can only be compared with the best in the United States, and instead of flagging, the excitement is on the increase."

The principal change in Jenny's career after her marriage was that now all strain and tension were removed. Otto looked after the details of writing letters, carrying on negotiations and making travel and concert arrangements. Josephine Åhmansson was a second mother to the children. Jenny could leave them in her care without apprehension for the month or two of the tour—seldom longer, for after a few weeks' absence, Jenny could not wait to get back to them.

There was no longer any pressure to make money, for besides her own fortune—she received $176,000 from her American tour alone—Otto had an income from his family's business. She gave concerts to help worthy causes, or to advance Otto in his career, and above all to bring to her listeners the noblest music. As the years went on, she confined her concerts more and more to the great oratorios, in particular those of Handel, Haydn and Mendelssohn. Eventually she became so associated with Handel's music that the memorial to her in the Poet's Corner of Westminster Abbey was placed next to that of Handel, and the plaque showing her head in profile was engraved with the words she had sung so many times with such conviction, "I Know That My Redeemer Liveth."

For a woman to be memorialized in Westminster Abbey was unprecedented. Among the many illustrious persons who petitioned Parliament to break the age-old rule in Jenny Lind's favor was Manuel Garcia, her singing teacher in Paris, who once had been skeptical about her ability.

In 1858, Jenny declined with thanks an invitation from P. T. Barnum for another American tour, and the Goldschmidts moved to England. Otto had enjoyed his teaching, but in conjunction with the concert tours, it was taking too much of his time. He wanted to be freer for composing. And England provided the best climate for the oratorios, which had become Jenny's chief interest in singing. They had not been in England very long when Jenny received word of her father's death. She did not go to Sweden, Judge Munthe attending to Niklas's burial, as he had to Anna Marie's. Jenny had no guilt feelings in connection with her father's death. She had had little communication with Niklas since the time she had spent with him at Hanover, other than his incessant demands for more pocket money. The image of the young Papa Niklas had been obliterated by that of the whining, wheedling, drunken spendthrift. Jenny was surprised and touched when Judge Munthe wrote that he had found, among Niklas's belongings, a portrait of Jenny painted when she was sixteen. It was a bad painting and a poor likeness, Jenny remembered, but she asked Judge Munthe to send it to her. The fact that Niklas had kept it all those years made Jenny feel that in her father's confused, muddled being, some genuine fondness for her had remained.

For several years the Goldschmidts lived in rented houses, in and about London. Then, in 1864, they built a home in a wooded tract overlooking Wimbledon Park, on the very ridge along which Jenny had often gone horseback riding with the Duke of Wellington. The house was semi-Tudor in style and stately, with many tall chimneys and many bedrooms, surrounded by a pleasant garden and paddock. Jenny thought to name it "Larkfield," for obvious reasons, but Otto preferred "Oak Lea" because of a huge, ancient oak tree that sheltered the front of the house, and so it was called. However, the shield they placed over the front entrance showed a lark winging upward, and engraved on the shield was the word "Excelsior."

With the move to England, Jenny's friendship with Queen Victoria was firmly established. The Queen often invited the singer to Buckingham Palace or Windsor. The Goldschmidts were always guests at the parties the Queen gave after her "shoots"—oddly, Victoria was an enthusiastic and expert riflewoman. Jenny sang at the brilliant wedding of the Prince of Wales to lovely Princess Alexandra of Denmark, and Jenny the Second first met Raymond Maude, whom she married, in Buckingham Palace. The Queen had expressed a desire to see her friend's little daughter, young Raymond was the son of a Court official. He comforted and reassured the child while she waited to be summoned to the august presence.

The Queen and Jenny, the two most prominent women in the world in their time, met and talked together as equals. They had another thing in common, now that Jenny was married. Both these uniquely situated women had found husbands who devoted themselves to helping their wives carry the burdens placed upon them by the work they had been given to do in the world. Both women enjoyed supreme domestic bliss, in addition to the adulation they received from the multitudes; both idolized their husbands.

There were some who liked to speculate that Jenny's marital felicity was feigned, that she was merely putting a good face on a bad bargain. But there has never been the slightest substantiation for this theory. On the contrary, the resemblances between the two prominent couples were so marked that first her friends and then the public began calling Otto "Jenny's Prince Consort"—though never in her presence. She fiercely resented any intimation that Otto was not as important a person as she was. "Why do people persist in saying, 'Jenny Lind was there with her husband?'" she demanded of Mrs. Grote. "They ought to say, 'Herr Goldschmidt was there with his wife!'"

[322]

After America

In 1860, Jenny rewarded Otto's assiduous and capable attention to their business and financial affairs by canceling the antenuptial contract she had drawn up and Otto had signed. The young husband now relieved the aging Judge Munthe of the burden he had carried so long, though Jenny's affectionate correspondence with the old man continued to the last. Otto became a full partner with Jenny in the handling of what she called her "private fund," that part of her earnings that she had placed aside for her scholarships and philanthropies. It thrived so well under his careful management that after setting up the Jenny Lind Stipendium in 1862, by 1864 the pair were able to found a hospital in Stockholm for the children of poor parents. This hospital performed an important and heretofore neglected service, and near the turn of the century was merged with the public welfare system of the city and nation. Every year there were smaller grants and gifts, some to institutions, others to help some struggling musician or painter or sculptor to complete his training.

All these things had come out of Jenny's throat, as she liked to say, and there were to be many more.

The concerts had continued. In 1859, Jenny made a tour of Ireland, assisted by Joachim and Belletti. The Italian, recovered from his breakdown, was the same retiring but always understanding and sympathetic Uncle Belletti, except that his dark eyes were perhaps a shade more melancholy. He sang a number of times with Jenny, but was not one of the frequent visitors to the Goldschmidt home. In 1862 he surprised everyone by retiring abruptly from the musical world, when he was at the very height of his career. He returned to Sargona, his native village in Italy, and remained there, a virtual hermit, until his death in 1890. Belletti never gave an explanation for his sudden withdrawal. If Jenny knew or suspected the reason, she gave no sign.

Also in 1859, Jenny sang again at the Lower Rhine Music Festival at Düsseldorf, there being no Liszt on hand this time to keep her away. She was invited back to Düsseldorf for the Rhine Festival of 1862, and replied that she would come, and what was more would sing for nothing, if the committee would employ Otto to conduct the entire Festival. For Otto was ambitious now to become established as a conductor. Her offer was accepted, and Otto gave such a good account of himself that Jenny declared he must have been born with a baton in his hand.

Otto's steady rise toward recognition on the basis of his own abilities was perhaps Jenny's greatest pleasure. In 1863, he was offered the position of Professor of Piano at the Royal Academy of Music, and before long was made Vice Principal of the Academy. One of London's outstanding musical events of that year was the Goldschmidts' revival of *L'allegro* and *Il pensoroso*, Milton's words, as they had been set to music by Handel. Jenny sang the leading role, Otto conducted.

Jenny, meanwhile, was busy filling in the gaps in that part of her education which had been supervised, not too capably, by Anna Marie. She had hardly had time for this before, between the necessity of learning new roles and songs and languages and constant travel. She went about it as painstakingly as when she had mastered the fundamentals of voice production, studying English grammar first, then going on to the English classics, with which she was unfamiliar. Only English was spoken in the Goldschmidt home after the move to England, and Jenny would read aloud to the children from Shakespeare's plays, unconsciously acting them out as she read. She judged literature in terms of music.

"For true music, we must have one feeling, one harmony, and not a series of broken lights, no matter how brilliant, and thus it is with true writing," she declared. "Take Milton. Every word that he wrote can be sung! And so with Dryden, for his words are simple and definite, like the notes on a scale. But Tennyson! Ha! Not even a Handel could compose for that man.

"Italian writing is *all* music, every word of it! How different from my own Swedish language! But this is not the Swedes' fault, no indeed. Italian has the warm, musical Mediterranean about it all the time, while Swedish is Norse, and the words are bits of ice frozen by our long winters. German? Well, Heine's poems run into music at once. They are music. But Goethe? His words *are* literature, perhaps, but he was influenced by Hegel, and this made him irreligious. And that is a tragedy, for there is no true music without religion."

The Goldschmidt home was filled with music. There were five pianos at Oak Lea, besides an old harmonium. Jenny Goldschmidt Maude said that as her mother grew older, her features took on a stronger and more Scandinavian cast, though the expressive, mobile mouth remained the same. The elder Jenny's character strengthened, too, grew more decisive, after she had thrown off her fears and her feelings of inferiority and guilt. She simply did not bother with people who were not her friends and did not interest her. When rash folk intruded on her out of curiosity, she held herself haughtily aloof, and Otto was constantly obliged to exercise his tact to smooth the feelings of harmless people who had not meant to offend.

But to those she cared for, or that she considered worthy of attention, Jenny gave her friendship and her voice as warmly and unstintingly as ever. Oak Lea was a center for artists and writers and interesting people of all kinds, from members of the nobility or scions of royal families, to the nice little man who kept the stationery store at the corner. Many an impromptu concert was held, and many amateur singers found themselves, like the Queen of Hanover, in the exhilarating and at the same time awe-inspiring position of singing duets with Jenny Lind. Arthur Coleridge, a constant visitor to the Goldschmidt home as was Arthur Sullivan, said it always scared him half to death to be called upon to sing with Jenny.

Just before the children's bedtime, Jenny would seat herself at the harmonium, and the young Goldschmidts and whatever guests happened to be present would gather round her. They would sing together the folk songs Jenny had learned from the old ladies at the Widows' Home in Stockholm, and the songs of Lindblad, Kjerulf and Taubert. When Jenny struck the first chords for Schumann's "Wann fromme Kindlein schlafen gehen" ("When tired children go to sleep"), the Goldschmidt youngsters knew that at the conclusion of the song their mother would close the harmonium, the signal for them to say goodnight. Jenny always played for the Christmas carols too, seated at the little harmonium, and she played the piano for the dancing at the children's parties. "Presently," her daughter wrote, "she would spring up and take part in the dance herself."

Moreover Jenny continued to sing in public long after her voice had gone off a bit; the lower notes had lost their purity and clarity and the high notes that once had floated out so effortlessly had to be forced. This was the harder to understand because to Jenny of old, the overriding dread of her life had been that she would wake some morning and the marvelous tones would no longer be there. Now that it had happened, Jenny sang on, with no intimation that she knew it had happened. She could still do good with her voice, as long as a vestige of it remained. She sang for such worthy causes as the Florence Nightingale Fund, sponsored by Queen Victoria; funds to aid retired clergymen, distressed needlewomen and other groups who needed help. The public still flocked to hear her. When Jenny sang the *Messiah* in 1863 as a benefit for a sailors' church and school at Victoria Docks, such a huge crowd gathered that the Bishop of London declared it took nearly an hour for his carriage to get through the Strand to Exeter Hall, where the concert was held. A letter to the *Times* of London inveighed bitterly against the hoop skirts which Empress Eugénie had lately made fashionable, declaring that at least four hundred seats in the hall were sacrificed to crinolines. "The ladies should dispense with these ornaments whenever Madame Lind-Goldschmidt sings," the writer declared.

In 1866, Jenny sang the *Messiah* at the Lower Rhine Festival at Düsseldorf again, and also sang Arthur Sullivan's "Orpheus with His Lute," dedicated to her, in Sullivan's Grand Orchestral Concert at St. James Hall, in London. In 1867, she sang the part of Ruth in Otto's oratorio of that name, a part her husband had composed with her voice in mind, as Mendelssohn had composed the soprano solos of his *Elijah* with Jenny's voice in mind.

For her audiences, she exerted the old magic, regardless of what time was doing to her face and voice. The Austrian critic, Eduard Hanslick, noted as early as 1862, that "even the well known, prophetically shining eyes had lost much of their former brightness, and obstinate wrinkles played undisguised round the mouth. . . . I recognized the glorious voice in much the same way as you recognize a beautiful old portrait, now partly faded and discolored. The notes were somewhat weak and veiled, and the higher, forte passages somewhat forced. Now and then, however, an occasional silver tone from of old would run like a golden thread through the clouds, to vanish hastily again as though scared. And yet I could not but recognize that everything it stood in human power to do with such a voice, Jenny Lind was doing to a higher degree than any other singer could have done.

"To judge by the rapturous applause of the public, however, no one could have guessed that Jenny Lind's voice was badly on the decline. The English public is unique in matters of piety. In Jenny Lind they honored virtuosity in a double sense, in art and in charity."

A critic who heard her sing in 1863 remarked, "I suppose her high notes are a little gone, but the matchless expression and heart-feeling will never go out of her voice." While Lady Westmorland—the same Lady Westmorland who had taken Jenny in hand in her youth and taught her to pay more attention to her appearance—when told the Lind had lost her voice, said, "If Jenny has still got her soul, she is more worth hearing than all the other singers in the world."

The elder Senator Henry Cabot Lodge heard Jenny sing when he was a young man and she was long past her prime, and said in after years that her voice seemed to him the most wonderful he had ever listened to. "It had a quality of beauty which dwells with me still and which I have never heard surpassed."

An unpleasant matter was disposed of in 1871. With the expansion of the British Empire, and possibly as a reaction against Queen Victoria's increasingly strict moralism, an era of journalistic muckraking arose, in which public idols were pulled from their pedestals in a way similar to the great "debunking" period that followed World War I. Every leader of Her Majesty's government came under vicious attack. Prime Minister William Gladstone was called a bumbler at best; at worst a traitor to his queen and country. It was inevitable that a person as well known and revered as Jenny Lind should be included among the victims.

There was much talk about her "vast wealth," accumulated, according to one journal, at the expense of the "gullible" public. Jenny cared little what the sensational publications said about *her*, but rose in wrath when a newspaper commentator said, "It is well known that Jenny Lind's husband, Mr. Otto Goldschmidt, has squandered the fortune of his wife by generally incompetent management. It is rumored that he is cruel toward Jenny, and has made her life definitely unhappy."

She sued the writer and the paper for libel, went into court armed with figures to show how her funds, both for her personal use and her philanthropies, had benefited by Otto's management. She testified to the unbounded happiness she had enjoyed ever since her marriage. She won the suit, and gave the nominal damages she had asked for to charity.

The children were growing up now, and in order to give young Jenny a wider social life, in 1874 the Goldschmidts regretfully left Oak Lea and bought a large house at 1 Moreton Gardens in South Kensington, London. At once young Jenny's parents, too, became an important part of the London social scene. They dined with Gladstone, and Jenny wrote

Judge Munthe that to see the great statesman's eyes light up with pleasure when she sang some Swedish songs was a joy to her heart. Otto rapidly collected all the honors open to a musician in England. He became a member of the Royal College of Organists, the London Company of Musicians and the Royal College of Music. Princess Helena, Queen Victoria's daughter, came to the house for piano lessons with Otto. They were visited by various members of the British and Swedish Royal families.

But dearest to Otto's heart was a group made up principally of amateurs who met in the Goldschmidt drawing room once a week to sing the music of older and less well known composers, whose works were ordinarily neglected. Arthur Coleridge was a member of the group. One night he brought with him a manuscript of the B minor Mass of John Sebastian Bach, which he had chanced upon.

Following the rediscovery of Bach by Mendelssohn, and due to his efforts and those of Robert Schumann and such English musicologists as Wesley and Crotch, more people were becoming interested in Bach's music. In 1850, when Bach had been dead a hundred years, a society was organized to arrange for the publication of all of Bach's works that could be found. Many were lost, including some major ones, it was believed, during the century of neglect that followed his death. Such of his works as could be recovered were being made available, but the B minor Mass had never been produced in England, and few people had ever heard of it.

Otto and Jenny marveled at its rich harmonies and the intricate blendings of the many voices of instruments and chorus. Jenny said, "To think that an old woman like me, who has lived music all her life, should have been told of *this* music by an amateur!" (Arthur Coleridge was not an amateur, in truth, but said, himself, that singing with Jenny had taught him the difference between professional competence and genius.)

The Goldschmidts determined to produce the Mass in a manner worthy of it. All that winter, Otto's little group, which called itself the "Madrigal Society," earnestly studied and rehearsed the music. All of England's leading musicologists were brought in—Steiner, Benedict, now Sir Julius Benedict, and others. Otto made several trips to Germany to dig into sources which might shed light on Bach's own intentions for producing the Mass, and to transcribe orchestral parts according to the original score. More singers were enlisted. The group grew too large for the Goldschmidt drawing room and the meetings were transferred to a house with a larger one. This was outgrown, and in the end the meetings and rehearsals were held in the lecture hall of the South Kensington Museum. The Prince of Wales sometimes attended the rehearsals, Princess Helena was often there.

Jenny demurred at taking a solo part, but she trained the soloists and led the soprano section of the chorus—considered a supreme act of abnegation on the part of the world's most renowned prima donna.

The entire Bach B minor Mass was performed for the first time in England on April 26, 1876, and what had started out as a handful of amateurs, meeting in the Goldschmidt drawing room, became the Bach Choir. Nine years later the Bach Choir celebrated the bicentenary of the birth of Johan Sebastian Bach by singing the Bach B minor Mass at Albert Hall, with an orchestra and chorus together numbering six hundred. The Lutheran Bach was now recognized as one of the greatest musical masters, firmly established as the equal of Beethoven. Otto conducted, then turned the choir over to a successor. Jenny listened from a seat of honor in the audience. She was nearly sixty-five, and felt herself too old even to lead the sopranos in the chorus.

But what would have been her joy if she could have known that in America, where many thousands heard their first great sacred music from her throat, the devotion and reverence she and Otto felt for the Bach B minor Mass would be shared in full, and that its glorious strains would be sung by great choruses, supported by native orchestras second to none in excellence.

When Jenny had turned fifty in October, 1870, an advanced age for a coloratura soprano, she had begun to think about retiring. Nevertheless, during the decade between 1870 and 1880, she gave an average of a dozen concerts and oratorios each year, notable among them being her Hyde Park Gardens appearance in 1871, with Clara Schumann and Alfredo Piatti; the Northumberland House concert in 1873 and the Turkish Refugee Benefit concert in 1877. At the special request of Queen Victoria, she took part in a command concert at Windsor in behalf of the Albert Institute, in 1880, but then begged the Queen to let her hide her "wrinkled face and gray hairs" from the public thereafter.

She had, however, refused for some time to sing in her native Stockholm, fearing the cruel comparison of her aging self with the Jenny who had had her first triumphs in the Royal Opera House. When she made what she had expected to be her last visit to Sweden in 1876, she had let no one but Judge Munthe know she was coming, and had seen only old friends.

But in 1881 Jenny returned to Sweden after all, though not to sing. This time she had been summoned by King Oskar II, to receive from him the highest honor it was in his power to give her. For the last time Jenny stood before her own King and Queen, surrounded by officials of the Royal Opera and scores of selected guests. She wore a white dress with a blue belt decorated with forget-me-nots—the blue and white ensemble that had been her favorite for concerts. Around her neck was the "good luck" locket containing the likenesses of George Washington and Daniel Webster, on her arm a diamond bracelet, one of Queen Victoria's many gifts. Her ash-blond hair was streaked with white now, but she wore it rolled about her face in the way that had created a long continuing fashion in the United States.

The King was speaking. "Fru Jenny Lind-Goldschmidt, who has so highly honored our Kingdom and our people with her matchless art of song, who has for so long dedicated her great talent to the benefit of humanity . . . for these accomplishments, and in everlasting gratitude, we present the Kingdom's medal of Litteris et Artibus." And King Oskar placed about Jenny's neck a blue seraphim ribbon, from which hung a gleaming medal of gold, set with diamonds. He grasped the Nightingale's hands, and as the company applauded, leaned over and kissed her cheek. (Greta Garbo, another greatly gifted Swede, who has had much the same kind of magical, mysterious appeal for the public as did Jenny Lind, was awarded the Litteris and Artibus medal by King Gustaf of Sweden.)

Jenny was made even happier when the next year King Oskar conferred upon Otto the Order of Wasa. Later Otto was given the gold medal of the Polar Star and elected to membership in the Swedish Musical Academy.

Still Jenny's work was not done. She had yielded to the urging of the Prince of Wales that she head the faculty of vocal instruction in the newly established Royal College of Music. Everyone said she was a hard teacher but a wonderful one. She exacted from her pupils the same perfectionism she had always exacted from herself, and could be devastating toward those who did not come up to her expectations. Liza Lehmann, one of Jenny's pupils, said that Jenny was always wonderfully kind to her, but "sometimes treated certain of her pupils with almost cruel harshness and sarcasm. No doubt her musical nerves were strained almost to the breaking point—in fact, looking back, I cannot imagine how she could tolerate any of us. But curiously enough, I believe she loved teaching.

"A stern and unrelenting kind of Puritanism seemed to emanate from her personality, but when she sang, all harshness vanished and her face became illuminated and suffused with lofty tenderness, as if inspired by Saint Cecilia herself."

Jenny did love teaching, for she had definite theories about it and welcomed an opportunity to carry them out. "To be able to sing, the whole character must be trained. . . . Anyone who would learn to sing must be informed about many other things. . . . A singing teacher's calling is difficult and important. Difficult because almost every voice has to be treated individually and the whole character widened out. No one learns to sing who is stupid. The teacher's calling is important because incautious studying ruins the health. For the whole body sings—yes, even the legs!" She mentioned that after she had sung in opera, her own legs could scarcely take her to her carriage, she had surrendered herself to the music so completely.

In 1883, Jenny gave up her teaching because of poor health, and realized finally her dream for a modest cottage in the country. She had heard much about the beauty of Herefordshire from Queen Victoria, and the Maude family, into which young Jenny had married, had a house near Malvern about a hundred and twenty-five miles from London. Jenny visited them a number of times and became enamored of the region. She and Otto bought two cottages in Malvern Hills and turned them into one house, reminiscent of a Swiss chalet, with a deep-sloping, many-gabled roof and green-painted verandas, and with porch pillars made of un-trimmed silver birch. They named the house "Wynd's Point." Once again, as when she had been a small child at Ed-Sollentuna, Jenny could roam through the woods and meadows and hear wild birds sing. The fields that surrounded Wynd's Point were full of daffodils in season; the paths over the hills were bordered with wildflowers. A music room ad-joined their little drawing room—Jenny called this her own "little golden cage," where she could sing when she was forced to remain indoors. To surprise Otto, she had a small rustic arbor built in Swedish style when he was away on a trip.

It was at Malvern Hills that Jenny gave her last concert. One day a railroad employee asked her diffidently if she would sing at a concert to raise money for the Railway Servants' Benevolent Fund. It was the kind of thing Jenny loved most to do, and she promptly accepted. The concert was held at the Malvern Hills Spa, and local legend had it that the applause was so vociferous it literally "brought down the house." At least, residents proudly displayed a split in the roof, and the hall could not be used again until it had been repaired.

At Malvern Hills, Jenny died. Both Jenny and Otto had suffered from rheumatic ailments as a result of the English climate, and in latter years had formed a habit of going to Cannes during the worst winter months. This was before Cannes had become a fashionable resort, and Jenny had liked to sit and sing among the vineyards. The only concert she ever gave in France was a benefit for a local charity, at the request of the towns-people of Cannes.

The winter of 1886, Jenny went to Cannes alone because Otto had engagements which kept him in England. She scoffed at the idea that she might feel lonely. "I *alone*, with God above me and such beauties of Nature as I shall have around me?" But shortly after Christmas, Jenny's doctor in Cannes wrote Otto that his wife had cancer, too far advanced to be operable, and he hurried to her. They remained in Cannes until May, with all the children paying visits. Then Otto took Jenny back to England and to Malvern, after a brief stay in London to permit her to rest from the journey.

For a long time Jenny was not told the nature of her disease, for she had a special horror of cancer, but when at last she knew, she was not disturbed. How could she complain, when God had given her a life so rich, so full, so wonderful?

It was a lingering death, but the doctors made it as painless as they could. Otto was always there, sometimes reading to her, sometimes playing the piano softly in the next room.

In September of 1887, Jenny suffered a stroke, and her right arm was paralyzed. Her mind was not affected, however. When Queen Victoria sent messages and Jenny was asked if she had understood them, she replied, "None better." On the thirteenth of that month, she received the holy Communion at her request and now was ready to die.

The morning of November 2, 1887, young Jenny entered the room softly and pushed back the curtains from the windows. A bar of sunlight fell across her mother's bed. Jenny roused herself and formed with her lips, for she could no longer make sounds, the opening bars of Robert Schumann's "sunshine song." Soon, however, she collapsed. Her doctors were sent for hastily, but there was nothing they could do.

Outside the house, the villagers gathered as the news spread, and stood in reverent silence. To them, and to the outer world, it was a death watch for one of the great of earth. At Jenny Lind's passing, flags would be lowered to half mast in England and Sweden, and messages would come from all over the globe. King Oskar of Sweden would say, "She was like a meteor, blazing its trail above the heads of a wondering world."

But to the little group gathered about Jenny's bed, it was a beloved mother, a greatly adored wife, who was slipping away from them.

There was no pain now, and Jenny was content to lie quietly, her eyes moving from one to another of her dear ones. To tall Walter first, for he had been her first-born—a miracle. Jenny was aware that some critics had said her voice was never as fine an instrument after his birth. But she had also known, when she held her own baby in her arms, that this was the greatest gift of all.

To young Jenny next, moving about the room, smoothing the covers or adjusting a curtain—so like her mother, everyone said. Only the mother knew the differences between them. *This* Jenny's coming had been awaited joyously, her birth proclaimed proudly. Throughout her growing years, she had known nothing but love, had been shielded from every hurt.

And now to Ernst, the last—dearest and closest of all, given her when her cup of happiness was already running over.

Otto was sitting beside her, clasping her cold hand. Her eyes were heavy; to lift them to his face had become too great an effort. But how well she knew and loved that strong, sensitive pianist's hand! The music it made, the thousand kindnesses it had dispensed. The poet Longfellow had called Otto a good man. Yes, if by that he had meant the gentlest and most thoughtful, the most faithful, the most devoted to all that was finest and best. She would have liked to speak to Otto, say something to him of their lives together, glorified equally by their love and the great music they had shared, if she had not been so very tired. Otto knew, after all, what she would have said. Otto would remember.

Ah, the ship was beginning to move, slowly, almost imperceptibly, and someone was singing. It was Mendelssohn's "Spring Song!" But never had Jenny heard it sung as it was now being sung. It was the voice of a young girl, piercingly sweet, leaping upward in sheer ecstasy at being alive, conveying all the freshness and wonder of the spring itself. Why, it was her own voice, before she had learned to school and control it so carefully through Garcia's teaching! But this is the way the "Spring Song" should be sung, Jenny thought. I must try to sing it this way for Mendelssohn. . . .

The current had caught them now, the ship was making headway, leaving behind the true, fresh, pure voice of Jenny's youth. She was standing on the stage, the great chorus behind her, dear Otto bent over the score before her and wielding his baton to make the music surge, or fall to a whisper.

They were weaving the gorgeous tapestry of Bach's B minor Mass. Yet at the same time, she was standing by the piano of the drawing room in South Kensington, her eyes racing rapturously over the manuscript Arthur Coleridge had brought, crying out to Otto, "But this is the finest, the greatest of all!"

And now here was a strange thing. Still standing on the stage, she was singing the Agnus Dei from the Mass, the notes warm and rich, infinitely tender and compassionate. Never had she sung that aria. Not because it was a contralto solo, for when she had coached the soloists for the Mass she had sung every part. But because whenever she had tried to sing the Agnus Dei, her throat had closed, no sound would come forth. Now there flashed into her mind another scene, long banished because to recall it was too painful—a little girl huddled against the wall in a shock of revelation, a squalling cat clutched in her arms. Grandma Tengmark's voice came from far away: "This child is God's lamb, I know it! You shall not sacrifice her to your mistaken principles!"

Jenny whispered, "Dear Lord, you did not let me be made a sacrifice, in any part, in any way. Dear Lord, how beyond all understanding has been your goodness to me!"

The people on the shore were calling to her. "Jenny, don't leave us, Jenny come back to us!" Tears came to her eyes as she thought how many times she had been speeded on her journeys and greeted on her arrivals by thousands who were strangers to her, and had never heard her sing. She ought to wave to them, she knew. But her hand felt so warm and sheltered, nestled in Otto's. She could not bring herself to remove it.

Already it was too late to wave. The ship was moving very swiftly, the shore and the people crowding it were growing dim. But from everywhere now came the music—the music! The mightiest of the anthems and the paeans of praise, those noblest of works of the greatest masters, which lift men's souls and bring them nearer to the angels. They rang out together, yet she could distinguish every phrase and every thread of melody; for she had steeped herself in them until the music had become Jenny, and Jenny the music.

If voices still called to her from the shore, Jenny did not hear them.

Index

Åhmansson, Josephine, 132, 134, 144, 147, 148, 154, 155, 164, 175-179, 184-187, 226, 233, 235, 239, 252, 253, 261, 263, 299, 303, 305, 316, 317, 320

Albert, Prince Consort, 94, 117, 135, 322

Alboni, 124, 142, 145, 311, 312

Alexandra, Princess, 251, 322

Amelia (Rådberg, Jenny Lind's half sister), 18, 19, 23-25, 28, 42, 44

American tour, principal engagements:
Baltimore, 235, 236, 276
Boston, 211-216, 218-222, 307
Buffalo, 286, 289
Charleston, 250-252
Cincinnati, 272-274
Columbus, 286
Havana, Cuba, 252-259
Louisville, 271, 272
Memphis, 266
Nashville, 269, 270, 278, 279
New Orleans, 259-261
New York City, 184-210; 211-216, 218-222, 233, 276-281, 307, 308
Northampton, Mass., 296, 307
Philadelphia, 226, 227, 235, 276
Pittsburgh, 274, 275
Richmond, 248, 249
Springfield, Mass., 295, 296
St. Louis, 268, 269, 273, 274
Toronto, 286, 289

Andersen, Hans Christian, 79-84, 94, 113, 122, 131, 244, 250

Andersen stories inspired by Jenny Lind:
"Angel, The," 82, 83
"Emperor's Nightingale, The," 82, 83
"Snow Queen, The," 82
"Ugly Duckling, The," 83

Annette, 48, 55, 108

Arnemann, Fru, 144

Arnemann, Herr, 113

Atwater, Taylor, 265

Bach Choir, 329

Bach's B minor Mass, 328, 329

Balfe, 115

Bates, Joshua, Baring Brothers, 153, 158, 224, 225

Barnum, Caroline, 223, 235, 236, 264, 266

Barnum, P. T., 148-159, 161-163, 175-286, 308, 309, 311, 315, 321

"Barnum's Parnassus," 182, 183

Bayard, Mademoiselle, 37, 40, 41

Belletti, Giovanni, 49-51, 58, 59, 61, 63, 70, 82, 86, 134-139, 142, 153-155, 161, 168-180, 184-187, 195, 219, 222-224, 239, 249, 251, 252, 261, 264, 289, 291, 298, 318, 323

Bellini, 103

Index

Index

Index

Index

Index